Hiroaki Kuromiya and Georges Mamoulia

The Eurasian Triangle

Russia, The Caucasus and Japan, 1904-1945

Hiroaki Kuromiya and Georges Mamoulia

The Eurasian Triangle Russia, The Caucasus and Japan, 1904-1945

Managing Editor: Katarzyna Inga Michalak

Series Editor: Irena Vladimirsky

Language Editor: Adam Tod Leverton

DE GRUYTER
OPEN

ISBN 978-3-11-046951-6
e-ISBN 978-3-11-046959-2

Published by De Gruyter Open Ltd, Warsaw/Berlin
Part of Walter de Gruyter GmbH, Berlin/Boston
The book is published with open access at www.degruyter.com.

Library of Congress Cataloging-in-Publication Data
A CIP catalog record for this book has been applied for at the Library of Congress.

Managing Editor: Katarzyna Inga Michalak
Series Editor: Irena Vladimirsky
Language Editor: Adam Tod Leverton

www.degruyteropen.com

Cover illustration: © Łukasz Połczyński

Contents

Acknowledgments and Notes

We would like to express our gratitude to all the libraries and archives, both public and private, in the many countries whose holdings we have utilized for the present book. We owe especial gratitude to the Institut für die Wissenschaften vom Menschen, Vienna, Austria, whose fellowship allowed one of us (Kuromiya) to work on this project. In addition, we have benefited greatly from the *Nowy Prometeusz* group in Poland with which we have been working for some years. Ester Ham of Indiana University kindly translated Dutch documents into English. Dr. Alexander Marshall of the University of Glasgow generously answered our queries. We are also indebted to anonymous reviewers for helpful comments which we took into consideration in revising the manuscript. Dr. Jan Ryder has carefully edited the manuscript.

The Japanese name order, the surname followed by the given name, causes much confusion in literature. To avoid confusion, we have adopted the Western order, the given name followed by the last name, for example Giichi Tanaka, instead of Tanaka Giichi. Although this sounds odd to the Japanese ear, we have consistently adhered to the Western norm.

We have tried to avoid acronyms except for some archival names:

AMAE:	Archives du ministère des Affaires étrangères, Paris, France
AVP:	Arkhiv vneshnei politiki Rossiiskoi Federatsii, Moscow, Russia
BBKT:	Bōeishō Bōei Kenkyūjo Toshokan, Tokyo, Japan
BDIC:	Bibliothèque de documentation internationale contemporaine, Nanterre, France
CAW:	Centralne Archiwum Wojskowe, Warsaw, Poland
CHAN:	Centre historique des archives nationales, Paris, France
GARF:	Gosudarstvennyi arkhiv Rossiiskoi Federatsii, Moscow, Russia
GGSK:	Gaimushō Gaikō Shiryō Kan, Tokyo, Japan
GSCHA:	Georgian State Central Historical Archive, Tbilisi, Georgia
HHStA, PA:	Haus-, Hof- und Staatsarchiv, Politisches Archiv, Vienna, Austria
JACAR:	Japan Center for Asian Historical Records, National Archives of Japan, Tokyo, Japan
NA:	National Archives, Kew, UK
NARA:	National Archives and Records Administration, College Park, USA
RGASPI:	Rossiiskii gosudarstvennyi arkhiv sotsial'no-politicheskoi istorii, Moscow, Russia

1 Introduction

The Caucasus lies far from Japan. The distance from Tokyo to Tbilisi, capital of Georgia, for example, is almost 8,000 kilometers or 5000 miles. It is difficult to see any immediate historical or cultural links. Oddly, however, from the beginning of the twentieth century, an area of mutual concern developed between them. Just as Poland and Japan found mutual benefit in their resistance to the Russian Empire and Soviet expansion,[1] so did Japan and the Caucasus. Relations began during the 1904–05 Russo-Japanese War and continued into the period of World War II. The former marked the first defeat in the modern era of a European power by a non-European power, followed by Russia's rapid decline and Japan's spectacular rise on the international scene. The latter marked the Soviet Union's rise to a world superpower and Japan's decisive defeat at the hands of the United States and Britain (and, at the very end, the Soviet Union). Three relative latecomers – Germany, Russia (later the Soviet Union), and Japan – defined much of the fate of Eurasia in the first half of the twentieth century. In the geopolitical scheme of these three countries, the Caucasus played a strategic role. Because Japan's role in this area is the least known and least studied,[2] most works on the modern history of the Caucasus do not even mention the remote Asian country.[3] Nor is Japan's Caucasian nexus well known in Japan itself. For example, the activity of Lieutenant Colonel Shigeki Usui of the Imperial Japanese Army, one of the major Japanese figures who worked closely with the Caucasian émigrés in the 1930s, is utterly unknown there. Even his son knew nothing about his work until one of the authors found and contacted him in Tokyo in 2010.

The present book, a vastly expanded version of our short essay published in 2009,[4] focuses on secret wars the Caucasus and Japan jointly fought against the Russian Empire and the Soviet Union. Although, unfortunately, many relevant Japanese documents were destroyed during World War II, existing pieces of information allow us to

1 See Hiroaki Kuromiya and Andrzej Pepłoński, *Między Warszawą a Tokio: Polsko-Japońska współpraca wywiadowcza 1904–1944* (Toruń: Adam Marszałek, 2009).

2 Jonathan Haslam has written a short yet pioneering work on the enigmatic relations between Moscow and Tokyo in the 1930s: *The Soviet Union and the Threat from the East, 1933–41: Moscow, Tokyo and the Prelude to the Pacific War* (Pittsburgh, PA: University of Pittsburgh Press, 1992). It does not, however, discuss the Caucasus factor.

3 See, for example, Charles King, *The Ghost of Freedom: A History of the Caucasus* (Oxford-New York: Oxford University Press, 2008), Donald Rayfield, *Edge of Empires: A History of Georgia* (London: Reaktion Books, 2012), and James Forsyth, *The Caucasus: A History* (New York: Cambridge University Press, 2013). An exception is Alex Marshall, *The Russian General Staff and Asia, 1800–1917* (London-New York: Routledge, 2006), whose discussion of the Japanese nexus is based largely on an earlier work by one of the authors of the present book: Georges Mamoulia, "L'histoire du groupe Caucase (1934–1939)." *Cahiers du monde Russe* 48, no. 1 (January-March 2007), 45–86.

4 Hiroaki Kuromiya and Georges Mamoulia, "Anti-Russian and Anti-Soviet Subversion: The Caucasian-Japanese Nexus." *Europe-Asia Studies* 61, no. 8 (October 2009), pp. 1415–1440.

Fig. 1.1. The Caucasus and Japan.

outline the clandestine operations of Japan and various Caucasian political groups. Published and archival sources – Russian, German, American, French, Georgian, Polish, British, and Japanese – document the lengths to which Japan and peoples from the Caucasus went in planning and executing subversion against their common enemy as well as the lengths to which the Soviet Union went to subvert such activities by penetrating the Caucasian groups supported by Japan. Then, as now, international schemes of this sort were not unusual. Many have simply never come to light. Yet the story of the Japanese-Caucasian connection raises issues of more than mere episodic significance in the history of the Russian Empire and the Soviet Union: indeed it symbolizes the globalization of the regional affairs of Asia and the Caucasus in the twentieth century.

* * *

The nexus between Russia and the Caucasus is centuries old. By the second half of the nineteenth century, the bulk of the Caucasus had come under Russian domination. During the Civil War of 1918–21 that followed the Russian Revolution of 1917, some southernmost areas (such as the city of Kars and its region) of the Russian Caucasus were incorporated into the Ottoman Empire. Sandwiched between the Black Sea and the Caspian Sea, the Caucasus is sometimes divided into the Southern Caucasus (Transcaucasia, roughly encompassing Azerbaijan, Georgia, and Armenia) and the Northern Caucasus. In terms of geographical size, the Caucasus is very roughly the size of France or Spain, and larger than Germany or the state of California in the United States. In 1897 the population of the Russian Caucasus was approximately nine million, increasing to some fourteen million by 1939. (Here the "Caucasus" is defined in rough terms without considering the various and complex administrative changes that have affected the region.) The Caucasus was an area long contested for influence by the Russian, Persian, and Ottoman Empires. It was an area where Islam and Christianity coexisted: Georgia (an autocephalous Orthodox church) and Armenia (an Oriental Orthodox Monophysite church), both among the oldest Christian communities in the world, and smaller Christian communities (in Ossetia, Abkhazia, and elsewhere) lived alongside the Muslims of Azerbaijan and the Northern Caucasus (such as Chechnia, Ingushetia, and Dagestan). Within each of these lands, Christians and Muslims created a complex web of relations. The Muslims in turn were divided among Shias (predominant, for example, in Azerbaijan) and Sunnis (predominant in Chechnia, Ingushetia, and Dagestan).

Most of all, the Caucasus is known as the embodiment of complexity, a mosaic of geographic, ethnic, linguistic, and cultural diversity. Since the days of Greek civilization, the Caucasus has dismayed visitors with its "tribal" and linguistic variations. It is estimated that more than fifty ethnic groups and corresponding numbers of languages exist there. As one anthropologist has noted:

> Again and again in the two and a half millennia since Herodotus's day, writers have commented on the ethnic and linguistic diversity of the Caucasus. Strabo, writing about four and a half centuries later, having discounted more exaggerated estimates, affirms that 70 tribes, all speaking different languages, would come down to trade in Dioscurias (the modern Sukhumi), and a few decades after Strabo, Pliny claimed that the Romans carried on business in the same city by means of 130 interpreters. Arab travelers in the middle ages bore continuing witness to Caucasian polyglossia, and it was one of them, the tenth century geographer al-Mas'udi, who named the Caucasus *ǰabal al-alsun*, "mountain of tongues."[5]

This diversity, especially prominent in the northern, mountainous regions of the Caucasus, may have something to do with the region's terrain (which isolated villages and settlements from one another) as well as with the practice of endogamy, intended to provide "a high level of guarantee that outsiders will not be able to lay claim to [arable] land," which was particularly scarce in the mountainous regions.[6] It was only after the

5 See J.C. Catford, "Mountain of Tongues: The Languages of the Caucasus." *Annual Review of Anthropology* 6 (1997), 283.

6 Bernard Comrie, "Linguistic Diversity in the Caucasus." *Annual Review of Anthropology* 37 (2008), 139.

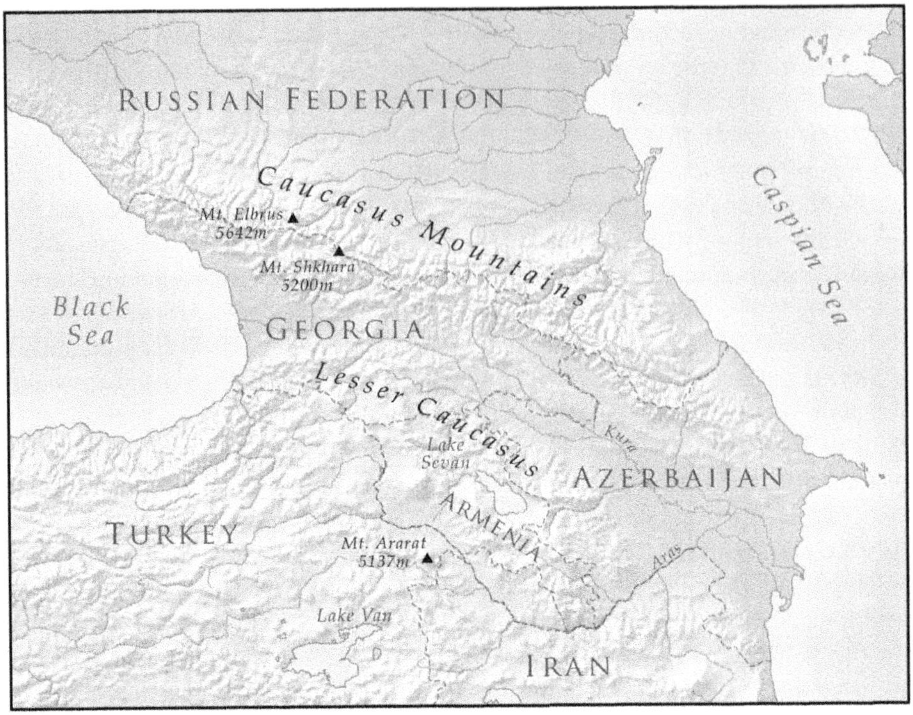

Fig. 1.2. The Geography of the Caucasus.

arrival of Russian rulers in the eighteenth and nineteenth centuries that the Caucasus had a lingua franca.

This diversity was replicated in major cities in the Caucasus with a twist. For example, in Tiflis (Tbilisi from 1936 onward), capital of Georgia and the administrative capital of the Russian Empire in the Caucasus, there were more Armenian and Russian speakers than Georgian in 1897, when the first comprehensive population census was taken.[7] It was only in the 1920s under the Soviet regime that Tiflis became more Georgian than Armenian. Until then Russians and Armenians had been predominant in commerce and administration in the Caucasus. In cities in the north, such as Vladikavkaz and Grozny, Russian speakers were the vast majority in 1897. In the same year in the city of Baku, Azerbaijan, Russian and Armenian speakers accounted for more than half the population. Not until the 1960s did Azeris become a majority in their own capital city.

7 The census data are now available online: http://demoscope.ru/weekly/ssp/census.php?cy=0 (accessed 17 March 2013).

Diversity also meant fragmentation. Consequently the fragmented Caucasus was historically at the mercy of neighboring empires' intent to divide and conquer. In the modern era it was the Russian Empire, succeeded by the Soviet Union, that came to control the Caucasus. Russia's contact with the area had begun much earlier: already in the seventeenth century Russia (Muscovy) had reached the Northern Caucasus with the help of Terek Cossacks. Under Peter I (1682–1725) and Catherine II (1762–96), Russia rapidly expanded, opening the way to eventual incorporation of almost all the Caucasus into the empire in the nineteenth century. There was a certain logic to this development. In 1722–23 during the war Peter was conducting against Persia, for example, both Armenia and Georgia joined Russia against Persia, considering the former as a counterweight to the latter, a bigger and stronger neighbor than themselves. Apart from Persia, the Caucasians had to contend with another neighbor, also a big empire, that of the Ottomans which, like Persia, had invaded the Caucasus repeatedly.

In the late eighteenth century, Russia skillfully and forcefully began its conquest of the Caucasus. Georgia became a Russian protectorate in 1783 with Persia serving as a common enemy. Much as the Pereiaslav Treaty of 1654 between Ukrainian Cossackdom and Muscovy led to the annexation of Ukrainian land to Russia, so too did the 1783 Treaty of Georgievsk lead in 1801 to Georgia's incorporation into Russia by armed force. Georgia's king was dethroned in violation of the 1783 agreement, resulting in an embittered Georgian population. Through numerous wars against Persia, Russia continued to expand in the Caucasus, annexing much of today's Azerbaijan by 1813 (Treaty of Gulistan) and part of Armenia by 1829.[8] It took much longer and more brutal armed struggles, however, to incorporate certain areas of the Northern Caucasus such as Circassia, Chechnia, and Northern Dagestan. Nearly half a century of war elapsed before these areas were subdued by force.[9] In the process, Russian authorities expelled numerous (possibly hundreds of thousands of) "mountaineers" from Circassia to the Ottoman Empire, in a manner reminiscent of later deportations of national groups in the 1930s and 1940s. Even today this Caucasian war, which ended in 1864, remains the symbol of the Caucasians' determined and unending resistance to Russian domination. Imam Shamil (1797–1871), who led the war against Russia not only in the Dagestan-Chechnia area (the core of the Caucasian resistance), but, albeit to a lesser extent, in the western Northern Caucasus (Circassia) as well, remains one of the

8 Later as a result of the war against Turkey in 1877–78, Russia also added Kars, Ardahan and Batumi (Batum) to its already vast territory.

9 There is much work on this war in English alone. See, for example, Michael Khodarkovsky, *Bitter Choices: Loyalty and Betrayal in the Russian Conquest of the North Caucasus* (Ithaca-London: Cornell University Press, 2011); Firouzeh Mostashari, *On the Religious Frontier: Tsarist Russia and Islam in the Caucasus* (London-New York: I.B. Tauris, 2006); and Austin Jersild, *Orientalism and Empire: North Caucasus Mountain Peoples and the Georgian Frontier, 1845–1917* (Montreal: McGill-Queen's University Press, 2002).

Fig. 1.3. The Russian Conquest of the Caucasus in the nineteenth century.

most celebrated heroes in the Northern Caucasus. Caucasians in general still enjoy the reputation of fierce warriors.

The Russian imperial conquest of the Caucasus was more than a mere domination. Together with Russia's subjugation of Central Asia in the second half of the nineteenth century, it was significant for the development of Russia's own identity in the Eurasian continent as well. Russian images of the Caucasus ranged from the "primitive and savage Other" (the antithesis to European civilization) to romantic idealizations of old and noble cultures long lost to Russia itself.[10] The Caucasus thus contributed to Russia's unsettled identity between Occident and Orient. This uncertainty is reflected in Russian literature, from Alexander Pushkin to Mikhail Lermontov and Lev Tolstoi, the latter two of whom in fact took part in the Caucasian War.[11]

10 In this sense, Russian Orientalism had something in common with German Orientalism. For the latter, see Franziska Torma, *Turkestan-Expeditionen. Zur Kulturgeschichte deutscher Forschungsreisen nach Mittelasien (1890–1930)* (Bielefeld: Transcript, 2011).

11 See Susan Layton, *Russian Literature and Empire: Conquest of the Caucasus from Pushkin to Tolstoy* (Cambridge: Cambridge University Press, 1994).

By the time the Caucasian War ended, however, Russia itself had begun to change rapidly. Its defeat in the Crimean War (1853–56) against Britain, France, and the Ottoman Empire was an impetus for what came to be known as the Great Reform. Initially with much hesitation, Russia ultimately embarked on rapid modernization if only to survive in an increasingly competitive world. It emancipated the serfs (one of the last states to do so in Europe) in 1861 and enacted other reforms (judicial, military, and administrative) in the following years. Russia did so, however, without reforming the political system, that is, without renouncing its autocracy. More generally, the Russian autocracy failed to see, let alone solve, fundamental contradictions in its body politic: while it wished to become a mighty state with modern military forces on a par with the most advanced European countries, it refused to acknowledge that its modernization program inevitably eroded the fabric of the old regime. In plain language, while Europe made its way into the modern era by way of bourgeois revolution, the Russian autocracy remained stuck in the absolutist mold.

This marked a sharp contrast with Japan, another latecomer, which, setting out on the path of modernization about the same time, assumed a constitutional monarchy following the Meiji restoration in 1868.[12] By the time Japan finally promulgated its constitution in 1889, Russia had reversed some of its earlier reforms in the wake of the assassination in 1881 of the Tsar-Liberator Alexander II by revolutionary terrorists (a process called "counter reform"). Nevertheless, the Russian autocracy even intensified its modernization and industrialization programs in the belief that they would strengthen, rather than undermine, the old, tradition-bound autocratic monarchy.

Modernization came to the Caucasus as well. Railways, the symbol of modern, industrial power of the time, reached Poti, on the western Black Sea coast of Georgia, in 1865 and Tiflis and Vladikavkaz in 1872 and 1875, respectively. In 1883 the railway network extended to Baku on the Caspian Sea of Azerbaijan, completing the Baku-Poti route. This allowed Caspian oil to be shipped from Baku to the Black Sea and then to other parts of the world. Yet the Caucasus remained Russia's colony, however enlightened some of Russia's viceroys may have become. The Great Reforms failed to reform Caucasian society very much. For instance, the zemstvo system, an elected body of local representatives with all estates (*sosloviia*) participating, was introduced in 1864 in European Russia. But although it contributed greatly to improving the provincial infrastructure, including administration, education, medicine, welfare, transport, and the like, it did not extend to the Russian periphery, including the Caucasus, where the Russian gentry was non existent or else weakly represented. Russian hegemony was thus impossible to secure.[13] The judicial reform enacted in the same year also improved the legal system of the empire greatly. Yet for this reform, too, the elective

12 See the classic work, Cyril E. Black et al., eds, *The Modernization of Japan and Russia: A Comparative Study* (New York: Free Press, 1975).

13 For the Great Reforms in general, see Ben Eklof, John Bushnell, and Larissa Zakharova, eds, *Russia's Great Reforms, 1855-1881* (Bloomington-Indianapolis: Indiana University Press, 1994).

justice of the peace was not introduced in the Caucasus. In any case, the reform itself did not extend to the vast majority of the population in Russia either, namely the peasantry.[14] Nor did the emancipation of serfs in 1861 satisfy any group in the Caucasus: not only did it take a few years to reach the area, but its effects were also much more limited there than in Russia proper. (In Dagestan, slavery persisted, abolished only later in the 1860s.)[15] In Georgia, the serfs were emancipated but received no land, while the landlords lost both the labor and income they had had from serfdom, leaving all important groups within Georgia dissatisfied.[16] Elsewhere in the Caucasus, especially in Azerbaijan, emancipation did not extend to most peasants because they were not living on private lands but instead on those belonging to the crown and treasury. Even those emancipated "had in effect been expropriated and forced to rent the land under [their] use from the landowners."[17]

Russian authorities wished to use the Great Reforms in the Caucasus to integrate unruly areas more closely into the Empire. Yet Russia remained a colonizer and its policies, including the Great Reforms, were meant in the last analysis to serve its colonial purposes. The reforms were palliatives, failing to adapt the old order to the demands of the modern era. In the Northern Caucasus, the presence of the Terek Cossacks, a privileged, landed warrior class of Orthodox Slavs who served the Empire, greatly complicated the ethnic, religious, and economic relations with the indigenous peoples.[18] In Armenia, the government decided to turn over the estates of the Armenian Church to the Ministry of Agriculture and the Department of State Properties, meaning that the clergy were to become "paid employees of the state." This blatant assault on Armenian national sentiment provoked violent protests, which were brutally crushed by military forces.[19] Combined with an intense cultural and linguistic Russification campaign in the last decades of the nineteenth century, Russia's modernization, without any substantive political or economic reforms, created a base for modern nationalism and modern forms of national resistance in the Caucasus.[20]

Georgian and Armenian nationalism appeared first in the Caucasus in the 1890s. This was in part because of their historic sense of distinctness (aided by the surround-

---

14 See Richard S. Wortman, *The Development of a Russian Legal Consciousness* (Chicago: University of Chicago Press, 1976).

15 See Elena Inozemtseva, "On the History of Slave-Trade in Dagestan," *Iran and the Caucasus*, 10, no. 2 (2006), 181–89.

16 Ronald Grigor Suny, *The Making of the Georgian Nation* (Bloomington-Indianapolis: Indiana University Press, 1988), 112.

17 Mostashari, *On the Religious Frontier*, 69.

18 See Thomas M. Barrett, *At the Edge of Empire: The Terek Cossacks and the North Caucasus Frontier, 1700-1860* (Boulder: Westview Press, 1999).

19 Ronald Grigor Suny, *Looking toward Ararat: Armenia in Modern History* (Bloomington-Indianapolis: Indiana University Press, 1993), 92.

20 For the most explicit work linking modernization and nationalism, see Ernest Gellner, *Nations and Nationalism* (Oxford: Blackwell, 1983).

ing milieu, which was largely Muslim) and in part because both groups produced larger numbers of educated people than did others in the Caucasus, and these went on to articulate and spread national ideologies.[21] Giorgi Dekanozishvili (Dekanozi) (1868–1910), an engineer who appears prominently in chapter 2, is merely one such educated Georgian. In Azerbaijan, the modern nation of "Azerbaijani" came much later, well after the 1905 Revolution, created from the official and disparate notion of "Tatars," or "Turks" and other generic designations, implying nonnational pan-Turkism and pan-Islamism.[22] Other regions in the Caucasus also produced educated people who brought forth new ideas and new movements. Haidar Bammat (Bammatov) (1889–1965), a Kumyk from Dagestan and one of the protagonists of the present book, belonged to the younger generation of educated Northern Caucasians, studying first at a classical gymnasium in Stavropol' and then law at St. Petersburg University.[23] The small and disparate ethnic groups in the Northern Caucasus, on the other hand, had a far harder time articulating a sense of nation than did the Armenians or Georgians. Consequently, when the Russian Empire collapsed, they tended, if only for the sake of survival against the forces of Russia, to band together as "mountaineers" and orient themselves politically toward a federation.

In a country where any organized political activity was illegal, all critical political expressions had to go underground. In the 1890s in particular, when Russia's industrialization was progressing particularly rapidly under its finance minister Sergei Witte (1849–1915, born in Tiflis to a Baltic German family), Russia's economic and social fabric was rent ever more widely. Social and political contradictions mounted and unrest became increasingly evident in town and country alike. In this last decade of the nineteenth century, numerous political parties emerged in the Caucasus as in Russia proper. In the Caucasus, as in most other borderlands in the Russian Empire, modern nationalism emerged together with socialism. One of the most famous Caucasians, Ioseb Jughashvili (Iosif Dzhugashvili), better known among English speakers as Joseph Stalin (1878–1953), started his political career first as a Georgian nationalist in the mid-1890s and then, within a few years, as a Marxist internationalist.[24] Where national oppression and class oppression often coincided, this was inevitable. The Georgian liberal nationalists, central players in the present book on the Russian-

---

21 For Georgia and Armenia, see Suny, *The Making of the Modern Georgian Nation* and also his *Looking toward Ararat*.

22 See Mostashari, *On the Religious Frontier*; Audrey Altstadt, *The Azerbaijani Turks: Power and Identity under Russian Rule* (Stanford: Hoover Institution Press, 1992); and Tadeusz Swietochowski, *Russian Azerbaijan, 1905–1920: The Shaping of National Identity in a Muslim Community* (Cambridge: Cambridge University Press, 1985).

23 Georges Mamoulia, K-M. Donogo, and M. Vatchagaev, *Gaidar Bammat i zhurnal "Kavkaz"* (Makhachkala–Paris: Akhul'go, 2010), 9.

24 See Donald Rayfield, *Stalin and His Hangmen: Au Authoritative Portrait of a Tyrant and Those Who Served Him* (London: Viking, 2004), ch. 1 and Simon Sebag Montefiore, *Young Stalin* (London: Weidenfeld & Nicolson, 2007), part one.

Caucasian-Japanese nexus, adopted in the beginning of the twentieth century the banner of Socialist-Federalism to attract the laboring population, even though they were much closer in conviction to political liberalism than to socialism.[25]

In Georgia, however, the Social Democrats (the so-called Menshevik faction) were much more dominant than the Bolsheviks and the Socialist-Federalists. As Marxist internationalists, the Mensheviks were interested in solving the question of national liberation in Georgia as elsewhere in the empire by a revolutionary change in the empire as a whole. For them, the national question was merely a subset of the class question. Under the influence of European socialism rather than Russian Bolshevism, they managed to appeal effectively to both workers and peasants.[26] In Armenia, the Social Democrat Hnchakian Party, formed abroad in 1887, was also nationally oriented. Likewise the Armenian Revolutionary Federation (Dashnaktsutyun), formed in Tiflis in 1890, was both socialist and nationalist. Both Armenian parties practiced political terrorism against Russian and Turkish autocracy.[27]

As one historian has put it, "In the years 1903 through 1905, between the organized terrorism of the Armenian revolutionaries, the increase in strike activity of workers, and the armed resistance of Georgian peasants, Transcaucasia was rapidly becoming ungovernable and previewed for the whole of Russia the revolutionary situation that developed in 1905."[28]

* * *

It was against this background of rapid modernization and political unrest that the Caucasus began to attract the attention of Japanese strategists. It is difficult to pinpoint exactly when Japan began turning its attention to the Caucasus. After all, it was only in the mid-nineteenth century that Japan had begun opening its doors widely to the outside world after more than two centuries of a largely isolated existence. Japan had always been aware of the big country to the north called Russia. Yet it appears that it was only with its imperial contention with Russia over Asia in the late nineteenth century that Japan began to concern itself with Russia's periphery (including the Caucasus) as the weak ring and therefore as suitable for political subversion. It is also likely that Japan acquired the expertise of Britain in Caucasian affairs because at

25 See K. Zalevkii, "Natsional'nyia partii v Rossii," *Obshchestvennoe dvizhenie v Rossii v nachale xx-go veka*, v. 3 (St. Petersburg: Obshchestvennaia pol'za, 1914) pp. 316–18. They were federalists in the sense that they initially sought a democratic federalist Russia in which Georgia was to enjoy full autonomy.
26 The Menshevik predominance is peculiar to Georgia in the Russian Empire. Whether there were objective conditions for this uniqueness is difficult to answer. See Stephen F. Jones, *Socialism in Georgian Colors: The European Road to Social Democracy, 1883–1917* (Cambridge: Harvard University Press, 2005), pp. 120–127 (stressing the "ecumenism" of Georgian Menshevism) and Suny, *The Making of the Georgian Nation*, pp. 158–164 (emphasizing the "strong elective tradition among Georgian workers").
27 See Suny, *Looking toward Ararat*, 24.
28 Suny, *Looking toward Ararat*, 92.

the time Japan and Britain were drawn increasingly closer against their common foe of Russia, culminating in the 1902 Anglo-Japanese alliance.

The career of Motojirō Akashi (1864–1919), a central figure in the initial phase of the Caucasian-Japanese nexus, is instructive of the speed with which Japan renounced isolationism and came to envision its place in the world. In the decades after Japan was forced by external powers (the United States in particular) to open its doors widely to the world, it made tremendous efforts to adapt to the modern age and cope with the advanced foreign powers by learning from them. Akashi was one of the Japanese elite of the time who became an internationalist. After graduating from the Imperial Japanese Military Academy and Army University, Akashi was sent to the Imperial General Staff, from which in 1894 he was dispatched to Germany, whose Prussian military models Japan was following. Soon, however, the Sino-Japanese War (1894–95) forced him back to Japan. A staff officer of the elite Imperial Guards, he served at this time in China (Taiwan). Afterwards, he observed the Spanish-American War in the Philippines in 1898, and in 1900 he was sent to China for negotiations with Russia regarding the settlement of the Boxer Rebellion by the Chinese. In 1901 he was appointed Japan's military attaché in Paris and in 1902 in St. Petersburg, where he became acquainted with the British spy Sidney Reilly (1873–1925), said to be the model for Ian Fleming's James Bond. (It appears that Akashi managed to convince Reilly to work for Japan as well. Reilly indeed opened a front business firm in Port Arthur in 1903, and provided to Britain and Japan valuable information on Russia's fortress there.) Akashi, fluent in both French and German (and Russian and English, according to some accounts), worked energetically in Europe until the end of the Russo-Japanese War. After a short stay in Tokyo, he returned to Berlin and later served in Korea (which Japan annexed in 1910), where he repressed Korean resistance to Japanese domination. In 1918 Akashi was appointed governor (viceroy) of Taiwan (which Japan had acquired from China as a result of its victory in the Sino-Japanese War).[29] In a word, he personally represented the ambitious new imperialist power of modern Japan.

Thus, in the increasingly mobile, imperialist, and contentious world of the early twentieth century, the Caucasus and Japan came to find each other. The following chapters discuss this unknown history.

The significance of this story is much more than episodic, however: it is an integral part of twentieth-century international history. In this era Poland, Germany, Japan, Britain, and other countries devised strategies to contain first the Russian Empire and then the Soviet Union and Communism on the Eurasian continent. It is our contention that of them, Japan's secret wars against its northern neighbor were the most comprehensive: whereas Japan envisioned these wars on a truly Eurasian scale, the European powers generally lacked an effective strategy in the vast Asian land-

29 See Tokuji Komori, *Akashi Motojirō*, 2 vols. (Tokyo: Hara Shobō, 1968) and Chiharu Inaba, *Akashi kōsaku: bōryaku no nichiro sensō* (Tokyo: Maruzen, 1995).

mass. The Caucasian-Japanese nexus was part of this history. Later during the Cold War, these secret wars, including those involving the Caucasus, were taken over and further developed by the West against the Soviet Union. Thus, the Eurasian triangle of Russia, the Caucasus, and Japan is an utterly forgotten history of cardinal importance that, stretching from the Russo-Japanese War to World War Two, ultimately influenced Western Cold War strategies.

2 The Russo-Japanese War

In the mid-nineteenth century, after more than two centuries of international isolation, Japan opened its doors and began to expand as a way to survive in a competitive world. Although its isolation from the outside world had also been a way of survival (indeed, its isolation was never complete), this seclusion was irrevocably broken by an expanding neighbor across the Pacific Ocean, namely the United States. This was classic gun-boat diplomacy. Like many other nations, Japan was forced to accept unequal treaties with foreign colonial powers, although it was itself never colonized. Overwhelmed by the military and economic might of the colonial powers, which had already colonized much of the world and were now doing the same to Japan's neighbor, China, Japan pursued a policy of "enrich the country, strengthen the military" (*fukoku kyōhei*). In this process, Russia and Japan came into conflict.

With regard to other Asian nations, Japan behaved like a colonial power: indeed, it became the first non-European imperial power in the modern era. This inevitably brought Japan on a collision course with other imperial powers. Already in 1894–95, Japan's imperialist ambitions clashed with China over the control of Korea (whose traditional overlord was China), while Russia was equally interested in extending its control to Korea. In the Sino-Japanese war itself, the rapidly modernizing Japan beat a China mired in tradition and torn by internal divisions. But fearing Japan's advance into Korea and China, Russia, together with France and Germany, intervened in the Sino-Japanese settlement, forcing Japan to return the Liaodong Peninsula to China (the so-called Tripartite Intervention). This in turn set the background for military confrontation ten years later between Russia and Japan.

The "Sleeping Tiger" proved to be rather fragile, and China's defeat stimulated the semicolonization of this giant country by imperial powers, Russia and Japan included. Russia's expansion in the Far East was long-standing. After its defeat in the Crimean War at the hands of Britain, France, and Ottoman Turkey, Russia's attention turned sharply to the East, leading to the annexation of much of central Asia in the 1860s and 1870s.[1] Russia also acquired the Maritime Province (including the Amur and Usuri regions and Vladivostok) from China in 1860. In return for helping China recover the Laiodong Peninsula from Japan, Russia gained the right to build railways in Manchuria, leading to the construction of the Chinese Eastern Railway linking Chita and Vladivostok through Manchuria. Russia also gained the lease of Dalian (now named Dal'nyj, literally meaning "Far" in Russian) and Lushun from China. Russia built railways linking these cities to Harbin and thereby to the Trans-Siberian Railway via the Chinese Eastern Railway. Northeastern China thus came under de facto Russian control. At the same time, Russia sought to extend its control further to Korea, which Japan interpreted as an explicit and direct threat to its own interests and security.

1 Orlando Figes, *The Crimean War: A History* (New York: Metropolitan Books, 2010), 453-56.

Russia's rapid expansion into Asia disquieted other imperial powers as well, although they, too, joined in the colonization of China. Britain, among other nations, also feared Russia's domination over China. Engaged in the so-called Great Game with Russia over control of Central Asia, Britain found in Japan a counterforce to Russia in the Far East. In 1902, abandoning its policy of "splendid isolation," Britain concluded a treaty of alliance with Japan with Russia in view. Japan in turn made great efforts to be accepted into the exclusive club of Western powers. In 1890 it had become a constitutional monarchy with a parliament. Compared to Russia's autocracy with no constitution or parliament, Japan appeared more acceptable to Russia's rivals. Like Britain, the United States also feared Russia's rapid expansion in Asia, where the Americans had their own imperialist ambitions. Therefore, they, too, courted Japan as a counterweight to Russia in the Far East.

2.1 War

It was under these international conditions that Russia and Japan came into military conflict in 1904. Some historians have called the Russo-Japanese War "World War Zero," the first global, imperial war.[2] Although this characterization may be somewhat far-fetched, the war, fought in neutral countries (China and Korea), was an imperial contest among imperial powers implicitly supporting one camp (France and Germany for Russia) or the other (Britain and the United States for Japan). Japan's intelligence operations thus had to become global. In this context, the Caucasus and Japan met each other, just as Poland, Finland, and Japan had found common interests against the Russian Empire.[3]

It was under the pressure of war that the Russian autocracy cracked for the first time in history and was forced to make concessions (the 1905 Revolution). This marked the beginning of the end of the Russian autocracy in 1917. In this context, the Russo-Japanese War was a signal event foreshadowing the tumultuous history of Eurasia in the twentieth century. Japan's engagements with non-Russian nationalities in the Russian Empire, including the Caucasians, before, during, and after the war are thus a matter of special historical significance.

Like the Habsburg Empire, the Russian Empire was multi-national. In the course of the nineteenth century, Russia had added to its already impressive size by conquer-

2 John W. Steinberg, Bruce W. Menning, David Schimmelpenninck van der Oye, David Wolff, and Shinji Yokote, eds, *The Russo-Japanese War in Global Perspective: World War Zero*, 2 vols. (Leiden-Boston: Brill, 2005-2007).

3 On Poland and Japan, see Hiroaki Kuromiya and Andrzej Pepłoński, *Między Warszawą a Tokio: Polsko-Japońska współpraca wywiadowcza 1904–1944* (Toruń: Adam Marszałek, 2009), and on Finland and Japan, see *Iznanka revoliutsii. Vooruzhennoe vozstanie v Rossii na iaposnkiia sredstva* (1906) (St. Petersburg: Tip. A.S. Suvorina, n.d.).

ing the Northern Caucasian peoples, the Southern Caucasian states (today's Georgia, Armenia, and Azerbaijani), and Central Asia. Yet some of the territory was gained only after bitter military struggle, as exemplified by the Caucasian War of 1817–64. This was an area where Russia's hold was particularly precarious. Schemes to break up Russia from within through "wars of nationalities" were old. During the Crimean War in the mid-nineteenth century and beyond, Britain entertained such plans, although how hard it pursued them is unclear.[4] It did, however, pursue similar plans in the 1880s. In the years leading up to the Russo-Japanese War and during the war itself, Britain considered the Caucasus crucial for its strategic purposes, that is, to maintain and expand its influence and control in Persia, India, and Central Asia at the expense of Russia. For this purpose, Britain entertained the idea of organizing armed uprisings in the Caucasus and apparently did at least supply weapons and ammunition.[5]

Japan likely learned lessons from the experience of other countries such as Britain and Ottoman Turkey that had fought against Russia in the past. As the Russo-Japanese competition in the Far East escalated, Japan increasingly paid attention to gathering intelligence on Russia. The Japanese military in particular was preparing for eventual armed conflict in great earnest. Tokyo sent many military officers to strategic parts of the Far East disguised as private citizens engaged in commerce, such as photographers, barbers, and brothel owners.[6] Like other countries, Japan of course used its diplomatic posts as well. In 1902, it opened a consulate in Odesa (or Odessa),[7] in today's Ukraine, to observe, among other matters, the movement of the Russian Black Sea fleet.

Japan's activity thus became global, reflecting the size and nature of modern conflict. By the turn of the century, the Caucasus had also begun attracting the attention of Japanese strategists. Giichi Tanaka (1864–1929) was probably the first Japanese to recognize the importance of this area to Japan's interests. In 1898 Captain Tanaka, a descendant of a samurai family who would become prime minister of Japan in the late 1920s, was sent to St. Petersburg as an assistant military attaché, although his status as such may not have been officially acknowledged. Going there to investigate the country, he not only learned the Russian language but also russified his name (Giichi Nobusukevich Tanaka). An atheist up to that point, he converted to Orthodox Chris-

4 Figes, *The Crimean War*, 401, 453.

5 See I.Sh. Menteshashvili, *Zakavkaz'e v anglo-russkikh protivorechiiakh v 1880–1914 gg.* (Tbilisi: [n.p.], 2001), 63–65.

6 The best-known example is Makiyo Ishimitsu who had studied in Russia and then in 1901 left his official position in the army to take up a special assignment: running first a laundry shop and then a photography shop in Harbin and becoming the official cameraman of the Russian troops stationed there and elsewhere in Manchuria. See his memoirs, Masato Ishimitsu (ed.), *Ishimitsu Makiyo no shuki* (Tokyo: Chūō kōron, 1988).

7 Here and hereafter, the Ukrainian spelling of "Odesa" is used.

Fig. 2.1. Giichi Tanaka, future prime minister of Japan (in the 1920s).

tianity and regularly went to church in Russia. He also learned to dance and led a very active social life in the Russian capital.[8]

In 1899 Tanaka traveled extensively in Russia, including the Caucasus: Saratov, Tsaritsyn, Astrakhan, Piatigorsk, Kislovodsk, Vladikavkaz, Batumi,[9] Novorossiisk, Sevastopol, Odesa, and Kyiv (Kiev). The following year he managed to have himself attached to a Russian military regiment: the Emperor Alexander III 145th Novocherkassk Infantry Regiment in St. Petersburg. He also learned to drink in a Russian way, became acquainted with Minister of War Aleksei N. Kuropatkin, and frequented gatherings of Russia's upper society.[10] Later, he used to tell Russians that "he had drunk so much vodka with Russian officers during his service in Russia that nothing could destroy the ties [between him and Russia]."[11]

Tanaka's ties to Russia were not limited to upper society. A hardline advocate of war with Russia, he energetically traveled around the country wherever he sensed revolutionary ferment. In the process he met many revolutionary activists. In 1901 he

8 *Tanaka Giichi denki*, vol. 1 (Tokyo: Tanaka Giichi denki kankō kai, 1958), 110–116.
9 Although its old name was "Batum," the present name of "Batumi" is used in this book.
10 *Tanaka Giichi denki*, 136–38, 140–64.
11 George Alexander Lensen (ed.), *Revelations of a Russian Diplomat: The Memoirs of Dmitrii I. Abrikossow* (Seattle: University of Washington Press, 1964), 268. Tanaka became famous as the alleged author of the infamous "Tanaka Memorial," a forged document purportedly detailing Japan's ambition for world conquest. This will be discussed in chapter 5.

again traveled to southern Russia and the Caucasus, where demonstrations and industrial strikes frequently took place. According to Tanaka, he even dreamed of becoming an industrial worker and a revolutionary himself. He also associated closely with some leaders. Subsequently, in the 1920s, he confessed they had become so famous that he could not reveal their names publicly.[12] His biographers further suspect that he met the young Stalin in the Caucasus. Tanaka himself stated that he had met Stalin and helped him with money, at least, this is what he told his emissary to Stalin in 1927 after becoming prime minister.[13] He did not say, however, where and when. Although one account mentions a meeting near Irkutsk in Siberia,[14] this cannot be correct, because in June 1902, having been promoted to major, Tanaka returned to Tokyo, whereas Stalin was exiled to Siberia for the first time in 1903. Although Tanaka's meeting with Stalin cannot be confirmed by other sources, it seems to be the case that Tanaka did cultivate close ties with revolutionaries in the Caucasus and elsewhere.

Tanaka returned home convinced that Russia was so big and rich in resources that merely winning war against it or capturing some territory from it would not help. What was important, according to him, was to facilitate Russia's own self-destruction by supporting destructive forces from within.[15] This idea was almost certainly shared by some strategists within and without the Japanese military.

In 1903, oddly in view of the growing tension between the two countries, Tanaka, along with twenty other Japanese politicians and military commanders, was decorated by the Russian government (in his case, with the Order of St. Ann Second Rank).[16] Those Russians who hosted Tanaka's tenure in the Novocherkassk regiment were in turn recommended for decoration by the Japanese government.[17]

2.2 The Akashi Operations

Tanaka's activities were followed by Motojirō Akashi, who as an intelligence officer became much better known than Tanaka. Colonel Akashi was appointed a Japanese military attaché in St. Petersburg in 1902 and stayed there until February 1904, when the Russo-Japanese War broke out. Akashi then moved from St. Petersburg to Stockholm in Sweden. But because his official position as a military attaché in Stockholm

---

12 *Tanaka Giichi denki*, 165.

13 Quoted in Kaoru Furukawa, *Yume harukanaru: kindai nihon no kyojin Kuhara Fusanosuke* (Tokyo: PHP Kenkyūjo, 2009), 356–57.

14 Furukawa, *Yume harukanaru*, 357.

15 *Tanaka Giichi denki*, p. 169.

16 The Japan Center for Asian Historical Records (National Archives of Japan; hereafter JACAR): http://www.jacar.go.jp (reference code: A10112576300).

17 JACAR, reference code: A10112549800.

Fig. 2.2. Motojirō Akashi (c. 1904).

was burdensome enough to hinder his intelligence work, he was relieved of his position to allow him to engage fulltime in his secret work throughout Europe.[18]

Initially, Akashi had much difficulty connecting with Russian revolutionaries. What if any contacts Tanaka passed on to Akashi is unknown.[19] It is quite possible that Tanaka's story about his connections with revolutionaries was in fact exaggerated. It was likely difficult for anyone, let alone a foreigner, to become acquainted with underground revolutionaries in Russia at the time. Whatever the case, Akashi familiarized himself with the anti-Tsarist forces in the country and recruited a few spies within Russia, including at least one Russian army captain. It is known that when the war ended in September 1905, Akashi had been operating seven "spies" (*kanchō*, six inside Russia and one in France), who were assisted by another five (all outside Russia). Some of them he deployed along the Trans-Siberian Railway – in Samara, Cheliabinsk, and Irkutsk. At first he used those introduced to him by his friends and colleagues, but he found that in the end those who worked for money were the most useful.[20] Indeed, he went through a lot of money, but in fact he appeared more successful in his work with those who worked for political reasons.

---

18 On Akashi's work, see Chiharu Inaba, *Akashi kōsaku: bōryaku no nichiro sensō* (Tokyo: Maruzen, 1995), and Motojirō Akashi, *Rakka ryūsui: Colonel Akashi's Report on His Secret Cooperation with the Russian Revolutionary Parties during the Russo-Japanese War*, tr. by Inaba Chiharu and ed. by Olavi K. Fält and Antti Kujala (Helsinki: Societas Historica Finlandiae, 1988).

19 Tanaka's biographer suggests that Tanaka introduced Akashi to his contacts but gives no details. See *Tanaka Giichi denki*, 181.

20 Motojirō Akashi, "Rakka ryūsui," *Gaikō jihō*, no. 1030 (1966), 97. This part of Akashi's report is not included in the English translation published in Helsinki in 1988.

Fig. 2.3. Motojirō Akashi (probably in the 1910s).

In the course of the war, the General Staff gave Akashi 1 million yen (amounting to as much as ten million in today's dollar values), of which he used 730,000 yen.[21] It was not easy for Akashi to extract this much money from Tokyo, which, and especially the Ministry of Foreign Affairs, feared that if Japan's secret funding of opposition movements in Russia became known, it would be a diplomatic disaster on a global scale. Tokyo therefore repeatedly rejected Akashi's requests for large-scale funding. It was only in the spring of 1905, more than a year after Akashi had initiated contact with leaders of the opposition movements, that Tokyo decided to meet his requests. Eager to force Russia to make peace under conditions favorable to Japan, Tokyo finally concluded that it would be politically expedient to fund subversive Russian forces on a massive scale.

21 Hisao Tani, *Kimitsu nichiro senshi* (Tokyo: Hara shobō, 1966), 258.

Assisted by Japanese diplomats and officers stationed in Europe as well as English socialists and Swedish officers and businessmen,[22] Akashi now cultivated extensive contacts with subversive elements. In his postwar report to the General Staff, Akashi discussed fifteen anti-Tsarist political parties and some forty important persons of these parties. The Russian Socialist Revolutionary Party, the Russian Social Democratic Party, the Liberal Party (the Union of Liberation), the Jewish Bund Party, the Armenian ("Droshak" or Dashnaktsutyun) Party, the Georgian (Sakartvelo) party,[23] the Lettish (Latvian) Social Democratic Party, the Finnish Constitutional Party, the Finnish Active Resistance Party, the Polish Nationalist Party (National League), the Polish Socialist Party, the Polish Progressive Party, the Ukrainian Socialist Revolutionary Party, the Belarusian (or Belorussian) Party (Hramada), and the "Gapon Party" – all came under Akashi's attention. The overall prejudices at the time in Europe, as well as Japan's peculiar ignorance and arrogance, were reflected in Akashi's own prejudices. Regarding the Georgian Sakartvelo Party, for instance, Akashi wrote: "Georgia is generally a backward civilization, and the Georgians are ferocious and brave. Consequently this party is not as moderate as other socialist groups, and frequently uses explosives."[24] Akashi, however, almost certainly would have agreed with H.C. Armstrong, who said regarding the Georgians of the time and their struggle for independence:

> Though only a people of three million souls in all, they revolted against the might and massed strength of Russia; and the Russians trod them down with fierce reprisals, sending thousands to the gallows and tens of thousands to exile in Siberia. But it was in vain, for though sometimes for a while crushed, their spirit remained unbroken and again, untamed and untamable, they revolted; and they carried on their "Unending Battle" for Freedom.[25]

Akashi's listing of the opposition leaders is almost a "Who's Who" in the Russian opposition movements, starting with N.V. Chaikovskii, Prince Kropotkin, G.V. Plekhanov , and V.I. Lenin, and ending with P.N. Miliukov, P.B. Struve, Maksim Gor'kii, and Roman Dmowski. Akashi also lists Prince Loris-Melikov (Hovhannes Loris-Meliov/Melikian) and Mikayel Varandian (Hovhannisian), both of the Droshak Party, and Varlam Cherkezishvili (Varlaam Cherkezov, a Georgian prince and anarchist). Akashi personally met many of the people he listed (although no one knows for sure whether he actually met Lenin.). Akashi maintained particularly intimate ties with Konrad Viktor (Konni) Zillicaus (1855–1924), head of the Finnish Active Resistance Party who had lived in Japan for two years; Witold Jodko-Narkiewicz (1864–1924), leader of the Polish

22 Michael Futrell, "Colonel Akashi and Japanese Contacts with Russian Revolutionaries in 1904–5." *St. Antony's Papers 2: Far Eastern Affairs* 4 (1967), 12.

23 The "Sakartvelo Party" used repeatedly by Akashi in fact signified the Georgian Party of Socialist Federalists. See footnote 26 of this chapter (page 21).

24 Akashi, *Rakka ryūsui*, 26.

25 H.C. Armstrong, *Unending Battle* (New York-London: Harper & Brothers, 1934), xii.

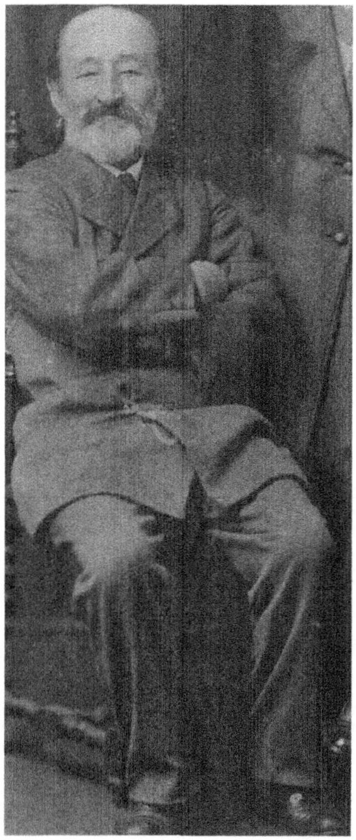

Fig. 2.4. Varlam Cherkezishvili (Varlaam Cherkezov), London, beginning of the twentieth century.

Socialist Party; and Giorgi Dekanozishvili (Dekanozi) (1868–1910), leader of the Georgian Revolutionary Party of Socialist Federalists (*sakartvelos socialist-federalisturi sarevolucio partiia*).[26] (Whether Akashi's view of Dekanozishvili differed from the

26 The Russian police often referred to Dekanozishvili erroneously as an "Armenian anarchist." The Socialist Federalist Party was formed in 1904 of Georgian intellectuals headed by Prince Artshil Dzhordzhadze. In 1901 these intellectuals formed an initiative group in Georgia aimed at restoring independence to Georgia. The following year the group sent two of its most active members, Dzhordzhadze and Dekanozishvili (a mining engineer known for his organizational skills), to Paris to publish a journal, *Sakartvelo*, in the Georgian and French languages. The French version was used to acquaint Europe with the Georgian question, while the Georgian version was smuggled into Georgia. The group advocated an autonomous Georgia within the larger framework of a Caucasian Federation within the Russian Empire that all peoples of the Caucasus were to join. This was to be the first step toward the eventual full independence of Georgia. In April 1904, the Sakartvelo group formed the core of a new Georgian Revolutionary Party of Socialist Federalists. See Giorgi Laskhishvili, *memuarebi [Memoirs] (1885–1915)* (Tbilisi: [n.p.], 1934), 138–41, 159–61; Dimitri Shvelidze and Giorgi Gaprindashvili, *giorgi dekanozishvili – mamulishvilis dabruneba* [Giorgi Dekanozishvili – the patriots return] (Tbilisi:

Fig. 2.5. Artshil Dzhordzhadze (beginning of the twentieth century).

view he held of Georgians in general just quoted is unknown.) Akashi's list included double agents such as "Dikanskii" (the famous E.F. Azef of the Socialist Revolutionary Party's terrorist units) and Father Gapon (G.A. Gapon), organizer of a peaceful demonstration in St. Petersburg on 9 January 1905 that was crushed in a bloody massacre, events that became known as Bloody Sunday and that led to the 1905 Revolution in Russia.

Together, Akashi and Zillicaus pursued two routes to subvert the Russian government. One was the unification of opposition parties, the other violent demonstrations and armed uprising. Tokyo gave some financial support for organizing a meeting of the opposition parties in Paris for the purpose of uniting them. This conference took place in September–October 1904, with eight parties taking part: the Union of Liberation, the Polish National League, the "Finnish opposition," the Socialist Revolutionaries, the Polish Socialist Party, the Georgian Socialist Federalist Revolution-

Universali, 2010), 30–31; and A. Dzhordzhadze, "La Géorgie et la Fédération du Caucase," *Géorgie, politique et sociale* (Paris), 1903, no. 4, 1–2. Shortly after the party formed, the young Stalin wrote a scathing attack on the Socialist-Federalists. See I.V. Stalin, *Sochineniia* vol. 1 (Moscow: Politizdat, 1946), 32–55.

Fig. 2.6. Giorgi Dekanozishvili (in a mining engineer's uniform) with his parents and sister, Tiflis, end of the nineteenth century.

ary Party, the Armenian Dashnaktsutyun Party, and the Latvian Social Democratic Party. The Bolsheviks and Mensheviks, concerned about the funding by Japan, did not participate. Although unification of these diverse groups (socialist and nonsocialist) proved impossible, the conference did issue a declaration advocating the overthrow of autocracy, the establishment of a free, democratic system, and the right of self-determination for all nations in the Russian Empire. Soon after the conference, the Georgian Socialist Federalist Party issued in Paris a leaflet in the name of itself, the Socialist Revolutionary Party, the Polish Socialist Party, and the Latvian Social Democratic Party. Written in the Georgian language for Georgian workers, it advocated the right to free choice, territorial autonomy, and secession for all nations in the Russian Empire.[27]

With Tokyo's strong support in sight, Akashi and Zillicaus convened another conference in Geneva, Switzerland, in early April 1905, in which the Russian Socialist Revolutionaries and Father Gapon took the initiative in inviting mainly socialist and revolutionary parties. This time the Belarusian Hramada, the Bolsheviks (represented by Lenin), the Bund, and the Armenian Social Democratic Workers' Party also joined in

27 Fonds Georges Dekanozichvili. Centre historique des archives nationales (CHAN), Paris, boxe 345AP/1.

Fig. 2.7. Giorgi Dekanozishvili (Paris, beginning of the twentieth century).

the meeting. Yet the Bolsheviks and other social-democratic parties questioned the hegemony of the Socialist Revolutionaries and raised other issues, eventually leaving the conference. The remaining seven parties managed to adopt a declaration in which they advocated the overthrow of the Russian autocracy by armed uprising and the foundation of a democratic republic.

Plans for such an armed uprising had already been detailed by Zillicaus and Akashi well before the Geneva meeting,[28] and they expended a great deal of money on preparations, though initially Japan's commitment was limited. Famously, Polish Socialist Party leader Józef Piłsudski traveled to Tokyo to solicit Japanese aid in arms with which to subvert Russia from within. But Piłsudski's efforts were thwarted by his rival Roman Dmowski (of the National Democratic Party), who also traveled to Tokyo.[29] Japan did, however, supply some money to provide weapons to the Russian Socialist Revolutionaries through Zillicaus, who held the financial sources hidden from Russian parties. By contrast, he openly courted non-Russian opposition parties with Japanese money. In July 1904 it was Zillicaus who introduced Loris Melikian and

28 On these conferences, see Antti Kujala, "March Separately – Strike Together: The Paris and Geneva Conferences Held by the Russian and Minority Nationalities' Revolutionary and Opposition Parties, 1904–1905," in Akashi, *Rakka ryūsui*, 85–167.

29 Kuromiya and Pepłoński, *Między Warszawą a Tokio:*, 32–36.

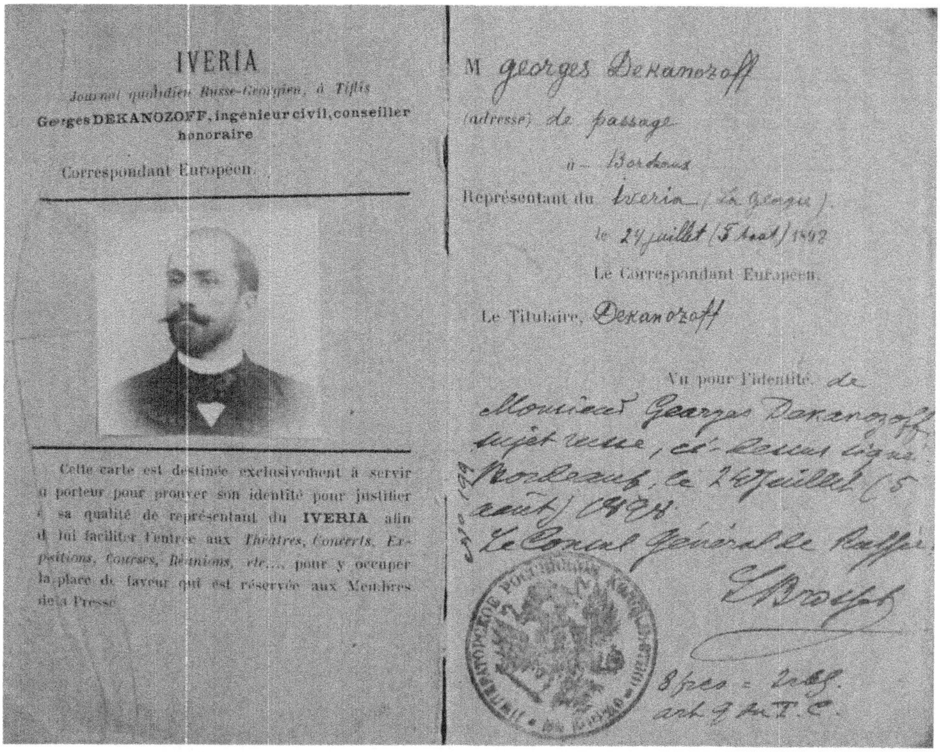

Fig. 2.8. Giorgi Dekanozishvili's identification card as a European reporter for the Georgian patriotic newspaper *Iveria*, 1898.

Dekanozishvili to Akashi in Paris.[30] (From circumstantial evidence, however, it is possible that Akashi's contact with Dekanozishvili in fact began several months earlier.) With Tokyo's approval of large-scale funding, preparations for armed uprising within Russia began in earnest in the spring of 1905.

Akashi knew that the Caucasus, like Poland and Finland, was fertile ground for subversion. The outbreak of the Russo-Japanese War in February 1904 accelerated political activities in the Caucasus as elsewhere in the Russian Empire. Shortly after the war broke out, the French consul in Tiflis reported that even though the Tsar's "loyal subjects" were mobilized for demonstrations in support of the war, a large section of the population sympathized with Japan. On 15 February 1904, for example, a large number of Georgians demonstrated in Batumi with a Russian flag (to mislead the police), then threw it on the ground, stomped on it, and raised a red flag instead with cries of "Down with the Tsar! Hurrah for the Japanese!" The meeting was dispersed by Cossacks and five people were arrested. (The French consul added that the pupils

30 Kujala, "March Separately – Strike Together," 100–101.

Le Numéro : 20 centimes

LA GÉORGIE

POLITIQUE & SOCIALE

RÉDACTION & ADMINISTRATION : 51, rue Saint-Sauveur, PARIS

LA GÉORGIE est en vente à la SOCIÉTÉ NOUVELLE DE LIBRAIRIE & D'ÉDITION (Librairie Georges Bellais) 17, rue Cujas, Paris (V).

SOMMAIRE

La Géorgie et la Fédération du Caucase

Fig. 2.9. Title page of *La Géorgie*, the first Georgian periodical published in Europe (1903).

of the Georgian school for nobles in Kutaisi shared the same sentiment.) In Baku, at about the same time, a terrible incident took place when at the end of a service being held in an Armenian church for the victory of the Russian army in the Far East, someone threw a bomb, killing "a large number of people."[31] From his observations, the consul concluded, quite rightly, that even though volunteer forces were being formed from "Cherkessians" referring to Muslims in the Northern Caucasus, the Caucasus was unlikely to be able to provide a large military force to the Far East.[32] For its part, the journal *Sakartvelo* took an openly pro-Japanese and defeatist position when the war broke out.[33]

Akashi, familiar with the political situation in the Caucasus, took advantage of it. The Georgians in particular attracted his attention. Already in April 1904, a con-

31 Archives du ministère des Affaires étrangères (AMAE), Correspondance politique et commerciale dite "nouvelle série," 1896-1918, Z (Europe), dossier Russie (Agitation révolutionnaire et anarchiste), no. 12, fol. 354–56.

32 AMAE, Z, dossier Russie, no. 12, fol. 335.

33 See "La guerre russo-japonaises," *Géorgie, politique et sociale* (Paris), 1904, no. 7, 4–6. It is possible that the publication of this journal was helped by Japan. See also GARF, f. 102, DP PP 1904-II, op. 316, d. 28, ll. 130, 163, 176, 191 (on Baud) and 132 (on Gabunia).

საქართველო

Fig. 2.10. Title page of *Sakartvelo* (Georgia), the first Georgian periodical published in Europe (1903).

ference of Georgian political groups in Europe had been convened in Geneva through the initiative of Dzhordzhadze and Dekanozishvili. The Georgian Socialist Federalists, anarchists, and Social Democrats sent their representatives to discuss a joint struggle against Tsarism. Cherkezishvili, filled with patriotic feelings, declared that he had come to the conference not so much as an anarchist as a Georgian.[34] Noe Zhordania, leader of the Social Democrats, however, refused to form a united front with the Socialist Federalists, who, he contended, ignored the class struggle of the Georgian people, and so left the conference.[35] (Ironically it was Zhordania who became the head of an

34 *okmebi kartvel revolutsionerta p'irveli konperentsiisa* [Minutes of the first conference of the Georgian revolutionaries] (Paris: "Sakartvelo," 1904), 15. In March 1904 the Armenian Dashnaktsutiun party resolved to work with the Russian Socialist Revolutionaries and the Georgian Sakartvelo group. See [A. Jorjadze], "ra gadmogvtsa ts'arsulma tse'lma? [The heritage of the last year]." *sakartvelo, kartvel sotsialist'-pederalist'ta sarevolutsio partiis organo* [Georgia, organ of the revolutionary party of Georgian socialist-federalists] (Paris) no. 1(13), 2.

35 Georgian State Central Historical Archive (GSCHA), Tbilisi, Georgia, f. 94, op. 1, d. 70, l. 2, and Shvelidze and Gaprindashvili, p. 70. See also Noe Zhordaniia, *chemi ts'arsuli. mogonebani* [My past. Memoirs] (Tbilisi: Sarangi, 1990), 45. According to the French police, who secretly monitored this con-

Fig. 2.11. Participants in the founding conference of the Georgian Party of Socialist Federalists, Geneva, April 1904. Dekanozishvili lying in the center. Sitting from left: Artshil Dzhordzhadze and Mikheil (Mikhako) Tsereteli. Standing from left: Aleksandre (Sandro) Gabunia, Komando Gogelia and Varlam Cherkezishivili (Cherkezov).

independent Georgia in 1918.) The conference adopted a resolution announcing the official creation of a new Georgian Revolutionary Party of Socialist Federalists on the basis of the Socialist Revolutionaries, anarchists, and the Sakartvelo group who were present, and the journal *Sakartvelo* became its official organ.[36] The conference further adopted a resolution emphasizing the necessity to combat not only the Russian autoc-

ference, they declared that their party regarded the struggle against the government as a task of the entire country, independent of "local interests and the question of nationalities" (see CHAN, F/7/12521). In return, members of the conference criticized the Social Democrats for ignoring the question of nationalities. See GSCHA, f. 94, op. 1, d. 70, ll. 52–52ob.

36 See *okmebi kartvel revolutsionerta pirveli konperentsiisa*, 3-4; "Congres des révolutionnaires géorgiens." *Géorgie, politique et sociale* 1904, no. 8, 6.

racy but a possible "centralist republic" that could hinder the "social, economic, and national liberation of Georgia."[37]

Shortly after the conference, the Socialist Federalists issued an appeal to the Georgian people in which it called on Georgian soldiers to boycott the war with Japan: "[T]ake every measure not to participate in this useless blood-letting .... Our oppressor and murderer is not there [in the Far East] but much closer .... We must fight not to enslave others but for our own freedom."[38] Already from late 1904 onward, a limited number of weapons (mainly revolvers) and revolutionary literature were being smuggled into Tiflis, Baku, Batumi and elsewhere in the Caucasus with the financial assistance of Japan.[39] In one case, the Georgians used the boat *Sidon* of the Messageries Maritimes Company to transport "illegal literature." Russian police agents suspected the boat of committing "more grave crimes."[40]

Despite the suspicions of the Russian police, Georgian revolutionaries were able to receive revolutionary literature through these channels because they had their own men in the customs authorities of the port of Batumi. As Tedo Sakhokia, a leader of the Georgian Socialist Federalists later reminisced, with the help of his old friend I. Gvaramadze he was able to deliver on shore, "almost freely," his party's organ *Sakartvelo* and other illegal literature sent by boat from Paris.[41]

By the autumn of 1904, the Socialist Federalists had attained considerable political influence in Georgia. Their antidraft campaign in Guria, for example, led the majority of the population to refuse categorically to serve in the military, proclaiming "Better to die in our Guria than in Manchuria." This led to a bloody confrontation with Cossacks, resulting in a large number of casualties on both sides. Some Gurians fled to the woods where, in view of an acute shortage of weapons, they manually manufactured simple Berdan rifles for partisan warfare. By contrast, the Social Democrats, whose political base was generally much larger in Guria, called on the population not to evade conscription but to join the military in order to conduct revolutionary propaganda there. Their tactic did not, however, enjoy popularity in Guria. On 7 November 1904, people in Kutaisi demonstrated with red banners against the call-up and ended up battling the Cossacks and the police, while in Khevsureti, in northeastern Georgia, conscription was suspended owing to popular discontent.[42]

---

37 GSCHA, f. 94, op. 1, d. 70, l. 2 ob.

38 "kartvel musha khalhs: mots'odeba no. 1" (kartvel sotsialist'-pederalist'ta sarevolutsio part'ia) [To Georgian Workers. Leaflet no. 1 (Georgian Revolutionary Party of Socialist Federalists)](1904), Fonds Georges Dekanozichvili, CHAN, boxe 345, AP/2.

39 GARF, f. 102, DP PP 1904-II, op. 316, d. 28, l. 12. According to Dekanozishvili, by May 1905 "a significant number of weapons" had been delivered. See ibid., l. 49ob.

40 GARF, op. cit., ll. 22, 28.

41 See Tedo Sakhokia, *tsimbirshi. mogonebani 1905 ts'lis revolutsiis droidan* [My exile in Siberia. Memoirs from the period of the 1905 revolution] (Tbilisi: literaturis muzeumi, 2011), 184.

42 *sakartvelo, kartvel sotsialist'-pederalist'ta sarevolutsio part'iis organo* (Paris) 1904, no. 7(19), 5-6.

Fig. 2.12. Giorgi Dekanozishvili and Mikheil Kiknadze (Paris, 1905).

Elsewhere in the Caucasus, especially in the Northern Caucasus, there seems to have been less resistance to the war. The Tsar's government recruited hundreds of volunteer soldiers from among the Dagestani, Karachais, Balkars, Ingush, and others. Many of them pledged allegiance to the Koran and traveled to the Far East, where they fought.[43] This does not, of course, mean that the war was universally popular in the Northern Caucasus.

Following Bloody Sunday in St. Petersburg, the situation in the Caucasus turned quite violent and revolutionary. As Luigi Villari, an Italian correspondent for *The Times* in London, witnessed:

> Since the general state of unrest in Russia spread to the Caucasus, Batum [Batumi] has been a perfect hotbed of revolt. . . . But unlike the strikes in St. Petersburg, those of Batum at once proceeded to violent measures, and from that day to this the town has not had a moment's real quiet. When I arrived things were peaceable enough in appearance; although the state of siege was in force there were no patrols, and hardly any policemen. Yet not a day passed without murders being committed in the streets, and no murderer was ever arrested.

43 See the History (Russo-Japanese War) at http://www.gazavat.ru (accessed 19 March 2012).

Fig. 2.13. Giorgi Dekanozishvili, his wife Henriette Frenois, and children Tinatin and Tariel (Paris, beginning of the twentieth century).

The real governor of Batumi was not the official Russian governor but someone living in one of its suburbs. His "word was obeyed as law":

> Orders will suddenly be issued that the workmen of such and such a factory must strike; the men obey without a murmur, and any manager or employee who attempts to stop the movement is assassinated.... It seemed incredible that in a town fortified like Batum, surrounded by batteries bristling with guns and garrisoned by large bodies of troops, murder and outrage should be so easy. No attempt was made to arrest the guilty, and in fact the word seemed to have been passed that the revolutionists be left alone.[44]

In the north of Batumi, in the Guria region of Georgia, people rejected any governmental authority, making instead "a practical experiment in peasant autonomy of a very interesting nature." The "Gurian Republic" impressed Lev Tolstoi, who commented with admiration that the Gurians organized "life in such a manner that there should be no need for any authority." But unlike the pacifist Tolstoi, the Gurians fought with arms against interference in their affairs: "If they (the Russians) wish to restore the old form of government, they must kill us to the last man; till then we shall go on resist-

44 Luigi Villari, *Fire and Sword in the Caucasus* (London: T. Fisher Unwin, 1906), 52, 53, 55.

ing." Indeed, the whole province resisted and, as Villari described it, was "drenched in blood."[45]

In the spring of 1905, Tedo Sakhokia, a Socialist Federalist leader and Dekanozishvili's close associate, was dispatched to Georgia to create party cells in Batumi, Poti, and Sukhumi and prepare for the receipt of weapons to be sent from Europe. He succeeded in creating party committees and taking over the editorial office of the Batumi newspaper *Chernomorskii vestnik* (*Black Sea Herald*). Secret military organizations led by Georgian officers serving in the Russian Army were also created. Information gained from them was then handed to Akashi.[46]

With Tokyo's approval of substantial funding in the spring of 1905, Akashi began working closely with Caucasian revolutionaries. In his work, he may well have been helped by Britain, which favored Japan's victory over Russia for its own strategic reasons. Indeed, Britain is said to have facilitated Japan's penetration of the Caucasus by its agents. For example, in 1904 the English steam boat *Hempsud* (Hampstead?) arrived in Batumi, most of whose crew, according to the Russian police, were Japanese spies. It was further reported that the Japanese government was sending more of its agents to Black Sea ports to destroy the Russian military fleet by mines and other explosives. The Russian police, suspecting that British boats were being staffed by Japanese spies, paid particular attention to ships run by the English company Samuel Samuelson servicing the route between Istanbul and Batumi.[47]

Akashi found Dekanozishvili reliable and significant. Moreover, Dekanozishvili's reach went beyond Georgia per se. According to Russian police information, he had informants in Azerbaijan and Dagestan as well, where his relatives (Khananov or Khananashvili) worked as high-ranking officials in the Russian police and administration. Only at the end of May 1906 did the Russian police find out that Dekanozishvili had maintained contact with them.[48] It was probably through his contact that the socialist-federalist ideas of the Georgians reached Azerbaijan. In early 1905, for instance, the Turkic Social-Federal Revolutionary Committee distributed leaflets of "separatist content" in Elizavetpol' (Ganja) in today's Azerbaijan. The committee called for the unity of Caucasian peoples and condemned the mutual massacres committed by Armenians and Azeris in Baku in February 1905. Accusing the Russian government of attempts to incite the Caucasian peoples against one another, the Committee issued an appeal: "Turkic brothers! The Baku massacres have pushed back us Muslims and Armenians by a hundred years and shamed us in the eyes of other

45 Villari, *Fire and Sword*, pp. 84–85, 98, 99. On the Gurian Republic, see also Stephen F. Jones, *Socialism in Georgian Colors: The European Road to Social Democracy, 1883–1917* (Cambridge: Harvard University Press, 2005), ch. 6.

46 Correspondence from Sakhokia to Dekanozishvili (3 April, 9 May, and 28 June 1905): Fonds Georges Dekanozichvili, CHAN, boxe 345, AP/1.

47 Menteshashvili, *Zakavkaz'e v anglo-russkikh protivorechiiakh*, 54.

48 GSCHA, f. 836, op. 1, d. 237, ll. 1, 1–5.

peoples. When bloodied Armenians and Muslims are lying on the streets of Baku, our enemy gloats and thinks that 'once these two peoples are at each other, my hands are freed.' So we should wake up and recognize our [true] enemy: the Russian government."[49] This proclamation by Azeris greatly alarmed the Russian authorities.[50] Thus, the far-reaching influence of Dekanozishvili in the Caucasus made him particularly attractive to the Japanese.

In his meeting with Dekanozishvili on 2 May 1905 in Paris, Akashi told him that he was not entirely happy with the direction of the revolutionary movement. He cautioned Dekanozishvili that it should not be directed against the private property of individuals but against the Russian autocracy. Dekanozishvili responded by saying that everything could not proceed as planned, and that one needed to consider the presence of military forces. Akashi sought to convince Dekanozishvili that, based on data obtained from a Russian officer, at the time there were approximately four- to five-hundred thousand soldiers in the country, and that one hundred thousand armed people could overcome the demoralized soldiers. For this purpose he was ready to provide funding. Akashi gave 125,000 francs in cash to his partner, urging him to "work energetically" and "get the work done promptly."[51] Later in Paris, Dekanozishvili met Sadakoto Hisamatsu, Japan's military attaché in Paris, and Baron Norizumi Suematsu, Japan's special envoy to Europe. Dekanozishvili befriended in particular Captain Yukio Takatsuka, an intelligence officer attached to the Japanese embassy in Paris.[52]

Russian authorities in Paris now sent alarming notes to St. Petersburg: Akashi was more than Japan's military agent. Indeed, he was seeking to create trouble (*smuta*), and armed uprisings in the Caucasus in particular. He was a political agitator and provocateur, and his work was directed against the very foundations of Russia's political regime.[53]

Purchasing arms was no easy matter, but the Poles were well prepared in this business. By Akashi's admission, Dekanozishvili gave "the Poles money in advance and a free hand, but other parties received money only after they had found arms for sale."[54] Whether the Japanese money contributed to the revolution in Poland (particularly the June uprising in Łódź) is not known. Akashi himself did not discuss this connection, although he did mention that some time in early 1905 he met "the chief of the Polish Intransigent Party Suddeniki" (Wojciech Dzieduszycki) in Vienna and

49 See I.S. Bagirova, *Politicheskie partii i organizatsii Azerbaidzhana v nachale XX veka (1900–1917)* (Baku: Elm, 1997), 165. This committee appears to have laid the foundation in the summer of 1905 for the political party Geirat (Honor) in Elizavetpol' (Ganja).

50 Bagirova, *Politicheskie partii i organizatsii Azerbaidzhana* , 166.

51 GARF, f. 102, DP PP 1904-II, op. 316, d. 28, ll. 48–50, 150.

52 GARF, f. 102, DP PP 1904-II, op. 316, d. 28, l. 212.

53 GARF, f. 102, DP PP 1904-II, op. 316, d. 28, ll. 169, 202–203.

54 Akashi, *Rakka ryūsui*, 45–46.

arranged to buy "tens of thousands of inexpensive rifles in Switzerland."[55] Eventually sixteen thousand rifles and 3 million bullets were bought in Switzerland to be sent to the Baltic regions, and likewise eighty-five hundred rifles and 1.2 million bullets were to be shipped to the Black Sea regions. The latter purchase was arranged by Dekanozishvili with the help of the Georgian anarchist Varlaam Cherkezishvili and the wealthy Swiss anarchist Eugène Baud.[56] Cherkezishvili's contact with anarchist networks in the Netherlands and Southern France proved especially useful. An anarchist organization based in Marseilles, a French port city on the Mediterranean coast, and led by R.O. Colombo (who, according to some data, was secretary of the Marseilles Sailors' Union),[57] rendered invaluable assistance in shipping small packs of arms, explosives, and political literature to the Caucasus via passenger boats on which some of their members worked.[58] Dekanozishvili was also aided in his work by his fellow Georgians in Paris, including Artshil Dzhordzhadze, publisher of the journal *Sakartvelo*, and "Miss Cholokashvili" and "Mr. [Aleksandr] Gabunia," couriers.[59] According to contemporary accounts, Dekanozishvili made sure that each Georgian returning home from France took along the journal *Sakartvelo*. Dekanozishvili also attempted to ship a printing press to the Caucasus, although he succeeded in this only in the spring of 1906.[60]

The transport of the purchased weapons to the Baltic regions and their fate are well known. Akashi bought a small steamship, the *John Grafton* for this purpose, but the shipment was delayed repeatedly for various reasons. Finally, in late July 1905, with the aid of the Japanese shipping company Takada in Rotterdam, the Netherlands, and the implicit support of British authorities, the *John Grafton*, with sixteen thousand rifles, three million bullets, three thousand revolvers, and three tons of explosives, left England for Russia. This first journey did not succeed because many revolutionaries (mainly Socialist Revolutionaries) had been arrested by the police and were not in a position to accept the arms. The Bolsheviks led by Lenin, however, were eager to acquire the weapons and arms from this shipment. On its second journey, staffed mainly by Finns and Latvians, the *John Grafton* was forced by weather and miscommunica-

55 Akashi, *Rakka ryūsui*, 45.

56 Akashi, *Rakka ryūsui*, 46–47. According to Russian records, Baud once worked as a correspondent in Russia for a French newspaper. French intelligence noted Baud's extensive travels to England, Germany, and Switzerland and his "conspiratorial contacts" with many individuals, concluding that he was an "international spy." GARF, f. 102, DP PP 1904-II, op. 316, d. 28, ll. 130–30ob.

57 "Personal Memoirs by Christiaan Cornelissen," International Institute of Social History, Amsterdam, the Netherlands, 331.

58 GARF, f. 102, DP PP 1904-II, op. 316, d. 28, ll. 78, 94–95, 125, 133, 162, 190. See also Sakhokia's letters to Dekanozishvili (28 June, 15 July, and 23 August 1905): Fonds Georges Dekanozichvili, CHAN, boxe 345 AP/1.

59 "Rapport sur la surveillance du colonel japonais AKASHI" (13 May 1905), Archives de la préfecture de la police de Paris, BA, Carton 1673, dossier "Missions japonaises venues en France (1879–1930)," 3.

60 GARF, f. 102, DP PP 1904-II, op. 316, d. 28, l. 190.

tion to divert first to Kemi and Jakobstad (Pietarsaari), on the northern and central coast of Finland, where some arms were unloaded. This was on 5 and 6 September, by which time the Russo-Japanese War had ended. But when the boat left Jakobstad to journey further south, it soon ran aground, well short of its eventual goal, St. Petersburg, the capital of Russia. On 6 September, unable to extract itself and in fear of Russian authorities, the crew blew up the boat and fled.[61]

Some of the Swiss-made weapons were, however, recovered by Russian authorities. In November 1905 the concerned Russian police sent an inquiry to the Swiss Department of Justice and the Swiss police: who had bought the 608 Swiss-made Vetterli Swiss rifles (and ammunition) recovered from a steamboat wrecked off the coast of Finland in August 1905 (apparently referring to the Russian calendar still then in force). In early January 1906, the Swiss Military Department, to which the inquiry was forwarded, responded that they could not honor the request and that, in any case, it was impossible to determine who had bought the weapons and ammunition. These older weapons were being liquidated, and the bulk of them were being sold retail by the Swiss army without regard to purchasers, most of whom were from Switzerland and neighboring countries.[62]

The Caucasus operation, on the other hand, though much less known, fared better. The shipment of arms to the Caucasus was organized by Dekanozishvili. Another Georgian, Leo Kereselidze, characterized Dekanozishvili as

> the driving force behind the revolt being prepared in Georgia. He was from Tiflis, a fanatical patriot, a revolutionary by instinct, a humanitarian kind at heart, but ready to be ruthless regardless of consequences, and to send his friends to death if his plans needed it. . . . Proud and thin-skinned, as every Georgian, he had, however, the ability to make friends with all manner of men and to get their help . . . . His voice was deceptive, for it was soft and musical, but what he said was always clear and decided and often harsh, for though he saw visions he was not all a dreamer but also a man of action, and his eyes were compelling and demanded obedience.[63]

Kereselidze was chosen by Dekanozishvili and the Tiflis Committee of the Socialist Federalists to take charge of the secret delivery of weapons and ammunition from Europe to the Caucasus by way of the Black Sea. Inspired by Japan's fight against Russia, Dekanozishvili came to be convinced that "what the Japanese could do they [Georgians] could all [*sic* also] do." He was "seeing visions of victory – Georgia full of men marching to battle: Georgia free and triumphant leading all the Caucasus States:

---

61 Michael Futrell, *Northern Underground: Episodes of Russian Revolutionary Transport and Communications through Scandinavia and Finland, 1863–1917* (New York: Frederick A. Praeger, 1963), ch. 4. Antti Kujala, "March Separately – Strike Together," 163–64; and Antti Kujala, "The Russian Revolutionary Movement and the Finnish Opposition 1905: The John Grafton Affair and the Plans for an Uprising in St. Petersburg." *Scandinavian Journal of History* no. 5 (1980), 257–75.

62 Fonds Georges Dekanozichvili, CHAN, boxe 345 AP/1.

63 Armstrong, *Unending Battle*, 17–18.

Fig. 2.14. Giorgi and Leo Kereselidze, Geneva, 1907.

Georgians rolling back the Russians over the mountains, avenging the brutalities and the misrule of a hundred years, and smashing the Russian Empire so that it would never again be a menace. He had no thought for himself, what success would mean to him. He did not work for any material advantages for himself, wealth, influence or power . . . . He worked only for Georgia, for their Georgia."[64]

A realist, Dekanozishvili of course did not exclude the eventuality of failure in his plan to deliver weapons to the Caucasus. Yet even were it to fail, he calculated that the mere fact of such attempts would force the Tsarist government, weakened by the defeat in the Far East and revolutionary upheaval within the country, to make concessions to the peoples of the Caucasus. Such concessions would include autonomy similar to that enjoyed (at least nominally) by Poland and Finland. On 13 November Dekanozishvili made note of this matter in his diary: "Even if a boat [with weapons

64 Armstrong, *Unending Battle*, 10, 19–20, 38.

Fig. 2.15. Steamship *Sirius*, Amsterdam, 1906.

and ammunition] cannot be received [in the Caucasus], this fact will scare the liberal [*sic*] government of Russia into thinking of reform in Georgia. Frightened, it will tell itself: 'If the Georgians were able to send one boat, then they will be able to send yet another. In this way they'll continue their fight and organize uprisings. The Caucasus will interfere with us at a difficult moment.' For this reason, Russia will be forced to think about our autonomy, as it does about autonomy in Poland and Finland."[65]

Kereselidze accepted the challenge Dekanozishvili presented to him. As in the case of the *John Grafton*, Japan financed the operation. By the time it actually took place, however, Tokyo had prohibited Akashi from funding further operations. Akashi's assessment of the Caucasian situation had not been very encouraging to begin with. He wrote: "During this time [of organizing the shipments of arms to the Baltic and Caucasian regions], the conflict incited by the Russians between Tatars and Armenians had begun in Baku in the Caucasus and Shusha in Georgia, and both provinces dissolved into total disorder."[66] (Obviously, Akashi's grasp of the situation was not very solid: for example, the Armenian-"Tatar" (Azeri) massacres in Baku had

65 Viktor Nozadze, "gardasrul zhamta ambavni da sakmeni" [Events and deeds of the past]. *kavkassioni* (Caucasus) (Paris) 1964, no. 9, 122–123.

66 Akashi, *Rakka ryūsui*, 52 (translation slightly modified).

taken place earlier in February 1905, and Shusha was in Nagorno-Karabakh, a land disputed by Armenians and Azeris.) Nevertheless, Akashi supported, financially and otherwise, the completion of the operation. In August he received information that "a plan had been completed" to transport eighty-five hundred Swiss rifles and 1.3 million bullets to the Caucasus and the Black Sea provinces.[67] For this purpose the *Sirius*, a tramp steamer of 2,500 tons, much larger than the *John Grafton*, was acquired for 2,900 pounds sterling. (Initially funds provided by an "industrial tycoon" in the Caucasus were used to purchase the steamship. Yet they soon proved inadequate to carry out the operation, and the Georgian revolutionaries used the money provided by the Japanese Embassy in Paris instead.)[68] This was on 6 September 1905, one day after the signing of the Portsmouth Treaty ending the Russo-Japanese War. Christiaan Cornelissen, a Dutch anarchist and nephew of Cherkezishvili's wife, was appointed to supervise the operation. The boat was manned by Dutch anarchists and French sailors (the latter of whom, unlike the former, did not know the aim of the journey).[69]

Money from the Japanese government, however, posed a moral challenge to the crew, who nonetheless in the end accepted and justified it. Cornelissen himself noted: "This concerned Finnish and Georgian nationalists who considered the government in St. Petersburg a more immediate threat and a more direct enemy to their homeland than the government in Tokyo which played one government against another. As an internationalist opposing the oppression of one people by another, of a weak people by a bigger and stronger, I could have understood their position."[70]

The original plan was to discharge the freight in Turkish waters, out of the reach of Russian authorities. The weapons and ammunition were then to be smuggled inland into the Russian Caucasus in small quantities. In June 1905, to obtain the Sublime Porte's agreement, Prince Mamed Abashidze, a Muslim leader with roots in both Adjara in Georgia and Ottoman Turkey, went to Istanbul, where he had contacts among the ruling elite. The Ottoman government was inclined to grant permission, although there is no record that it ever did officially.[71] The following month Dekanozishvili secretly dispatched from Paris to Georgia a group of conspirators (representatives of Socialist Revolutionaries, anarchists, and Socialist Federalists) to organize propaganda. One of them was Mikheil Kiknadze, a compositor of the newspaper *Sakartvelo*, who carried to the Tiflis committee of Socialist Federalists a missive on armed uprisings de-

---

67 Akashi, *Rakka ryūsui*, 53.

68 "Personal Memoirs by Christiaan Cornelissen," 330.

69 Markoz Tugushi, "giorgi dekanozishvili (tskhovreba da mokmedeba). sakartvelos sotsialist'-pederalist'uri sarevolutsio part'ia (1901-1906 ts'.ts'.)" [Giorgi Dekanozishvili. Life and Activity. Georgian Socialist-Federalist Revolutionary Party (1901-1906)], *kavkassioni* [Caucasus] (Paris) 1964, no. 10, 137-138.

70 "Personal Memoirs by Christiaan Cornelissen," 331.

71 See Sakhokia to Dekanozishvili (19 and 28 June, 15 and 21 September). Fonds Georges Dekanozichvili, CHAN, boxe 345 AP/1.

vised by Dekanozishvili with Akashi. In Tiflis, an underground bomb factory was to be built.[72] (An Italian eyewitness reported at the time that in Tiflis, "bomb factories were being perpetually discovered."[73]) The military organization of the Socialist Federalists also drew up a plan to conduct partisan warfare.[74]

By August 1905 the situation in Tiflis was chaotic and menacing. A large number of Russian soldiers appeared to control the city under martial law. Yet bombs were frequently hurled at them by revolutionaries, and the soldiers were forced to scatter and patrol in disorder to minimize casualties. By this time, Socialist Federalists in Tiflis had drafted plans to capture the city by arms.[75] Well aware that the Social Democrats were much more influential in Georgia than the Socialist Federalists, Dekanozishvili once again proposed to the former the creation of a united front. Offering to share with them the weapons to be smuggled into Georgia, Dekanozishvili proposed that the Social Democrats agree to convene a Constituent Assembly in Georgia and gain territorial autonomy after the model of Poland and Finland. Supporting political centralism in the Russian Empire, however, the Social Democrats refused the proposal, demanding, instead, "Give us the money and the sticks [rifles], we'll get the job done."[76]

The journey of the *Sirius* encountered its own problems. Once the war ended in the Far East, the Porte appeared less willing to support the Caucasian operation for armed rebellions. It was uncertain whether it would allow passage of the *Sirius* through the Straits (the Bosphorus and Dardanelles) to the Black Sea. At the last moment, in any case, Dekanozishvili's comrades in Georgia telegraphed to him that they could not accept the arms: when the time had come for action, many lost their nerve and were in a panic because they were convinced the Russian authorities knew about the shipment and were about to arrest and execute them all.[77] Moreover, on 16 September, Tedo Sakhokia informed Dekanozishvili that, now that the war with Japan had

72 Ibid. (from Kiknadze to Dekanozishvili, 3 August 1905). In this missive, one can detect hints of the Japanese connections of these clandestine operations, Kiknadze mentioning "Maksimov" (whose service Akashi and Dekanozishvili discussed using) and "the embassy."

73 See Villari, *Fire and Sword*, 127.

74 Laskhishvili, *memuarebi*, 213.

75 Kiknadze to Dekanozishvili (3 August 1905). Fonds Georges Dekanozichvili, CHAN, boxe 345 AP/1.

76 See Laskhishvili to Dekanozishvili (21 October 1905), Fonds Georges Dekanozishvili, CHAN, boxe 345 AP/1.

77 This fear resulted probably from a massacre that took place in Tiflis on 11 September. The Social Democrats organized a meeting in the city council building to discuss whether to take part in the elections for the newly introduced zemstvo. Some two thousand people, mainly Georgians, gathered, but then Cossacks and infantry fired at the crowd, kiling approximately one hundred people and injuring another two hundred. Most of the dead were "buried at the dead of night in a common grave without any religious ceremony, permission being refused to the relatives to carry the bodies away." Four days after the massacre, "when the *panikhida* of the dead was held (a funeral ceremony of the orthodox Church), nine bombs burst in different parts of the town – all in the vicinity of Cossack barracks." See Villari, *Fire and Sword*, 123–25.

ended, the government had decided to send an additional ninety thousdand soldiers with artillery units to the Caucasus.[78] Ten days later Sakhokia wrote again, urging Dekanozishvili to suspend the operation temporarily, because it would be impossible to receive and distribute weapons from abroad: "An enormous number of troops are advancing from all directions . . . . They have no mercy. If they suspect that you are hiding something, they'll take it, if you resist, they'll kill you. They have orders to spare no one."[79] Meanwhile, the loading of the cargo of weapons and ammunition had been completed by 21 September.[80]

Dekanozishvili despaired of success in the Caucasus and, apparently, was about to commit suicide when Kereselidze visited him in Paris to receive his final approval. Dekanozishvili declared: "But don't they realize that I have given my word of honour to the Japanese? I have taken their money and used it. Our people will rise whether they get the arms or not. It is too late to turn back. Unless they get the arms they will be defeated. The whole success of this revolt depends on it. I shall be dishonoured. I shall have betrayed them. All the blame and disgrace will fall on me. I can see no way out but suicide." Dissuading Dekanozishvili from taking such a drastic step, Kereselidze traveled to Georgia and won their comrades back to carrying out the planned revolt.[81] He also travelled to Istanbul where, with the aid of high-ranking officials from the Muslim areas of Georgia, he met with Sultan Abdul Hamid II, who sympathized with the Caucasians fighting against Russia. The sultan said to him: "It was in Asia that she [Russia] raised her great empire by the spilling of much oriental blood, and it is in Asia that she has just received the blow from which she will never recover. . . . . Russia is the common enemy of your country and mine." The sultan, through his emissary, wished Kereselidze good luck in Georgian: "*Gum arjoba* – may success be with you and Victory yours."[82] The sultan thus allowed the *Sirius* passage to the Black Sea, although all available evidence suggests that he did not permit the cargo (weapons and ammunition) to be discharged on Turkish territory. Therefore, a decision was made for the *Sirius* to unload its cargo at a Georgian port.

Finally on 7 October 1905, the *Sirius* left Amsterdam and proceeded toward Gibraltar.[83] Meanwhile, the political situation in Russia was turning more favorable for the revolutionaries. "In spite of repressive measures," a foreign observer reported later

78 Sakhokia to Dekanozishvili (16 September 1905). Fonds Georges Dekanozichvili, CHAN, boxe 345 AP/1.

79 Fonds Georges Dekanozichvili, CHAN, boxe 345 AP/1 (letter dated 26 September 1906).

80 "Stoom-Journaal van het Stoomschip Sirius, gevoerd door Kapitein W. van Oppen" (the Sirius log kept by the captain W. van Oppen, entries for 19, 20, 21 September). The log shows that the crew took extraordinary care to guard the boat throughout. Fonds Georges Dekanozichvili, CHAN, boxe 345 AP/2.

81 Armstrong, *Unending Battle*, 41.

82 Armstrong, *Unending Battle*, 36–37.

83 The log by Captain van Oppen suggests that the boat may in fact have left Amsterdam around 7 October. He received 1,000 francs from Dekanozishvili on 6 October 1905 in "Algiers," possibly a code name for Amsterdam. See his receipt: Fonds Georges Dekanozichvili, CHAN, 345 AP/1.

from Tiflis, "the weakness and impotence of the [Russian] Government were everyday more manifest. Although the town was under martial law and the streets were ceaselessly patrolled and no one was supposed to carry arms, hardly a man or boy was without his revolver and *kinjal*, and political murders were of frequent occurrence."[84] The day the *Sirius* left Amsterdam, general strikes erupted across Russia, forcing the Tsar on 17 October (old style, 30 October new style) to declare significant political concessions (the October Manifesto). This led to the release of many Georgian revolutionaries (including Socialist Federalists and Social Democrats) from the infamous Metekhi prison fortress in Tiflis. The Tsar's concession also led to a sharp conflict between the Russian and Georgian populations in Georgia's capital (as elsewhere in the Caucasus and beyond). On 21 October (old style), Russian colonists and officials demonstrated on Tiflis's main thoroughfare in a show of patriotism and fealty to the Tsar, holding portraits of the Tsar and singing the national anthem "God Save the Tsar." The local Black Hundreds (extreme Russian nationalists) also managed to attract Russian railway workers to the demonstration. In a show of force, albeit ostensibly to protect the demonstration, the Russian government mobilized a large number of dragoons, Cossacks, and soldiers. At some point, shots were fired and bombs were thrown at the demonstrators from buildings. The soldiers then fired indiscriminately at the buildings and the pedestrians on the street, resulting in approximately seventy people killed and a hundred injured.[85]

The western provinces of Georgia were cut off from Tiflis by popular uprisings. On 21 October (old style), it was reported to Dekanozishvili from Georgia that "our country has been caught completely by disturbances. There is no need for agitation. Our misfortune is that we don't have sticks [guns]."[86] A few weeks later Sakhokia wrote to Dekanozishvili with relief that the situation had improved and that a constitutional reform promised by the Manifesto would not be enough: the Georgians would not surrender until they had forced the Tsar to introduce a democratic republic.[87] An experienced revolutionary, Dekanozishvili had calculated well the best time for the *Sirius* operation. On 11 November (old style) 1905, the Russian Black Sea Fleet revolted in Sevastopol'. Most of the Russian troops were withdrawn from the Black Sea ports of Batumi and Poti and sent to suppress insurrections in Kutaisi and Tbilisi. The insurrections disrupted telegraph and other means of communication in the Caucasus.[88]

Meanwhile, Dekanozishvili and his comrades successfully misled Russian authorities about the *Sirius*. For example, Russian foreign minister Vladimir N. Lamsdorf in-

---

84 Villari, *Fire and Sword*, 126–27.

85 Laskhishvili, *memuarebi*, 220–21.

86 From G. Laskhishvili to Dekanozishvili (21 October 1905). Fonds Georges Dekanozichvili, CHAN, boxe 345 AP/1.

87 Sakhokia to Dekanozishvili (15 November 1905). Fonds Georges Dekanozichvili, CHAN, boxe 345 AP/1.

88 Nozadze, "gardasrul zhamta ambavni da sakmeni," 127.

Fig. 2.16. Steamship *Sirius* log.

formed his governor in the Caucasus on 9 September (22 September) that based on the information he had received from Amsterdam the boat had left the port on the same day with weapons and explosives for London, whence it appeared to proceed either to Finland or to the Caucasus.[89] Although Lamsdorf instructed the Russian mission in London to watch for the boat, it was not to be found there. Because of the failure of the *John Grafton*, the *Sirius* crew were extremely careful and kept their activities strictly confidential. Christiaan Cornelissen's brother Pierre, a wholesale merchant in coffee, provided coffee barrels as a cover for the weapons. The whole scheme was kept in strict secrecy.

Meanwhile, by 24 October (old style) the *Sirius* had already reached the port of Valetta on Malta. The boat then moved to Sète (Cette) in France, where the crew awaited further instructions. But by 1 November, Captain W. van Oppen and First Machinist H. Buff had abandoned the boat, apparently fearing the possible consequences of the risky operation to the Caucasus. Cornelissen was dispatched, along with two Dutchmen who replaced Buff, to help with the operation on board under the

89 GSCHA, f. 13, op. 29, d. 54, ll. 1–2.

Fig. 2.17. Steamship *Sirius* tin container of registration documents.

new captain, Leendert Groendijk.[90] On 2 November the *Sirius* journeyed to Marseille, where additional weapons and political literature were loaded, necessary repair work

90 Cornelissen spoke of "the captain, the brave Leendert Groendijk from Terschelling [an island in The Netherlands]." See "Personal Memoirs by Christiaan Cornelissen," p. 334. Armstrong, *Unending Battle*, 48–52, states that this change of command took place in Valetta and that van Oppen was arrested and the crew who stayed on were promised generous remuneration. On 24 October 1905, Dekanozishvili noted that a day earlier, Cornelissen had left for Sète to which the *Sirius* was also journeying. See Nozadze, "gardasrul zhamta ambavni da sakmeni," 121. According to the *Sirius* log, the boat arrived in Sète on 28 October. See "Stoom-Journaal van het Stoomschip Sirius," 4. Other sources indicate that Cornelissen and the two Dutchmen were dispatched to Marseille where the crew change took place.

was done on the boat, and a new crew hired. Four days later the *Sirius* left Marseille, arriving in Nikolo, Greece, where additional crew members were taken on.[91]

Successfully navigating through the Turkish Straits on 16 November with the help of bribes and the implicit sympathy of Turkish officials, the *Sirius* reached the Black Sea the following day and proceeded to the Caucasus coast, avoiding an encounter with enemy forces. On that day Dekanozishvili telegraphed to Batumi and Tiflis that the boat would reach the coast between 21 and 24 November. Considering that a large garrison of Russian troops was stationed in Batumi at the time, a decision was made for the *Sirius* to discharge its freight in Poti, a Black Sea coastal port in Georgia and fifty-five kilometers north of Batumi. On 22 November the boat stood sixty-four kilometers from the port. Waiting for night, the boat navigated to a point previously agreed upon and sent a signal by lighting lamps to alert the rebels to its arrival,[92] though only on 24 November did the rebels find the *Sirius*. Taking advantage of the general chaos of the time, they managed to unload 226 barrels of weapons and 330 of ammunition using longboats. They then asked the captain to wait for further unloading until 27 November, by which time they promised to return with empty longboats. If they could not return by then, the captain was authorized to dump the cargo and return home.[93]

Meanwhile, one of the longboats loaded with weapons was blown off course by a storm into Poti Bay, whereupon it was decided to unload the boat there. But a brawl broke out between the Socialist Federalists and Social Democrats over the weapons, during which the barrels were opened. The rebels were not familiar with the foreign weapons, and one of them, loading a rifle, accidentally set off some shots. Alarmed, Port authorities called in military units,[94] and the Poti detachment of the Black Sea Border Control Brigade and the rebels exchanged fire. As a result, on the night of 27 November, seven hundred rifles were confiscated in Poti.[95] A gunboat was then deployed to capture a fully loaded longboat, reportedly with twelve hundred rifles and ammunition.[96] (Some of the weapons seized by the Russians were subsequently bought back by rebels from Russian soldiers!) One longboat, however, succeeded in delivering its load (sixteen hundred rifles and ammunition) to Gagra, Abkhazia, where the weapons and ammunition were hidden at the estate of Prince Aleksander Inalishvili (Inal-ipa) in the village of Alakhadzy.[97] There they were divided up and deliv-

91 "Stoom-Journaal van het Stoomschip Sirius," 5 and Nozadze, "gardasrul zhamta ambavni da sakmeni," 123.

92 Nozadze, "gardasrul zhamta ambavni da sakmeni," 124–125, 130–131.

93 Nozadze, "gardasrul zhamta ambavni da sakmeni," 130–31 and Tugushi, "giorgi dekanozishvili," 147–148.

94 Tugushi, "giorgi dekanozishvili," 146.

95 GSCHA, f. 13, op. 29, d. 5, l. 2.

96 GSCHA, f. 13, op. 29, d. 5, l. 3. See also M. Tugushi, "giorgi dekanozishvili," 146.

97 Sakhokia, "tsimbirshi. mogonebani 1905 ts'lis revolutsiis droidan," 28—29, 38.

ered, in small consignments, to western Georgia,[98] where, as a leader of the insurgents later recalled, the weapons and munitions delivered by the *Sirius* played a "notable role in the revolts of 1905."[99] After waiting another five days and coming to understand that the rebels were unable to collect the rest of the load, the *Sirius* crew finally threw overboard the remaining weapons and ammunition.

The steamer then left the Caucasus coasts and reached Varna, Bulgaria, by 4 December. Moving on to Algiers,[100] from there, the boat returned to Amsterdam on 15 January 1906.[101]

Thus, although many arms were lost or confiscated, some at least did reach the rebels. In Poti, shortly after the arms were delivered, fighting went on all day. In the end, however, the Russians regained control and "had hung a large number of men and declared martial law in the district." In Batumi, the situation was similar. After heavy fighting, this busy port city turned into a ghost town: buildings were "pitted with rifle bullets and pieces of bombs . . . . The trains had stopped, and outside the station dangled a row of corpses – insurgents hung by court martial as examples . . . . [and] business, trade, even the ordinary buying and selling of food and necessities had ceased, for only a few people would risk going into the streets where the patrols of Russians, nervous and expecting to be attacked, fired at anything or anybody on the least provocation."[102]

Returning to Japan after the war, Akashi received a letter from one of his contacts (probably Dekanozishvili) dated 24 December 1905:

> Our movement has a bright future. We were not able to overthrow the Russian government at a stroke, but will try to do it step by step. No one doubts that the authority of the Tsarist government will collapse. The arms transported to the Black Sea arrived there safely. We were able to buy back the arms confiscated by the *Aziia*, a converted cruiser. They number 8,400 rifles.[103]

Even though the war was over, Akashi must have been pleased. His postwar memorandum to the General Staff ends with the delivery of arms to the Black Sea regions. Dekanozishvili, in turn, kept his honor.

The Japanese-Caucasian cooperation of this period marked a significant stage in the national liberation movement of the Caucasus. Japan's goal was not a socialist

98 Laskhishvili, *memuarebi*, 206. See also Mikheil Ts'ereteli, "giorgi dekanozishvili," *sakhalkho sakme. sakartvelos sotsialist'-pederalist'uri part'iis daarsebis 50 ts'listavi. sagangebo rveuli* ([Buenos Aires]: n.p., 1952), 10–14.

99 Giorgi Kereselidze's letter to the director of the Ministry of Foreign Affairs of the German Federal Republic, 25 March 1958, 1, N. Badual-Kereselidze Family Archive (Aix-en-Province, France).

100 The *Sirius* log entries for December 1905, Fonds Georges Dekanozichvili, CHAN, boxe 345 AP/2.

101 "Personal Memoirs by Christiaan Cornelissen," 334.

102 Armstrong, *Unending Battle*, 73, 77.

103 Akashi, *Rakka ryūsui*, 53.

revolution but the weakening of the Russian Empire. In this Japan and the Caucasian national movements found common ground.

2.3 Japan and "Total Espionage"

Yet despite the massive spending, Akashi's operations did not achieve their ultimate goal of instigating mass armed uprisings in the Russian Empire. Moreover, Akashi had been deceived by Azef, a Socialist Revolutionary and police double agent, apparently entrusted with some of the operations in the Caucasus. Believing that the money he used had contributed to the famous Battleship Potemkin mutiny in June 1905, Akashi wrote: "Dikanskii [Azef], the most powerful leader of the Socialist Revolutionaries, reported that he had gone to Odessa with 40,000 yen to canvass and to seek ways to obtain arms. In June he provoked a disturbance there and escaped to Moscow. Vakulinchuk and Feldmann, both of whom were Dikanskii's disciples and Caucasians, organized a mutiny on the *Potemkin* which started the Black Sea Revolt."[104] Of course, Azef kept the money for himself, and had nothing to do with the Potemkin uprising.[105] Nor were Vakulinchuk and Feldmann from the Caucasus. Akashi's operations did, however, have a "powerful impact" on the uprisings in the Caucasus, as acknowledged in Russia, by providing a substantial amount of weaponry and ammunition there: it was precisely those areas of the Caucasus such as Poti, Ozurgeti, Zugdidi, and Sukhumi, where arms and ammunition from the *Sirius* actually reached, that the uprisings were most serious.[106]

Part of the reason Akashi's operations were ineffective was that Russia's counterintelligence was well informed about them. Initially *Okhrana* (the Russian secret police) failed to grasp the Akashi-Dekanozishvili nexus. In Paris the Okhrana began following Dekanozishvili only from October 1904 on. Although Akashi naturally came to its notice, at first the Okhrana failed to see through the nature of his activity.[107] After the 1891 Franco-Russian Alliance, French intelligence (*Sûreté générale*) provided assistance to the Okhrana (and vice versa), and informers were rewarded for valuable intelligence.[108] Aware of this, Akashi based his activity instead in London, where Okhrana

---

104 Akashi, *Rakka ryūsui*, 45–46.

105 Akashi knew that his agent in Odesa, likely Azef, overstated the political situation and his role in it. See GARF, op. cit. ll. 48–49.

106 *Iznanka revoliutsii. Vooruzhennoe vozstanie v Rossii na iaposnkiia sredstva* (St. Petersburg: Top. A.S. Suvorina, 1906), 20. See also Pavlov, *Iaponskie den'gi*, 180. Some of the weapons may have reached Moscow as well. See *Iznanka revoliutsii*, 19.

107 GARF, f. 102, DP PP 1904-II, op. 316, d. 28, ll. 203–204ob.

108 For the Franco-Russian intelligence collaboration, see Archives de la péfecture de la police de Paris, BA, Box 1693, File "Police russe à Paris (1913)." Significantly two Okhrana chiefs, P. Pachkovskii (1885–1902) and L. Rataev (1902–1905) were decorated by the French government.

activity was limited. Japan had also concluded an alliance with Britain in 1902. From London Akashi traveled to Europe. Well aware of surveillance, he took precautions.[109] Nevertheless, Russia achieved a breakthrough in Akashi's case in February 1905, when a French cleaning woman (named "Mason") at the International Hotel Jena (Iéna) in Paris informed the Russian ambassador in Paris, A. Nelidov, of Akashi's suspicious contact with Zillicaus and "Empilov," a pseudonym used by Dekanozishvili. (Mason had rummaged through the trash can in Akashi's room.)[110]

The Okhrana in Paris, headed by I. F. Manasevich-Manuilov, thereupon followed Akashi and his contacts everywhere in Europe, tapped their conversations in hotel rooms, opened and read their postal correspondence, and intercepted and decoded Japanese diplomatic codes.[111] In August 1905, Dekanozishvili, working near Lausanne, Switzerland, wrote in his diary: "Russian agents surround me from all directions. They bribe local postmen and telegraph carriers in order to find everything out that way. But I don't sleep . . . . I have no assistants, but they have a whole army of collaborators working for them."[112] Asian-looking men from the Caucasus were also watched carefully by Russian agents, particularly in port cities like Istanbul and Batumi.[113] Those few Japanese and Chinese residing in the Caucasus at the time were deported.[114]

In 1906 the Russian government published some of the Akashi correspondence in facsimile to discredit politically those opposition groups that had received Japanese money.[115] The exposé was also intended to cause a diplomatic scandal. Although after the war Akashi had returned to Tokyo, he was soon sent to Berlin as a military attaché to study Russian affairs. Considering him dangerous, Russia sought to drive him out of Europe with the publication, and the scandal indeed made it impossible for Akashi to remain there. In 1907 he returned to Japan, subsequently serving in Korea and Taiwan, where he died in 1919.

---

109 See GARF, f. 102, DP PP 1904-II, op. 316, d. 28, ll. 39, 71–72, 74, 150, 156, 164.

110 GARF, f. 102, DP PP 1904-II, op. 316, d. 28, ll. 205–6.

111 This happened with the help of a Dutchman in The Hague (Den Haag). See "Tainaia voina protiv Rossii." *Istoricheskii arkhiv* 1994, no. 3, 29–30, 53. At the time the French *Sûreté* succeeded in breaking the Japanese diplomatic codes and may have helped the Russians. See Christopher Andrew, "Codebreakers and Foreign Offices: The French, British and American Experience," Christopher Andrew and David Dilks, eds., *The Missing Dimension: Governments and Intelligence Communities in the Twentieth Century* (Urbana-Chicago: University of Illinois Press, 1984), 36.

112 Nozadze, "gardasrul zhamta ambavni da sakmeni," 121.

113 E.M. Osmanov, comp., *Iz istorii russko-iaponskoi voiny 1904–1905 gg.* (St. Petersburg: Izd-vo S.-Peterb. un-ta, 2005), 444, 449–50, 455.

114 See N.F. Bugai, *L. Beriia – I. Stalinu: 'Posle Vashikh ukazanii provedeno sleduiushchee . . .'* (Moscow: Grif i K, 2011), 58–61.

115 *Iznanka revoliutsii*. See also Chiharu Inaba, "Franco-Russian Intelligence Collaboration against Japan during the Russo-Japanese War, 1904–05." *Japanese Slavic and East European Studies* vol. 19 (1998), pp. 1–23.

Dekanozishvili himself died of consumption in France in 1910. He missed Georgia greatly. Before he died, he said:

> I'm finished, but it is not the Russians who have finished me. It's the want of some good Georgian air to clear my lungs . . . . I wish I could smell the mountain air and the pines below Kazbek [a mountain in Georgia: it was here that, according to Greek mythology, Prometheus was chained to a rock as punishment for stealing fire for human use] just once more . . . . I have never given way to the Russians. They put me in prison. They beat me. After I escaped they always hunted me. After that they tried to bribe me to submit, and they even promised to let me live in Tiflis – think of it, to go back and live again in Tiflis – if I would not work against them. I never agreed. God curse them.[116]

He died a Georgian patriot: until his death he believed that "one day God will make Georgia free and triumphant. I can see it. Georgia triumphant. Georgia great and Georgia free."[117]

Behind the scenes, however, Akashi's operations did contribute invisibly but substantially to Russia's defeat in its war against Japan. As Abraham Ascher has noted regarding Poland:

> For the Tsarist government, unrest in Poland proved to be very costly indeed. Even before the revolution [of 1905], early in 1904, it maintained an army of 250,000 men in Poland, larger than the one then in the Far East; and by mid-1905, the government felt obliged to increase it by 50,000 men, this at a time when every soldier was needed at the front. It can also be argued that because such a large military force was tied down in Poland, the government found it more difficult to cope with unrest in other parts of the Empire, which compelled it eventually to grant concessions when it would have preferred not to.[118]

Whether Tokyo considered the results sufficient to justify Japan's vast expenditure on its European intelligence operations is unknown. In any event, in Asia Japan's operations proved far more effective than Russia's. Russia failed to take Japan's threat seriously enough: it was to be a short, victorious little war over "little brown monkeys," as Tsar Nicholas was said to have called the Japanese. But Russia had few specialists on Japan and few speakers of the Japanese language when the war began and so Russia miscalculated its enemy.[119] By contrast, Japan had been training Russian specialists for some years and had been practicing elaborate intelligence and counterintelligence operations since well before the war. According to incomplete data collected by the

---

116 Armstrong, *Unending Battle*, 196–97.

117 Armstrong, *Unending Battle*, 198.

118 Abraham Ascher, *The Revolution of 1905: Russia in Disarray* (Stanford, Calif.: Stanford University Press, 1988), 158.

119 See Bruce W. Manning, "Miscalculating One's Enemies: Russian Military Intelligence before the Russo-Japanese War." *War in History* 13, no. 2 (2006), 141-70.

Russian police, when the war began in 1904, about five hundred Japanese spies were operating in Russia.[120]

In Asia, as in Europe, Japan's nexus with the Caucasus was evident. To be sure, for obvious reasons, the main forces of Japanese intelligence in Asia were Asians of third-party neutral countries: Chinese, Koreans, Mongolians, and others.[121] Japanese spies often camouflaged themselves as Chinese or Koreans or Mongolians. Yet quite a few people from the Caucasus also ended up in the battle ground in various capacities in Manchuria. Official Russian military reports during the war, for instance, mentioned measures taken to neutralize "European spies" working for Japan, specifically mentioning "Jews, Greeks, Armenians and Turks."[122] Another report discussed the influx of European adventurers and speculators to Manchuria during the war, believing that Japan recruited spies from among them such as former prisoners who had served their terms in Sakhalin and deserters from prisons. Among them were mentioned Jews, Caucasians, Greeks, Turks, Armenians, Germans, French, and English. The report went on to say that Caucasians were particularly troublesome: about 150 of whom were brought to Manchuria by "Gromov," a contractor.[123] Of course, Russia used precisely the same groups of people for its own operations; Japan noted, for instance, Greeks working for Russia.[124]

Clearly, both Russia and Japan understood that the Caucasus was a region of strategic importance and acted accordingly. Japan, for instance, used Odesa for intelligence in the Caucasus. Before the war, the Japanese consul in Odesa had cultivated an intelligence network in Turkey, Persia, Bulgaria, Serbia, and the Caucasus.[125] When the war broke out, the Japanese consulate was closed and the staff moved to Vienna and Istanbul ("in order to engage in intelligence against Russia").[126] Odesa's role in turn attracted the attention of Russian authorities. From there the remaining Japanese, protected by the US consul, continued to supply information to the Japanese legation in Vienna. In the end, the former secretary at the consulate, Giichi Tagashi, was arrested on 31 July 1904 and expelled from Russia on 3 August.[127]

120 Osmanov, *Iz istorii russko-iaponskoi voiny*, 330.

121 On Japan's use of Chinese agents, see David Wolff, "Intelligence Intermediaries: The Competition for Chinese Spies," in Steinberg et al., *The Russo-Japanese War in Global Perspective: World War Zero*, vol. 1, 305–330.

122 D. Pavlov and S. Petrov, *Iaponskie den'gi i russkaia revoliutsiia: russkaia razvedka i kontrrazvedka v voine 1904–1905 gg.* (Moscow: Progress, 1993), 201. On Greeks working as Japanese agents, see also I.N. Kravtsev, *Tainye sluzhby imperii* (Moscow: Izd-vo RAGC, 1999), 102, 105.

123 Pavlov and Petrov, *Iaponskie den'gi*, 236–237 and 261–62.

124 Rei Hasegawa, "Nichiro sensō to senjō no chōhōsen." *Gunji shigaku* 42, no. 2 (2006), 125.

125 Osmanov, *Iz istorii russko-iaponskoi voiny*, 354.

126 Merthan A. Dündar and Nobuo Misawa, "Isutanburu no nakamura shōten o meguru ningen kankei no jirei kenkyū." *Tōyō daigaku shakaigakubu kiyō*, 46, no. 2 (2009), 191.

127 GARF, f. 102, DP PP, 1904, op. 316, d. 15, ll. 92, 119.

In 1906, soon after the war ended, Japan's consulate reopened in Odesa. Likewise, Japan used Istanbul, where many people from the Caucasus took refuge, for operations against Russia. The Ottoman Empire and Japan did not have official diplomatic relations at the time. Yet, with the support of the sultan (according to Russian authorities), a Japanese businessman ("K. Nakamura") acted as a "secret" consul and intelligence officer under whom a reserve military officer ("T. Yamada") worked with two Japanese assistants, Japanese newspaper correspondents ("Ito" and "Tarō Matsumoto"), to develop an "extensive network."[128] Although there is no evidence that the reserve officer (Torajirō Yamada) had anything to do with the Japanese military forces, during the war he conducted intelligence work for Japan at the request of the Japanese ambassador in Vienna. It is also known that another Japanese working with him at the time, Kenjirō Nakamura (probably the "K. Nakamura" referred to in Russian documents), had traveled to Istanbul as a naval officer as early as 1897.[129] More significantly, the journalist "Matsumoto" was in fact the former consul in Odesa, Kametarō Iijima working under cover. In Istanbul Iijima employed a Swiss and a Greek as informants, followed the movement of Russian vessels through the Turkish Straits, and acquired valuable information from the local British legation.[130] In 1907, although Japan and Turkey still lacked official diplomatic relations, Japan even managed to station a "military attaché" in Istanbul!

Japan's extensive operations in Eurasia, however, proved costly. Almost certainly Japan spent much more on intelligence than did Russia. as noted earlier, Japan earmarked 1 million yen in 1905 for Akashi's operations. According to Russian estimates, in the years leading up to the war Japan expended 12 million rubles, whereas Russia spent annually a little more than 100,000 rubles on military intelligence.[131] It is unclear whether the figure for Japan is cumulative or annual,[132] and the figures for both Japan and Russia do not appear to include expenditures on counterintelligence. Rus-

128 "Tainaia voina protiv Rossii," 41–42. See also Osmanov, *Iz istorii russko-iaponskoi voiny*, 446-9, 455-56.

129 See Selçuk Esenbel, "Seiki matsu Isutanbūru no nihonjin," in *Kindai nihon to toruko sekai*, edited by Masaru Ikei and Tsutomu Sakamoto (Tokyo: Keisō shobō, 1999), 80 and 96, Kuniki Yamada and Toshio Sakamoto, *Meiji no kaidanji toruko e tobu: Yamada Torajirō den* (Tokyo: Gendai shokan, 2009), 155–60, and Dündar and Misawa, "Isutanbūru no nakamura shōten," 189, 191. See also "Tainaia voina protiv Rossii," 160.

130 Chiharu Inaba, "The Question of the Bosphorous and Dardanelles during the Russo-Japanese War: The Struggle between Japan and Russia over the Passage of the Russian Volunteer Fleet in 1904," Selçuk Esenbel and Chiharu Inaba, eds, *The Rising Sun and the Turkish Crescent: New Perspectives on the History of Japanese-Turkish Relations* (Istanbul: Boğaziçi University Press, 2003), 127–30.

131 I.V. Derevianko, "Russkaia agenturnaia razvedka v 1902–1905 gg." *Voenno-istoricheskii zhurnal* 1989, no. 5, 76.

132 A. Votinov, *Iaponskii shpionazh v russko-iaponskuiu voinu 1904–1905 gg.* (Moscow: Voenizdat, 1939), 4 states that espionage and diversion accounted for 10 percent of Japan's war expenditure in 1904.

sia's *Okhrana* in Paris was spending more than 8,000 French francs a month in 1905,[133] while its cumulative expenses during the war in Paris amounted to millions in today's Euros.[134]

In the realm of Russian finance, the Caucasus occupied a special place. Whereas the annual expenditure on military intelligence ranged from about 4,000 to 12,000 rubles per military district in Russia, the Caucasus military district alone received 56,890 rubles for maintaining secret agents in "Asiatic Turkey."[135]

One of the most important lessons Russia learned from its encounter with the Land of the Rising Sun was the significance of intelligence. It was not that Russia was unaware of it. Indeed, at the time Russia's intelligence was as good as that of any other European country. Certainly once the war started, Russian police placed every Japanese and everyone suspicious under careful and thorough surveillance.[136] Yet Japan's innovations took Russia by surprise. Preparing for war against a formidable European power, Japan recognized itself as an underdog and so went to extraordinary lengths, often beyond the imaginable for the Russians. What Japan did at the time foreshadowed what came to be called in the 1930s "total espionage." Japan sought to enlist all Japanese everywhere, from businessmen and journalists to maids and prostitutes, to gather intelligence. Moreover, it deployed its spies widely under the guise of stokers, cooks, and waiters on boats traveling between Russia and foreign countries, orderlies in Russian hospitals, prostitutes, nannies, and maids in Russian households in Manchuria and beyond, construction workers, bakers, clerks at foreign businesses, stevedores, barbers, owners of inns, hostels, and brothels, Buddhist priests, entertainers such as circus performers, and many others. In 1905, for example, expecting the Russian Baltic fleet to stop for coal stocking on its way to Japan, Japanese agents were working in Singapore, Saigon, and elsewhere as Chinese coal stevedores. Russian reports of the time were full of warnings of these deceptions.[137] Japan's activities should not have been a surprise because, after all, espionage was a deception game. What was unimaginable to Russians was that many educated and capable Japanese officials, including those from noble families, would willingly disguise themselves as humble laborers such as cooks, barbers, and coolies. In a strictly hierarchical organization like the Russian military, this was almost unthinkable.

As an English observer noted at the time:

> With characteristic pertinacious care, the Japanese have for years pried into other nations' affairs. With them espionage has been bred in their bones, and fostered by custom, approved and rewarded by Government. They have collated information about all places, of late more especially

133 "Tainaia voina protiv Rossii,"52.

134 Inaba, *Akashi kōsaku*, 160.

135 Derevianko, "Russkaia agenturnaia razvedka," 76.

136 See many reports in GARF, f. 102, PP DP 1904, op. 316, d. 14.

137 See, for instance, Osmanov, *Iz istorii russko-iaponskoi voiny*, 341, 345, 398, 424-25.

> about Russia. Natives, much above the rank of the middle class in Japan, as well as coolies and common women, have been systematically sent out to gather information, and make reports to the Mikado's Government . . . . Officers of the Japanese army and navy have thought it no shame to pass as barbers, cheap-jacks, photographers, and what not, in order to be enabled to spy out important and State secrets . . . . They [the Japanese] know as much about Wei-hei-Wei and Hong-Kong as our own authorities, and of San Francisco and the Philippines as the Americans."[138]

After all, in the view of Westerners, Japan was a country of *ninja*s. Years later, a German report noted likewise: "[T]his preoccupation with espionage is ingrained in the Japanese, since for very many years under the shogunate a system of secret police was extensively active whose main task was to secure the shoguns against plots on their lives and against their positions."[139]

It is possible that in 1904-05, Japan "subjected Russia, not only in Asia but in Europe as well, to invasion by the largest secret army ever put into the field up to this time."[140] A British military observer subsequently noted that "in the course of history, there have been few wars in which espionage was so widely practiced as during the Manchurian campaign."[141] A Soviet commentator observed similarly: "Never in the history of war was espionage used so extensively as in the Russo-Japanese war of 1904–1905."[142] Before the war between Russia and Japan began, even the British military attaché in Beijing, "with the help of *the Japanese who have agents at every railway station in Manchuria*, ha[d] just completed an accurate summary of all the Russian troops from Lake Baikal eastwards."[143]

This image of an army of Japanese spies became entrenched in the minds of Russians and later continued to influence the Soviet government. However far the distance of the Caucasus from Japan, Moscow never failed to see there the shadow of its Far Eastern foe.

---

138 Bennet Burleigh [war correspondent of *London Daily Telegraph*], *Empire of the East or Japan and Russia at War, 1904–5* (London: Chapman & Hall, 1905), 72–73.

139 Quoted in Ronald Seth, *Secret Servants: A History of Japanese Espionage* (New York: Farrar, Straus and Cudahy, 1957), 151.

140 Speth, *Secret Servants*, 144.

141 Quoted in David Wolf, "Intelligence Intermediaries: The Competition for Chinese Spies," in Steinberg et al., *The Russo-Japanese War in Global Perspective: World War Zero*, vol. 1, 305.

142 Votinov, *Iaponskii shpionazh*, 4.

143 Quoted in Ian Nish, "Japanese Intelligence and the Approach of the Russo-Japanese War," in Andrew and Dilks, *The Missing Dimension*, 30 (emphasis in original).

3 A Lull

The turmoil of the 1905 Revolution did not end quickly or easily in the Russian Empire, the Caucasus included. In April 1906, Leo and Giorgi Kereselidze and Nestor Magalashvili (Magalov), the heads of the combat organization of Georgian Socialist Federalists, staged a raid against a state bank office in Dusheti, Georgia, capturing 315,000 rubles.[1] The money was most likely used to publish political propaganda in Georgia.[2] Pursued by the police, they fled to Switzerland, where they were tried but acquitted on the grounds that they had acted for a justifiable political cause against Russian oppression.[3] The trial even helped publicize in Europe the plight of Georgians under Russian rule.[4] The following year they sent a petition to a disarmament conference in The Hague, Netherlands (Second Hague Conference for Peace), in which they accused Russia of occupying Georgia and appealed to the world powers (which included Germany, Britain, France, the United States, and Japan, as well as Russia) to help reinstate autonomy in Georgia.[5] By 1907, however, the Russian autocracy had succeeded in restoring peace and order to much of the empire through a combination of concessions (most notably, the creation of the national Duma and a form of quasi-constitutional monarchy) and violent repression.

3.1 "Pacification"

In western Georgia, where weapons from the *Sirius* had reached, turmoil ended with brutal suppression by the Tsarist forces. In 1905 the region consisted "not so much of anarchy as of an independent state made up of self-governing communes which recognized no authority but that of the revolutionary committees." The political situation in the Kutaisi province, according to one account, was "so amazing when witnessed against the general background of the political structure of the Empire that foreigners are making special trips to the Caucasus with the aim of observing on the spot this

1 See GSCHA, f. 153, op. 1, d. 1835, ll. 169–223.

2 See GARF, f. 102, DPOO 1909, op. 239, d. 202, ll. 5, 59.

3 See Commissariat d'Annemasse, Surveillance générale des révolutionnaires russes. Au sujet des vols commis à mains armée en Russie (reports of 14 and 15 September 1906 and of 14 February of 1907). CHAN, Box F 7, 12521.

4 G. Kereselidze, "sakartvelos damoukideblobis komit'et'i (1914-1918)" [Committee for the independence of Georgia], *kartuli emigratsia* [Georgian emigration] (Tbilisi: n.p., 2013), vol. I (4), 149.

5 Werner Zürrer, *Kaukasien 1918–1921: Der Kampf der Großmächte um die Landbrücke zwischen Schwarzem und Kaspischem Meer* (Düsseldorf: Droste Verlag, 1978), 8.

Fig. 3.1. Nestor Magalashvili, Tiflis, 1906.

new manifestation of Russian political organization." In January 1906, however, these "self-governing communes" were brutally destroyed by Russian troops and Cossacks.[6]

The commander leading this military operation, General M. Alikhanov-Avarskii, known for his savagery ("Bloody Alikhanov"), was subsequently interviewed by American journalist Kellogg Durland (1881–1911), who visited Kutaisi soon after the event. Durland asked the general point-blank:

> Your Excellency, I have come to you on a strange errand. I have heard worse stories about you than I have ever heard about any living human being. As an American I do not wish to repeat these stories to my countrymen, if they are not true. On the other hand, if they are true, I want to hear your side of the case, your justification – if such there be.

The general asked Durland what stories he had heard, to which Durland responded:

> "The people of this province," I replied, "tell me that your soldiers are burning the homes of the people indiscriminately at your order, – the homes of people against whom there is no legal

6 Quotations in this paragraph are from David Marshall Lang, *A Modern History of Soviet Georgia* (New York: Grove Press, 1962), 167–68 and *Revoliutsiia 1905–07 gg v Gruzii. Sbornik dokumentov* (Tbilisi: Sakhelgami, 1956), 347.

> evidence, only suspicion; that your soldiers are encouraged to loot and to pillage the shops; that not only the women and the girls, but also little children, fare very badly at their hands."
> The general received these words quietly, but answered with some heat: "The people of this province are bad, all bad, very bad. There is no other way to repress them than as my soldiers are now doing."
> "There are many people here," I added, "many different tribes and races – are none good?"
> "No! they are all bad! The Georgians are the worst, but they are all against the government, and must be put down."
> "By putting down, do you mean arresting them and burning their homes, or are these stories false?"
> The general showed slight irritation at this, and replied: "There are more than one hundred thousand houses in this province, one hundred and twenty have been ordered burned since I came to Kutais. What are one hundred and twenty out of so many?" Then, flashing his eyes directly upon me, he added, in excellent French: "These people are terrorists, they are socialists, and revolutionists. When I hear that a man is a socialist or revolutionist, I order my soldiers to burn down his house. It is the only way."[7]

When Durland replied that his casual observation suggested that far more than 120 houses had been burned, the general replied that "my soldiers are ordered to burn down a certain house, but of course they do not always have time to see that other houses do not catch fire and so burn also." As for hundreds of women and young girls who were raped by his soldiers, the general denied the charges, adding that "his soldiers were frequently forced to shoot women, but that was because women were often revolutionists."[8] A year and a half after this interview, on 16 July 1906, the general was assassinated. Deeply affected by the violence in the Caucasus, Durland wrote that if "I lived in the Caucasus, suffering and bleeding under Russian misrule, I would be a revolutionist." He came to understand "why assassination is deemed a legitimate weapon of warfare by the people of the Caucasus." In fact, "I think I might reply to these barbarous weapons – sanctioned and approved by the Czar's government – with the most effective weapons I could command – possibly even the revolver, the knife, and the bomb."[9] Such was the terrible state of affairs in Georgia.

Everywhere in the Caucasus repression was rampant. Even though Count Illarion Vorontsov-Dashkov, viceroy of the Caucasus appointed in 1905 by Tsar Nicholas II with the task of restoring order to the Caucasus, was a relatively liberal administrator, the whole Caucasus soon "turned into one big prison." By the first half of 1909 thirteen thousand people had been exiled from the Caucasus, and another eight thousand people had been tried for political crimes. Even so, Petr Stolypin, Russia's prime minster, complained about the viceroy's leniency toward "criminal organizations" of revolu-

---

7 Kellogg Durland, *The Red Reign: The True History of an Adventurous Year in Russia* (New York: The Century Co., 1908), 111–12.
8 Durland, *The Red Reign*, 112–13.
9 Durland, *The Red Reign*, 120.

tionaries.[10] From 1905 to 1911, more than five thousand state officials were killed by terrorists in Russia as a whole, Stolypin himself being murdered in 1911. Georgia's Exarch, Archbishop Nikon, a vehement opponent of the autocephalous Georgian Church, was assassinated on 22 May 1908, probably by former members of the Socialist Federalist combat organization.[11] The Russian autocracy in turn executed nearly three thousand people for political crimes between 1905 and 1909.[12]

Despite the setbacks, Dekanozishvili continued shipping arms to Georgia, which apparently the Russian authorities failed to intercept.[13] He also succeeded in delivering printing presses to Georgia after the 1905 revolution.[14] A small group of Georgian Bolsheviks also revived political terrorism, the most famous event of which was the 1907 raid on the Tbilisi State Bank. Nevertheless, the revolutionary and national movements in the Caucasus were generally contained by the Tsarist government. The political parties tended to be fragmented under Stolypin's repression. Some Socialist Federalists chose legal methods of work, while others adhered to illegal ones. Those rightists who, abandoning socialist ideas, focused on the nationalist cause joined other forces in 1917 to form the National Democratic Party of Georgia.[15]

In the meantime, Japan and Russia began mending relations following the Russo-Japanese War, and during World War I they stood on the same side, that of the Triple Entente. Little trace of a Japanese-Caucasian link can be found in these years. But the interwar period was just a lull, soon to be interrupted by the world war, the Russian Revolutions, and the independence of four Caucasian states.

3.2 The Impact of Japan's Victory

The 1905 victory of Japan, an Asian constitutional monarchy, over Russia, a European autocracy, had an immediate impact on other nations in the world that had to contend with the European colonial powers, Russia included. As a German naval officer noted

10 Ronald Grigor Suny, *The Making of the Georgian Nation* (Bloomington and Indianapolis: Indiana University Press, 1988), 174.

11 See GSCHA, f. 153, op. 1, d. 1835, l. 4.

12 See Anna Geifman, *Thou Shalt Kill: Revolutionary Terrorism in Russia, 1894–1917* (Princeton, NJ, 1993), 21, 228.

13 See letters from Sh. Iosava to Dekanozishvili (25 January and 2, 5, and 6 February 1906), Fonds Georges Dekanozichvili. Centre historique des archives nationales (CHAN), Paris, box 345 AP/1, and GSCHA, f. 13, op. 29, d. 64, ll. 11–14.

14 See V. Nozadze, "gardasrul zhamta ambavni da sakmeni" [Events and deeds of the past], *kavkassioni* (Caucasus) (Paris), 1964, no. 9, pp. 123–28, and GARF, f. 102. DPOO 1904, op. 316, d. 28, ll. 133, 162 and f. 102, DPOO 1909, op. 239, d. 202, ll. 15–16, 23.

15 D. Shvelidze, *polit'ikuri part'iebis ts'armoshoba sakartveloshi. pederalist'ebi* [The origins of the political parties in Georgia. Federalists] (Tbilisi: "Arsi," 1993), 256.

at the time, "This is the beginning of a new era in world history."[16] In the Caucasus and its surrounding areas, too, the euphoria over the humbling of Russia by a tiny Asian power was palpable.

The Ottoman Empire, a colonial empire long in decay under the pressure of European imperial powers, was also emboldened by Japan's victory over Russia, an empire that more than any other had contributed to its own decline. Its defeat in the last war against Russia, in 1877–78, was still fresh in the memory of the Ottomans. In 1908, inspired at least partly by Japan, the Young Turks staged a successful revolution against the sultan's autocratic power, ushering in a progressive, modernizing, and constitutional era.[17]

Japan's victory was hailed in Persia as well, as it signaled the weakening of its oppressive neighbor to the north. The victory also represented the triumph of the transformation of a tradition-bound society into a modern, industrial one. Japan thus became "the model of Asian progress for the Iranian nationalists." Persia, too, aspired to become a constitutional polity; after all, Russia had also been forced to adopt a quasi-constitution. Japan's constitution was even translated into Persian. Persia's constitutional revolution, however, did not last long, eventually being nullified by Russia and Britain's partitioning of Persia, according to the Anglo-Russian Convention of 1907.[18]

The repercussions of Japan's victory went much further still, affecting national groups within the Ottoman and Persian realms. Having witnessed the defeat of their patron (Russia) in the Far East, the Slavic states in the Balkan Peninsula became convinced that "ultimately they would have to rely upon themselves to realize their national aspirations against the Ottomans." The Great Power equilibrium thus disrupted, Bulgarian, Greek, and Serbian nationalists adopted "Japanese methods" of fighting in the Balkan Wars of 1912–13, namely, offensive warfare characterized by "direct infantry assaults and indirect artillery support" and reinforced by self-sacrificing élan. Although this tactic was often merely a metaphor for scaring the enemy (the Ottomans), it nevertheless was effective and indeed frightened the Ottoman soldiers.

---

16 Quoted in Rotem Kowner, ed., *The Impact of the Russo-Japanese War* (London–New York: Routledge, 2007), 304.

17 On Japan's impact on Turkey, see Handan Nezir Akmese, *The Birth of Modern Turkey: The Ottoman Military and the March to World War I* (London–New York: I. B. Tauris, 2005), 72–79; on Japanese-Turkish relations, see Selçuk Esenbel and Chiharu Inaba (eds.), *The Rising Sun and the Turkish Crescent: New Perspectives on the History of Japanese Turkish Relations* (Istanbul: Boğaiçi University Press, 2003).

18 See Janet Afary, *The Iranian Constitutional Revolution, 1906–1911* (New York: Columbia University Press, 1996) (quoted passage, "the model of Asian progress . . . ," on p. 181). For Japan's impact on the Middle East in general, see also Renée Worringer, ed., *The Islamic Middle East and Japan: Perceptions, Aspirations, and the Birth of Intra-Asian Modernity* (Princeton, NJ: Markus Wiener, 2007).

But it also resulted in colossal casualties on both sides.[19] Armenians and Kurds in Eastern Anatolia, became equally emboldened and defiant of the Turks. The efforts of the Young Turks to modernize and centralize the country met with stiff resistance in Eastern Anatolia where Istanbul's control had always been rather limited. In that land, the Ottomans had long sought to use the Muslim Kurds, Christian Armenians, and others (such as Christian Assyrians) to subvert its imperial rival to the north. Likewise, Russia sought to do the same against its rival to the south. Because these minority groups were often pitted against one another, mutual pogroms were not uncommon, as was also the case in the Russian Caucasus between Christian Armenians and Muslim Azeris. Major population centers such as Tiflis and Baku were in fact afflicted by ethnic and religious violence at the time of the 1905 Revolution.[20]

What changed after 1905 was that Muslims as a whole came to be deliberately targeted by Western imperial powers for political operations. All imperial powers had been scheming for a piece of the enormous pie of the Ottoman Empire. This was the core of the century-old "Eastern Question." Famously, Germany's ambitions to become a global power led to Anglo-German naval competition, drawing Germany to Asia Minor and the Middle East, where it saw a good chance of competing successfully against its rivals – Britain, France, and Russia. Thus, Germany courted Turkey. German ambitions went much further, however, eyeing the Muslims in the Caucasus, Persia, Afghanistan, and Central Asia. The promotion of pan-Islamism (which itself had emerged to contest Western colonial domination of Muslim lands) under German aegis was intended to subvert the imperial extensions of Germany's competitors. In the case of Russia with its large Muslim population, German support of pan-Islamism had the additional effect of subverting Russia from within. The German plan to extend its railways from Berlin to Baghdad became the symbol of German imperial ambitions in the east of Europe.[21]

Japan, too, found among the Muslims a tool with which to satisfy its imperial ambitions. Even after the war against Russia ended successfully in 1905, Japan continued to collect, openly and secretly, detailed information on political, economic, religious, and national conditions in the Caucasus and Persia.[22] No evidence seems to exist to suggest that Japan maintained any sustained contact with Muslims (or Chris-

19 Richard C. Hall, "The Next War: The Influence of the Russo-Japanese War on Southeastern Europe and the Balkan Wars of 1912–1913." *Journal of Slavic Military Studies*, 17, no. 3 (2004), 563–577 (quotes on p. 574.)

20 See the first-hand account by an Italian correspondent: Luigi Villari, *Fire and Sword in the Caucasus* (London: T.F. Unwin, 1906).

21 See Sean McMeekin, *The Berlin-Baghdad Express: The Ottoman Empire and Germany's Bid for World Power* (Cambridge, MA: Harvard University Press, 2010).

22 See scanned documents (pertaining to the period from 1908 to 1911) available at JACAR, the Japan Center for Asian Historical Records (National Archives of Japan): http://www.jacar.go.jp, reference codes: B03050608300, B03050608400, B03050608500, B0213056620.

tians for that matter) in the Caucasus at the time. It is remarkable, however, that having gained the admiration of the Ottomans, Japan managed to station a "military attaché" in Istanbul from 1907 onward, at a time when Japan and Turkey had not even established official diplomatic relations. Moreover, Japan did have contact with Muslims from Russia. Abdrashid Ibragimov (Abdürreşid Ibrahim, 1857–1944), a Tatar from Western Siberia had already visited Japan before the Russo-Japanese War, but was expelled at the Russian government's demand.[23] In the wake of Japan's victory over Russia, Ibragimov wrote about Japan and Islam, predicting (more correctly, expressing his wishful thinking) that the Japanese nation might convert to Islam. In 1908–10 he visited Japan again, met many influential Japanese, and praised Japan as a force that could help the Muslim peoples become liberated from the European yoke.[24] Japan, in turn, found Ibragimov and other Muslim activists useful allies for a possible future war against Russia and provided them financial support.[25]

Japan's courting of Muslims, however, complicated its relations with the Sublime Porte. Ottoman admiration was tempered by fear that Ottoman hegemony over the Muslim world might slip into the hands of Japan. In Southeast Asia, for example, some Muslims came to see Japan as an "alternative savior from Dutch colonialism": Japan might even become a "Second Mecca."[26] In fact, Japan's imperialist schemes ultimately had the opposite effect of undermining its own credibility in Asia.

Even though hidden in the euphoria over its victory, Japan's imperial ambitions were evident. The Ottoman Porte and Japan had intended to open formal diplomatic relations even before the Russo-Japanese War, yet they never succeeded because Japan insisted on the same privileges (including extraterritoriality) that the Western imperial forces imposed on the Porte. These claims fundamentally undermined Japan's trustworthiness. The absurdity was evident even to many Japanese diplomats and military leaders. In 1910, the head of military intelligence, for example, advised strongly that the Japanese government forge close relations with the Ottomans on equal footing because the country's importance to Japan was unmistakable: Japan's renunciation of extraterritoriality would win the hearts and minds of "220 millions of Muslims" in the

---

23 Larisa Usmanova, *The Türk-Tatar Diaspora in Northeast Asia. Transformation of Consciousness: A Historical and Sociological Account between 1898 and the 1950s* (Tokyo: Rakudasha, 2007), 7, states that Ibrahim (Ibragimov) "had close ties with Colonel Motojirō Akashi," and that Ibrahim's son Murad, helped by Akashi and others, studied at Waseda University in Tokyo from 1908 to 1911.

24 See Abdürrechid Ibrahim, *Un Tatar au Japon – voyage en Asie (1908–1910)*, tr. and ed. François Georgeon (Arles: Actes Sud, 2004.).

25 See the diary entries of the chief of Japan's military intelligence in 1909 to 1912 discussing Ibragimov: *Nihon rikugun to Ajia seisaku: rikugun taishō Utsunomiya Tarō nikki*, vol. 1 (Tokyo: Iwanami, 2007), 235–36, 243, 321, and vol. 2 (Tokyo: Iwanami, 2007), 248.

26 Kowner, ed., *The Impact of the Russo-Japanese War*, 220, 234. More generally on the impact of Japan's victory on the Muslims, see Klaus Kreiser, "Der Japanische Sieg über Russland (1905) und sein Echo unter den Muslimen." *Die Welt des Islams*, 21, nos. 1–4 (1981).

world, including nearly 14 million in Russia.[27] Nevertheless, the Japanese government failed to understand this important point, and it became a symbol of Japan's extraordinarily inept diplomacy.

The possibility of the establishment of Turko-Japanese diplomatic relations (and even an "alliance" between the two countries) greatly concerned Russia.[28] Indeed, Russia suspected that after Akashi was forced to leave Europe in 1907, he made a stop in Istanbul on his way back to Japan to conclude "a military alliance with Turkey."[29] Akashi's ghost was evident in the Caucasus as well: rumors circulated that the Japanese had covered the Caucasus with secret spies.[30] In the end, however, Tokyo's ineptitude in Turkey benefited Russia greatly.

3.3 A New Global Political Configuration

Russia's defeat in the war against Japan had tremendous global repercussions in another respect as well: it changed the global political balance of power, particularly in Europe and Asia.

Humbled in Asia, Russia returned to its historic interests in Europe, that is, in the west and south. Yet there Russia faced her now emboldened imperial rivals and oppressed nationalities.

After the war, Russia's modus operandi was to secure peace and the restoration of its military might severely weakened by its defeat. In 1907, in a sharp departure from the historic Great Game with Great Britain, Russia concluded an agreement with its archenemy (the Anglo-Russian Convention of 1907), dividing Asia (Persia, Afghanistan, and Tibet) into their respective spheres of influence, most notably splitting Persia into three zones (Russian, neutral, and British). Although of course this did not eliminate the rivalry of the two countries in Asia,[31] it did help Russia gain time to recover from the war with Japan. On the eve of the agreement's signing, A.P. Izvol'skii, Russia's foreign minister, noted that "Russia must be assured of peace from Kamchatka to Gibraltar for about ten years . . . or else we will be in the position of a half-forgotten Asian power."[32] With the Franco-Russian alliance from the 1890s and the Anglo-French Entente Cordiale of 1904, the Russian-British rapprochement now created the Triple Entente.

---

27 JACAR, reference code: B06151024000.

28 See Rossiiskii gosudartsvennyi voenno-istoricheskii arkhiv, f. 450, op. 1, d. 146 (pertaining to 1906).

29 GARF, f. 102, DP PP, 1907, op. 316, d. 38ch1, ll. 97–98.

30 GARF, f. 102, DP PP, 1907, op. 316, d. 38ch1, ll. 97–98.

31 See Jennifer Siegel, *Endgame: Britain, Russia and the Final Struggle for Central Asia* (London–New York: I.B. Tauris, 2002).

32 Quoted in David MacLaren McDonald, *United Government and Foreign Policy in Russia 1900–1914* (Cambridge, MA: Harvard University Press, 1992), p. 109.

The Anglo-Russian Convention was prompted at least in part by the rapid rise of the German Empire, an empire that had been changing the political map of Europe since 1871. Together with the Habsburgs in Austria-Hungary, Russia's old continental rival, and Italy, an upstart colonial power, the German government had long belonged to the Triple Alliance of Central Powers. Russia's weakness as exposed in the war against Japan now emboldened the Central Powers. Austria-Hungary, for example, supported by Germany, delivered to Russia a "diplomatic Tsushima," a humiliating defeat akin to Japan's routing of the Russian Fleet in the Tsushima Straits, Japan, in 1905. In 1908 the Habsburgs almost unilaterally annexed Bosnia-Herzegovina through cunning diplomatic manoeuvers. Although, in return, Russia secured the independence of Bulgaria from the Ottomans, it failed to exact territorial and political concessions for Serbia and Montenegro or gain freer access to the Turkish Straits. This event, forced upon a weakened Russia, set the stage for the confrontation between Russia and Austria-Hungary in World War I.[33]

Germany itself proved even more formidable, for it, unlike Austria-Hungary, strove to become a global power, and so inevitably clashed with Russia, Britain, France, and even Japan and the United States. Russia felt most threatened by Germany's growing influence in its southern borderlands: the Ottoman Empire, the Caucasus, and Persia. As noted, Germany sought to use these to challenge its rival imperial powers of Britain, France, and Russia. The Ottomans, long in decline under the pressure of these European powers, found in Germany (with which it did not share a border) a convenient counterweight to them. But the ties of the two countries, which were becoming ever closer, greatly unnerved the other imperial powers, Russia included. The so-called Liman von Sanders incident in 1913–14 is symbolic of the growing German influence in the Ottoman Empire: when the German general was put in charge of the Ottoman army corps defending the Straits, the other European imperial powers strongly reacted. But although in the end Germany was forced to make a concession,[34] the affair did not break German ambitions in this part of the world.

Likewise, the Russo-Japanese War changed significantly the international environment in which Japan operated. One of the most important changes was that after Japan's victory, the United States now viewed the new Asian empire as a potential threat to US interests in Asia. Originally the United States, like Britain, had regarded Japan as a convenient counterweight to Russia's imperial expansion in Asia. Japan's victory, however, fundamentally changed the American position. True, the

33 For this Bosnian crisis, see McDonald, *United Government and Foreign Policy in Russia 1900–1914*, ch. 6. For a detailed analysis of the Balkan crisis and its consequences, see Andrew Rossos, *Russia and the Balkans: Inter-Balkan Rivalries and Russian Foreign Policy, 1908–1914* (Toronto: University of Toronto Press, 1981).

34 See Michael A. Reynolds, *Shattering Empires: The Clash and Collapse of the Ottoman and Russian Empires 1908–1918* (Cambridge: Cambridge University Press, 2011), 40–41.

United States did tolerate Japan's annexation of Korea in 1910 (in exchange for security in its colonies in the Philippines). Yet soon after the Russo-Japanese War, the end of which it brokered in Portsmouth, New Hampshire, the United States began preparing for a possible future war with Japan. Indeed, it was "the first time in American history that the United States prepared war plans in peacetime directed at a specific adversary."[35] A political configuration that would lead to the Pacific War in 1941 was thus already emerging soon after the Russo-Japanese War.

By contrast, Japan and Russia began drawing closer, in part to protect their interests in Asia from the United States, which was beginning to claim its own stakes aggressively.[36] In 1907, Russia and Japan came to an agreement, demarcating their respective spheres of influence in Manchuria, which meant that Japan could annex Korea in 1910 without Russia's objection. In 1910 Russia and Japan concluded another agreement aimed at consolidating their respective spheres. In 1911–12, faced with the consequences of the 1911 Xinhai Revolution in China, the two powers also secretly agreed to demarcate Inner Mongolia under their respective areas. In turn, Japan reluctantly acknowledged Russia's special interests in Outer Mongolia (which in 1912 declared independence from China). However strange it may appear, their rapprochement was merely part of their imperial schemes, allowing Russia to concentrate its attention on Europe and Japan to guard against Russia's "war of revenge." In 1916 their diplomatic dance would culminate with a formal alliance between them.[37]

Despite the rapprochement, however, the world remained in doubt about its endurance, expecting that Russia and Japan would fight again in due course. A Georgian reporting from Persia in 1909 noted that people there were asking whether Japan indeed would start a war against Russia and what, in that case, "Giurzhistan" (Georgia) would do. Local people thought that it "necessary to drive out the Russians from the Caucasus."[38] Indeed, the Russo-Japanese rapprochement did not alleviate the mutual suspicions of either side.

---

35 Tal Tovy and Sharon Halevi, "America's First Cold War: The Emergence of a New Rivalry," in Kowner, ed., *The Impact of the Russo-Japanese War*, 150.

36 The latest Russian work on the subject is Ia. A. Shulatov, *Na puti k sotrudnichestvu: Rossiisko-iaponskie otnosheniia v 1905–1914 gg.* (Khabarovsk-Moscow: Izd-vo Instituta vostokovedeniia RAN, 2008).

37 See Peter Berton, "A New Russo-Japanese Alliance?: Diplomacy in the Far East during World War I." *Acta Slavica Iaponica*, no. 11 (1993), 58–59. For more detail, see Michio Yoshimura, *Zōho: Nihon to Rosia* (Tokyo: Nihon keizai hyōronsha, 1991).

38 GARF, f. 102, DP PP, 1910, op. 239, d. 24ch79lA, l. 3.

3.4 "Spy Mania"

Despite Russia and Japan's political rapprochement, they never stopped considering each other potential foes. On the contrary, both sides, or to be more exact, a considerable section of military leaders in both countries, continued to regard the other as a dangerous rival.

Russian war planning in 1910, for example, included Japan: the plan, which was "the first in Russian imperial history that developed full mobilization schedules for combat on the entire Eurasian continent," provided for "war against China, Japan, China and Japan in alliance, war in the Caucasus, and war in Turkestan, while at the same time continuing to provision for the traditional European threat." In general, the Russian military were "unplacated by the assurances of their diplomatic counterparts that the 1907 Anglo-Russian Convention and later agreements with Japan had effectively neutralized the threat from that direction."[39] Russia's strengthening of its military forces in Asia in general unnerved Tokyo, which in turn enlarged its military presence in Korea.

Moreover, Russia's virtual control of Outer Mongolia greatly alarmed Japan. Having long engaged in various political machinations to extend its influence to Inner Mongolia and eventually to Outer Mongolia as well, Japan in turn schemed to detach Manchuria and Inner Mongolia from China under Japanese aegis.[40] Although Japan's attempt failed, owing to pressure from Britain and Russia, numerous independent Japanese schemers (called continental *rōnin*) continued to engage in political and military intrigues in China and Inner Mongolia in response to the perceived Russian threat. Often the Japanese government was unable to control these independent schemers, who were assisted by sympathizers in the Japanese military. Japan's operations had also already extended to Xinjiang (Chinese Turkestan) during the Russo-Japanese War.[41] In 1912, when Japan and Russia negotiated a clear demarcation of their respective spheres of influence in Inner Mongolia, Russia demanded exclusive "special interests" in "Western China" (i.e., Xinjiang). Tellingly, Japan refused,[42] although this was an area lying directly on Russia's borders but thousands of kilometers from Japan! (The distance between Tokyo and Urumqi, the capital of Xinjiang, for example, is approximately 4,500 kilometers, or 2,800 miles.) Because it was a strategic area that would link Japan to Central Asia (Russian Turkestan), the Caucasus, and the Middle East, Japan refused to give in.

---

39 Alex Marshall, *The Russian General Staff and Asia, 1800–1917* (London–New York: Routledge, 2006), 101.

40 See Masaru Hatano, *Manmō dokuritsu undō* (Tokyo: PHP Kenkyūjo, 2001).

41 JACAR, reference code: B03050330700. See also Michio Yoshimura, "Nichiro sensō ki no Nihon no tai-Mōko seisaku no ichimen: 'Kharachin ōfu kenbunroku' i tsuite." *Seiji keizai shigaku* 300 (1991), 183.

42 Michio Yoshimura, "Dai san kai nichiro kyōyaku seiritsu zengo: romō kyōyaku to no kanren ni oite." *Kokusai seiji* 31 (1966), 74.

Russia's fear of Japan became an impetus for reforming and strengthening its military intelligence: "In a broad sense, the experience of Russian MI [military intelligence] during the Manchurian campaign [of 1904–05] laid the corner stone of the establishment of one of the most powerful secret services in the history of the twentieth century."[43] Russia's military intelligence budget shot up. From 1906 to 1910 it increased more than five-fold, from 344,140 to 1,947,850 rubles. Even in 1913, on the eve of World War I, the intelligence budget for the East (i.e., Asia) was 50 percent higher than that for the West.[44] The Caucasus occupied an equally important position. In 1914, for instance, the Caucasus military district received the highest intelligence budget of all districts.[45]

With the rise of intelligence budgets came increased spy mania and spy hunting. Russia's fear of Japanese spies did not abate at the end of the Russo-Japanese War.[46] The memory of Japanese spies masked as Japanese Buddhist priests or Mongolian lamas during the war remained fresh.[47] If anything, spy mania in Russia intensified with the suspicion that, under the guise of peace, Japanese spies were afoot everywhere.

The famous story "Staff Captain Rybnikov" (1906), by Aleksandr Kuprin, is symptomatic of the psychic state of Russia after the war. In this story, Kuprin describes a Japanese spy, cleverly disguised as a patriotic Russian military captain. It is assumed that his somewhat Asiatic facial features are shared by many Cossacks from Orenburg and the Urals. But eventually Rybnikov's clever disguise is uncovered by true Russian patriots, and the spy is caught. Indeed, Russia's spy mania after the war was extraordinary. Nearly all Japanese came to be suspected as military spies. Many were arrested. Japanese consulates were depicted as centers of espionage. Likewise, Russian authorities treated Koreans and Chinese as potential Japanese spies and began excluding them from working in the country as laborers. The Russian military spread the view of all-pervasive Japanese espionage widely, while Japanese diplomats in Russia described the Russian attitude as "terrifyingly suspicious."[48] In 1913, Army Major Sadao Araki, on his return journey to Japan after serving as military attaché in St. Petersburg,

---

43 Evgeny Sergeev, *Russian Military Intelligence in the War with Japan, 1904–05: Secret Operations on Land and at Sea* (London–New York: Routledge, 2007), 185.

44 Marshall, *The Russian General Staff and Asia*, 99-100.

45 Marshall, *The Russian General Staff and Asia*, 110.

46 For Russia's spy mania during the war, see Leonid Heretz, *Russia on the Eve of Modernity: Popular Religion and Traditional Culture under the Last Tsars* (Cambridge: Cambridge University Press, 2008), 153–54.

47 For these examples, see Hisao Tani, *Kimitsu nichiro sen shi* (Tokyo: Hara shobō, 1966), 287, 291, and Yoshimura, "Nichiro sensō ki," 179.

48 Michio Yoshimura, "Nichiro sensō go ni okeru nihonjin gunji tantei kengi mondai." *Kokushigaku* 105 (May 1978), 13 (referring to 1910). Of course, Japan had its own mania against Russian spies (*rotan*), but it did not quite match the level of the Russian obsession. See Michio Yoshimura, "Rotan to nihonjin shakai." *Rekishi dokuhon* 49, no. 4 (2004), 140–43.

was arrested in Chita, Siberia, on suspicion of espionage, causing a diplomatic scandal.[49] In reaction, the Russian government itself admitted that "spy incidents" had become an "infectious disease" in Russia.[50]

It is true that Japan, like Russia, engaged in clandestine operations. Some Japanese disguised themselves as priests or lamas or Koreans and engaged in intelligence work, while others masked themselves as barbers, dentists, photographers, and the like. Japan also used entertainers such as circus performers and "professional fighters" (judo and karate masters) who reached Central Asia and the Caucasus as well.[51] In 1907 a Japanese ("Major Takenouchi") was spotted by Russian authorities around Baku, while in Batumi another Japanese, a convert to Islam, one "Abdul Hamid Saishi Nakashima" was observed.[52] In fact, in February 1907 Major Takeo Takenouchi, with his interpreter "Nobuhiko Okawa," visited Baku, Tiflis, Erevan, and Batumi before moving on to Odesa.[53] Another Japanese, "Kazioto Ito," age thirty-two, was arrested in Vladikavkaz and another, "Oiyama" in Batumi in July 1907. Ito was arrested for his close connections with Ossetians in the Vladikavkaz area. Their activity, according to the Russian police, indicated "espionage, revolutionary agitation, and financial and military support [for the Caucasians]."[54] Yet immediately after these arrests, in September 1907, three Japanese officers, "Major Nabussi Muto," "Major Takayanagi" and "Uchiya" visited Baku. Although Uchiya fell ill there, Muto and Takayanagi went on to visit Tiflis, Batumi, and Odesa. At about the same time, another Japanese, "Matsuyosuki Kawai," visited Batumi and Tiflis before moving on to Baku.[55] In 1910 Colonel "Hagino" of the Japanese army was spotted in Tiflis, Vladikavkaz, Mineral'nye Vody, and Krasnovodsk (today's Turkmenbashy).[56] In 1913, on the eve of World War I, Russian police suspected that a "troupe of Japanese artists" ("Hanako Ōta," "Konstantin Aleksandrovich Saratori" [Shiratori?], and an Orthodox Christian who had worked at

49 Manabu Kikkawa, *Hiroku Rikugun rimenshi: shōgun Araki no shichijūnen* (Tokyo: Yamato Shobō, 1954), pp. 224–38 and N.V. Grekov, *Russkaia kontrrazvedka v 1905–1917 gg.: shpionomaniia i real'nye problemy* (Moscow: Mosk. obshch. nauch. fond, 2000), 190–192.

50 Yoshimura, "Nichiro sensō go," p. 19.

51 GARF, f. 102, DP PP, 1907, op. 316, d. 38ch2, l. 1–2 (Rostov on the Don), 1908, op. 316, d. 381G, l. 58 and 79 (Kyiv, Kazan, Tomsk, Chita, and Khabarovsk). See also Grekov, *Russkaia kontrrazvedka*, 145.

52 Alex Marshall, "Imperial Russian War Planning for the Eurasian Space and the Impact of the War," in *Rethinking the Russo-Japanese War, 1904–05: Centennial Perspectives*, ed. Rotem Kowner, v. 1 (Folkestone: Global Oriental, 2006), 301.

53 GARF, f. 102, DP PP, 1907, d. 316, d. 38ch1, ll. 27, 50–52, 68.

54 GARF, f. 102, DP PP, 1907, d. 38ch2, ll. 1–2, 8. In this connection, two Japanese, "Saimoto" and "Ochiri" in Moscow and a certain "Brublevskii," likely a Pole, as well as a circus troop in Rostov on the Don (see note 51 above) were arrested.

55 GARF, f. 102, DP PP, 1907, d. 38ch2, ll. 195–97, 201, 206.

56 GARF, f. 102, DP PP, 1910, op. 316, d. 38lv, ll. 88–89, 93.

the Japanese embassy for many years, as well as others) who were visiting Tiflis were in fact military spies because they "walked a great deal around the town."[57]

It is also quite likely that Japan sought to use as spies and informers Russian citizens (including those from the Caucasus) working as conductors, waiters, and in similar capacities on the railways connecting Russia and China. A number of people from the Caucasus were indeed in the Far East in one capacity or another. On his way to Japan in early 1910, Abdrashid Ibragimov was surprised to see so many different peoples (including Georgians and Ossetians) on the Japanese boat from Vladivostok to Tsuruga, Japan, even though there were not many passengers.[58] It is difficult to confirm that any of the Caucasians actually spied for Japan. Suspicions remained strong, however: many years later, under Stalin, some of those Caucasians who had lived in the Far East were to be accused of espionage for Japan and executed (see chapter 6).

Among these was Giorgi Pitskhelauri, born in Telavi, Georgia, in 1873, who had lived in Harbin in Manchuria from 1899 to 1926 before returning to Georgia. Arrested in 1937 on charges of espionage for Japan, Pitskhelauri stated under questioning that at the time of the Russo-Japanese War a sizeable colony of Georgians formed in Harbin, mainly traders, speculators, and owners of canteens, supplemented by "adventurists," fugitives, and exiles.[59] Among them were strong anti-Russian sentiments. There were also Georgians who ran dining cars in railways covering the Chinese Eastern Railway and the Trans-Siberian Railway, an excellent base for military and economic intelligence. Simon Ordzhonikidze, who had been persecuted by Tsarist authorities, lived in Harbin under the name of Mikhail Nazarov and, according to Pitskhelauri, worked for Japanese intelligence. It was through Ordzhonikidze that Pitskhelauri was allegedly recruited by an official of the Japanese consulate in Harbin to spy for Japan. The Japanese, according to Pitskhelauri's confessions, promised support for Georgia's struggle against Tsarist Russia and, in the event of success, Japan's guarantee of Georgia's independence. In return he, as a merchant, was to promote Japanophilic work, provide intelligence, and create intelligence and diversionary agents along the railway lines.[60]

Pitskhelauri further stated, according to the Soviet secret police, that nearly all leaders of the Georgian colony in Harbin had been "recruited" at the time by Japan: Ivlian Khaindrava, Beglar Robakidze, Giorgi Mgaloblishvili, Nikoloz Tsulukidze, Ilia Pateishvili, and others, each of whom had his own agents both in Manchuria and in Russia. In 1906, allegedly to cover its clandestine operations, Japan created the Georgian Society in Harbin, the head of which was Pitskhelauri. It had three hundred to four hundred members and used philanthropic covers "for intelligence purposes."

57 GARF, f. 102, DP PP, 1913, op. 316, d. 38lia, l. 42-42ob.

58 Ibrahim, *Un Tatar au Japon*, 96.

59 By 1905 the Georgian community in Harbin had grown substantially to justify the foundation of a national library. See *Rubezh* (Harbin-Shanghai), 4 October 1941, 14.

60 File of K.O. Gelovani, Archive of the Ministry of Internal Affairs of Georgia (Tbilisi).

Pitskhelauri himself allegedly operated twenty-four agents (many of whom ran dining cars) scattered along the railways who, according to his confessions, provided excellent intelligence: Egor Gdzelidze, Grigol Dzhaparidze, Irakli Matikashvili, Abel' Tatulov, Ismail Abashidze, Noe Muskhulia, Grigol Danelia, Antimos Tskhomelidze, Sokrat Revia, Aslan Bakradze, Lavrenti Abashidze, David Dvali, Platon Dadiani, Ivan Metreveli, Egor Dzhakeli, and others.[61]

Needless to say, one cannot take these confessions, made at the time of the Great Terror, at face value. What they do suggest is that Japan was targeting ethnic non-Russians (including Georgians and other peoples from the Caucasus) for intelligence operations, and that the Russian government remained keenly aware of this link between Japan and the ethnic national minorities. Obviously, the Soviet government inherited those suspicions.

In any case, the message Russia projected to the nation was that of Japan's "total espionage," as discussed in the previous chapter. Discussing foreign espionage, one Russian book sounded a tocsin:

> No other country in the world has organized a military espionage network on such a large scale as Japan. Because the Japanese have a special, innate ability as military spies, it is very easy for the Japanese Emperor to increase ten-fold the number of military spies now placed in various countries. In fact he has no need for it, because today military spies have already been placed in many countries in the world . . . Japan has no ordinary general moral senses such as we have in Europe . . . Japanese behavior is not restricted by any morality but their patriotism for Japan.[62]

On the eve of 1914, the number of those suspected of being Japanese spies in Russia was the second largest (309), after Austro-Hungarian spies (353).[63]

Of course, Russia had learned a bitter lesson from Japan, and so emulated and enriched its own total espionage. In the autumn of 1912, for example, "at least four Russian army officers dressed and disguised as Kurds crossed into Ottoman lands in order to incite the Kurds." Meanwhile, Russia was running its own intelligence operations using in part its banks in Ottoman Turkey.[64] Of course, Russia was well aware of the Ottomans' similar use of Kurds against Russia.

Whatever the case, Russia's spy mania created a "tendency to view whole nationalities within the sensitive border zones as potential intelligence threats."[65] Clearly,

---

61 File of K.O. Gelovani, Archive of the Ministry of Internal Affairs of Georgia (Tbilisi).

62 Quoted in Yoshimura, "Nichiro sensō go," 15–16. Unfortunately we have been unable to identify the Russian original.

63 Grekov, *Russkaia kontrrazvedka*, 175.

64 Reynolds, *Shattering Empires*, 64. Regarding the use of banks, Russians suspected during World War I that "the very epicenter of German espionage in Russia was the banking system." See Alex Marshall, "Russian Military Intelligence, 1905–1917: The Untold Story behind Tsarist Russia in the First World War." *War in History* 11, no. 4 (2004), 413.

65 Alex Marshall, "Russian Intelligence during the Russo-Japanese War, 1904–05," *Intelligence and National Security*, 22:5 (October 2007), 695–96.

the spy mania originated not in the Soviet period but well before the Bolsheviks ever came to power in 1917. It was deeply rooted in the memory of the Tsarist rout in 1904–05, and was already available for Stalin to exploit in the 1930s and 1940s. In the 1930s Kurds, Koreans, and those of many other national groups came to be suspected as foreign spies.

The mutual suspicion of Japan and Russia often led to curious events. After the war, Imperial Japanese Army Lieutenant Colonel Giichi Tanaka, whose work in the Caucasus and Russia before the Russo-Japanese War was discussed in the previous chapter, began providing confidential military information to the Russian military attaché in Tokyo, General V. K. Samoilov. Exactly when Tanaka began helping Samoilov is unclear. It was certainly before the 1907 rapprochement between the two countries. In late 1906, for Tanaka's great contribution, Samoliov even recommended to the Russian government that he be decorated with an order.[66] How much confidential information did Tanaka reveal to the Russians, and why? Tanaka was author of the draft on the top-secret "Imperial Defense Strategy" of 1907, which detailed Japan's fundamental military strategies. Was this also leaked to Russia? No one knows. It is difficult to believe Tanaka sold out his own country; he even became prime minister in the 1920s. Did he provide disinformation to Samoilov? Was he a crypto Russophile? Was he blackmailed by Russians for some reason? Whatever Tanaka's intention, he almost certainly revealed too much. Immediately after his death in 1929, he was described as the author of the infamous "Tanaka Memorial" of 1927, which, though apparently a Soviet forgery, purportedly laid out Japan's strategy to conquer Asia.

3.5 The Caucasus on the Eve of World War I

Meanwhile, Caucasian national political forces continued to fight against Russian domination. As Count Vorontsov-Dashkov, Tsar's viceroy in the Caucasus, wrote: "In Central Russia the police are rarely forced to act against an armed mass, in the Caucasus, constantly."[67] Tsarist oppression of national sentiments following Stolypin's coup in June 1907 further complicated the already complex relations in the Caucasus. Still, Georgian, Armenian, Polish, Ukrainian, Finnish, and other nationally oriented political groups managed to maintain contact and work together.[68] When the long-standing autonomy of Finland (the Grand Duchy of Finland) within the Russian Empire came

66 See P.E. Padalko, *Iaponiia v sud'bakh Rossiian: Ocherki istorii tsarskoj diplomatii i rossiiskoi diaspory v Iaponii* (Moscow: Kraft+, 2004), 96–98.

67 Quoted in Firouzeh Mostashari, *On the Religious Frontier: Tsarist Russia and Islam in the Caucasus* (London-New York: I.B. Tauris, 2006), 106.

68 See, for example the testimony of Giorgi Laskhishvili, *memuarebi (1885–1915)* [Memoirs] (Tbilisi, 1934), 246–248.

to be drastically curtailed in 1910, the Georgian Socialist Federalists protested against the Russian government in support of the Finns.[69]

The thrust of Stolypin's policy in the Caucasus as elsewhere in the Empire was not merely Russification, but the advancement of Russian hegemony in non-Russian provinces. It was to be carried out by ethnic Russians. Russian peasants, in particular, were encouraged to "colonize" the Caucasus by buying land from impoverished landlords. Thus under Stolypin tens of thousands of Russian peasants settled in Georgia alone. The Black Sea coastal areas and the southern part of Azerbaijan (the Mugan steppe) were also settled by Russians. Altogether, by 1910 one hundred thousand had settled in the Caucasus.[70] Naturally their settlement, supported by the Russian government, deeply disturbed local sentiments. Indeed, the Georgian Socialist Federalists, without excluding terrorism as a weapon against Russian colonization, set up a secret national land fund to keep Georgian lands from being bought by Russian peasants.[71]

The insistence on national autonomy by the Georgian Socialist Federalists made their position particularly dangerous in the eyes of Russian authorities. They were in fact more dangerous than the Social Democrats (who dominated Georgian politics) in one particular respect: whereas the latter, as Marxist internationalists, considered nationalism as particularistic and separatist and sought to "solve" national issues within the framework of "Russia" itself, the former regarded Russia as an occupier and colonizer. As repression continued, some Socialist Federalists became even more radicalized, advocating outright independence from Russia. By 1910, they were targeted for destruction, and in April of that year, most of the central figures of the party were arrested.[72] In a further blow to the party, in November, the most prominent member abroad, Dekanozishvili, died in Cannes, France.

Nonetheless, the Socialist Federalists persisted politically. In 1912, for example, Prince Varlaam Gelovani (1878–1915), a Georgian lawyer who had studied at St. Petersburg University and a member of the Socialist-Federalist Party, was elected in Kutaisi to the Fourth State Duma of the Russian Empire. In a speech at the Duma, he demanded Georgia's autonomy within the empire.[73] Moreover, the Romanov tercentenary in 1913 led the government to grant amnesty to many of those arrested and exiled.

In 1911, Peter Surguladze, a Socialist Federalist who had fled Russia in December 1910, had already founded the Foreign Committee of the Party of Georgian Separatists in Geneva.[74] The committee included Leo Kereselidze and his brother Giorgi, Nestor

69 GSCHA, f. 94, op. 1, d. 369, ll. 1–2.

70 See Mostashari, *On the Religious Frontier*, 107.

71 GSCHA, f. 153, op. 1, d. 1835, l. 11ob and 18ob, and GARF, f. 102 DPOO 1909, op. 239, d. 202, ll. 174–75, f. 102 DPOO 1910, op. 240, d. 2479, ll. 13, 16–17, 30–31, 33, 47–48, 58, 64.

72 GARF, f. 102 DPOO 1910, op. 240, d. 2479, ll. 45–45ob.

73 Laskhishvili, *memuarebi (1885–1915)*, 279.

74 G. Kereselidze, "sakartvelos damoukideblobis komit'et'i (1914-1918)" [Committee for the independence of Georgia], *kartuli emigratsia* [Georgian emigration] (Tbilisi: n.p., 2013), vol. I (4), 151.

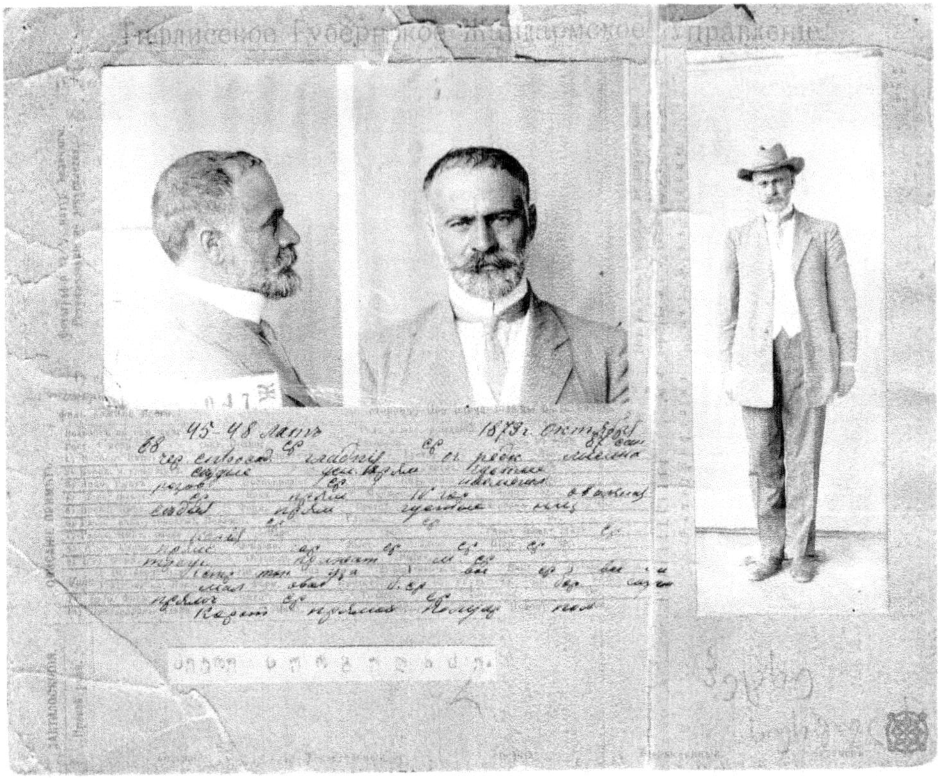

Fig. 3.2. Peter Surguladze.

Magalashvili, and others.[75] In 1913 the committee began publishing *Free Georgia*.[76] During World War I this committee was transformed into a Committee for the Liberation of Georgia with Germany's support.

Among Muslims in the Caucasus, non-national, pan-Islamic ideas still predominated. In certain areas, however, they evolved into more articulate national sentiments. The Russian government suspected that "pan-Islam had succeeded in planting 'fanatical hatred towards the Russians' in the hearts of natives; they were asking for 'Daghestan [Dagestan] for the Daghestanis [Dagestanis]'."[77] In 1911, Mammad Amin Rasulzade (Mehmet Emin Resulzade) and other formerly Social Democratic Azeri in-

75 Nozadze, "gardasrul zhamta ambavni da sakmeni," 121.

76 GSCHA, f. 94, op. 1, d. 695, l. 1ob.

77 Mostashari, *On the Religious Frontier*, 144.

Fig. 3.3. Members of the Georgian Student Association in Switzerland "Iveria" in commemoration of the 350th anniversary of the University of Geneva: Seated in the center is its chairman, Leo Kereselidze; on his right, Giorgi Kereselidze; far left, Nestor Magalashvili with a banner in hand. Geneva, 1909.

tellectuals founded a secret political party Musavat (meaning "equality"), oriented toward pan-Islamism and restoration of the "lost independence of Muslim countries."[78]

The Armenians went much further: they became a "mobilized nationality." Viceroy Vorontsov-Dashkov himself was pro-Armenian, especially in view of his using ethnic Armenians in the Ottoman Empire against the sultan.[79] His policies did not always help, however, because they raised the suspicions of other Caucasian groups. The conflict with Muslim Azeris and the resentment of Georgians against the "material and political power of the Armenians in Tiflis and other Georgian cities" contributed to making the Armenians a "mobilized nationality."[80] As a result, the Dashnaktsu-

78 See Ronald Grigor Suny, *The Baku Commune 1917–1918: Class and Nationality in the Russian Revolution* (Princeton, NJ: Princeton University Press, 1972), 18–19. See also Aidyn Balaev, *Azerbaidzhanskoe natsional'noe dvizhenie; ot "Musavata" do Narodnogo Fronta* (Baku: Elm, 1992), 4–5.

79 Note his famous letter to the Tsar: "Pis'ma I.I. Vorontsova-Dashkova Nikolaiu Romanovu (1905–1915 gg.)." *Krasnyi arkhiv* no. 26 (1928), 118–120 (10 October 1912).

80 Ronald Grigor Suny, *Armenia in the Twentieth Century* (Chico, CA: Scholarly Press, 1983), 15.

tiun, or nationalist party, continued to increase its influence throughout Armenian society, especially between 1903 and 1917.[81]

In these developments, it is difficult to detect Japan's presence or direct influence, although its indirect influence stemming from its victory over the Russian Empire in 1905 was a constant factor. While after the war Russia and Japan began drawing nearer for political reasons, they remained suspicious of each other. Invariably, the Russian police regarded a constant stream of Japanese visitors to the Caucasus as spies.

81 Suny, *Looking toward Ararat*, 93.

4 War, Independence, and Reconquest, 1914–21

Even though the events leading up to World War I may have appeared to be purely European affairs, they had deeper Eurasian roots: the change in the European balance of power caused by the rise of Germany as an imperial power after the 1871 unification and the decline of Russia following the Russo-Japanese War was the single most significant factor. According to one historian, the "long fuse that lit the Balkan powder keg originated in Manchuria."[1]

World War I involved four empires in East-Central Europe – the Ottoman, the Russian, the German, and the Habsburg Empires – and it led to the destruction of all four. With their collapse, numerous nations, willingly or unwillingly, became independent states. In the Caucasus, at least four new states emerged: Georgia, Armenia, Azerbaijan, and the Mountaineer Republic of the Northern Caucasus. By the spring of 1921, however, all of them had been conquered by the Red Army, and in 1922 they ended up in the newly created Soviet Union.

During the war Japan fought on the same side as Russia until the Bolsheviks seized power in the autumn of 1917. Consequently, Japan was no longer in a position to subvert Russia from within by supporting the independence movements of Russia's national minorities. Instead, those within the Russian Empire who aspired to independence turned to Russia's foes, Germany in particular. After the Bolshevik Revolution led to civil war in Russia, more than a dozen countries intervened militarily, including Japan, Britain, France, Germany, the United States, and others. In the end, however, the intervention failed to overthrow the Bolshevik government, and the Russian Empire reconstituted itself as the Soviet Union (*sans* Poland, Finland, and the Baltic states). This created new ground for Caucasian-Japanese collaboration against Moscow.

4.1 World War I

Soon after the outbreak of hostilities, Russia suffered a crushing defeat by Germany at the Battle of Tannenberg (described by Aleksandr Solzhenitsyn in his epic novel *August 1914*). Russia's initial success on the Galician front, too, was soon nullified by the German-Austrian joint forces. In the course of 1915, Russia was forced to retreat and abandon Galicia and Russian Poland (including Warsaw).

Turkey, initially maintaining neutrality, resisted Germany's pressure to join the Central Powers while simultaneously toying with the idea of striking a deal with Russia. But in the end, the Ottomans closed the Straits and stood against Russia, which

1 Keith Nelson, "The War and British Strategic Foreign Policy," in Rotem Kowner (ed.), *Rethinking the Russo-Japanese War, 1904-05*, vol. 1 (Folkestone: Global Oriental, 2007), 317.

on 31 October 1914 declared war on the Sublime Porte.[2] Compared with the European front, the Caucasian campaign proved much more propitious to Russia, which by the spring of 1916 had captured Erzurum and Trabzon and advanced deep into Eastern Anatolia.

Russia's military gains, however, masked the tremendously complex political situation in the Caucasus. Both Russia and Turkey sought to use the Armenians for subversion against each other while at the same time treating them with suspicion. For example, both courted the Dashnaktsutiun party of Armenian revolutionaries, simultaneously suspecting they were separatists and agents of the respective enemy. The party did, however, receive funds from Russia to organize armed rebellions by Armenians within Turkey,[3] and some Armenians did put up armed resistance against the Ottomans, most famously in the city of Van in Eastern Anatolia in May 1915. These factors led the Ottoman Porte to deport ethnic Armenians on a large scale. In the process, up to one million Armenians died or were killed. This is commonly considered a genocide among Armenians.[4] Along with Armenians, Christian Assyrians suffered similarly.[5] The "Armenian question" became a valuable political weapon in the hands of Russia against its foe, the Ottomans. Yet Russia had no intention of granting autonomy, let alone independence, to the Armenians in the Russian Caucasus.

Just as Moscow was leery of the Christian Armenians, it did not fully trust the Caucasian Muslims. Unlike Muslims elsewhere in Russia (including Volga and Crimean Tatars), Muslims in the Caucasus and Central Asia were exempt from military service for the empire.[6] Caucasian Muslims, however, could volunteer to fight, and indeed, in the summer of 1914 several cavalry regiments were formed from Dagestan, Chechen, Kabard, Ingush, Cherkess, Ossetian, and other volunteers. Admired and feared for their bravery, they were called the "Wild (Savage) Division," about whom N. N. Breshko-Breshkovskii published a namesake novel in Riga in 1920. They

2 For Turkey's negotiations with Russia for an alliance, see Michael A. Reynolds, *Shattering Empires: The Clash and Collapse of the Ottoman and Russian Empires 1908–1918* (Cambridge: Cambridge University Press, 2011), 110–12.

3 Reynolds, *Shattering Empires*, 116–17, and Firuz Kazemzadeh, *The Struggle for Transcaucasia (1917–1921)* (New York: Philosophical Library, 1951), 26–27. In Japan, ethnic Armenians who were Ottoman citizens were protected by Russian diplomatic legations from being treated as enemy aliens. See JACAR, reference cods: B11100646500 and B11100654800.

4 The literature on the subject is legion and controversies abound. For the most recent treatment, see Ronald Grigor Suny, Fatma Müge Göçek, and Norman M. Naimark, eds, *A Question of Genocide: Armenians and Turks at the End of the Ottoman Empire* (Oxford-New York: Oxford University Press, 2011).

5 At the same time, a large number of Muslims, indeed a larger number of Muslims in absolute terms than Armenians and Assyrians, are said to have died or have been killed in Anatolia during World War I, many of them at the hands of Armenians and Russians.

6 Armenians, unlike Caucasian Muslims, served in the regular Russian army; they also served in voluntary units, which were disbanded in 1916.

were, however, used in the west against Europeans and not in the south against the Ottomans.

Meanwhile, the Central Powers, particularly the Porte, sought to use pan-Turkic, pan-Islamic, and, more grandly, pan-Turanian movements to their advantage (this last referred to the movement to unite all "Turanian" peoples – mainly Muslims but not necessarily restricted to them – in Turkey, the Caucasus, Central Asia, Siberia, and, in a wider sense, even Hungarians, Finns, Mongols, Koreans, and Japanese). During World War I, émigrés from the Russian Empire began organizing themselves against Russia. Already in August 1914, under Ottoman aegis, a Caucasian Committee was formed under the guise of the Turkish Medical Mission, uniting the representatives of Cherkessia, Dagestan, Georgia, and Azerbaijan.[7] Although this committee was dissolved in 1916 owing to internal conflict, a different political group emerged in Turkey in the same year, namely the Committee for the Defense of the Rights of Turko-Tatar Muslim Peoples of Russia, formed from representatives of Volga Tatars, Crimean Tatars, Azeris, and "Bukharan Turks." These and similar groups proposed to the Central Powers that they support armed uprisings of the Caucasian peoples and create buffer states, which would put the insatiable Russian desire for conquest to an end.[8] In its October 1915 appeal to German foreign minister Gottlieb von Jagow, the Caucasian Committee requested Germany's support for creating a Confederation of Caucasian states.[9] In 1916, in Lausanne, Switzerland, non-Russian peoples of the Russian Empire (including those from the Caucasus) took part in the congress of the Union of Nationalities (formed in 1911 in Brussels) to acquaint the world with the plight of national minorities in Russia.[10] Yet these activities amounted to very little in terms of actual political results within Russia itself.[11] Nor did the attempts to recruit and employ Russian-Muslim prisoners of war as military forces go very far, apparently because Turkish officers did not treat them well.[12]

---

7 Wolfdieter Bihl, *Die Kaukasus-Politik der Mittelmächte. Teil I: Ihre Basis in der Orient-Politik und ihre Aktionen 1914–1917* (Wien-Köln-Graz: Böhlaus, 1975), 61, 239, 269.

8 Bihl, *Die Kaukasus-Politik der Mittelmächte*, 128, 240, 243.

9 Haus-, Hof- und Staatsarchiv, Politisches Archiv (HHStA, PA) (Vienna, Austria), I 947 Krieg 21 k Türkei: Georgisch-grusinischer Aufstand im Kaukasus 1914–1918, fols. 88–90.

10 See Seppo Zetterberg, *Die Liga der Fremdvölker Russlands 1916-1918. Ein Beitrag zu Deutschlands antirussischem Propagandakrieg unter der Fremdvölkern Russlands im Ersten Weltkriegs* (Helsinki: Finnische Historische Gesellschaft, 1978), 60-61, 70, 91-92, and Gotthard Yaschke, "Le peuples opprimé de Russie et la Conférence de Lausanne en 1916." *Prométhée* 1937, no. 132, 12–21.

11 In 1916 a revolt did take place against labor conscription in Russian Central Asia. Britain and Russia ascribed it to the influence of German, Austrian, and Turkish agents. Although there were many prisoners of war of the Central Powers in Central Asia, there is little evidence that they or their agents played any role in the revolt of 1916. See Edward Dennis Sokol, *The Revolt of 1916 in Russian Central Asia* (Baltimore, MD: The Johns Hopkins Press, 1954), 75–76 and 147–153.

12 Bihl, *Die Kaukasus-Politik der Mittelmächte*, 245–247.

Fig. 4.1. Mikheil (Mikhako) Tsereteli, Istanbul, 1915.

Many Georgians also organized themselves against Russia during World War I under the aegis of the Central Powers. In August 1914, Archimandrite Nicolas, who previously oversaw the largest monastery in Georgia, founded with other Georgians a nationalist organization in Trabzon.[13] In September in Berlin the Georgian National Committee (also known as the Committee for the Liberation of Georgia [see p. 70]) formed under the direction of Prince Giorgi Machabeli (1885–1935) and Mikheil (Mikhako) Tsereteli (1878–1965), formerly a close collaborator of Dekanozishvili.

The committee collaborated with Finnish and Ukrainian organizations against Russia. They all believed that the Caucasus would rise against Russia once the Central Powers invaded and that within two or three months, a combat-ready army of five hundred thousand men could be deployed there.[14] In their September 1914 appeal to the German Ministry of Foreign Affairs, Machabeli and Tsereteli, emphasizing the history of Georgia's struggle against Russia, reminded the Germans of the Japanese precedent: during the Russo-Japanese War, a "certain power (*eine Macht*)" (that is, Japan) assisted the Caucasians with weapons and ammunition to stand up against the Russians. They suggested that assistance of the same kind by the Central Powers to the

13 Reynolds, *Shattering Empires*, 131.
14 Bihl, *Die Kaukasus-Politik der Mittelmächte*, 60–61.

Caucasus would make it impossible for Russia to continue this war, prompting it to conclude peace with the Central Powers. This would extend Germany's influence to the Caucasus and all the way to Central Asia as well.[15] In 1916–17 Germany did help the Georgians transport weapons and ammunition and political activists to the Caucasus using submarines,[16] enterprises clearly influenced by the expedition of the *Sirius*. Hidden by local National Democrats (see p. 80) in secret stores in Georgia, the weapons and ammunition delivered from the German U-boats played an important role in arming the military units of National-Democrats and Socialist Federalists. Using these weapons, they subsequently conducted secret operations against Russian authorities and troops in 1917 and in the spring of 1918 resisted the Ottoman troops invading the Caucasus.[17]

The Georgian National Committee also organized a special Georgian Legion, a legion of fighters for Georgia's independence, funded by the Germans and deployed by the Ottomans. Both Germany and the Porte promised independence for Georgia in exchange for their service. Comprising both Christian and Muslim volunteers and refugees (including the Northern Caucasian "mahajirs" or immigrants and refugees who settled in Turkey in the nineteenth century) and fighting under a Georgian flag, the Legion was not generally trusted by the Turks. Small in numbers (formed only on a battalion level) and poorly armed, they made little contribution in military terms.[18] The legion's commander, Leo Kereselidze (discussed in Chapter 2) and his brother Giorgi also sent agents inside the Russian Caucasus, where in 1915 a clandestine branch of the Georgian National Committee was created.[19] In June 1916, Prince Machabeli himself, Selim Bey Bebutov, an Azeri, Murat Gazavat (Uzden Arzamakov), a Chechen, and two other Georgians were successfully dispatched by a German U-boat to Georgia. It is difficult to confirm whether their work had any significant impact. But soon the Russian autocracy collapsed. By the summer of 1917, Prince Machabeli returned to Berlin by way of Petrograd (as St. Petersburg was renamed in 1914), Japan, and the United States.[20] Whether he made any contact with Japanese authorities is unknown.

There is little indication of Japan's contact with Caucasian independence fighters during the war. This is partly explained by Japan's brief alliance with Russia: in 1916,

15 HHStA, PA, I 947 Krieg 21 k Türkei: Georgisch-grusinischer Aufstand im Kaukasus 1914–18, fols. 42-49.

16 Georges Mamoulia, *Les combats indépendandistes des Caucasiens entre URSS et puissances occidentales: Le cas de la Géorgie (1921–1945)* (Paris: L'Harmattan, 2009), 198.

17 See Davit Vachnadze, "samshoblos samsakhurshi" [On the service of the Motherland]. *Iveria* (Paris), 1990, no. 35, 35–68.

18 Bihl, *Die Kaukasus-Politik der Mittelmächte*, 63, 82, 238. Among the leaders of the Legion was the Georgian Muslim Osman Bey Kartsivadze (79 and 81).

19 Mamoulia, *Les combats indépendandistes des Caucasiens*, 15.

20 Bihl, *Die Kaukasus-Politik der Mittelmächte*, 72.

Japan and Russia concluded an alliance and adhered to the London Declaration of 1914, according to which Britain, France, and Russia pledged not to conclude a separate peace treaty with the Central Powers during the war. Suffering an acute shortage of ammunition, Russia needed Japan's help, and Japan in turn needed Russia's tacit consent to its expansion in China.[21] In fact, from early on in the war, Russia benefited greatly from the purchase of Japanese armaments and remained appreciative of Japan's contribution to its war efforts. This helped the two countries to sign the 1916 alliance.[22] But soon after the alliance was concluded, the Russian autocracy collapsed.

Russia's spy mania, fostered by the bitter experience of the Russo-Japanese War, also gathered momentum during the war. Fears of total espionage now focused on Germany. German citizens in Russia, Russian citizens of German descent, and Jews (assumed to be sympathetic toward German and Austrian cultures) were singled out as suspects. Studying Japan's experience,[23] Germany and Austria deployed espionage extensively against Russia, employing businessmen, financiers, merchants, prostitutes, nurses, and the like, for indeed "total war necessitated total espionage."[24] Of course, Russia resorted to the same methods, although how effective they were is a matter of debate. In any event, pogroms and lootings against Germans and Jews took place in Russia, of whom hundreds and thousands were deported from the western borderlands to inland Russia.[25] Even the Russian government and the Russian court, where people of Germanic heritage (including Empress Alexandra, originally Alix of Hesse, herself) were quite prevalent, became suspect in the eyes of many Russians.[26]

In the Caucasus, Muslims, who were in general suspected of harboring sympathy for the Ottomans, fared better than did the Germans in Russia. Although some (ten thousand or so) were indeed deported to the Ottoman Empire, protests by Georgian deputies to the Duma ultimately prevented the mass deportation of Muslims in the southern borderlands.[27] This did not, however, mean there were no massacres of Muslims. In 1915, for example, the Russian military slaughtered Muslim Laz and Atchars

---

21 See Peter Berton, *Russo-Japanese Relations, 1905–1917: From Enemies to Allies* (Milton Park, Abingdon–New York: Routledge, 2012).

22 For Russia's appreciation of Japan's contribution, see Eduard Baryshev, "The General Hermonius Mission to Japan (August 1914–March 1915) and the Issue of Armaments Supply in Russo-Japanese Relations during the First World War." *Acta Slavica Iaponica*, v. 30 (2011), 40–41.

23 In 1910 Karl Haushofer, who subsequently became "Hitler's teacher," was sent to to Japan as a "military observer" to study the Japanese army. For Haushofer, see Bruno Hipler, *Hitlers Lehrmeister: Karl Haushofer als Vater der NS-Ideologie* (St. Ottilien: EOS Verlag, 1996).

24 Curt Riess, *Total Espionage* (New York, NY: G.P. Putnam's Sons, 1941), vii.

25 See Eric Lohr, *Nationalizing the Russian Empire: The Campaign against Enemy Aliens during World War I* (Cambridge, MA: Harvard University Press, 2003).

26 There were some sensational cases, one of which was the Miasoedov Affair: in 1915 Colonel Sergei N. Miasoedov was hanged as a German spy. See William C. Fuller, Jr., *The Foe Within: Fantasies of Treason and the End of Imperial Russia* (Ithaca–London: Cornell University Press, 2006).

27 Lohr, *Nationalizing the Russian Empire*, 152–153.

in Georgia because their sympathies favored the Turks. In the Chorokhi (Çoruh) river valley, some forty-six thousand Muslims were purportedly killed, leaving only seven thousand.[28] Although these figures cannot be taken at face value, the massacres were openly and passionately condemned by the Baku deputy Muhammad Jafarov at the State Duma.[29] Yet suspicions of disloyalty never died. During the Russo-Japanese War, Greeks had been suspected of spying for Japan. During World War I, Russia suspected Greeks (Pontic Greeks) of spying for Turkey, even though they were never trusted by the Porte.[30]

4.2 Revolution

In February 1917 (old style, March 1917 new style), Tsar Nicholas II abdicated and the Russian autocracy fell. Whatever plans Marxists and other revolutionaries may have had to overthrow the government, the turmoil leading up to the collapse was triggered by spontaneous demonstrations, staged in the capital on International Women's Day, on 22 February (7 March new style), by a large group of women and hungry citizens demanding bread. The demonstrations led to strikes and other disturbances. Troops refused to obey orders to suppress the unrest and mutinied in their turn. Finally, on 2 March (15 March new style), Nicholas abdicated, but his brother refused to succeed and the autocracy collapsed. Thus, various plans of subversion, some prepared by people from the Caucasus with foreign help, were overtaken by popular actions.

All the same, the end to the autocracy brought much joy to the Caucasus as elsewhere in the empire. M. Philips Price, a British journalist, observed the following scene in Tiflis on Sunday, 5 March (18 March new style) 1917:

> I passed down the Golovinsky street [the main thoroughfare today named Rustaveli Avenue] of Tiflis, and crossed the bridge over the Kura to the outskirts of the city. The streets were full of silent and serious people walking in the same direction. They were all going to a great mass meeting of the Caucasian people on the Nahalofsky square to welcome this great day in the history of Russia. In a large open space six raised platforms had been built, and round them was assembled a vast multitude composed of almost every element in the multiracial population of the Caucasus. There were wild mountain tribesmen, Lesgians, Avars, Chechens and Swanetians in their long black cloaks and sheepskin caps. The eddies of the wave of revolution had swept up into the recesses of the Caucasus, where they had lived sunk in patriarchal feudalism until yesterday. Many of them did not know whether they were subjects of the Tsar of Russia or the Sultan of Turkey. Yet

28 David Marshall Lang, *A Modern History of Soviet Georgia* (New York: Grove Press, 1962), 185.
29 Tadeusz Swietochowski, *Russian Azerbaijan, 1905–1920: The Shaping of National Identity in a Muslim Community* (Cambridge: Cambridge University Press, 1985), 81.
30 For a "'very well organized' espionage network along the Black Sea coast involving Greek businessmen, bankers, and clergy among others as well as Muslims," see Reynolds, *Shattering Empires*, 163.

> they had come across miles of mountain tracks out of curiosity to confirm the rumours they had heard, and in order to pay their humble tribute to the Russian Revolution.[31]

Of course, Georgians, Armenians, and Azeris also came:

> There were the picturesque peasants of the fair provinces of Georgia, who had driven in on bullock-wagons. Doubtless many of them during the last ten years had been exiled to Siberia, where they had learnt from Western Socialists to appreciate the principles of Marxism, and had caught the breath of the International [i.e., an international organization of labor and socialist parties]. Then there were Armenian merchants from Tiflis, the staunch supporters of all progressive movements in Russia. There were educated Tartars of the East Caucasus, who had helped to inspire the revolutionary movement in Persia in 1909. There were the representatives of the urban proletariat of Tiflis and some from the Baku oil-fields, the grimy products of Western European industrialism which is slowly creeping into the East. Among them were the intellectual Russian student, the Georgian poet and the Armenian doctor, who had hitherto been forced to hide their talents . . . . The spirit of Demos had suddenly risen out of a multitude of suppressed individualities, and had manifested itself in the form of that great gathering of mediaeval mountaineers and twentieth-century working-men, all inspired by the same idea of brotherhood and freedom.[32]

The Mensheviks (Social Democrats) were in control, urging, along with the Socialist Revolutionaries, the people to elect delegates to the soviets. Price commented that the meeting was "a genuine international movement, for it refused to consider any of the questions of nationality which had so long been troubling the Caucasus, and dividing the proletariat into hostile factions."[33] Soldiers also joined and appealed to the crowd: "Comrades, let us not forget that over there in Germany we have brothers crushed under the same tyranny from which we have now been delivered. May God grant that the hour of their deliverance has also struck!" Prisoners, too, came out: "The political prisoners, who since 1906 had been pining in the dungeons of the Tiflis prisons, were being liberated and brought to the meeting. They were carried on the shoulders of comrades to the platforms, whence they addressed the multitude. The massed bands then struck up the Marseillaise."[34]

Despite the euphoria, the question of the future of the Caucasus remained uncertain. In Georgia there emerged a national democratic movement that led in 1917 to the formation of the party of National Democrats with Spiridon Kedia as its leader. It sought the restoration of Georgia's national sovereignty and a democratic body politic in Georgia.[35] In July 1917, the Berlin-based Georgian National Committee wrote to the Central Powers, under the names of Giorgi Machabeli, Mikhako Tsereteli, Giorgi Kere-

---

31 M. Philips Price, *War & Revolution in Asiatic Russia* (New York: The Macmillan Company, 1918), 280–81.

32 Price, *War & Revolution*, 281–82.

33 Price, *War & Revolution*, 283.

34 Price, *War & Revolution*, 284.

35 The party originated in the Georgian movement for national independence created in 1906 by Prince Ilia Chavchavadze. Although in 1907 he was assassinated by local Marxists who feared his po-

selidze, and Peter Surguladze, that the Georgians aspired for "indépendence complète." Germany financed their political activity. In December 1917, after the Bolshevik takeover, the German government pledged support for the idea of creating an independent state in the Russian Caucasus.[36] Those for favoring the independence of Georgia, Armenia, and other areas (Azerbaijan, the Northern Caucasus, or larger entities like Transcaucasia) were decidedly a minority, however. Many thought that if Russia became truly democratic, there might be a way for them to live, as they had done since the nineteenth century, within the framework of "Russia."

In Georgia, the overwhelmingly popular political party of the Mensheviks was concerned more with the future of "All-Russian" affairs than with Georgia per se. Nikolai (Karlo) Chkheidze (1864–1926), a Georgian Menshevik, worked as chairman of the Petrograd Soviet in 1917. Irakli Tsereteli, an influential Georgian Menshevik, even joined the second Provisional Government in Petrograd as Minister of Post and Telegraph and held the position of defending Russia against its war-time enemies while pursuing peace to end the war. Naturally, Machabeli and other supporters of independence accused the Mensheviks of being "averse" to the independence of the Caucasus.[37]

Armenian political groups were reluctant to become independent of Russia for different reasons: they saw in Russia a counterweight against the Turks, whose political domination they dreaded. The Azeris had their own logic. The most popular political party, the Musavat originally supported the equality and independence of all Muslim nations in the Russian Empire. Yet in 1917 it, too, asserted that the Azeris could live within the framework of a democratic Russian republic. (Another important pan-Islamic and pro-Russian party, Ittihad [Union], took a similar position regarding the future of Caucasian Muslims.) Nonetheless, everything, including the future of the Caucasian body politic and such matters as the autonomy or independence of the Georgian Orthodox Church from the Russian ecclesiastical order, was to be decided at a future Constituent Assembly.

Meanwhile, in May 1917 in the Northern Caucasus, bordering on Russia, the people had created the Union of United Mountaineers. Hoping to build on the achievements of the February Revolution, the Union also envisioned the Northern Caucasus within a federated and democratic Russia. Despite the large number of ethnic Slavs and Cossacks with whom the Northern Caucasians had had contentious relations, the Union nevertheless foresaw a coexistence with them in a future body politic (the Southeastern Union of Cossack Hosts, Mountaineers of the Caucasus, and Free Peoples of the

---

litical influence, his like-minded associates maintained a group that published a journal *Klde* (rock) in Tiflis. See Mamoulia, *Les combats indépendandistes des Caucasiens*, 11.

36 Wolfdieter Bihl, *Die Kaukasus-Politik der Mittelmächte. Teil II. Die Zeit der versuchten kaukasischen Staatlichkeit (1917–1918)* (Vienna-Köln-Graz: Böhlau, 1992), 32–34.

37 Bihl, *Die Kaukasus-Politik der Mittelmächte*, vol. 2, 38.

Steppes).[38] The leaders of the Georgian National Democrats understood the cardinal significance of the solidarity of all peoples in the Caucasus. Some (Shalva Karumidze, Davit Vachnadze, Shalva Amiredzhibi, and Dmitri Chiabrishvili) attended the founding congress of the Union of the United Mountaineers in May 1917 for this reason.[39]

But when the October 1917 coup took place in Petrograd before the Constituent Assembly was able to meet (not until January 1918, when it was promptly disbanded by Lenin), the political groups of the Caucasus found themselves in an awkward position: as the Georgian Menshevik leader Noe Zhordania remarked, "Now a misfortune has fallen on us. The connection with Russia has been broken and Transcaucasia has been left alone. We have to stand on our own feet and either help ourselves or perish through anarchy."[40] Yet the separation also helped introduce the idea of independence into the political life of the Caucasus.

In fact, even before the October coup, all Caucasian national groups had begun forming military units in view of the unforeseeable military situation: Russian forces were progressively disintegrating amid the revolutionary confusion, while Turkish forces threatened to take over Transcaucasia. In February 1918, the Turkish army broke the December 1917 Armistice of Erzincan between the Ottoman Empirea and the Transcaucasian Commissariat, created in Tiflis shortly after the October coup as a self-governing body, and advanced toward the Caucasus. In response, the Union of the United Mountaineers sought to unite the Northern Caucasus, Dagestan, and Transcaucasia into an independent state with the economic and military support of Turkey and the Central Powers.[41]

Meanwhile in March 1918, Bolshevik Russia concluded the Treaty of Brest-Litovsk with the Central Powers, abandoning the Caucasus to its fate but affirming the independence of Finland, Estonia, Latvia, Lithuania, Belarus', and Ukraine. The treaty also restored the territory the Ottomans had lost to Russia in the 1877–78 Russo-Turkish War (including the port city of Batumi, the fortress city of Kars, and the city of Ardahan).[42] For its part, Turkey wished to create as its protectorate an independent state or states in the Caucasus as a buffer zone against Bolshevik Russia (although the Caucasians suspected Turkey's imperial ambitions in the Caucasus in general). The Georgian National Democrats also sought to proclaim Transcaucasia's independence, as

38 See *Soiuz ob"edinennykh gortsev Severnogo Kavkaza i Dagestana (1917–1918 gg.), Gorskaia Respublika (1918–1920 gg.): dokumenty i materialy* (Makhachkala: Institut istorii, arkhelogii i etnografii DNTs RAN, 1994), 28–29, 74.

39 *Shalva Amirejibi (1886-1943)*, vol. 1 (Tbilisi, 1997), 271–274.

40 Quoted in Kazemzadeh, *The Struggle for Transcaucasia*, 55.

41 Haidar Bammat's 28 February 1918 telegram to the Georgian National Council, M. Bammat Family Archive, Paris, France.

42 See John Wheeler-Bennett, *The Forgotten Peace, Brest-Litovsk, March 1918* (New York: W. Morrow, 1939) and Fritz Fischer, *Griff nach der Weltmacht. Die Kriegszielpolitik des kaiserlichen Deustchland 1914/18* (Düsseldorf: Droste Verlag, 1961), 483-484.

Fig. 4.2. Members of the Georgian diplomatic delegation in Berlin, 1918. Standing from left: Spiridon Kedia, Giorgi Machabeli, and Mikheil Tsereteli. Seated from left: Niko Nikoladze, Akaki Chkhenkeli, and Zurab Avalishvili.

ultimately did the Musavat. Yet the Sejm, or legislative body of the Transcaucasian Commissariat, which was headed by Nikolai Chkheidze, hesitated, nor did it heed the call by the Union of the United Mountaineers for a United Caucasus. In the end the Sejm delegation accepted the Brest-Litovsk terms in Trabzon in view of the overwhelming Turkish forces threatening the Caucasus. Yet the Sejm itself rejected the treaty and even declared war against the Ottomans. But overwhelmed by the advance of Turkish forces, on 22 April the Sejm finally accepted the Turkish conditions and declared independence, creating the Democratic Federative Republic of Transcaucasia and resuming peace negotiations with Turkey.[43] The government of the new independent state was led by Prime Minister Akaki Chkhenkeli (1874–1959), a Georgian Menshevik, and staffed by an equal mix of Georgian, Azeri, and Armenian ministers. Within a week, the Ottoman government recognized the new government of Transcaucasia.[44]

43 The Sejm's debate and declaration are in *Dokumenty i mater'ialy po vneshnei politike Zakavakz'ia i Gruzii* (Tiflis: Tipgrafiia Pravitel'stva Gruzinskoi Respubliki, 1919), 220–23.

44 *Dokumenty i mater'ialy po vneshnei politike Zakavakz'ia i Gruzii*, 253.

Fig. 4.3. Noe Ramishvili (left, minister of internal affairs), and Noe Zhordania (right, prime minister), Tiflis, 1918.

Nonetheless, the Ottomans continued their military advance, demanding further concessions from the new state and threatening to take over Tiflis, its capital. The Ottoman goal was to place Transcaucasia and Persian Azerbaijan under its control and secure the oil fields of Baku. Although this move did not disturb the Azeris, it greatly disquieted the Georgians and Armenians. The Ottoman territorial demands amounted to a virtual destruction of Armenian territory and a vast erosion of what Georgia claimed as its own. Moreover, the Ottoman move perturbed Germany, which also eyed the Baku oil fields and the manganese deposits in Georgia. The Ottomans thus wrought divisions within the brand-new Transcaucasian government. Georgia decided to turn to Germany for protection, and, with Germany ready to oblige, de-

Fig. 4.4. The delegation of Union of the United Mountaineers in Istanbul, 1918.

clared independence from the newly minted state, effectively destroying it. On 26 May 1918 the Sejm dissolved itself, and Georgia declared the formation of the Georgian Democratic Republic. The government was headed by Menshevik Noe Ramishvili as prime minister, with Chkhenkeli serving as foreign minister. Berlin, Istanbul, Paris, Vienna, London, Rome, Washington, Moscow, Sofia, Tokyo, Bucharest, Tehran, Madrid, The Hague, Kyiv, Stockholm, Copenhagen, and Kristiania (Oslo) were notified.[45] Two days later Armenia and Azerbaijan followed suit, declaring independence with Erevan and Ganja as their respective capitals. Within a week the three independent states signed peace treaties with Turkey, who largely dictated the terms.[46]

The Northern Caucasus, bordering on Russia, faced threats not from the Ottomans but from Russia, both Red and White. After the Bolshevik seizure of power in the capital, the Union of the United Mountaineers cut its ties to the Bolshevik government, although the Union itself fragmented politically. Whereas the Union adhered to the

45 *Dokumenty i mater'ialy po vneshnei politike Zakavakz'ia i Gruzii*, 330–31, 335, 338. Two months later Noe Zhordania became prime minister, and Ramishvili minister of internal affairs.

46 For the Turkish territorial gains, see the map on p. 36 of Richard G. Hovannisian, *The Republic of Armenia. Vol, 1: The First Year, 1918–1919* (Berkeley-Los Angeles, CA: The University of California Press, 1971).

idea of creating a unified Caucasian state as the only viable option, it also accepted the demand of some German military commanders that it constitute itself as an independent state to be recognized as the legitimate representative of the Northern Caucasus peoples. (In truth, the German commanders were interested in eventually annexing the Northern Caucasus to the German Empire.)[47] Thus, on 11 May 1918, the Union (or at least those who claimed to represent it), appealing to Germany and Turkey for support, declared independence and created the Republic of the Mountaineers of the Northern Caucasus and Dagestan (the "Mountaineer Republic").[48] The new Republic was headed by Tapa (Abdul Medzhid) Chermoev (1882–1937), a Chechen, with Haidar Bammat (Bammatov) (1890–1965), a Dagestani lawyer, serving as foreign minister.[49] Chermoev and Bammat were the two who signed the 11 May declaration. While Russia denounced this move, it was recognized by Georgia.

There was a serious problem, however: the Mountaineer Republic claimed areas that it did not control, such as the Terek and the Kuban regions. In fact, it hardly controlled other regions it claimed, such as Chechnia and Dagestan.[50] Moreover, the independence proclamation had been issued in Batumi, which was under Turkish control. The political situation in the Northern Caucasus had also grown complex, with insurgents and Cossack fighters rising in various places against whoever controlled them. But, in October and November 1918, both Turkey and Azerbaijan came to the aid of the new republic to expel the Bolsheviks and the Entente-oriented White Russian forces from the Northern Caucasus.[51] Germany, far from united in its policy toward the Northern Caucasus, was deeply disturbed by the advance of Turkish forces into the area, yet it did not dare jeopardize the Brest-Litovsk Treaty with Russia.[52] Ultimately, as Bammat bitterly complained later, Germany failed to keep its earlier promise to support

47 See Werner Zürrer, "Deutschland und die Entwicklung Nordkaukasiens in Jahre 1918." *Jahrbücher für Geschichte Osteuropas*, 26, no. 1 (1978), 38.

48 See *Soiuz ob"edinennykh gortsev*, 121.

49 On Bammat, see Georges Mamoulia, Khadzhi Murad Donogo, and Mairbek Vatchagaev, *Gaidar Bammat i zhurnal "Kavkaz"* (Makhachkala–Paris: Akhul'go, 2010).

50 The Republic left the question of its southern borders open for future unification with the Southern Caucasus.

51 See Vassan-Giray Jabagi (Cabagi), "Revolution and Civil War in the North Caucasus–End of the 19th—Beginning of the 20th Century." *Central Asian Survey* 10, nos. 1-2 (1991), 124–125 and Pshemakho Kosok, "Revolution and Sovietization in the Northern Caucasus." *Caucasian Review* (Munich) 1956, no. 3, 51. For more details, see Georges Mamoulia, "Kavkaz i derzhavy Chetvernogo soiuza v 1918 g." *Nowy Prometeusz* 5 (2013), 156–158.

52 Winfried Baumgart, "Das 'Kaspi-Unternehmen' – Größenwahn Ludendorffs oder Routineplanung des deutschen Generalstabs?" *Jahrbücher für Geschichte Osteuropas* 18, no. 1 (1970), 99–106.

the Republic's independence.[53] Although the Allied countries, including Japan, supported the Republic with "Platonic sympathy," they failed to recognize it officially.[54]

4.3 Reconquest

In the end, all these republics and the entire Caucasus itself were reconquered by the Bolsheviks. One might fault in part the new republics with failures in internal reforms. The question of land reform, for instance, was certainly a vexed question. In the Caucasus the land question was not merely a class issue; it was deeply connected to the national question and the matter of Cossack privileges as well in the Northern Caucasus. In Georgia, although the Menshevik government did enact land reform by taking land from large landowners and redistributing (selling) it to the poorer peasants, it also saved the landowners from wholesale confiscation of their land. In western Georgia in particular, where agricultural land was scarce and most nobles tilled their lands themselves, little land was available for the peasants. The reform satisfied neither the poor nor the rich.[55]

Many other factors undermined the new independent states. In the spring of 1918, for instance, a power struggle in Baku between the Bolsheviks and the Dashnaktsutiun on the one hand and the Musavat on the other led to the mutual massacre of Muslims and Armenians (the former suffering larger losses estimated at twelve thousand).[56] This incident (March Events) ushered in the Bolshevik-led Baku Commune,[57] which in turn was quickly overthrown by the Centro-Caspian Dictatorship (an alliance of Socialist Revolutionaries, Mensheviks, and Dashnaks) with the assistance of British forces. In September 1918, when the British forces left, Ottoman and Azeri forces occupied Baku and overthrew the Centro-Caspian Dictatorship, while Baku's Armenians were massacred by the Azeri population (the September Events). Death estimates ranged from ten thousand to thirty thousand.[58] Shortly afterward, the Democratic Republic of Azerbaijan moved its capital from Ganja to Baku.

---

53 Haidar Bammate, *The Caucasus Problem: Questions concerning Circassia and Daghestan* (Berne: Staempfli & Cie, 1919), 32.

54 On "Platonic sympathy," see *Soiuz ob"edinennykh gortsev*, 174.

55 For a Menshevik view emphasizing "absolutely no problem" in implementing the land reform in Georgia, see G.I. Uratadze, *Obrazovanie i konsolidatsiia Gruzinskoi Demokraticheskoi Respubliki* (Munich: Institut zur Erforschung der UdSSR e. V., 1956), 93.

56 See Jean Loris-Melicof, *La Révolution Russe et les nouvelles républiques transcaucasiennes* (Paris: Librairie Félix Alca, 1920), 115–117.

57 Ronald Grigor Suny, *The Baku Commune 1917–1918: Class and Nationality in the Russian Revolution* (Princeton, NJ: Princeton University Press, 1972), ch. 7.

58 Richard G. Hovannisian, *Armenia on the Road to Independence, 1918* (Berkeley-Los Angeles, CA: University of California Press, 1967), 227.

Territorial issues also contributed to discord among the new republics. As one observer aptly noted, the Caucasian peoples, after long years of submission and oppression, were enjoying independence and power for the first time. Some of their politicians were given to flaunting power, displaying pomp, and showing jealousy over haughty titles. Some became megalomaniacal.[59] A newly acquired sense of power also spilled over into dreams of territorial grandeur, prompting these republics to fight over tiny territories: Lori, Borchalo, Nakhichevan, Karabakh, and so on. To be sure, these disputes were understandable, given that each territory, however small, had almost always had an ethnically mixed population. Baku, an Azeri city, was dominated by ethnic Russians and Armenians. The mayors of Tiflis, the capital of Transcaucasia and a Georgian city, were mostly ethnic Armenians, the last being Alexander Khatisyan, 1910–17, who later became prime minister and foreign minister of independent Armenia (1919–20).

It was perhaps unrealistic to imagine that these new republics, sandwiched between two contentious imperial powers, could have easily survived on their own. The Northern Caucasians understood this issue well. Bammat, then a socialist, for instance, was convinced that "only if all the peoples of the Caucasus worked together would they be able to defend a region of such strategic importance against attack, and to make the most of its abundant but unequally distributed resources."[60] He publicly proposed a Caucasian Federation made up of Azerbaijan, Armenia, Georgia, and the Northern Caucasus. Turkey, too, supported this vision in its own strategic interests,[61] although how sincere it was is open to debate. Yet this vision, like earlier ones envisioned by others,[62] failed to materialize. Bammat feared that as time passed, the Christian Georgians and Armenians might be absorbed into Russia and emphasized the centrality of Muslims to the Caucasus.[63] Bammat also believed that the Northern Caucasians belonged historically and culturally to Europe, which was "not the case with the Turks." Therefore, he rejected any notion of uniting the Northern Caucasus with Turkey.[64] Indeed, when the Mountaineer Republic welcomed Turkish troops to Dagestan in October 1918 to protect itself from the Bolsheviks, the Republic emphasized its ecumenical nature of treating all religions and nationalities equally.[65] The Mountaineer Republic and Bammat repeatedly proposed to form a "single political

---

59 See Loris-Melicof, *La Révolution Russe et les nouvelles républiques transcaucasiennes*, 157, 159–160, 171.

60 Haidar Bammate, "The Caucasus and the Russian Revolution (from a Political Viewpoint)." *Central Asian Survey* 10, no. 4 (1991), 14–15.

61 Reynolds, *Shattering Empires*, 201, 206–7.

62 See Mamoulia, *Les combats indépendandistes des Caucasiens*, 17–18 and Alex Marshall, *The Caucasus under Soviet Rule* (London-New York: Routledge, 2006), 66.

63 Bihl, *Die Kaukasus-Politik der Mittelmächte*, vol. 2, 311.

64 Bihl, *Die Kaukasus-Politik der Mittelmächte*, vol. 2, 311.

65 *Soiuz ob"edinennykh gortsev*, 162–63.

entity in the Caucasus," which was "imperative in view of all the strategic, economic and political considerations."[66] But it bore little fruit. It was only in April–June 1919 that the four republics held a conference in Tiflis. The threat of Anton Denikin's White Army drew the Georgians, Azeris, and Mountaineers closer. Georgia and Azerbaijan agreed to render military assistance to each other, regional unity being their goal.[67] Yet the conference failed to reach an agreement: the Azeris were absorbed in territorial issues with the Armenians, while Armenia, wishing for a Great Armenia and supporting Denikin's forces, showed no interest in forming a single federative state.[68] Meanwhile, the Northern Caucasus was being destroyed by Denikin's Volunteer Army.

Ultimately, internal discord and international politics combined to cause the eventual demise of the newly independent republics of the Caucasus. Bammat's complaint about Germany's breach of promise owed largely to the fact that at the time Germany was seeking a supplementary agreement to the Brest-Litovsk Treaty with Bolshevik Russia, to be concluded in August 1918. In exchange for receiving oil from Baku and the recognition of Georgia as an independent state, Germany promised not to support any third-party military operations beyond Georgia's borders and the areas of Ardakhan, Kars, and Batumi.[69] In August 1918 Germany and Russia also agreed to the eventual return of Baku to the Soviet government.[70] These agreements in turn prompted the Turks and Azeris to occupy Baku the following month (see p. 87), seriously complicating German-Soviet-Turkish relations.[71]

Subsequently, the end of World War I in November 1918, with the defeat of the Central Powers, presented both opportunity and danger for the Caucasian republics. The Ottoman defeat afforded Armenia an unprecedented opportunity for survival and unification with Ottoman Armenia in Eastern Anatolia. But to Azerbaijan and Georgia, the Central Powers' defeat meant the loss of their respective patrons.

For now each country went its own way, despite the fact that Bammat and other federalists continued advocating for the unity of the Caucasus as a whole.[72] In Georgia, the most stable of all the new states in the Caucasus, the Georgian language replaced Russian, while the Red banner gave way to the black-white-red tricolor national flag.

---

66 Bammat, "The Caucasus and the Russian Revolution," 16.

67 See Dzhamil' Gasanly, *Russkaia revoliutsia i Azerbaidzhan. Trudnyi put' k nezavisimosti 1917–1920* (Moscow: Flinta, 2011), 398–399.

68 See Bammat, "The Caucasus and the Russian Revolution," 17; and Hovannisian, *The Republic of Armenia*, 355–60; and Mamoulia, *Les combats indépendandistes des Caucasiens*, 20–21.

69 See *Dokumenty vneshnei politiki SSSR*, vol. 1 (Moscow: Politizdat, 1959), 436–444 and Winfried Baumgart, *Deutsche Ostpolitik 1918. Von Brest-Litowsk bis zum Ende des Ersten Weltkrieges* (Vienna-Munich: Oldenbourg, 1966), 201–202.

70 See Baumgart, *Deutsche Ostpolitik 1918*, 203–204.

71 Kazemzadeh, *The Struggle for Transcaucasia (1917–1921)*, 143.

72 Bammat's indefatigable efforts to secure independence and international recognition is detailed in G. Mamoulia, Vatchagaev Mairbek, and Donogo Khadzhi Murad, eds, *Gaidar Bammat – izevestnyi i neizvestnyi. Sbornik dokumentov i materialov* (Baku: Azerbaijanskoe istoricheskoe obshchestvo, 2015).

Fig. 4.5. The Constituent Assembly of Georgia, Tiflis, 1920.

Now with British instead of German forces stationed in the capital, the new republic held elections for the Constituent Assembly in February 1919. Mensheviks took 109 seats out of 130, with the National Democrats and the Socialist Federalists accounting for eight seats each. Noe Zhordania headed the newly formed government. By 1920 Tiflis, its capital, had been significantly "Georgianized,"[73] although it never lost its multinational character. In the end, however, Georgia and all of the Caucasus would be conquered by the Bolsheviks.

The first to fall was the Mountaineer Republic, even though in late 1918 it had been "recognized" by British Major General William M. Thomson, who was acting as the Allies' representative.[74] Thomson was the commander of the British expeditionary forces that had arrived in Baku, in agreement with the Azerbaijan government, in November 1918, in the wake of the departure of the Ottoman forces. The British forces, however, also supported Denikin's Volunteer Army, operating in the Don, Kuban, and Northern Caucasus, in the fight against the Bolsheviks. But Britain's double game was not viable because Denikin's goal was not merely the overthrow of the Bolshevik government but also the maintenance of "one and indivisible Russia." This latter objective meant rejecting independent states such as the Mountaineer Republic. By mid-1919

73 Loris-Melicof, *La Révolution Russe et les nouvelles rêpubliques transcaucasiennes*, 163–164. In the autumn of 1918, however, Germany entertained the possibility of a coup against the Menshevik government as it had the previous spring against the socialist government of Ukraine (the Skoropads'kyi coup). See Mamoulia, *Les combats indépendandistes des Caucasiens*, 17.

74 Bammate, "The Caucasus and the Russian Revolution," 17.

the Mountaineer Republic, riven by internal strife, was overrun by Denikin's Volunteer Army. Those who claimed to represent the government moved to Tiflis, where they set up an émigré government (Medzlis). From Tiflis, Bammat and others appealed to European socialists and foreign countries for assistance.[75] In June 1920, for example, Bammat, "an unctuous gentleman of a sophistication remarkable in a representative of Caucasian mountain tribes," approached a British representative in Tiflis for help.[76] But little or no help came from anywhere, including the British forces, which appealed to the peoples of the Northern Caucasus to accept Denikin's forces in the fight against the Bolsheviks. Insurgency thus became the order of the day in that area, and the situation became so complex that it was difficult for anyone to assess.[77]

The Soviet Red Army, however, succeeded in mobilizing the dissatisfied mountaineers to defeat the Volunteer Army, promising to honor the independence of the Mountaineer Republic.[78] Ultimately, like the peasants in Russia, many mountaineers of the Caucasus may have regarded the Bolsheviks as the lesser evil, because the power of Denikin and his White forces meant the restoration of the old regime, whereas Bolshevism promised its destruction. Moscow thus effectively divided the anti-Bolshevik forces. The Volunteer Army's defeat in spring 1920 by the Red Army did not, however, spell freedom. The Northern Caucasus virtually lost its independence with the Bolshevik conquest. Only on the verge of its defeat did the White Army recognize the Mountaineer Republic. It came too late.[79]

Even after the Bolsheviks conquered Northern Caucasus and occupied Azerbaijan at the end of April 1920 (see p. 94), the mountaineers of the Caucasus did not cease fighting. In September 1920, Georgia helped the insurrection of Colonel Kaitmaz Alikhanov in Dagestan and the military operations of Muhammad Said Shamil (grandson of Imam Shamil) in Dagestan and Chechnia. Georgians, Azeris, and Northern Caucasians worked together to explore ways to ensure their political survival. All options required outside military assistance. Working with the Georgians, the French military mission in the Caucasus devised a grand plan of spreading insurrections to other parts of the Caucasus and cutting links between Russia and the Southern Caucasus along the Baku-Petrovsk (Makhachkala) line, where mountains soar sharply from the Caspian shorelines. Weapons and ammunition were to be supplied by France via

---

75 See *Soiuz ob"edinennykh gortsev*, 321–327, 407–409.

76 See a memoir by Sir Harry Luke, *Cities and Men: An Autobiography*, vol. 2 (London: Geoffrey Bles, 1953), 155. Luke added that "Bamakov" (Bammat) did not look to him as "the type to be a leader of such a venture [military operations against the Bolsheviks]."

77 See Marshall, *The Caucasus under Soviet Rule*, 118–32.

78 Tiflis did send a detachment of troops, under General Leo Kereselidze, to the Northern Caucasus in August 1919 to fight the Denikin forces. See Leo Kereselidze, "Curriculum Vitae." *tanamemamule* (Tbilisi), 2007, No. 3(24), 16. The detachment was later recalled in the spring of 1920 when Tiflis, with the Azerbaijan government, sought to reach an agreement with Moscow.

79 See Bammat, "The Caucasus and the Russian Revolution," 20–21.

Georgia. Yet Paris adhered to the idea of a Federative Russia in which the Caucasus was to enjoy autonomy, not independence. Units of the White Army, now headed by the newly appointed commander General Petr Vrangel' (Wrangel), were to be dispatched from the Crimea to the Northern Caucasus to lead the anti-Bolshevik forces. Only through the general were weapons and ammunition to be handed to the rebels. The mountaineers and Azeris, however, were willing to fight alongside the Vrangel' forces only in so far as the general officially supported the independence of the North Caucasus and Azerbaijan. But Vrangel' had no such intention. His venture in the Northern Caucasus, however, failed in the summer and autumn of 1920. (By then Armenia was divided up by Soviet Russia and Turkey [see p. 96]). The insurgents, with no heavy weapons (which the French had earlier promised), were also doomed: when in December 1920 they struck their way out of the mountainous terrain to the Caspian shore areas in Dagestan, they faced formidable enemy forces.[80] Although the fighting did not stop, by mid-1921 the insurgents had been largely defeated by the Reds.[81] Only after the invasion of Georgia by the Red Army in February 1921 (see p. 98), did France finally begin supplying weapons to the Caucasus. It was, however, too late.

Although the other three republics fared better, their ultimate fate was the same: Bolshevik conquest. Yet they did enjoy a brief period of international recognition.

The Paris Peace Conference (which lasted from January 1919 to January 1920) proved favorable only to Armenia. The Democratic Republic of Armenia, with few resources but flooded with refugees from Turkish Armenia, was constantly on the brink of famine and collapse, although the American Relief Mission provided vital help. While the Western powers were unsympathetic to Georgia, Azerbaijan, and the Northern Caucasus with their ties to the defeated Central Powers, they showed much sympathy for Armenia which was free of such ties and whose sufferings bought the sympathy of the Great Powers. Nevertheless, Armenia failed to achieve its goals. Even though its territorial claims (which included Turkish Armenia) did not differ from the proposals of the Entente powers, Armenia was "hypnotized by the grandeur and the magnificence of their future state." It could not be satisfied with being a "small country" like Belgium, as some Europeans suggested. The delegates' inordinate de-

80 For the details of these events, see Georges Mamoulia and R. Abutalybov, *Strana ognei. V bor'be za svobodu i nezavisimost'. Politicheskaia istoriia azerbaidzhanskoi emigratsii 1920–1945 gg.* (Paris-Baku: CBS, 2014), 32–86.

81 Mamoulia, *Les combats indépendandistes des Caucasiens*, 23–24. Alikhanov and his three sons were killed in action, and Said, injured, fled to Turkey. See Marshall, *The Caucasus under Soviet Rule*, 139, and Marie Bennigsen Broxup, "The Last *Ghazawat*: The 1920–1921 Uprising" in *The North Caucasus Barrier: The Russian Advance towards the Muslim World*, ed. by Marie Bennigsen Broxup (London: Hurst, 1992), 141.

mands and complaints did not help their cause,[82] and in the end Armenia was not recognized, nor was any mandate issued regarding it.

Part of the reason for this indecision was that at the time, in mid-1919, the Council of Four (Britain, France, the United States, and Italy) and Japan, were hoping that the government of Admiral Aleksandr Kolchak might well conquer the Bolsheviks, and recognized this government as Russia's. In return, Kolchak recognized the independence of Poland and Finland and promised autonomy to the Baltic states of Estonia, Latvia, Lithuania, and Transcaucasia. (The Mountaineer Republic sent its own delegates, including Bammat, to Paris, but in general they were not taken seriously there. By mid-1919, as discussed already, the Republic had been overrun by Denikin.)[83] It was only in early 1920, when the Great Powers' hopes for the victory of Kolchak (or Denikin) were dashed by the Bolsheviks, that they and Japan recognized de facto Georgia, Azerbaijan (12 January), and Armenia (19 January).[84] Soon the newly independent Poland also recognized Georgia, with which it sought to establish a military alliance against Soviet Russia.[85] At the beginning of 1920 the international situation of the three republics was therefore more firmly consolidated.

On 7 May 1920, the Democratic Republic of Georgia and the Russian Soviet Socialist Federal Republic concluded a formal treaty in Moscow whereby the latter, following the Western powers and Japan, acknowledged de jure the "independence and self-sufficiency of the Georgian state" and pledged " to renounce any kind of interference in the internal affairs of Georgia." The two states pledged not to allow any foreign military forces onto their respective soils.[86] But this treaty, which was secretly negotiated in Moscow, was not well received in Georgia, where it was published a month later on 7 June and denounced by the public as a "veiled subjection of Georgia to Russia."[87] Indeed, the provisions and consequences of this treaty, as David Marshall Lang has observed, contained "striking parallels with the treaty concluded in 1783 between

82 Loris-Melicof, *La Révolution Russe et les Nouvelles Républiques transcaucasiennes*, 157–60. For the Paris Conference and Armenia, see also Hovannisian, *The Republic of Armenia*, vol. 1, 250–340.

83 Its desire for independence and international recognition was not entirely ignored, however. US President Woodrow Wilson, with whom Bammat had a personal talk, was sympathetic with the cause of the Mountaineer Republic. See AMAE, correspondance politique etcommerciale (CPC) 1914-1940, série E (Levant), Caucase-Kurdistan, dossier no. 4, fol. 230–232.

84 See Richard G. Hovannisian, *The Republic of Armenia. Vol. II: From Versailles to London, 1919–1920* (Berkeley-Los Angeles: University of California Press, 1982), 499–517. The United States, "opposed to the drastic dismemberment of the Russian Empire," did not initially approve this decision but shortly reversed its position. See also Zourab Avalishvili, *The Independence of Georgia in International Politics 1918–1921* (London: Headley Brothers, 1940), 172, 219–226.

85 See Wojciech Materski, *Georgia rediviva: Republika Gruzińska w stosunkakh międzynarodowych 1918–1921* (Warsaw: Instytut Studiów Politycznych PAN, 1994), 168–169.

86 This treaty was published in *Izvestiia*, 10 May 1921, 2.

87 An eyewitness account is given by Luke, *Cities and Men*, 153.

Catherine the Great of Russia and King Erekle II of Georgia, which proved to be the prelude to Georgia's complete annexation."[88]

The Georgians' suspicions proved correct, for the treaty contained a secret supplement. Immediately after taking power, the Bolsheviks had denounced the secret diplomacy of the Russian imperial government as well as of the Provisional Government (which existed briefly between the February and October 1917 Revolutions) and revealed many of the secret agreements they had concluded with foreign countries. Now the Soviet government was doing exactly what it had denounced as imperialist. The secret supplement contained a stipulation: "Georgia pledges itself to recognize the right of free existence and activity of the Communist party . . . and in particular its right to free meetings and publications (including organs of the press)."[89] As Firuz Kazemzadeh has noted, this clause in fact amounted to curtailing Georgia's sovereignty and annulling the clause by which Russia pledged not to interfere in its internal affairs.[90] Moscow knew well that the Georgian Mensheviks, close in political orientation to Western liberalism, could be tempted by such an ostensibly respectable clause, and that they also believed that Moscow's official recognition of Georgia's independence signified Moscow's renunciation of aggression. But the Bolsheviks were far shrewder than the Georgian Mensheviks.

The Bolsheviks almost certainly had a plan to reconquer the Southern Caucasus. As soon as the Whites were driven out of the Northern Caucasus in the spring of 1920, the Bolsheviks began penetrating the Southern Caucasus. Moscow was in desperate need of the oil in Baku and was determined to capture it by all means.[91] Turkey, now with its new Kemalist leaders (followers Mustafa Kemal Atatürk) and new geopolitical orientations (see p. 96), even helped Moscow by demanding that the Azeris allow Soviet forces to advance into their country in order to link up with the Turks and jointly defend Turkish borders from the British.[92] The Turks even assured the Azeris that the Red Army would not occupy their country. Instead, the Red Army invaded Azerbaijan on 27 April 1920, overthrew the government, and on 30 April set up the Azerbaijan Soviet Socialist Republic in Baku. The Azeris thus "accused Mustafa Kemal's men of having sold them out to Russians in order to save themselves."[93] Anti-Russian, anti-Bolshevik rebellions followed, with Georgians assisting. Plans were made to retake Baku. Yet the Menshevik government in Tbilisi ultimately canceled them for fear of

---

88 See Lang, *A Modern History of Soviet Georgia*, 226.

89 Kazemzadeh, *The Struggle for Transcaucasia*, 299.

90 Kazemzadeh, *The Struggle for Transcaucasia*, 299–300.

91 See A.V. Kvashonkin, O.V. Khlevniuk, L.P. Kosheleva, et al., eds., *Bolshevistskoe rukovodstvo. Perepiska. 1912-1927. Sbornik dokumentov* (Moscow: POSSPEN, 1996), 120–121.

92 At the time Moscow and Ankara signed a mutual military action against the British. Kvashonkin, Khlevniuk, Kosheleva et al., eds., *Bolshevistskoe rukovodstvo*, 121.

93 Reynolds, *Shattering Empires*, 257.

Fig. 4.6. The cabinet of the Azerbaijan Republic, Baku, 1920. Seated in the center is Nasib Yusifbeyli (Ussubekov), prime minister, murdered in May 1920, apparently by Bolsheviks.

an all-out confrontation with Bolshevik Russia.[94] Rebels were mercilessly repressed, causing a stir even among the Kemalists in Turkey who were collaborating with the Bolsheviks.[95] The Great Powers, which had de facto recognized Azerbaijan's independence, hardly took action against Moscow's annexation of the state,[96] in which there was little Bolshevik influence outside Baku.[97] Later, in January 1921, Azeris and Northern Caucasus mountaineers created in Tiflis a committee aimed at "liberating Azerbaijan and the Northern Caucasus from the Russian occupation, restoring Democratic republics, and creating a Caucasian confederation." In February Tiflis recognized the committee as the provisional government of Azerbaijan and the Northern Caucasus.[98] Three days later, however, Tiflis itself fell to the Red Army (discussed shortly).

94 See G.I. Kvinitadze, *Moi vospominaniia v gody nezavisimosti Gruzii, 1917–1921* (Paris: YMCA Press, 1985), 194.

95 See Kvashonkin, Khlevniuk, Kosheleva et al., eds., *Bolshevistskoe rukovodstvo*, 173–174.

96 Kazemzadeh, *The Struggle for Transcaucasia*, 276–85.

97 See Audrey L. Altstadt, *The Azerbaijani Turks: Power and Identity under Russian Rule* (Stanford, CA: Hoover Institution Press, 1992), 110.

98 Mamoulia, *Les combats indépendandistes des Caucasiens*, 24.

The Georgian-Russian treaty of May 1920 took place within this context of Moscow's reconquest of Azerbaijan. With hindsight, it appears evident that Moscow used the treaty to subvert Georgia from within by mobilizing the Communists in Georgia. By internal subversion and frontal attack, Moscow was to reconquer Georgia the following year.

Before Georgia fell, Armenia came under Moscow's subjugation. Armenia was the strongest of the three Southern Caucasian independent republics from an international perspective because it had the sympathy of the Western powers. Although its megalomaniac position alienated it at the Paris Peace Conference, in early 1920 Armenia was internationally recognized de facto as an independent state. In August 1920 a peace treaty was signed between Turkey and the Allied powers (including Japan but excluding the United States). The Treaty of Sèvres amounted to the dismemberment of the Ottoman Empire, with its territory reduced by nearly three quarters, its military forces drastically curtailed, its finances to be controlled by the Allied powers, and Istanbul, Trabzon, Batumi, and several other cities to become free ports. The treaty also recognized Armenia as an independent state whose exact borders with Turkey were to be decided by the United States. (Even though the United States refused to be involved in the matter of Armenian affairs, it was assigned this task.) In the end, in November 1920 President Woodrow Wilson granted a large section of Turkey's eastern Anatolia (including the Black Sea port of Trabzon) to Armenia.[99]

But the treaty was never ratified by Turkey because Turkish nationalists now founded an alternative government (in the form of the Grand National Assembly in Ankara) led by Mustafa Kemal Atatürk, which then formed a united front with Soviet Russia against the Allied powers. Their cooperation started in 1919 and strengthened in 1920.[100] With Soviet gold, the Turkish nationalists created new armed forces equipped with Soviet arms. Unlike the Ottoman political leaders of 1918, they did not regard the Southern Caucasus as a buffer zone against Russia; rather, they cooperated with Soviet Russia to divide the entire region, with Moscow and Ankara secretly agreeing to partition Armenia between them. In September 1920 the Turkish Nationalist Army invaded Armenia and quickly defeated it, but as Turkish forces advanced deeply into Armenia, Moscow feared Turkey might breach the agreement.[101] Not to be overtaken by the Turks, Moscow, too, intervened militarily in Armenia, removed

99 For "Wilsonian Armenia," see Richard G. Hovannisian, *The Republic of Armenia. Vol. IV: Between Crescent and Sickle: Partition and Sovietization* (Berkeley-Los Angeles: University of California Press, 1996), 40–44.

100 Swietochowski, *Russian Azerbaijan, 1905–1920*, pp. 162–164 and Kvashonkin, Klevniuk, Kosheleva et al., eds., *Bolshevistskoe rukovodstvo*, 121.

101 See Kvashonkin, Khlevniuk, Kosheleva et al., eds., *Bol'shevistskoe rukovodstvo*, 170 and Hovannisian, *The Republic of Armenia*, vol. 4, 343.

the Dashnaktsutiun-controlled Armenian government, and made it into a soviet.[102] Several Bolsheviks from the Caucasus, such as Stalin and G.K. (Sergo) Ordzhonikidze, were in charge of this operation, which was completed by early December.[103] Both the Allied powers and Georgia, while sympathetic to Armenia's plight, extended little help. Armenia, like Azerbaijan, was thus written off. Stalin declared that the Dashnaks, "agents of the Entente," had been overthrown by Armenians for having led Armenia to "anarchy and misery." He displayed much satisfaction with the fact that, for all their rhetoric, the Western powers did not come to rescue Armenia, which, he contended, was saved only by the new Soviet Republic of Armenia.[104]

Having conquered Armenia, Moscow now set its eyes firmly on Georgia. Russia's official recognition did nothing to help Georgia. The Bolsheviks in Georgia, having gained their freedom in the wake of the May 1920 treaty, made every effort to arouse popular uprisings against the Menshevik government. Already Lavrenti Beria, future chief of the Soviet secret police, had created an intelligence network in Georgia. He and other Bolsheviks were soon arrested but released on condition they leave Georgia within three days. Beria, however, assumed the false name of Lakerbaia and worked in the Russian embassy in Tiflis. Arrested soon again, he was now imprisoned in Kutaisi. In June 1920, when Sergei M. Kirov was sent to Tiflis as Soviet ambassador, he brought with him "a large staff, which at once took charge of the Bolshevist movement inside Georgia." Kirov successfully negotiated the release of Beria and others. At the time, as Kirov noted, Georgia was considered a "convenient back-door to Europe." As soon as the backdoor was no longer needed, Georgia's fate was sealed. Kirov frankly stated: "We don't consider the Georgians as a Government, but as a tool."[105] In autumn 1920, a delegation of Western socialists, including Karl Kautsky, an outspoken critic of Bolshevism, visited Georgia. Shortly afterwar, Kautsky penned a laudatory book on the Georgian Social Democratic government.[106] By then, however, having observed the Allied powers' reaction to the Soviet conquest of Azerbaijan and Armenia, Moscow no longer needed Georgia's backdoor to Europe. Instead it began military

---

102 Hovannisian, *The Republic of Armenia*, vol. 4, 374–75. Turkey accepted the Sovietization of a portion of Armenia as a guarantee of its own security in the Turkish part of Armenia. See Kvashonkin, Khlevniuk, Kosheleva et al., eds., *Bol'shevistskoe rukovodstvo*, 170.

103 Stalin was actively working in various parts of the Caucasus at the time: from 21 October to 20 November he traveled to Vladikavkaz, Baku, Temir-Khan-Shura (today's Buinaksk in Dagestan), and back to Vladikavkaz. See I.V. Stalin, *Sochineniia*, vol. 4 (Moscow: Politizdat, 1953), 470–71.

104 Stalin, *Sochineniia*, vol. 4, 413–414.

105 C.E. Bechhofer, *In Denikin's Russia and the Caucasus, 1919–1920* (London: W. Collins Sons, 1921), 318. On the episodes involving Beria, see Amy Knight, *Beria: Stalin's First Lieutenant* (Princeton, NJ: Princeton University Press, 1993), 18–19. An eyewitness account says that the Georgians were "alarmed at its [the Russian Mission's] size and have protested, but Bolsheviks continue to pour in." See Luke, *Cities and Men*, p. 156.

106 See *Georgien, eine sozialdemokratische Bauernrepublik: Eindrücke und Beobachtungen von Karl Kautsky* (Wien: Verlag der Wiener Volksbuchhandlung, 1921).

preparations against the Georgian government in late 1920. At the Eighth All-Russian Congress of Soviets held in December 1920 (the last in which the Mensheviks were allowed to take part), Lenin declared: "You know that a final peace has been signed with a number of states bordering on the Western frontiers of Russia that were part of the former Russian Empire. The Soviet government has unequivocally recognized their independence and sovereignty, in accordance with the fundamental principles of our policy."[107] But Lenin omitted mentioning Georgia altogether, a manifest sign of his scheme against it, which was immediately noticed by the Mensheviks present.[108]

By January–February 1921, Moscow, aware that internal subversion in Georgia was hopeless, had made up its mind to conquer and sovietize it.[109] Officially Moscow displayed a friendly face even on the eve of the Red Army's invasion of Georgia in February 1921. On 7 February 1921, a banquet was held in Tiflis to celebrate the Georgian state's de jure recognition by Western powers, which had taken place ten days earlier, on 27 January,[110] the day the Bolsheviks secretly decided to invade and conquer Georgia.[111] Diplomats from Germany, France, Italy, Turkey, Poland, and Russia attended. The following day, Kirov's successor, Aron L. Sheinman, insisted that Russia "wanted to live in peace and friendship with the Georgian republic."[112] Three days later, peasants of the Borchalo district, an area under dispute with Armenia, staged a revolt instigated by the Bolsheviks to justify military invasion. Indeed, within days the Eleventh Red Army had invaded Georgia to "assist the Georgian people." Simultaneously Georgian Bolsheviks, headed by Filipp Makharadze (1868–1941), Mamia Orakhelashvili (1883–1937), and Shalva Eliava (1893–1937), formed a Revolutionary Committee, which then proclaimed a Soviet regime. A week of intense battle followed, with Georgian forces led by G.I. Kvinitadze and supported by the Mountaineer Republic and Azeri émigrés in Tiflis such as Bammat. Three days later, however, Tiflis itself was taken by the Red Army, accompanied by Ordzhonikidze. The Bolshevik Revolutionary Committee formally dissolved the Georgian government and declared the formation of the Georgian Soviet Republic. Most Georgian political and military leaders (including Zhordania, Ramishvili, and Kvinitadze) left to go abroad, as did other Caucasian fighters such as Bammat.[113]

107 See V.I. Lenin, *Polnoe sobranie sochinenii* vol. 42 (Moscow: Politizdat, 1970), 131.

108 See David Dallin, "Between the World War and the NEP," in Leopold Haimson (ed.), *The Mensheviks* (Chicago: University of Chicago Press, 1974), 236.

109 See Kvashonkin, Khlevniuk, Kosheleva et al., eds., *Bol'shevistskoe rukovodstvo*, 173, 175, 177.

110 For the recognition of Georgia and the Baltic states, see AMAE, correspondance politique et commerciale 1914-1940, série Z, dossier no. 649. Fol. 128–129.

111 Kvashonkin, Khlevniuk, Kosheleva et al., eds., *Bolshevistskoe rukovodstvo*, 177–178.

112 Kazemzadeh, *The Struggle for Transcaucasia*, 313.

113 Lang, *A Modern History of Soviet Georgia*, 233–35, and Kazemzadeh, *The Struggle for Transcaucasia*, 314–24.

In conquering Georgia, Moscow regarded Turkey's cooperation as necessary for success and coordinated its own military operations, implicitly or explicitly, with the Turks: while the Red Army assaulted Georgia, Turkey made territorial demands (for Artvin, Ardahan and Batumi) on Georgia.[114] Forced to evacuate Artvin and Ardahan, the Georgians successfully defended against the Turks the port franc of Batumi, abandoned by Britain in July 1920.

The Bolshevik-Kemalist alliance did not, however, mean the parties trusted each other. Moscow constantly feared a betrayal by Kemalists: seeing Ankara's hands in the numerous insurgencies in the Northern Caucasus and Azerbaijan. In invading Armenia and Georgia, it assumed the possibility of fighting the Turks as well.[115] Well aware of the fragility of Bolshevik-Kemalist cooperation, foreign countries such as France maneuvered in turn to break up the alliance to their own advantage.[116] Nor did Ankara for its part trust the Bolsheviks, who indeed schemed against the Kemalists in Turkey itself (see p. 100).

As for Armenia, during the brief Russo-Georgian War, Dashnaks in Armenia who had escaped Russian repression staged an uprising and deposed the Soviet Armenian government in Erevan. The anti-Soviet insurgents were "welcomed in euphoric celebration with the strains of 'Mer Hairenik' [Armenian national anthem] and the unfurling once more of the republic's red, blue, and orange tricolor flag."[117] Following Tiflis, however, Erevan was retaken by the Red Army on 2 April. All of the Caucasus thus came under Soviet control.

By this time, Stalin had become firmly entrenched in revolutionary fervor. Earlier in 1917, he may have been inclined to help his Georgian friends who were not Bolsheviks. For example, the day after the Bolsheviks seized power in Petrograd in October, Spiridon Kedia, head of the Georgian National Democratic Party, received a stamp on his passport from Stalin to travel to Stockholm.[118] But by 1920 and 1921 both Stalin and Ordzhonikidze were advocating a forceful conquest of the Caucasus dominated by non-Bolsheviks and, in the end, succeeded. In July 1921, after the takeover of Georgia, Stalin returned to Tiflis as a conqueror. Accompanied by secret police guards, he attended a meeting organized in the town's working-class district. But he was greeted, according to an unsymapthetic account, with cries of "traitor" and "murderer." The

---

114 See an ex post facto account by the Georgian government of the history of the invasion: *Mémoire sur l'invasion de la Géorgie par les Armées de la Russie des Soviets* (Paris: A. Simon, 1921).

115 Kvashonkin, Khlevniuk, Kosheleva et al., eds., *Bolshevistskoe rukovodstvo* 177.

116 See for example, AMAE, CPC 1914-1940, série Z, dossier no. 631. fol. 234 (Mission militaire française au Caucase. Exposé de la situation politique pour la période du 1 au 15 novembre 1920, Tiflis, 16 November 1920).

117 Hovannisian, *The Republic of Armenia*, vol. 4, 405.

118 See Bihl, *Die Kaukasus-Politik der Mittelmächte*, vol. 2, 282. It appears that Kedia went to Stockholm to collect money in order to fight against the Mensheviks who refused to fight for Georgia's independence (p. 38). This may be why Stalin helped Kedia, although the National Democrats soon began working with the Mensheviks in Georgia, seeing no other way to influence the political life of Georgia.

crowd would not let him speak. Instead he stood at the meeting accused of treason by the old Social Democrat Isidor Ramishvili and others. Later that day, Ramishvili and some one hundred other Mensheviks were arrested. It was said that Stalin then convened another meeting of Tiflis workers, only to face the same fate. Humiliated, Stalin stormed into Bolshevik party headquarters in Tiflis and berated Filipp Makharadze, the Bolshevik leader in Tiflis. Having denounced the Mensheviks and Georgian nationalism, Stalin was said to have left for Moscow in a huff.[119]

4.4 The Caucasus and the World

By the time Moscow had conquered all of the Caucasus, the world – excepting Japan, the United States, and several other countries – had already begun accepting Soviet Russia. Most countries showed at most merely token sympathy towards the Caucasian states, which in essence were written off. The Kemalists of Turkey and the Bolsheviks circumvented the Sublime Porte and cooperated to reshape the recalcitrant Caucasus. Their cooperation led to the Treaty of Moscow signed in March 1921. This treaty confirmed the "existing solidarity between the two [governments] in the fight against imperialism," annulled all treaties concerning Turkey, and demarcated common borders, giving to Turkey most of the former Kars Oblast' (including the cities of Kars and Ardahan) and to Georgia Batumi and its surrounding area (as well as Akhalkalaki and Akhaltsikhe).[120] It was a settlement favorable to Turkey: except for Batumi, it virtually restored the borders before the 1877–78 Russo-Turkish War. Moscow acted on behalf of the new Caucasian Soviet Republics (or, more accurately, usurped their authority) in concluding this treaty. To correct this inconvenient situation, in October 1921 a new treaty was signed between Kemalist Turkey and the three Caucasian Soviet Republics in Kars. The new Treaty of Kars affirmed the previous Treaty of Moscow.[121]

Although Moscow worked with the Kemalists to divide and conquer the Caucasus, it never trusted them, as noted earlier. For instance, in December 1920 both Lenin and Stalin insisted that the Bolsheviks not trust the Kemalists and instead concentrate all their efforts on the victory of the "Soviet party."[122] A few months later, in April and May 1921, that is, after the signing of the Treaty of Moscow, Lenin approved a plan to arm the White forces (the forces of Vrangel', then a refugee in Istanbul) with Soviet weapons in order to conquer the Ottoman capital and then hand the city over to the Turkish Communists (and not to the Kemalists based in Ankara/Angora)! Leon Trotsky objected to this plan, a risky venture that he insisted would fail 95 percent and that, in

---

119 Joseph Iremaschwili, *Stalin und die Tragödie Georgiens* (Berlin: Verfasser, 1931), 60–62. See also Hiroaki Kuromiya, *Stalin: Profiles in Power* (Harlow, UK: Longman, 2005), 45–46.

120 *Dokumenty vneshnei politiki*, vol. 3 (Moscow: Politizdat, 1959), 597-604.

121 *Dokumenty vneshnei politiki*, vol. 4 (Moscow: Politizdat, 1960), 420–429.

122 See *V.I. Lenin: neizvestnye dokumenty, 1891–1922* (Moscow: ROSSPEN, 2000), 404.

Fig. 4.7. The Caucasus after the Treaty of Kars, 1921.

any case, would discredit the Bolsheviks even if it succeeded. Eventually the scheme was abandoned.[123]

Just as the conquest of Ukraine in 1920 was not enough to satisfy Moscow, the conquest of the Caucasus was not enough for some Bolsheviks, who now eyed Persia on its other side. In May 1920, shortly after the fall of Baku, Communists and their sympathizers in northern Persia set up the Soviet Republic of Gilan with the help of Soviet Bolsheviks and Soviet military forces.[124] Yet the Persian Republic soon turned, according to a retrospective Soviet assessment, into a "*Soviet-imperialist* enterprise."[125] Even

123 M.A. Persits, *Zastenchivaia interventsiia: O sovetskom vtorzhenii v Iran i Bukharu v 1920–1921 gg.* (Moscow: Muravei-Gaid, 1999), 187–89.

124 See Cosroe Chaqueri, *The Soviet Socialist Republic of Iran: Birth of the Trauma* (Pittsburgh, PA: University of Pittsburgh Press, 1995), *Persidskii front mirovoi revoliutsii: dokumenty o sovetskom vtorzhenii v Gilian (1920–1921)* (Moscow: Kvadriga, 2009), and Vladimir Genis, *Krasnaia Persiia: bol'sheviki v Giliane 1920–1921* (Moscow: MNPI, 2000).

125 Persits, *Zastenchivaia interventsiia*, 119 (assessment given in April 1921 by V.G. Tardov, Chief of Soviet Information Bureau in Persia: emphasis added).

in January 1921, Lenin still hoped to create a Soviet republic in Khorasan, Persia, as well "by the spring [of 1921]."[126] He remained cautious about waging revolutionary war in Persia,[127] however, ultimately choosing rapprochement with Britain (whose influence in Persia Moscow wished to dislodge). In February 1921 Moscow and Tehran concluded a friendship treaty, and the following month London and Moscow signed a trade agreement. But although the Gilan Republic soon collapsed, this did not end the ambition of some Bolsheviks towards Persia. Kirov and Ordzhonikidze, for instance, proposed to create an "illegal committee for the liberation of Persia" in Azerbaijan and organize revolutionary forces in Gilan. In November 1921 the two Bolsheviks were severely reprimanded by Lenin for subverting Moscow's agreement with Tehran.[128]

Of all the conquered Caucasian lands, Georgia was the most difficult and inconvenient case for Moscow to deal with. Moscow had formally recognized Georgia as an independent country but then destroyed it by force. Although Lenin repeatedly urged Stalin, Ordzhonikidze, and others to be "extra careful" in scheming to occupy Georgia,[129] in the end he went along with the more radical advocates within his party. But though Moscow succeeded in conquering Georgia, it did not conquer the hearts and minds of the Georgian people. Stalin, who triumphantly returned to Tiflis after the conquest, was instead humiliated and left the city indignantly. And whereas the Allied powers accepted the Soviet conquest of Georgia, France proved more protective of Georgia than did Britain. It was Aristide Briand, French Prime Minister and president of the Allied Supreme Council, who played a decisive role in the council's de jure recognition of Georgia in 1921, overriding Britain's reluctance. Indeed, France was the only country to provide military assistance to Georgia to fight the Red Army. But France also had no intention of going to war with Soviet Russia and so its military assistance was limited, leaving the Georgians unhappy.[130] The weakness of Soviet power in Georgia, however, remained a matter of political interest to the Allied powers, one that could be exploited in case of necessity.

4.5 The Caucasus and Japan

Japan did not figure prominently in the delicate international politics concerning the Caucasus at the time. But generally following the Great Powers of Europe, Japan kept

126 *V.I. Lenin*, 412 (26 January 1921 instruction).

127 See the resolution of the Communist Party Politburo (27 November 1920) in *V.I. Lenin*, p. 403, where he also advocated avoiding war in Georgia, Armenia, and Turkey.

128 See *V.I. Lenin*, 467, 484.

129 See Lenin's letters in November 1920 and February 1921 in *V.I. Lenin*, 403–404, 415.

130 Werner Zürrer, *Kaukasien 1918–1921: Der Kampf der Großmächte um die Landbrücke zwischen Schwarzem und Kaspischem Meer* (Düsseldorf: Droste Verlag, 1978), 448, 450, 454–455, 460, 708, and Mamoulia, *Les combats indépendandistes des Caucasiens*, 24.

watch on the Caucasian situation mainly from Istanbul, sometimes seeking intelligence from the British Army.[131] Records show that Japan treated the new Caucasian republics well. Armenia opened a legation in Japan in 1919,[132] and Consul Diana Agabek Abcar energetically worked in Japan to have Armenia accepted as an independent state, while Japan in turn "facilitated the relief activities and refugee services of Diana Abcar."[133] In 1920 Japanese financiers formed a consortium with Armenians to build railways in Armenia,[134] although, given the Soviet conquest that followed, this resulted in nothing concrete. After Japan's de-jure recognition of Georgia in 1921 (possibly even earlier, after its de facto recognition in February 1920), Georgians living in the Far East opened, with mandates from Tiflis, consulates in Vladivostok and Harbin in China. With the aid of Japan, Georgians in the Far East even apparently formed a Georgian national military unit within Ataman Semenov's White Army, which Japan supported. The unit was commanded by Ilia Pateishvili and supported by Ilia Mikeladze.[135] The Japanese Ministry of Foreign Affairs also regarded the Soviet conquest of the Caucasus as a prelude to Soviet exportation of Communism to Persia and India.[136]

In military terms, although Japan's moves did not have immediate impact on the Caucasus, they did have implications for subsequent development of cooperation with peoples from the Caucasus. As early as 1917 there were expectations that Japan would turn against Russia. Shortly after the Bolshevik Revolution, for example, the Japanese naval attaché in Petrograd noted persistent rumors in the capital that Russia's unilateral peace treaty with the Central Powers would lead Japan to declare war against Russia.[137] Indeed, some Japanese political and military leaders advocated military intervention immediately after the Bolshevik seizure of power. But there were others in Japan who urged restraint and careful coordination with other powers, particularly the United States. It took Japan more than six months to decide to intervene militarily in Siberia in coordination with the United States and other Allied powers.[138]

Soon, however, Japan began taking unilateral action in Siberia, deeply angering the United States, which feared giving away control of economic interests in the Russian Far East. Japan's forces, with some seventy-three thousand soldiers on Russian

131 Reports from Constantinople, Gaimushō Gaikō Shiryō Kan (Hereafter GGMK), Tokyo, Japan, 1,6,3, "Rokoku Kakumei ikken," vol. 2.

132 Hovannisian, *The Republic of Armenia*, vol. II, p. 527.

133 Hovannisian, *The Republic of Armenia: Vol. III: From London to Sévres February – August 1920* (Berkeley-Los Angeles: University of California Press, 1996), 430. However, Armenians could not freely dispose of their assets in Japan, because Armenia was yet a "non-treaty country" (a country with no commercial treaty with Japan). See JACAR, reference code: B06151142900.

134 Hovannisian, *The Republic of Armenia*, vol. III, 281.

135 File of K.O. Gelovani, Archive of the Ministry of Internal Affairs of Georgia (Tbilisi).

136 JACAR, reference code: B03051060400 (a survey of Russia in 1922), Section "Georgia."

137 JACAR, reference code: B03051400500 (29 November 1917 telegraph).

138 See James W. Morley, *The Japanese Thrust into Siberia, 1918* (New York: Columbia University Press, 1957).

soil, were the largest of all the countries militarily involved except for Russia itself. The Japanese forces quickly occupied the cities of Blagoveshchensk and Chita, eventually reaching as far west as Irkutsk to the west of Lake Baikal. Japan's undeclared goals were to detach the Russian Far East and Siberia from Soviet Russia and establish a puppet government or one friendly to Japan, thereby securing its political and economic interests there. In the end, however, Japan failed to achieve any of these goals. Its military hold was limited, and Bolshevik partisans rolled back the Japanese forces. Even after all other countries had withdrawn from military intervention against the Bolsheviks, Japan stayed on until 1922, when it finally withdrew from the Asian continent.[139] Japan's occupation of Northern Sakhalin (in support of an "independent Sakhalin") lasted even longer from 1920 to 1925.[140] This episode of Japan's intervention, which did not affect the Caucasus directly, suggest that Japan was the most uncompromising power toward the Bolshevik regime, which in turn meant that anti-Bolshevik forces naturally turned to Japan for assistance. And so a new chapter in Caucasian-Japanese relations was opened.

In the longer term, Japan's actions in the Far East likely affected the Caucasus directly. Chapter 3 discussed Japan's alleged recruitment of Georgians for espionage after the Russo-Japanese War. The Society of Georgians in Harbin was said to have been created by Japan for this purpose. Such societies were created elsewhere as well. In Vladivostok, for example, the Society of Georgians was founded in 1919, according to one account, by the instruction of the Menshevik government in Georgia to fight against Soviet Russia and mobilize world support for an independent Georgia. Its chairman, Kirill Gelovani, was later arrested, in 1937, in Soviet Georgia. According to Gelovani's confession under interrogation, the chairman of the Society of Georgians in Harbin, Ivlian Khaindrava (see p. 66), had called him to Harbin and told him that Japan's occupation of the Far East was beneficial to the Georgians, most of whom were engaged in commercial activities protected by Japan. Gelovani said that Khaindrava practically proposed that he recruit members of the society for intelligence for Japan. Meanwhile, Georgians in the Far East sent the Socialist Federalist David Rostomashvili to Tiflis. Rostomashvili returned to Vladivostok at the end of 1919 with a mandate to found a consulate in Vladivostok. "Tumanov" (Tumanishvili) was appointed consul, and after his death in 1922, Rostomashvili took over. According to Gelovani, Rostomashvili agreed with Khaindrava about the necessity of Georgians working for Japan, and Gelovani and Rostomashvili together worked to recruit members for "espionage for Japan." Allegedly to cover its intelligence operations, the Japanese occupation forces created the "Railway Bureau," with which the Soci-

139 See Teruyuki Hara, *Shiberia shuppei: kaukemi to kanshō, 1917–1922* (Tokyo: Chikuma shobō, 1989).

140 See Teruyuki Hara, "The Japanese Occupation of Northern Sakhalin (1920s)," in Stephen Kotkin and David Wolff, eds., *Rediscovering Russia in Asia: Siberia and the Russian Far East* (Armonk, NY: M.E. Sharpe, 1995).

ety of Georgians communicated through Melkhisedek Menabde, a merchant. Gelovani stated to Soviet authorities that he had worked to inculcate Japanophilic sentiments in the Georgian colony in Vladivostok. He then sent promising men such as Vasili Kipiani to the Japanese.[141]

These Georgians in the Far East, according to Gelovani, maintained contact with both the Social Democratic government in exile and the Georgian National Democrats. Yet when a National Democratic organization was created in Harbin, the entire leadership of the Georgian colony joined it, including Khaindarava, Rostomashvili, Mikeladze, Giorgi Pitskhelauri (see p. 66), and the "Ordzhonikidze brothers."[142]

In any event, there is no reason to take at face value the confessions made by Gelovani and others later in the 1930s under Soviet captivity. What was clear was that there was a mutual attraction between Japan and the Caucasians in the Far East. Both sides remembered the cooperation they had forged during the Russo-Japanese War. Both hoped that the Soviet regime would be short-lived and that the day of Caucasian autonomy and independence would come sooner or later. The strategists of both sides understood this very well and acted accordingly. Espionage or not, Soviet suspicions about the Caucasian-Japanese nexus existed even at the time, only to be colossally inflated in the 1930s.

---

141 File of K.O. Gelovani, Archive of the Ministry of Internal Affairs of Georgia (Tbilisi).

142 File of K.O. Gelovani, Archive of the Ministry of Internal Affairs of Georgia (Tbilisi). For Simon Ordzhonikidze, see p. 66 of the present book.

5 Renewal

Among the significant consequences of World War I is that Japan now grew into an international power. Its victory in the Russo-Japanese War fifteen years earlier had already made it a formidable power in Asia. Even though Japan's participation in actual battles was limited during World War I, it diligently assisted the Entente on a Eurasian scale. As discussed earlier, Japan rendered a great deal of material assistance to Russia; it also "ejected German forces from Qingdao, China, and German Micronesia, protected convoys of Australian and New Zealand troops from the Pacific to Aden, hunted German submarines in the Mediterranean, and provided desperately needed shipping, copper, munitions, and almost ¥640 million in loans to its allies."[1] Japan took part in the Paris Peace Conference at Versaille in 1919 as one of the "Big Five" and acquired from Germany rights to Shandong province in China and Pacific islands north of the equator. (The conference, however, rejected Japan's proposal for including a "racial equality clause" in the charter for the League of Nations.) Along with Great Britain, France, and Italy, Japan also became one of the original four permanent members of the Council of the League of Nations.

Meanwhile, the establishment of the Soviet regime produced large numbers, an estimated two million or more, of political émigrés in Poland, Romania, Yugoslavia, Czechoslovakia, Germany, France, Britain, Turkey, Persia, Afghanistan, China, Japan, and elsewhere. Foreign countries, including France, Poland, and Japan, took note of these people as being potentially useful in politically subverting and even ultimately destroying the Soviet Union. The Soviet Union's fear of external and internal subversion and Stalin's use of it for political purposes became a consistent theme in Soviet foreign and domestic policy. As described by one historian regarding the war, revolution, and civil war of 1914–21: "For both Soviet official historians and the Russian émigré movement the belief that tsarist Russia had been fatally undermined by German espionage formed a central bastion of their ideological thought."[2] The Soviet government was thus obsessed with the "myth of all-encompassing enemy espionage" and "internal betrayal."[3] Once again Russia came to deeply fear Japan as an espionage super power.

1 Frederick R. Dickinson, "Toward a Global Perspective of the Great War: Japan and the Foundations of a Twentieth-Century World." *The American Historical Review* 119, no. 4 (2014), 1160–1161.

2 Alex Marshall, "Russian Military Intelligence, 1905–1917: The Untold Story behind Tsarist Russia in the First World War." *War in History* 11, no. 4 (2004), 421.

3 Marshall, "Russian Military Intelligence," 421.

5.1 "Pacification"

In 1922 the three Southern Caucasian Soviet Republics were merged into one and then incorporated as a constituent republic, the Transcaucasian Socialist Federative Soviet Republic, of the newly created Union of Soviet Socialist Republics. (Later, in 1936, the Transcaucasian Republic was dissolved into the Armenian, Azerbaijan, and Georgian Soviet Socialist Republics.) The Northern Caucasus was incorporated into the Russian Soviet Federative Socialist Republic, the dominant constituent republic of the Union. Much of the Northern Caucasus, however, underwent a complex process of regionalization: the Mountaineer Autonomous Soviet Socialist Republic, created in 1921, spawned various autonomous units (such as Balkar, Chechen, Kabardian, Karachai, and Ingush), which, in 1924, were incorporated into the Northern Caucasus Krai (Region).

This administrative Sovietization did not mean that the Caucasus was politically Sovietized; indeed, rebellions against Soviet rule continued, for although the Soviet government had conquered the Caucasus, it could not easily "pacify" the region. Soon after the Civil War ended, rebellions again came to characterize the Caucasus. As one Russian historian has noted: "Rebellions in Chechnia, Dagestan, Terek *Oblast'* and Transcaucasia for all practical purposes did not subside, one growing into the next. The Civil War in the Caucasus was protracted and complex. The Soviet government only succeeded in containing the rebellions by March 1922, and rebellions continued to flare up in 1925 and in the 1930s, with no end in sight."[4] With respect to Muslims, pacification of the Caucasus proved much harder than that of Turkestan because the former, unlike the latter, had few native Muslims on the Soviet side: the Mountaineer Autonomous Soviet Socialist Republic was completely dominated by (mostly Christian) Ossetians and Russians.[5] As another historian has noted, "From 1922 to 1943, the history of Chechnia and Dagestan was an almost uninterrupted succession of rebellions, counter-expeditions and 'political banditism' " with uprisings occurring in 1924, 1928, and 1936.[6] Even in non-Muslim areas, the insurgency died hard: as late as the summer of 1921 the People's Army of the Northern Caucasus, the Kuban Insurgent Army" (led by M. A. Przheval'skii), and other units were operating many thousands strong, some of whom were coordinating with similar movements in Ukraine.[7]

---

4 N.E. Eliseeva, "Chechnia: vooruzhennaia bor'ba v 20-30-e gody." *Voenno-istoricheskii arkhiv*, no. 2 (1997), 123.

5 Alex Marshall, *The Caucasus under Soviet Rule* (London-New York: Routledge, 2006), 163.

6 Marie Bennigsen Broxup, "The Last *Ghazawat*: The 1920–1921 Uprising," in *The North Caucasus Barrier: The Russian Advance towards the Muslim World*, ed. by Marie Bennigsen Broxup (London: Hurst, 1992), 143.

7 Tat'iana Simonova, "Ustanovlenie Sovetskoi vlasti na Severnom Kavkaze, 1918–1921 gg." *Dialog* 2001, no. 12, 67.

To “pacify” the region, Moscow took various measures, including forcibly resettling and deporting people and disarming locals. In Chechnia, for example, in the summer and autumn of 1925, Moscow carried out a massive disarmament campaign using artillery and aerial bombardment by forces of the Red Army and OGPU (Soviet secret police).[8] Shortly afterward similar operations were carried out elsewhere in the Caucasus. In Dagestan, for instance, where 55,000 people were said to have taken part in anti-Soviet uprisings in 1925, several divisions of the Red Army were deployed to disarm the population. In the process, 1,867 people were arrested and of them, 139 people were tried extra judicially, with 52 sentenced to be shot.[9]

The Georgians were not far behind in taking a stand against the Soviet government. In 1922 popular uprisings spread across Georgia and parts of Dagestan, only to be suppressed by Soviet forces, although the rebels did receive sympathy (but no material support) from Poland.[10] In the same year the Georgian political parties united to create a clandestine organization, the Committee for the Independence of Georgia, with a military branch (United Military Center). In 1923 the committee, in collaboration with anti-Bolshevik forces in Azerbaijan and the Northern Caucasus, began planning an insurrection, only for the Soviet secret police to preempt their plans by arresting the leaders of the United Military Center. Simultaneously, Moscow implemented concerted campaigns nationwide to liquidate the Mensheviks as an organization, forcing them to proclaim their “self-dissolution.”[11]

In 1924 the August Uprising took place in Georgia. After the 1923 debacle, the Committee for the Independence of Georgia soon reconstructed itself. During that time the international situation turned unfavorable, with Britain formally recognizing the Soviet Union in February 1924, and expectations that France would follow Britain’s suit in the wake of a new French cabinet formed by the pro-Soviet prime minister Édouard Herriot in June 1924. (Indeed, France recognized the Soviet Union de jure six months later). To counter this move and draw the attention of the world to the Bolshevik occupation of Georgia, the Georgian Menshevik (Social Democratic) leaders in exile prepared for new popular uprisings. In February 1924 they secretly dispatched Valerian Dzhugeli, the former chief of the people’s guard in Georgia, for this purpose, but he was arrested on 6 August. Gogita Pagava, one of the Menshevik leaders charged with

8 See “Vtoroe pokorenie Kavkaza: Bol’sheviki i chechenskie povstantsy.” *Rodina* 1995, no. 6, 43–45.

9 *Lubianka: Stalin i VChK-GPU-OGPU-NKVD. Arkhiv Stalina. Dokumenty vyschikh organov partiinoi i gosudarstvennoi vlasti. Ianvar’1922–dekabr’1936* (Moscow: Mezhdunarodnyi fond Demokratiia, 2003), 793.

10 Georges Mamoulia, *Bor’ba za svobodu i nezavisimost’ Kavkaza (1921–1945)* (Tbilisi-Paris: Meridiani, 2012), 82–85, and Georges Mamoulia, “‘Prometei’ do prometeizma: neizvestnye stranitsy iz istorii natsional’no-osvoboditel’nogo dvizheniia na Kavkaze (1922 g.).” *Nowy Prometeusz*, no. 2 (2012), 286–287.

11 Georges Mamoulia, *Les combats indépendandistes des Caucasiens entre URSS et puissances occidentales: Le cas de la Géorgie (1921–1945)* (Paris: L’Harmattan, 2009), 30, 68, 74–75, 82.

coordinating resistance with the Azeris, had already been arrested in February. Consequently their plans for insurrection became known to the Soviet government and thus appeared infeasible. But in view of the international situation, the Menshevik leaders decided to proceed with their plans. On the eve of Britain and France's diplomatic recognition of the USSR, they wanted to prove that the Georgian people did not accept the Soviet occupation. Taking into account that Georgia was the only Caucasian republic recognized de jure by the Allies, the Social Democrats hoped that mass uprisings there would force France (which hosted the Georgian government in exile in Paris) to preserve the international stature of Georgia as an independent state. The Georgian government in exile also hoped that on the eve of the USSR's recognition by Western powers, the Kremlin would be obliged to refrain from massive repressive measures against the rebels.[12]

While the general uprising was planned for 29 August, already on 28 August the small village of Chiatura in eastern Georgia had revolted. There, Russian troops deployed an airplane and machine-gunned the rebels, who carried slogans such as: "Liberate Georgia and Restore its Independence," "Liberate the Country from the Communist Traitors," "Protect Private Property," and "Protect Religion." As during the Russo-Japanese War, Guria became a major center of rebellion, where nearly ten thousand men were armed.[13] But the rebels fought against insurmountable odds; the enemy forces, familiar with the insurrection plans through intelligence, appropriately deployed military forces. Additionally, the insurrection failed to spread to major centers such as Tiflis and Batumi or national minority regions, although parts of Abkhazia did join the rebels. After a week of fighting, the rebellions were crushed (although those in Abkhazia continued a few more days, and in some areas the Red Army fought against the "bandits" well into October 1924).[14] In these few days of uprising, as many as 12,578 prisoners were killed by the Communist government (not counting those who died in action).[15]

---

12 See Mamoulia, *Les combats indépendandistes des Caucasiens*, 81–85. The Menshevik leaders abroad knew that without working together with the Azeris and peoples of the Northern Caucasus, the plan would be suicidal. See Markus Wehner, "Le soulèvement géorgien de 1924 et la réaction des Bolcheviks." *Communisme* nos. 42/43/44 (1995), 158. Some historians suspect that the Georgian secret police deliberately "encouraged the rebellion so they would have a pretext for destroying all political opposition." See Amy Knight, *Beria: Stalin's First Lieutenant* (Princeton, NJ: Princeton University Press, 1993), 32.

13 Mamoulia, *Les combats indépendandistes des Caucasiens*, p. 85.

14 Note the military records in Rossiiskii gosudarstvennyi voennyi arkhiv (hereafter RGVA), Moscow, Russia, f. 25873, op. 1, d. 1113.

15 Wehner, "Le soulèvement géorgien de 1924," 160 and Wojciech Materski, "Powstanie narodowowyzvoleńcze 1924 r. w Gruzii." *Studia dziejów Rosji i Europy Środkowo-Wschodniej* v. 34 (1999), 63–64. See also the account by a Polish diplomat held in a prison in Georgia at the time: Andrzej Furier, "Relacja Józefa Łaszkiewicza o gruzińskim powstaniu antybolszewickim 1924 r.," *Pro Georgia* vol. 7 (1998), 147–148.

The mass executions of rebels disquieted Moscow, which, concerned about international repercussions, prohibited further executions without its authorization. (Indeed, the League of Nations adopted a resolution, as it had in 1922 concerning the suppression of rebellions at that time, drawing the attention of the world to the plight of the Georgians under Soviet rule.)[16] Nevertheless, the Transcaucasian Regional Committee of the Communist Party, headed by Sergo Ordzhonikidze, continued with the executions without Moscow's permission. Stalin deplored this action, which he saw as damaging the authority of the Communists and helping turn the executed into national heroes.[17] But with Stalin's implicit support, Ordzhonikidze and other Caucasian Communist leaders escaped formal reproof.[18] A month and a half after the incident, Stalin spoke about the Georgian uprisings, characterizing them not as a demonstration of national sentiments but as a manifestation of peasant economic discontent in areas where, according to him, Communists were well represented in local governments.[19] Stalin thus refused to acknowledge any national or religious content to the uprisings in his home land. Yet Moscow could not kill the "Georgian soul," which one writer declared "should rule in Georgia." As Stephen Jones has noted, Russians "who remained an insignificant minority of the [Georgian] republican population until the 1930s, were under considerable pressure to adapt to Georgian customs in the 1920s."[20]

The political situation in the Caucasus had long been a bone of contention within the Politburo of the Communist Party in Moscow. Well known is Lenin's irritation with the high-handed policy (forcible Sovietization) by Ordzhonikidze and other Caucasian Communists such as Filipp Makharadze and Budu Mdivani toward their native lands. There was also disagreement among them regarding the degree of centralization to be imposed on the Caucasus. This issue became known through Lenin's "Last Testament" as a source of conflict between Lenin on the one hand and Stalin and Ordzhonikidze on the other, the former accusing the latter of "Great Russian chauvinism." Recent studies, however, have suggested that in fact the conflict may not have been between Lenin and Stalin (although disagreements did exist between them). The authenticity of the relevant part of Lenin's testament has also come under scrutiny.[21] In any event,

16 Mamoulia, *Les combats indépendandistes des Caucasiens*, 69 and 86, and Materski, "Powstanie narodowowyzvoleńcze 1924 r. w Gruzii," 64–65.

17 *TsK RKP(b)–VKP(b) i natsional'nyi vopros. Kniga 1. 1918–1933 gg.* (Moscow: ROSSPEN, 2005), 232–33 (Stalin's memorandum to the Politburo dated 5 September 1924).

18 Wehner, "Le soulèvement géorgien de 1924," 162, 164–65.

19 I.V. Stalin, *Sochineniia*, vol. 6 (Moscow: Politizdat, 1947), 308–309.

20 Stephen Jones, "The Establishment of Soviet Power in Transcaucasia: The Case of Georgia 1921–1928." *Soviet Studies* 40, no. 4 (1988), 266, 269. Note that in 1904 the young Stalin criticized the "philosophical absurdities" of Georgian nationalists, insisting that there was no such thing as a "national spirit." See I.V. Stalin, *Sochineniia*, vol. 1 (Moscow: Politizdat, 1946), 53.

21 See Eric van Ree, "'Lenin's Last Struggle' Revisited." *Revolutionary Russia* 14, no. 2 (December 2001), 85–122; Jeremy Smith, *The Bolsheviks and the National Question, 1917–1923* (London, 1999), chs.

the Caucasus as a whole, regarded as an unruly region of long-standing defiance, continued to plague Moscow.

Moscow linked the insurgents to foreign powers, accusing them of being Turkish agents. Poland was equally implicated in the anti-Soviet incidents in the Caucasus. Poland ran an international effort (the Promethean movement, see p. 116) to dismember the Soviet Union by supporting the independence of national minorities within its borders. Georgia and the Caucasus were among Poland's major targets. Poland also maintained a consulate in Georgia (until early 1938, at the time of the Great Terror, when it was forced by Moscow to shut down). An Italian diplomat based in Tbilisi from 1928 to 1931, received numerous reports of the sabotage of the Baku-Batumi oil pipelines and the destruction of the rail tracks.[22] The year 1928 further witnessed massive arrests of former Musavats and Dashnaks in Azerbaijan and Armenia, accused of belonging to clandestine nationalist organizations, supported by foreign governments. The Persian consulate in Baku was placed under close police surveillance, and peasants and nomads who were Persian citizens were threatened with arrest unless they left Azerbaijan immediately. Even Soviet officials in the border regions were suspected of being "Trojan horses" of the Persian government.[23] In 1931 some former members of the Menshevik (Social Democratic) party were executed in Azerbaijan. Shortly thereafter, a number of local people associated with the Polish legation in Tbilisi were arrested and executed. The Italian diplomat Paolo Vita-Finzi noted that it was evident that Moscow wanted to isolate the Poles completely in the capital of Georgia.[24]

In all these reports there is little mention of Japan. But in view of the close relations between Japan and Poland in the realm of intelligence against the Soviet Union (see below p. 117), Japan's shadow was, not surprisingly, evident in the Caucasus. Indeed, in 1930 in Ingushetia, a land far from Japan, an elaborate scheme of provocation was devised by the Soviet secret police to uncover and arrest anti-Soviet elements, and involved a "Japanese agent" as its key figure (see below p. 126).

In 1929–31, when Stalin's policy of collectivizing agriculture and liquidating the kulak reached the Caucasus, the local peoples revolted again with arms in hand. In some areas of Chechnia and Karachai, whole regions rebelled against the Soviet government with "almost the entire population taking part in armed actions."[25] The po-

---

7–8; and V.A. Sakharov, *"Politicheskoe zaveshchanie" Lenina. Real'nost' istorii i mify politiki* (Moscow: Izd-vo Moskovskogo universiteta, 2003). For a concise discussion of this controversial issue, see Hiroaki Kuromiya, *Stalin* (Profiles in Power) (Harlow: Longman, 2005), ch. 3.

22 Paolo Vita-Finzi, *Journal caucasien (1928–1931) suivi de Carnet moscovite (1953)*, tr. Jean-Marc Mandosio (Paris: Inventaire, 2000), 155.

23 Jörg Baberowski, *Der Feind ist überall: Stalinismus im Kaukasus* (Munich: Deutsche Verlags-Anstalt, 2003), 401, 561, 563.

24 Vita-Finzi, *Journal caucasien*, 155–56.

25 Eliseeva, "Chechnia," 137.

litical situation in Chechnia was such that its party secretary declared that the Soviet government had been replaced by the OGPU.[26] Uprisings broke out in Azerbaijan, Georgia, and elsewhere, only to be brutally crushed.[27] In Abkhazia, thousands of peasants met to demand concessions from the party regarding its agricultural policy. Local party organizations were forced to meet their demands (which Moscow characterized as preparations for armed uprisings). The leader N. Lakoba was denounced by Moscow as opportunist.[28] In the Borchalo area of Georgia, the spring of 1931 witnessed a resumption of resistance to the collectivization drive, with peasants staging guerrilla war. Armed forces from the Red Army and the OGPU were mobilized to crush the rebellions. Rebels took refuge in mountainous areas, from where they continued their armed actions. In response, the OGPU took the rebels' parents as hostages, some of whom were executed and others exiled to Russia.[29]

Simultaneously, political repression intensified. In western Georgia, for example, in the spring of 1931, the police uncovered a "counter-revolutionary insurgent organization" allegedly headed by Georgian Social Democrats, with as many as two thousand members (most of whom were poor and middle-level peasants). This organization was formed in response to "systematic hunger and starvation." Armenian Dashnaks and Azeri Musavats, as they were called by the Soviet secret police, were likewise hounded in the Caucasus.[30]

Turmoil and violence inevitably produced large numbers of refugees fleeing to neighboring countries. In 1930 hundreds of Georgians seeking to cross the border with Turkey were caught by Turkish authorities and handed back to Soviet authorities. A large number were reportedly shot. Meanwhile, thousands of Azeris and Central Asians took refuge in Persia. Fearing political complications, the Persian government sent the politically active elements away from the Soviet border areas or extradited them back to the Soviet Union. In 1931, Moscow even dispatched military forces

26 Eliseeva, "Chechnia,", p. 138.

27 Mamoulia, *Les combats indépendandistes des Caucasiens*, 126–27, and *TsK RKP(b)–VKP(b) i natsional'nyi vopros*, 673–75.

28 *TsK RKP(b)–VKP(b) i natsional'nyi vopros*, 675–80. For more detail of the uprising, see Timothy K. Blauvelt, "Resistance and Accommodation in the Stalinist Periphery: A Peasant Uprising in Abkhazia." *Ab Imperio*, 2012, no. 3, 78–108.

29 Mamoulia, *Les combats indépendandistes des Caucasiens*, 132 and Georges Mamoulia, ed., *Kavkazskaia Konfederatsiia v ofitsialnykh deklaratsiiakh, tainoi perepiske i sekrethykh dokumentakh dvizheniia "Prometei." Sbornik dokumentov* (Moscow: Sotsial'no-polititsheskaia mysl', 2012), 30.

30 *TsK RKP(b)–VKP(b) i natsional'nyi vopros*, 667–78, 670. One ought to be careful, however, in evaluating these rebellions. In the case of the "Sheki rebellion" in Azerbaijan in 1930, it may well have been a provocation organized by a "leader" under the control of the Soviet secret police. See a suggestive essay by Bruce Grant, "An Average Azeri Village (1930): Remembering Rebellion in the Caucasus Mountains." *Slavic Review*, 63, no. 4 (2004), 705–731. For cases of uprisings led by police agents, see Aleksei Tepliakov, " 'Otrabotannyi material': massovaia likvidatsiia sekretnoi agentury sovetskikh spevsluzhb v 1920–1930-e gody." *Rossiiskaia istoriia*, 2013, no. 4, 110–111.

into Iranian territory to liquidate military detachments of émigré Azeris.[31] (Technically speaking, this sort of expedition was allowed by the 1921 Soviet-Persian treaty.) Nonetheless, the Sovietization of the Caucasus remained a difficult task for Moscow.

5.2 International Realignments

By the mid-1920s, the consolidation of the Soviet government had led to its international recognition by Finland, Turkey, Iran, the Baltic states (Estonia, Latvia, and Lithuania), Germany, Poland, Britain, Italy, France, and China, followed by Japan in 1925. The United States, which did not open diplomatic relations with Moscow until 1933, was the most notable exception. (Bulgaria and Romania recognized the Soviet Union in 1934, but the Kingdom of Yugoslavia did so only in 1940.) In 1926 the US House of Representatives discussed the issue of recognizing the Georgian government-in-exile in Paris, but did not carry its deliberations to the end.[32]

These events made it difficult for supporters of the independence of national minorities within the Soviet Union to gain international support. The Caucasian émigré groups knew well that a political struggle against the behemoth of the Soviet Union required their solidarity. At the same time, the differences in their political orientations made it almost impossible to maintain political unity. Thus, the interwar period was characterized by a desire for unity matched by the reality of political fragmentation.

Against this background of international isolation, the efforts of the Caucasian émigrés and their supporters were noteworthy. In June 1921, for example, representatives of the four Caucasian states (Georgia, Armenia, Azerbaijan, and the Northern Caucasus) submitted a joint declaration to the League of Nations, in which, "desirous of assuring the peoples of the Caucasus the benefits of independence, democratic government and economic prosperity" and "anxious to eliminate all ground for disputes between these republics and to establish their intimate union on a firm foundation," they declared:

> The above mentioned representatives unanimously recognise that Caucasia, a clearly defined isthmus between Europe and Asia, is, owing to its geographical location, the great international highway connecting the Black Sea and the Mediterranean with the countries in Central Asia and Western Asia, and that the freedom of this highway cannot be ensured to all peoples except by the

31 Mamoulia, *Les combats indépendandistes des Caucasiens*, 132.

32 See *National Republic of Georgia: Hearings before the Committee on Foreign Affairs, House of Representatives, Sixty-ninth Congress, first session, on H.J. Res. 195, Providing for the Appointment of a Diplomatic Representative to the National Republic of Georgia, April 1 and 2, 1926* (Washington: Govt. Print. Office, 1926).

> complete independence of the Caucasian Republics and the establishment of an alliance between them.[33]

In September 1922, in connection with anti-Bolshevik rebellions in Georgia, European socialists and Georgian émigrés led the League of Nations to adopt a unanimous resolution calling for the "normalization" of the Georgian political situation (i.e., the restoration of Georgia's independence) according to international law and by peaceful means. In 1924, in view of the uprisings in Georgia of that year, the League of Nations adopted the same call as its 1922 resolution.[34]

Some countries were more sympathetic than others toward the aspirations of the Caucasian émigrés. France, for example, as the Georgian government-in-exile hoped, allowed Georgia's diplomatic legation in Paris until 1933, thus continuing to recognize Georgia as an independent state. In a conversation with Noe Zhordania in 1921, French Prime Minister Aristide Briand emphasized that France would not abandon Georgia and that it wanted to "encircle Russia by Caucasian states."[35] Although Briand's desire was not to be fulfilled, Paris did provide a refuge for the Georgians abroad.

Warsaw, equally receptive, hatched its own political strategies to use the Caucasians against the Soviet Union. Poland and the Caucasus (Georgia in particular) had a close history: many Polish patriots had been exiled to Georgia by the Tsarist government, and many Georgian revolutionaries (including Zhordania) had studied in Poland. Sympathizing with the Poles, they supported the Polish cause, while Poland in turn supported the Georgian cause. Already in 1920 the two countries had attempted to forge a political-military alliance against Russia (see p. 93). In October 1924, under the aegis of the Polish ambassador in Turkey, Roman Knoll, a Committee for Caucasian Confederalists was set up in Istanbul for unifying Caucasian émigré political groups. Although the Armenians did not join, there was representation by Georgian National Democrats, such as Davit Vachnadze and Mikheil Tsereteli (former representative of Georgians in Berlin during World War I), Azeris (Hosrovbek Sultanov, the former minister of war of the Azerbaijan Democratic Republic), and Northern Caucasians, such as Vassan-Giray Dzhabagi and Alikhan Kantemir. The Committee declared that victory would be possible only if the Caucasians formed a united and confederate state to be supported by European states. By linking the committee to the Georgian Social Democrats, Azeri Musavats, and supporters of Said Shamil from the Northern Caucasus, Poland dreamed of creating a Union for the Liberation of the Caucasus. This union in turn was to be linked to the Ukrainian and Turkestan (Central Asian) orga-

---

33 Anita L.P. Burdett, ed., *Caucasian Boundaries: Documents and Maps 1802–1946*, v. 1 (London: Archive Editions, 1996), 763–68. See also Mitat Çelikpala, "The North Caucasian Émigrés between the World Wars." *International Journal of Turkish Studies*, 9, no. 1–2 (2003), 290. The French original is in Mamoulia, *Les combats indépendandistes des Caucasiens*, 358–361.

34 Mamoulia, *Les combats indépendandistes des Caucasiens*, 69 and 86.

35 Mamoulia, *Les combats indépendandistes des Caucasiens*, 45.

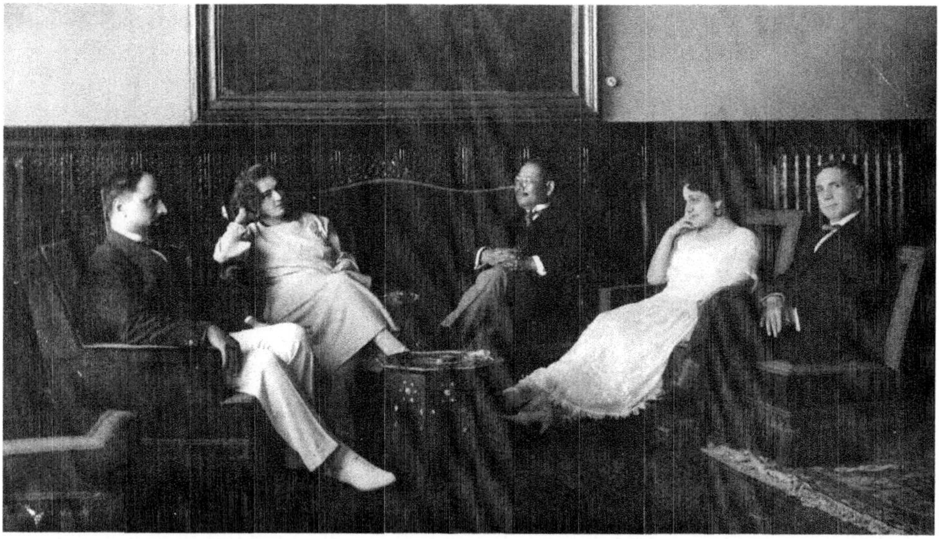

Fig. 5.1. Władysław Baranowski, Polish ambassador in Turkey with his wife; Sadazuchi Uchida, Japan's plenipotentiary at the League of Nations and ambassador in Turkey; and Konstantin Gvardzhaladze, representative in Turkey of the Paris-based Georgian government-in-exile, with his wife in Istanbul, 1922.

nizations for the same purpose. In this connection, in November 1924 a committee of Caucasians was created in Paris to coordinate the future form of the federation and its constitution. The committee was represented by Georgian Social Democrats (Akaki Chkhenkeli and Noe Ramishvili) as well as National Democrats (Spiridon Kedia), Azeris (Alimardan Topchubashi, former foreign minister of the Azerbaijan Democratic Republic, and Dzheikhun Khadzhibeili), and Northern Caucasians (Tapa Chermoev and Haidar Bammat). Meanwhile, Warsaw financially supported the clandestine dispatch of Vachnadze and Kantemir to the Caucasus to establish links to those areas under Soviet occupation.[36]

Japan, like Poland, did not cease to view the Soviet Union as it had Russia before World War I, and it remained strikingly active in the Caucasus. In the spring of 1922, a Japanese steam boat and its crew were detained by the Soviet government in Sukhumi, Abkhazia. Although the boat, owned by the Nitta Steam Boat Company

36 Mamoulia, *Les combats indépendandistes des Caucasiens*, 91–95, 367–72 and Mamoulia, ed., *Kavkazskaia Konfederatsiia*, 8–10, 47–54. At the time there were other secret dispatches of people into the Soviet Caucasus. Samson Kruashvili, or Samson Themur, who had left Batumi for Turkey in 1924 and then for France with a Turkish passport, was sent to Soviet Georgia in 1926. Kruashvili went to Trabzon, from where he crossed the border on foot. He spent seven to eight months in Georgia investigating the "Bolshevik movement," then, fearing arrest, left for Persia. See the French police report: *Service historique de l'armée de Terre (Château de Vincennes)* Series 7 N-3086.

in Kobe, Japan, and based in Istanbul, was hired out to other businesses, the Nitta company often failed to pay its debts on time and had also had some trouble in the Black Sea regions. Officially this led to its detention in Sukhumi, although the boat and its crew were released in the end. What exactly the commercial boat was doing in this region is not clear. Moscow certainly suspected more than commercial interests in the operation of a Japanese boat in the Black Sea.[37] In Turkey, with which Tokyo opened official diplomatic relations in 1924, the first Japanese ambassador, Sadazuchi Uchida, who had been stationed in Turkey since 1920, maintained close relations with the envoy of the Paris-based Georgian Social Democratic Government in Turkey Konstantin Gvardzhaladze. Japan appears to have maintained contact with other émigré Caucasian groups as well throughout the 1920s.[38] From Istanbul, Odesa (after 1925), and elsewhere, Japan followed Caucasian affairs, both political and economic; for example, Tokyo was aware of the 1924 rebellions in Georgia. According to Tokyo, even part of the Red Army (i.e., Georgian units in the Red Army) joined the Georgian rebels.[39]

At the time, Poland was far more committed to the Caucasus than was Japan, for the obvious reason that the Caucasus was much closer to Poland than to Japan. Indeed, Poland maintained a consulate in Tiflis until 1937. After Józef Piłsudski, a former leader of the Polish Socialist Party, took power through a coup, Warsaw made renewed efforts to strengthen ties with the Caucasian groups, with clear preference for Georgian Social Democrats and Musavats over Georgian National Democrats and other rightists. In the summer of 1926, Warsaw helped found the Committee for the Independence of the Caucasus in Istanbul, its aim being to "prepare the peoples of the Caucasus for the battle of restoring the independence of their republics and for their unification on a federalist base." The committee was represented by three presidents, Ramishvili (for Georgia), Mammad Amin Rasulzade (a Musavat, for Azerbaijan), and Said Shamil (for the Northern Caucasus).[40]

This was the beginning of the movement known as Prometheanism, which Timothy Snyder has called an "anticommunist international, designed to destroy the Soviet Union and to create independent states from its republics." Accordingly, it "brought together grand strategists of Warsaw and exiled patriots [Ukrainians, Georgians, Azeris, and others] whose attempts to found independent states had been thwarted

37 See JACAR, reference code: B11092836400.

38 This is based on documents and photographs of the residence of the exiled Georgian Social Democratic government in Leuville-sur-Orge (France).

39 See JACAR, reference codes: B03051163700 and A03023720600.

40 G. Targalski, "Les plans polonais concernant l'éclatement de l'URSS, le mouvement 'Prométhée' et le Caucase." *Bulletin de l'Observatoire de l'Asie centrale et du Caucase* 1997, no. 3, 11, and Mamoulia, ed., *Kavkazskaia Konfederatsiia*, 11-14, 67-68. On Rasulzade, see Aidyn Balaev, *Mamed Emin Rasulzade. Na chuzhikh beregakh 1922–1943* (Moscow: Maska, 2013).

by the Bolsheviks" and it was "supported by European powers hostile to the Soviet Union, morally by Britain and France, politically and financially by Poland."[41]

Poland further subsidized the publication of numerous periodicals and other publications by respective national groups, including Ukrainians and Central Asians. Although the Committee for the Independence of the Caucasus initially planned to publish its organ, *Nezavisimyi Kavkaz* (*Le Caucase indépendant*), in Istanbul in Russian, it abandoned its intention under the pressure of Turkish authorities (which feared complicating relations with Moscow). Instead, in the autumn of 1926 publication began in Paris of the journal titled *Prométhée* in French under the editorship of Georges Gvazava, a Georgian National Democrat. Allegedly, name of the monthly itself was proposed by Haidar Bammat and the first number composed in his flat in Paris.[42] Resisting the opposition of some members and supported by its Polish sponsors, the journal's first issue carried the subtitle "The National Defense of the Caucasus and Ukraine." From the spring of 1927, accepting the demands of the Azeris, it expanded to include Central Asia, hence the addition of Turkestan to the subititle: "The National Defense of the Caucasus, Ukraine, and Turkestan," with Mustafa Chokai joining the editorial staff as Turkestan's representative.[43]

To the extent that the Promethean movement depended on the support of foreign powers, it returned their favor with intelligence on the Soviet Union useful to them. The Eastern Section of Ekspozytura No. 2 (Bureau No. 2) of the Polish General (Chief) Staff Second Department (charged with intelligence, counterintelligence, and diversionary activity) was placed in charge of the Promethean movement and was headed by Edmund Charaszkiewicz.[44] Georgian military officers in exile also served in the Polish army. In 1926 in Warsaw, a new academic Institute of the East (*Instytut Wschodni*) was created, which was also closely linked to the Promethean movement.[45]

In this regard, it is worth noting that since the time of the Civil War in Russia, Poland and Japan had been closely cooperating in intelligence. Even though the political orientations of the two countries often diverged, they exchanged intelligence about the Soviet Union because of the common interests they shared against their gi-

---

41 Timothy Snyder, *Sketches from a Secret War: A Polish Artist's Mission to Liberate Soviet Ukraine* (New Haven: Yale University Press, 2005), 40. For more on this movement, see the monograph by Sergiusz Mikulicz, *Prometeizm w polityce II Rzeczypospolitej* (Warsaw: Książka i Wiedza, 1971).

42 Mamoulia, *Les combats indépendandistes des Caucasiens*, 101 and Mamoulia, ed., *Kavkazskaia Konfederatsiia*, 15.

43 Mamoulia, *Les combats indépendandistes des Caucasiens*, 101–2, 373–74, and Mamoulia, ed., *Kavkazskaia Konfederatsiia*, 15–16, 69, 71–72. On Chokai, see Bakhyt Sadykova, *Mustafa Tchokay dans le mouvement prométhéen* (Paris: L'Harmattan, 2007).

44 See Andrzej Grzywacz, Marcin Kwiecień, and Grzegorz Mazur, eds., *Zbiór dokumentów ppłk. Edmunda Charaszkiewicza* (Kraków: Fundacja CDCN and Księg. Akademicka, 2000), 12–15.

45 See Ireneusz Piotr Maj, *Działalność Instytutu Wschodniego w Warszawie 1926–1939* (Warsaw: Instytut Studiów Politycznych PAN, 2007).

Fig. 5.2. Georgian officers in the Polish Army in the 1920s, Warsaw.

ant neighbor.[46] Japan was thus familiar, to an extent, with the Promethean movement. As will be discussed, Japan sought to create a competing movement while also seeking to benefit from the Promethean movement by working with Poland.

At the time, Germany's Weimar Republic also took note of the Caucasian émigrés. The republic maintained at least superficially amicable relations with the Soviet Union (which was not a party to the Versailles Treaty) by signing the Rapallo Treaty in 1922 (implicitly directed against Poland). As is well known, the two countries even engaged in secret military cooperation in the 1920s. The German establishment, however, was not united in its policy toward the Soviet Union, and in 1925 Germany achieved a rapprochement with Western powers (Britain and France in particular) by signing the Locarno Treaty.

Moreover, those Germans disposed in favor of European democracies carried out political plans against the Soviet Union using anti-Soviet émigré forces, including those from the Caucasus.

The best-known case is that of the "counterfeit chervonets" (the Soviet currency of the time), an operation to unsettle the Soviet economy by massively infusing it with counterfeit money. This was to be followed by military operations in the Soviet-

46 See Hiroaki Kuromiya and Andrzej Pepłoński, *Między Warszawą a Tokio: Polsko-Japońska współpraca wywiadowcza 1904–1944* (Toruń: Adam Marszałek, 2009).

occupied Caucasus. In 1925–26, German General Max Hoffmann (who had led the German offensive against the Bolsheviks in February 1918), Alfred Nobel (whose oil interests in Baku had been confiscated by Moscow), and Henri Deterding (chairman of Royal Dutch/Shell, whose oil wells had also been confiscated by the Bolsheviks) conspired to use two Georgian National Democrats, Spiridon Kedia and Shalva Karumidze, for this purpose.[47] Kedia was charged with uniting all rightists of Georgia and the Caucasus. Counterfeit bills printed in Germany did reach the Soviet Union in 1927, although the impact on the Soviet economy was by all indications negligible since the Soviet secret police effectively forestalled clandestine operations. By 1928 the grandiose plan against the Soviet Union, which would have far exceeded the financial means of Deterding and others, was abandoned, and some of those involved were arrested in Germany.[48]

The political cohesion of the Caucasian émigrés was, however, undermined by the absence of the Armenians. Even though central figures of the Promethean movement and others sought reconciliation and cooperation with them, the latter's distrust of Turkey and Muslims made it difficult to join forces. Within each group there also occurred internal fighting over leadership and command (among the Northern Caucasians, for instance, Shamil did not get along with Bammat, Chermoev, or Kantemir). Moreover, Moscow made every effort to subvert the émigré movement directed against the Soviet Union through political manipulation and provocation. Mutual suspicion among political activists was widespread, as were accusations of connections with the Soviet secret police, who spread disinformation and carried out provocations intended to divide the émigré communities. The Poles in turn erroneously suspected that some Caucasian political activists, especially rightists such as Alikhan Kantermir and Haidar Bammat, were Soviet agents.[49]

---

47 The Foreign Office of Britain as well as Russian monarchists were also a party to this operation. In 1927 the British government severed diplomatic relations with the Soviet Union over Soviet espionage in Britain. In addition, at the time London was greatly disturbed by the Soviet construction of railways near the Soviet-Afghanistan frontier which London considered a preparation for invasion of Afghanistan and/or Persia by the Soviets. Britain drew up plans to bomb Baku and Grozny, the center of the Soviet oil industry. See Patrick R. Osborn, *Operation Pike: Britain versus the Soviet Union, 1939–1941* (Westport, CT-London: Greenwood Press, 2000), p. xvii. On Karumidze, see Françoise Thom, *Beria: Le Janus du Kremlin* (Paris: Les Éditions du Cerf, 2013), 74, 87–89.

48 See A. Norden, *Fälscher: Zur Geschichte der deutsch-sowjetischen Beziehungen* (Berlin: Dietz Verlag, 1960), and Andreas Dornheim, *Röhms Mann fürs Ausland. Politik und Ermordung des SA-Agenten Georg Bell* (Münster: Lit Verlag, 1998), 46. See also Mamoulia, *Les combats indépendandistes des Caucasiens*, 107–111 and Oleg Mozokhin, *VChK-OGPU na zashchite ekonomicheskoi bezopasnosti gosudarstva i v bor'be s terrorizmom* (Moscow: Iauza-Eksmo, 2004), 253–58.

49 See S.M. Iskhakov (ed.), *Iz istorii azerbaidzhanskoi emigratsii. Sbornik dokumentov, proizvedenii, pisem* (Moscow: Izd-vo Sotsial'no-politicheskaia mysl', 2011), 40. On an incident of Soviet provocation against Kantemir, see Mamoulia, *Les combats indépendandistes des Caucasiens*, 115–16.

While striving to divide émigré communities, Moscow also applied considerable pressure to Turkey to expel their leaders and activists. Thus in 1928, Simon Mdivani, the Georgian government's representative in Turkey, and his close collaborators (some of whom tried to penetrate the Soviet-Turkish borders for clandestine work in the Soviet Caucasus) were expelled from Turkey.[50] In 1929 the flats of both Shamil and Rasulzade were searched by the Turkish police and many documents confiscated. Soon the Committee for the Independence of the Caucasus in Istanbul disintegrated after the Georgians withdrew because Turkish authorities had paralyzed their activity.[51] Even before then, Bammat, Chermoev, Vachnadze, Kantemir, Sultanov, and other rightists had left the committee and sought to create a movement distinct from the Promethean group. Some rightist Georgians, such as Mikheil Kedia came under the influence of Italian fascism and Benito Mussolini. The legendary and charismatic figure of the Georgian émigré Leo Kereselidze supported the patriotic youth group Thethri Giorgi, sympathetic toward Italian fascism. In 1929 Bammat, who had distanced himself from the Promethean movement soon after its inception, and other confederalists began publishing in Paris a Russian-language journal, *Nezavisimyi Kavkaz* (the same title originally planned in 1926 for the organ of the Committee for the Independence of the Caucasus, which, however, adopted *Prométhée* in the end). They planned to issue the journal in French as well, but the journal ceased existence in 1930 after only three issues owing to financial difficulties. Nonetheless in that same year the Committee for the Independence of the Caucasus reconstituted itself in Warsaw, with just a small office left in Istanbul.[52]

The reinforcement of the Promethean movement and the spread of the committee's leaflets smuggled into the Caucasus alarmed the Kremlin because of the region's deep destabilization by Stalin's forced collectivization. The leaflets called on Caucasians to unite their forces in a common struggle against Red imperialism. Moscow's stance toward the Caucasian émigré activists now hardened, even to the point of terrorism. For example, Noe Ramishvili, one of the Georgian Social Democratic leaders and the main champion for reconstituting the Committee for the Independence of the Caucasus, was assassinated by Parmeni Chanukvadze, an OGPU agent in Paris, in 1930.[53]

50 Mamoulia, *Les combats indépendandistes des Caucasiens*, 123–24. Earlier the Soviet government had hatched a plan to assassinate Mdivani but did not carry it out (p. 104). The "North Caucasian publications in exile, without making any difference among them, were forbidden to enter Turkey by government decrees." See Çelikpala, "The North Caucasian Émigrés between the World Wars." 295.

51 Mamoulia, *Les combats indépendandistes des Caucasiens*, 125–26.

52 Mamoulia, *Les combats indépendandistes des Caucasiens*, 111–13, 128–29.

53 For the OGPU involvement, see K. Bylinin, A.A. Zdanovich, and V.I. Korotaev, "Organizatsiia 'Prometei' i 'prometeiskoe' dvizhenie v planakh pol'skoi razvedki po razvalu Rossii/SSSR," in *Trudy Obshchsetva izucheniia istorii otechestvennykh spetssluzhb* v. 3 (Moscow: Kuchkovo pole, 2007), 392. On Chanukvadze, see Józef Piłsudski Institute of America Archive, New York, Papers of Edmund Charaszkiewicz, sygnatura 3-1, fol. 25.

5.3 The Renewal of Japan's Interests in the Caucasus

Having grown into a major international power in the aftermath of World War I, Japan now sought to become an empire comparable to the world superpowers of the time. Going along with them to gain international respectability, Japan accepted a degree of disarmament and engaged in "liberal internationalism," which was "less dependent upon continental expansion than upon global trade and participation in the new international framework for peace."[54]

There was another aspect to this "new Japan": imperialist arrogance and ambitions tempered by the perception of disrespect on the part of Western powers. Famously, Japan's proposal for including a racial equality clause at the Versailles Peace Treaty had been rejected. The United States had already been alarmed by Japan's victory over the Russian Empire in 1905 and went so far as to devise war plans against Japan soon afterward (see p. 62). By 1923, the Anglo-Japanese alliance itself was terminated: despite Japan's contribution to British war efforts during World War I, Britain feared Japan's rise and preferred closer ties to the United States.[55] Moscow in turn willingly sought to exploit the rift between Japan and the Anglo-American alignment. Thus emerged the basic configuration of powers for the Pacific War twenty years later. But in the 1920s, the Soviet Union was still Japan's most important potential foe, especially for those Japanese strategists who dreamed of Japan's continental expansion.

Following the end of the Russian Civil War, Japan continued to be involved in Caucasian affairs. There was a considerable movement of people between the Caucasus and the Far East, especially Manchuria, which Japan closely monitored. Simon Ordzhonikidze (or Mikhail Nazarov, see p. 66), for example, was allegedly dispatched to Tbilisi in 1923 as chief of Japanese intelligence in Georgia; there he ran a cinema in the city. Fearing arrest, he "illegally" returned to Harbin in 1930, and his duty was taken over by the Socialist Federalist David Rostomashvili (see p. 104), who, like Ordzhonikidze, had moved to Georgia from Harbin. Also, between 1923 and 1930 three others (Giorgi Pitskhelauri, "Gurgenidze," and "Kobaliani") were sent to Georgia as "resident spies" for Japan, ten additional agents being dispatched with them. Kirill Gelovani and Serge Dzhokhadze were also consigned from Vladivostok to Georgia, along with thirteen other agents. Gelovani allegedly recruited additional agents in Tbilisi: in his 1937 confessions to Soviet authorities, he listed Zakharii Mirianashvili, a former board member of the Society of Georgians in Vladivostok, "Kutateladze," a government official, and Aleksi Purtskhvaladze, also a former board member of the Society of Georgians who settled in Kutaisi. Pitskhelauri was said to have used the wine trade as a cover for his work as a "Japanese spy" and to have reported to Japan

---

54 Frederick R. Dickinson, *World War I and the Triumph of a New Japan, 1919-1930* (Cambridge-New York: Cambridge University Press, 2013), 8.

55 Phillips Payson O'Brien, ed., *The Anglo-Japanese Alliance, 1902–1922* (London-New York: Routledge Curzon, 2004).

that shortly after the suppression of the rebellions in 1924, "counterrevolutionary [i.e., Georgian patriotic] elements" had revived in Georgia. Moreover, Rostomashvili and Dzhokhadze had allegedly created a "spy network" of twenty-two agents and collected information on the Caucasus railway, the timber and manganese industry, the Batumi and Poti ports, the composition and garrisons of the Transcaucasia Military District, and the coastal guard of the Black Sea.[56]

Even relatives of the future Soviet secret police chief Lavrenti Beria were among those who traveled between Georgia and the Far East. In 1915 Beria's maternal uncle Kapiton Kvaratskhelia moved to Harbin to join the business of another uncle of Beria's, Egor Dzhakeli. Kvaratskhelia returned to Tbilisi in 1926 or 1927, lived with Beria's family for a few months, and then moved back to Harbin, where he was joined by his daughter, who had lived with Beria. A few years later he went back to Tbilisi, and died in Sukhumi in western Georgia in 1951.[57]

There is no evidence that these and other movements were ordered by Japanese intelligence or that these people maintained any connections to Japanese authorities. In fact, as will be discussed in chapter 6, some of these Caucasian residents in Manchuria were Soviet agents working secretly for Moscow. Given Japan's presence in Harbin and elsewhere in Manchuria, these Caucasians no doubt had business and commercial connections with Japan and Japanese concerns. Soviet allegations about Japan's involvement came later in the 1930s. Pitskhelauri, for instance, stated under captivity in Soviet Georgia in 1937 that in 1924–26, his agents, Egor Dzhakeli, David Dvali, and Ivan Metreveli (all three mentioned on p. 67 in Chapter 3 as having been recruited as "Japanese agents" before World War I) had organized a number of incidents of sabotage on the Chinese Eastern Railway against Soviet interests.[58] These allegations made at the time of the Great Terror in 1937–38 are hardly credible. What is clear is that both Japanese and Soviet Intelligence were monitoring the movements of people between Manchuria and the Soviet Caucasus with suspicion.

Japanese Intelligence also undoubtedly regarded people from the Caucasus as potentially useful. In Japan's scheme against the Soviet Union, the Caucasus, far as it was from Tokyo or Harbin, occupied an important place, just as it had at the time of the Russo-Japanese War. In May 1928, Japan's ambassador to Turkey Yūkichi Obata, visited Baku and Batumi with his secretary and military attaché. Another group of Japanese headed by "Baron Ōkura" (likely to be Kishichirō Ōkura, a powerful businessman) had visited the Caucasus cities "three days earlier."[59] In 1928 Japan's military and naval attachés based in Moscow also traveled to the Caucasus, venturing

56 File of K.O. Gelovani, Archive of the Ministry of Internal Affairs of Georgia (Tbilisi).

57 O.B. Mozokhin, ed., *Politbiuro i delo Beriia. Sbornik dokumentov* (Moscow: Kuchkovo pole, 2012), 183.

58 File of K.O. Gelovani, Archive of the Ministry of Internal Affairs of Georgia (Tbilisi).

59 See AVP RF, f. 08, op. 11, papka 67, d. 340, ll. 1–2.

further from there to Persia, Afghanistan, India, and even to Central Asia.[60] Masatane Kanda, a Russian specialist working in Japan's military mission (Special Intelligence Agency) in Harbin, emphasized the Caucasus's significance in his report "Materials on Military Operations against the Soviet Union" (1928). His goals included: "To organize anti-Communist organizations in Southern Manchuria, Korea, and Sakhalin, and, responding to opportunity, to advance them into Northern Manchuria and Russian territory, thereby restraining the action of Russian military maneuvers; to establish an anti-Communist government in Russia depending on the situation of military developments, and to plan the overthrow of the Communist government in coordination with Siberia and the *Caucasus*."[61]

The importance of the Caucasus was not lost to another Russian specialist working in Turkey. Major Kingorō Hashimoto, Japan's military attaché in Istanbul from 1927 to 1930, became an ardent admirer of Mustafa Kemal Atatürk, the dynamic leader of modern Turkey, with whom he was said to have been personally acquainted.[62] In November 1929, Hashimoto submitted to Tokyo a memorandum, "The Situation in the Caucasus Region and Its Use for Diversion."[63] Hashimoto prefaced his memorandum:

> The Caucasus is geographically far from the center of the Soviet Union, and its nationalities and religions are diverse. It is an important point in the strategy against the Soviet Union in view of the fact, among others, that Russian culture is relatively limited there. The various nationalities in the Caucasus are, however, in conflict with one another and are not in a position to coordinate and carry out a mission. One has to say that it is very difficult to mobilize the entire Caucasus as a group against the Soviet Union, unless one occupies it militarily and forces it.[64]

Even though the Anglo-Japanese Alliance ceased in 1923, Hashimoto still believed that Britain would be a useful partner in Japan's strategy against the Communist regime. He noted:

> It is not impossible for Japan and Britain to work together and stimulate the territorial desire of Turkey and Persia and to use the two countries in order to mobilize the Caucasian Muslim states.

---

60 AVP, f. 0146, op. 11, papka 23, d. 2, l. 53, 110, 120.

61 National Archives and Records Administration (hereafter NARA), College Park, Maryland, USA, RG331, Doc. 2460A, 5–6 (emphasis added). As discussed in chapter 6 (see p. 140), Kanda later became Japan's military attaché in Turkey and played an important role in involving the Caucasians in Japan's strategy against the Soviet Union.

62 Subsequently Hashimoto became involved in radical military coup attempts in Japan. After their failures, he was dismissed to the reserve units. After World War II, the Occupation Forces regarded Hashimoto's involvement in coup attempts as having set the tone for Japan's subsequent military expansion and tried him as a war criminal. He was sentenced to lifetime imprisonment.

63 NARA RG331, Doc. 1989. This document fell into Soviet hands and is available only as a document submitted by Moscow as evidence of Tokyo's war crimes. See below p. 134 for the likely cause of the Soviet capture of this document.

64 NARA RG331, Doc. 1989, 2.

> At any rate it is absolutely necessary for Japan to maintain good relations with Britain in the event of conflict between Japan and the Soviet Union.[65]

Hashimoto then went on to discuss the "Great Armenianism" (a movement to construct a Great Armenian State from Armenian territory in the Soviet Union and Turkey), which he felt could be useful, if, and only if, Turkey turned against the Soviet Union. As long as Turkey was on friendly terms with Moscow, Great Armenianism was unrealistic. Although the Georgian independence movement would weaken the Soviet Union, according to Hashimoto, it would be necessary to guarantee Georgia's independence internationally. For this purpose, the support of Britain would be necessary. Hashimoto displayed a typical prejudice of the time: the Northern Caucasian mountaineers were of "such low cultural development" that even though they could be used for partisan warfare, they could not be depended on for important political purposes. As for using White Russians in the Caucasus, it would be disadvantageous because they would alienate the Caucasians.[66]

Having reviewed the Muslim movement, Great Armenianism, the Georgian independence movement, and the partisan activity of the mountaineers, Hashimoto concluded that a possible option would be to let the Caucasus fall into chaos by pitting these political movements against one another. The most important trigger for this scenario would be Great Armenianism, which would antagonize Turkey, Georgia, Azerbaijan, and others against Armenia and lead the Caucasus into disarray.[67]

In his memorandum, Hashimoto described Georgia as culturally closer to Europe than to Russia and as eager for independence. Therefore, Georgia, particularly its many intellectuals within the Soviet Union, was worth exploiting for subversion in the event of war. Hashimoto then noted that the Armenian people, by nature hardworking, were supported by the Armenian diaspora in Turkey and the United States. Again, typical of the racial and cultural stereotyping of the time, Hashimoto characterized Azerbaijan as culturally and politically less dynamic and less useful for Japan's strategic goals. The Caucasian "mountain peoples," Chechens, Dagestanis, Ossetians and others who had given the most trouble to the establishment of Soviet power in the Caucasus, Hashimoto emphasized, were difficult to use politically because of their ethnic diversity and their "low cultural development."[68]

---

65 NARA RG331, Doc. 1989, 2.

66 NARA RG331, Doc. 1989, 2.

67 NARA RG331, Doc. 1989, 2.

68 NARA RG331, Doc. 1989, 6–13. At the time, taking note of the presence in Turkey of Leon Trotsky, who had been expelled from the Soviet Union, and foreseeing his potential as a political ally, Hashimoto stationed a Japanese official named Nemoto (a Russian speaker married to a Russian) on Principo Island where Trotsky lived (Eitarō Tatamiya, *Hashimoto Kingorō Ichidai* [Tokyo: Fuyō shobō, 1982], 29). In April 1929, Hashimoto recommended to a meeting of Japanese military attachés in Berlin that they consider using Trotsky and his supporters exiled in Turkey for Japan's intelligence. This doc-

It is likely that Hashimoto associated with Caucasian émigré groups in Turkey. It is striking, however, that his views of the Caucasus were purely strategic and expedient. The Caucasus was important to him only insofar as it was useful for Japan's strategy against the Soviet Union. Not all Japanese military officers were like him, however. There were those who genuinely sympathized with the cause of the Caucasians, as will be seen. Yet the geographical distance of the Caucasus from Japan and the lack of common interests except for their anti-Russian/Soviet common front made Japan's Caucasian strategy innately weak. This weakness was to haunt Japanese-Caucasian relations throughout the period.

Hashimoto's interest in the "Caucasian Muslim states" outlined above is significant. By this time already, Tokyo had been energetically cultivating political relations with Muslim leaders from the former Soviet Union, developing what was called *Kaikyō kōsaku* or the Muslim Operation. After the Civil War's end in Russia, some ten thousand Tatar émigrés settled in the Far East, many of whom volunteered to work for Japan. Mukhammed Gabdulkhai Kurbangaliev (Muhammed Abdulhay Kurabn Ali in Turkish, 1892–1972), a former commander of the Bashkir military who fought alongside the White forces of Aleksandr Kolchak and Ataman Semenov in the Far East, was prominent among them. In 1922, he addressed a letter to Japanese authorities, stressing the importance of "Japanese-Turkish friendship" and the founding of "a world of equality and of humanity based on the principle of just world humanism." Kurbangaliev's missive was characterized by "an eclectic combination of Pan-Turkism and Pan-Islamism that appealed to Pan-Asianists in Japan, assuring that the vast Turkish populations in the Euro-Asian and North African continents befriended by Japan [would] aid the achievement of a just future for the peoples of Asia under the leadership of Japan."[69] He ended his letter with practical suggestions for the study and promotion of Turkic languages and cultures in Japan and an offer to help.[70] Whether Kurbangaliev wrote this letter on his own or in collaboration with Japanese supporters of the Islamic world, it found a ready response in Japan. Emigrating to Japan in 1924, he created Muslim societies, began printing offices, taught Islam at Muslim schools he created, and was closely associated with Japan's influential military leaders and politicians. He also assisted Japan's anti-Soviet intelligence from the 1920s to 1940s. In turn, Japan dreamed of a grand Muslim alliance against the Soviet Union extending from Japan and Manchuria to Xinjiang (Chinese Turkestan) and Central Asia and all the way to Afghanistan, Persia, Turkey, the Caucasus, and beyond.[71]

---

ument also fell into Soviet hands. NARA RG331, Doc. 1682. It is not known whether any contact was ever made between the Japanese military attaché and Trotsky.

69 Selçuk Esenbel, "Japan and Islam Policy during the 1930s," in *Turning Points in Japanese History*, ed. by Bert Edström (Richmond: Japan Library, 2002), 183.

70 Esenbel, "Japan and Islam Policy during the 1930s," 184.

71 Selçuk Esenbel, "Japan's Global Claim to Asia and the World of Islam: Transnational Nationalism and World Power, 1900–1945." *The American Historical Review*, 109, no. 4 (October 2004), 1157–70; Fu-

Also, Abdürreşid Ibrahim, a Russian Tatar (expelled earlier from Japan at the Russian government's demand [see chapter 3, p. 59]), again became involved with Japan in the 1930s. After emigrating to Turkey following the Russian Revolution, Ibrahim was from 1925 prohibited from engaging in pan-Islamic activity in Turkey. In 1929, however, "Japanese Military Attachés" in Turkey, likely Hashimoto and his assistants, visited him with an invitation to move to Japan,[72] which he did in 1933 (and where he died in Tokyo in 1944).

Although there is little evidence of close relations between Japan and Caucasian Muslims at the time, Moscow suspected Japan's influence among them and took appropriate actions through disinformation and provocation. Aleksandr Uralov (Abdurakhman Avtorkhanov), a Chechen historian, told the following story about Ingushetia in the Northern Caucasus in the autumn of 1930, about a year after Hashimoto sent his report to Tokyo on the Caucasus. A man claiming to be a secret envoy "from Japan" went around villages, held illegal meetings with authoritative Ingush figures, and made announcements about Japan's plans for war against the Soviet Union. The "envoy" set up "headquarters" in the house of former Tsarist army officer Radzhat Evloev in Dolakovo, Ingushetia. After visiting the villages, he convened an "inter-village united conference" to which influential Ingush known to be disposed against the Soviet government were invited. The conference took place in the house of Evloev who commanded much respect among those attending: Khadzhi Ibragim Tashkhoev, Mulla Geliskhanov, Shibilov Chada, Shibilov Said, Dalgiev Rans Uzhakhov Murad, and others. They knew one another, and they were also known among the Ingush people as loyal, energetic, and determined individuals.

At this illegal meeting, the "Japanese envoy" and Evloev had everyone present pledge individually with their hand on the Koran that they would never betray one another or the Japanese envoy. Then the envoy announced that Japan intended to declare war against the Soviet Union in the near future, and that other world powers would fight on Japan's side as well. Moreover, many oppressed peoples within the Soviet Union were supporting Japan. In the Caucasus, all the peoples but the Ingush had pledged support for Japan in the coming war. The envoy declared that he was authorized by Japan to invite the Ingush to take part in this peoples' liberation front. He spoke with considerable persuasive power and clear logic. The envoy announced at the end of his speech that until the start of the war, Japan would support its allies with money and weapons. To demonstrate that his were not empty promises, he offered money and weapons to the Ingush commanders and asked whether those present would approve Japan's plan for the liberation of Ingushetia. When they ex-

jio Komura, *Nihon isrāmu shi* (Tokyo: Nihon isrāmu yūkō renmei, 1988), 305–19, and Larisa Usmanova, *The Türk-Tatar Diaspora in Northeast Asia: Transformation of Consciousness: A Historical and Sociological Account between 1898 and the 1950s* (Tokyo: Rakudasha, 2007).

72 See http://www.archive.gov.tatarstan.ru/magazine/go/anonymous/main/?path=mg:/numbers/2010_1_2/05/03/ (accessed 7 July 2012).

pressed their agreement, the Japanese envoy appointed them commanders of military companies. The commanders received weapons of Japanese make and Japanese military badges. They were to receive money as their military underground work developed. As the war approached, they would receive orders for action. The commanders buried the weapons and badges in anticipation of war and their orders. They waited, but the war never came.

Instead, there came OGPU troops from Vladikavkaz. Massive arrests of Ingush took place, including those who had attended the meetings held at Evloev's house. Material evidence of their crime was dug up from under the ground. Evloev and the Japanese envoy, however, were not arrested. The latter turned out to be a Mongolian from Central Asia. Twenty-one people were executed, and up to four hundred were exiled without trial. For this operation, almost all major officials of the OGPU in Vladikavkaz were decorated by the Soviet government. Among them was one agent of the Ingushetia OGPU.[73]

Is this story true? If yes, it is one of numerous similar provocations carried out by the Soviet secret police: using fake anti-Soviet individuals and organizations, they uncovered real and potential enemies, the most famous provocation being the "Trust" (*Trest*) operation in the 1920s.[74] Even if untrue, the mere rumor about such an elaborate operation is indicative of the degree to which Moscow was concerned about Japan's renewed presence and influence and so strove to use its shadow to exterminate political opposition in the Caucasus.

However limited Japan's actual involvement in the Caucasus during the 1920s may have been, Moscow was ever vigilant of Japan's secret activities. If need be, it even faked them in the Caucasus as elsewhere. Such was the extent of Moscow's precautions and paranoia aroused by Japan's practice of total espionage during the Russo-Japanese War.

---

73 Aleksandr Uralov (A. Avtorkhanov), *Narodoubiistvo v SSSR. Ubiistvo chechenskogo naroda* (Munich, Svobodnyi Kavkaz, 1952), 31–33. We are grateful to Jeffrey Burds for drawing our attention to this book.

74 For the most recent work, see A.S. Gasparian, *Operatsiia "Trest." Sovetskaia razvedka protiv russkoi emigratsii. 1921–1937 gg.* (Moscow: Veche, 2008).

6 The Caucasus Group and Japan

The year 1931 marked an important turning point in the interwar history of the world. In September of that year, the Kwantung Army of Japan faked an attack on the railways under its control, then blaming the Chinese, began a full-scale military invasion of Manchuria. Although the Mukden Incident (or Liutiaohu/Jiuyiba [September 18] Incident) was not engineered or even sanctioned by Tokyo, the radical conspirators who staged it enjoyed enough support in the government and army for it to succeed. Their long-held ambition was to capture Manchuria in order to force it to serve the imperial needs of resource-poor Japan. Such blatant imperial aggression was bound to complicate Tokyo's international standing to the extreme. Once presented with a fait accompli, however, Tokyo went along, willingly or not, with the military conspirators, who escaped very lightly as Japan struggled with the political, diplomatic, and military consequences of the invasion. Ultimately, in February 1932, Tokyo let the radical military wing set up a puppet government in Manchuria, known as Manchukuo (or Manzhouguo), with Puyi, the last emperor of the Qing dynasty, installed as its nominal emperor. Seven months later Tokyo "recognized" the new state with its capital in Changchun (now renamed Xinjing, "New Capital").

Manchukuo encompassed not only Manchuria but also part of Inner-Mongolia (Hsingan or Xing'an or Barga). The foundation of Japan's puppet state thus brought Japan and the Soviet Union face-to-face over borders stretching some 4,000 kilometers (2,500 miles). (In addition, Manchukuo shared several hundred kilometers of borders with Outer Mongolia, or the Mongolian People's Republic, the first satellite state of the Soviet Union.) Moscow's offers of a nonaggression pact were refused by Japan. As tensions mounted in the east, Moscow fought hard to ease tensions in the west. In 1932 Moscow concluded a nonaggression pact with Finland, Latvia, Estonia, Poland and France, followed in 1933 by a similar treaty with Italy. The sharp realignment of international relations led inevitably to a realignment of émigré forces against the Soviet Union. Poland and the Polish-sponsored Promethean movement gave way to the rightist movements sponsored by Japan and Nazi Germany (after Hitler's ascension to power in 1933). The "Caucasus group" led by Haidar Bammat and financed by Japan now became the most active in subversion against Moscow.[1]

6.1 Moscow versus Tokyo

Japan's invasion of Manchuria and the foundation of Manchukuo were the cause of the instability that led eventually to the Pacific War. In this Moscow played a promi-

1 See Georges Mamoulia, *Les combats indépendandistes des Caucasiens entre URSS et puissances occidentales: Le cas de la Géorgie (1921–1945)* (Paris: L'Harmattan, 2009), ch. 3.

nent role. Although Moscow was not averse to recovering the territory the Russian Empire had lost to Japan in the war of 1904–05, it was keen to avoid any confrontation with Japan, at least one coordinated with a clash (most likely with Poland) in the West. Indeed, Stalin admitted, according to Karl Radek, that he feared a simultaneous Japanese-Polish attack at the time.[2]

Stalin's reaction to the Manchurian invasion is noteworthy. Even before the Mukden Incident of 18 September, Stalin was cautious. On 14 September, for example, he wrote to Lazar' Kaganovich (who, during Stalin's holidays away from Moscow, represented the Politburo's discussion of stronger measures against Japan's economic interests in the Far East) that it "is necessary to be more careful with Japan" and that, taking a principled position, the Politburo should be more flexible.[3] Five days after the Mukden Incident, Stalin wrote: "Most likely, Japan's intervention is undertaken in agreement with all or some great powers on the basis of expanding and strengthening the spheres of influence in China." He even suspected that some of the Chinese war lords supported Japan. Excluding Soviet military intervention and even regarding diplomatic intervention as undesirable, Stalin instructed the Soviet press to express opposition to any foreign military intervention in general, and the party newspaper *Pravda* to condemn severly the Japanese occupants, and to portray the League of Nations as a weapon of war (and not peace) and the United States as supporting the division of China. In addition, Stalin suggested that *Pravda* denounce loudly "the imperialist pacifists of Europe, America, and Asia" who were dismembering and enslaving China, and that the government newspaper *Izvestiia* do the same, but more moderately, which was "absolutely necessary."[4]

Stalin's remarkable restraint toward Japan's aggression did not satisfy everyone in Moscow. Stalin suspected that Commissar of Foreign Affairs Maksim M. Litvinov supported a much tougher stand. A few weeks after the Mukden Incident, when the Kremlin's "court poet" Dem'ian Bednyi published a poem in *Izvestiia* critical of Moscow's apparent inaction against Japan, Stalin attacked both men.[5] In 1932, when Moscow was alarmed by the increasing incursion of Japanese airplanes into Soviet airspace, Kliment E. Voroshilov, the head of the Soviet military forces, ordered they be shot down. Stalin immediately reprimanded Voroshilov on the grounds that the Soviet Union might be provoked into armed conflict with Japan. Stalin "categorically" prohibited shooting "without Moscow's permission."[6] Likewise, in the summer of 1932, Stalin was angered by the subversive work in Manchuria by the Soviet secret police and Soviet military intelligence that resulted in the arrest by Manchukuo-

2 Louis Fischer, *Russia's Road from Peace to War: Soviet Foreign Relations 1917–1941* (New York: Harper & Row, 1969), 222.

3 *Stalin i Kaganovich. Perepiska. 1931–1936 gg.* (Moscow: ROSSPEN, 2001), 103.

4 *Stalin i Kaganovich.*, 116.

5 *Stalin i Kaganovich.*, 32, 119–20, 122.

6 *Stalin i Kaganovich.*, 135, 141.

Japanese authorities of underground Korean operatives. Stating that such activities might provoke war with Japan, Stalin ordered that "draconian" measures be taken against the criminals in the secret police who were "agents of our enemies."[7] Even in May 1933, Stalin angrily denounced the party organization in Chita, across the border from Manchuria, for propagating slogans in Chinese directed against "Japanese imperialists and Manchukuo representatives."[8]

Needless to say, Stalin did not remain passive. His strategy was two-fold. At the same time he he was working to secure the western frontiers of the Soviet Union and embarking on a massive military buildup in the Far East, he was also making every effort to use the United States against Japan.

In the West, the Soviet Union courted Poland, Estonia, Latvia, and Finland and signed non-aggression pacts with each of them between January and August of 1932. But Moscow's offers of a nonaggression pact with Japan were rejected repeatedly. Further, Moscow concluded a non-aggression pact with France in November 1932 (ratified the following year) and even with Fascist Italy in September 1933. Although relations with Germany began to deteriorate even before Hitler's ascension to power in 1933, Moscow's security in the west was significantly enhanced by these treaties. Simultaneously, in view of Japan's aggression in the Far East, Moscow sharply increased military expenditure and expanded the armament industry.[9] The true scale of the military buildup was, however, carefully hidden from the world. In 1933, for instance, the People's Commissariat for Military and Naval Affairs claimed to have spent 1,421 million rubles, when in fact it spent 4,299 millions.[10] In February 1932, German diplomats in Siberia reported to Berlin that Soviet military forces with heavy artillery, armored cars, and air squadrons were being dispatched to the Far East at night under strictest secrecy.[11] At the same time, Japan estimated that within a year of the Mukden Incident, the number of Soviet infantry divisions in the Far East increased by three or four to eight or nine. In addition, in April 1932, Moscow ordered the formation of naval forces in the Far East. In Vladivostok, a naval port was resurrected and naval facilities were rapidly strengthened.[12] By 1933, Moscow had decided to replace its defensive position by an aggressive political offensive in the Far East.[13]

---

7 *Stalin i Kaganovich.*, 208.

8 RGASPI, f. 558, op. 11, d. 45, l. 135.

9 R. W. Davies, "Soviet Military Expenditure and the Armaments Industry, 1929–33: A Reconsideration." *Europe-Asia Studies*, 45, no. 4 (1993), 577–608.

10 Mark Harrison and R. W. Davies, "The Soviet Military-Economic Effort during the Second Five-Year Plan." *Europe-Asia Studies*, 49, no. 3 (1997), 369.

11 Intercepted cable in RGVA, f. 4, op. 19, d. 13, l. 131.

12 Saburō Hayashi, *Kantōgun to kyokutō sorengun* (Tokyo: Fuyō shobō, 1974), 53–54.

13 See recollections by Ivan Gronskii, editor of *Izvestiia*: Ivan Gronskii, *Iz proshlogo. Vospominaniia* (Moscow: Izvestiia, 1991), 147.

Simultaneously, Moscow sought to strengthen the home front in the Far East. In January 1932, for example, the Japanese general consul in Vladivostok reported to Tokyo that the Soviet secret police had been "feverishly" arresting people. On the night of 17 to 18 January 1932, as many as four hundred politically suspect people were arrested in the city, and the atmosphere there had become "very disquieting." According to the consul's secret agent, the situation in Nikol'sk (Nikol'sk-Ussuriiskii, today's Ussuriisk) in the north of Vladivostok was similar: all schools were closed to accommodate mobilized soldiers, and government facilities were evacuated to surrounding villages.[14] Here and there the Soviet secret police "uncovered" espionage-diversionary groups allegedly organized by the Japanese.

Moscow also sough to use the United States against Japan. Since the end of the Russo-Japanese War, American-Japanese tensions in the Far East had become ever more pronounced (see p. 62). Shortly after the war's end, Washington began drafting war plans against Japan, the first such undertaking by the United States in peace time. After the October 1917 Revolution, the Bolsheviks disclosed the many secret treaties the Tsarist government had concluded with imperialist powers and deliberately sought to pit the United States against Japan by misrepresenting the 1916 secret convention between it and tsarist Russia.[15] Although the secret convention was aimed against Germany, the two countries' common enemy at the time, the Soviet government published it under a sensational headline: "Secret Convention between Russia and Japan Had in View a Joint Armed Action against America and England in the Far East before the Summer of 1921."[16] This claim was, as Peter Berton has noted, a "patent falsehood and propaganda."[17] The participation of Japan and the United States in the Civil War in Russia's Far East had made their conflicting interests all the clearer,[18] and Moscow was keen to exploit the conflict to maximal effect. With this in mind, Leon Trotsky frankly noted in 1919 during the Civil War:

> The strengthening of Japanese forces in Siberia, in conjunction with the eclipse of Kolchak, would mean for America the Japanization of Siberia, and this she cannot accept lying down. In this event we probably might even reckon on direct support against Japan from the scoundrels in Washington. In any case antagonism between Japan and the United States would create a situation favorable to us in the event of our advancing into Siberia.[19]

In the wake of the Mukden Incident, Japan's aggression further spread to Shanghai in early 1932, greatly disquieting and ultimately antagonizing other imperial powers

14 RGVA, f. 4, op. 19, d. 13, ll. 191–92.
15 See p. 78 for the 1916 treaty, which included a secret convention.
16 *Gazeta Vremennago Rabochago i Krest'ianskago Pravitel'stva*, 8 (21) December 1917, 2.
17 Peter Berton, "A New Russo-Japanese Alliance?: Diplomacy in the Far East During World War I." *Acta Slavica Iaponica* no. 11 (1993), 72.
18 See p. 103 of the present book.
19 Jan M. Meijer, ed., *The Trotsky Papers, 1917–1922*, pt. one (The Hague: Mouton & Co., 1964), 622–23.

– Britain, France, Italy, and in particular the United States – all of which maintained extraterritoriality and had great economic stakes in the city. This incident thus provided an impetus to the eventual rapprochement between Moscow and Washington.[20] Japan's further expansion in China only aggravated the matter. In January 1933, to secure the southern borders of the newly created states, Japanese/Manchu forces invaded Rehe (Jehol) Province and eventually subdued it. The conquest resulted in the Tanggu Truce, a de facto recognition of Manchukuo by the Chinese Kuomintang government. This Japanese/Manchukuo military advance led one witness to later observe:

> In 1933 I went up to the province of Jehol as guide, interpreter, and ghostwriter to an Englishman who was reporting for an American news syndicate, and together with an American reporter and a couple of American military observers watched the Japanese overrun 100,000 square miles of territory in ten days. They did it by the use of motorized transport and by cutting through the Chinese forces and driving deep, paying no attention to their exposed flanks. This Japanese campaign in 1933 and not the German campaign in Poland in 1939, was the first tryout of the modern blitzkrieg. Only the Germans and the Russians seemed to have paid much attention. Other people thought it was just a lot of Japanese overrunning a lot of Chinese, and not worth study by professional soldiers.[21]

In response, Stalin made full use of the Marxist understanding of "contradictions between imperial powers," to pit Japan and the United States against each other. Most significantly, he sought diplomatic relations with the United States. Until then Washington obstinately refused to recognize the atheist Marxist state, but alarmed by Japan's expansion into China, President Franklin D. Roosevelt secretly began exploring a rapprochement with the Soviet Union, a move Stalin happily welcomed. Negotiations were conducted behind the scenes, the secrecy being necessary given the anticipated negative public reaction to a US recognition of the atheist state.[22]

Roosevelt planned his move carefully so that the United States' recognition would not expose the Soviet Union to Japanese threat. Fearing that Japan, reacting violently to the US-Soviet rapprochement, might attack the Port of Vladivostok, Roosevelt went out of his way to protect the Communist state by waiting for the port to freeze before announcing the recognition, since it would be difficult for Japanese battleships to strike

---

20 For the importance of the Shanghai Incident, see Tetsuya Sakai, "Nihon gaikō ni okeru soren kan no hensen (1923–37)." *Kokka Gakkai zassi* 97, nos. 3–4 (1983), 307–308.

21 Quoted in Robert P. Newman, *Owen Lattimore and the 'Loss' of China* (University of California Press, 1992), 21. See also Owen Lattimore, *Pivot of Asia: Sinkiang and the Inner Asian Frontiers of China and Russia* (Boston: Little Brown, 1950), 211.

22 On the United States, see Beatrice Farnsworth, *William C. Bullitt and the Soviet Union* (Indiana University Press, 1967), ch. 5, and on the Soviet Union, see Stalin's coded telegram on Litvinov's visit to the United States, RGASPI, f. 558, op. 11, d. 82, l. 43 and the Politburo directive to Maksim Litvinov (25 October 1933), f. 17, op. 162, d. 15, l. 119.

the port when frozen.[23] Thus Moscow and Washington formed a virtual united front against Japan.

This was a remarkable development whose significance for the course of international politics in the 1930s and 1940s cannot be overemphasized. By the end of 1933, the two countries had resumed diplomatic relations. In December of that year, Soviet Foreign Commissar Maksim Litvinov rang the tocsin of Japan's threat to American Ambassador William C. Bullitt soon after the latter's arrival in Moscow, stating that:

> he [Litvinov] and all other members of the Soviet Government considered an attack by Japan in the spring [of 1934] so probable that everything possible must be done to secure the western frontier of the Soviet Union from attack; that he did not fear an immediate attack by Germany or Poland or both combined, but that he knew that conversations had taken place between Germany and Poland looking toward an eventual attack on the Soviet Union if the Soviet Union should become embroiled in a long war with Japan; that he feared that a war with Japan might drag on for years and that after a couple of years Germany and Poland combined might attack the Soviet Union, Poland with the hope of annexing the Ukraine and parts of Lithuania and Germany with the hope of annexing the remainder of Lithuania, as well as Latvia and Estonia.[24]

Other Soviet leaders repeated Litvinov's concerns, except one: Karl Radek, a former Trotskyite supporter turned Stalin follower. Characteristically, Radek spoke too much and too frankly. According to Bullitt, Radek contradicted the foreign minister: "I had a long talk with Karl Radek, who does not believe that Japan will attack this spring, contrary to the belief of the members of the Government."[25] Still Litvinov sought American cooperation against Japan, telling Bullitt that:

> he felt that anything that could be done to make the Japanese believe that the United States was ready to cooperate with Russia, even though there might not be basis for the belief would be valuable. He asked whether it might not be possible for an American squadron or an individual warship to pay a visit during the spring to Vladivostok or to Leningrad. I said that I could not answer that question, but would submit it to my Government.[26]

Hoping to coordinate actions against Japan, Stalin sent the old Japan hand Aleksandr A. Troianovskii from Tokyo to Washington as first Soviet ambassador to the United States. In 1934, Karl Radek, acting as Stalin's personal diplomat, frankly noted that Moscow wanted to sabotage US-Japanese relations.[27]

---

23 AVP, f. 146, op. 16 papka 153, d. 10, l. 250 (Ambassador William C. Bullitt's remark to the Soviet side on 13 December 1933.) The Soviet diplomat G.Ia. Sokol'nikov, who received Bullitt, had to assure the United States that the climatic issue was no longer so vital because of the importance of air forces.

24 *Foreign Relations of the United States. The Soviet Union, 1933–1939* (Washington DC: U.S. Government Printing Office, 1952), 60.

25 *Foreign Relations of the United States. The Soviet Union, 1933–1939*, 57.

26 *Foreign Relations of the United States. The Soviet Union, 1933–1939*, 61.

27 RGASPI, f. 558, op. 11, d. 792, l. 1.

Despite these moves to contain Japan's aggression, Moscow was still in a vulnerable position. Even though the western borderlands were secured for now, a large-scale famine had struck Ukraine, resulting in millions of deaths, while an even more devastating one hit Kazakhstan. Meanwhile, in the neighboring Xinjiang, or Chinese Turkestan, Muslim rebellions threatened Han Chinese rule. In the Mongolian People's Republic, hasty socialist transformations (modeled on the Soviet experience) of pre-capitalist Mongolian society led to widespread rebellions, which Moscow sent armed forces to crush in 1932. All these developments destabilized the Soviet Union politically and raised questions about Stalin's leadership.[28] Moscow thus could not face the possibility of a confrontation with Japan. It is symptomatic of its position that in the spring of 1932, Moscow de facto recognized Manchukuo by allowing it to open two legations (in Chita and Blagoveshchensk), while Japan allowed Moscow to retain the already-existing Soviet diplomatic posts in Manchuria. Moscow's 1935 sale of the Chinese Eastern Railway to Manchukuo once again signified its recognition of Japan's puppet government.

Nevertheless, by 1934 Moscow appeared confident that it was more in control of Japan's aggression than in 1931 or 1932, while remaining ever vigilant about Japan's seemingly unpredictable behavior. To begin with, Soviet military forces were being strengthened at an accelerated pace. Washington further appeared to Moscow to be willing to work together to contain Japan in the Far East. Last, Moscow's intelligence operations had penetrated Japan and Manchukuo and their overseas legations quite successfully. In Moscow itself, Japan's legation had been repeatedly compromised by Soviet operations.[29] One of the most significant Soviet disinformation ploys involving Japan was Operation General, which started by sexually compromising the Japanese military attaché to Moscow in the late 1920s and continued into the period of the Great Terror.[30] As Georges Agabekov, a Soviet secret police official who defected to the West, testified, the Japanese embassy in Istanbul, the center of Japan's links to the Caucasian groups, was also penetrated by a "night-watchman there": "Through him we got hold of many despatches, which we deciphered." Using "two professional picklocks of the highest skill," the Soviet agent opened the Ambassador's strong-box and stole his cipher.[31] In Tokyo, Soviet military intelligence agent Richard Sorge began working successfully from 1933 onward. In Manchukuo, where Japanese authorities found it difficult to control order, let alone the constant migration of people, Soviet intelligence

---

28 See Hiroaki Kuromiya, "The Soviet Famine of 1932–33 Reconsidered." *Europe-Asia Studies*, 60, no. 4 (June 2008), 663–75.

29 See Hiroaki Kuromiya, "The Mystery of Nomonhan, 1939." *The Journal of Slavic Military Studies* 24, no. 4 (December 2011), 659–77.

30 See Arekusei [Aleksei] Kirichenko, "Kominterun to Nihon, sono himitsu chōhōsen o abaku." *Seiron* 2006, no. 10, 103–5, and "Duel' razvedok: Rossiia – Iaponiia," broadcast by Rosteleradio on 2 March 2005.

31 Georges Agabekov, *OGPU: The Russian Secret Terror* (New York: Brentano's, 1931), 209.

operations set up large and extensive networks using ethnic Chinese, Koreans, and other minorities (including some émigré White Russians) against Japan.[32] Indeed, the situation was almost the reverse of that of the Russo-Japanese War thirty years earlier. In the summer of 1937, the Japanese government estimated there were approximately two thousand Soviet "spies" in Japan and Manchukuo and fifty thousand "Soviet agents."[33]

Moscow's confidence was apparent in the statement made by Mikhail Kalinin (the nominal "Soviet president") in 1934. After speaking with Stalin, he noted that it was very difficult to understand Japan's policy (which he characterized as "endless adventurism") and that every year things were becoming easier for the Soviet Union. He went so far as to state:

> It's necessary for it to be widely believed that Japan is strong . . . . It'd be very good for us to have a fight with Japan and beat it soundly. If we beat Japan, no scoundrel in the West would poke his nose into our affairs. A war with Japan would not carry a direct danger.[34]

Clearly, Kalinin's statement reflected Stalin's judgment. How well Tokyo was informed of Moscow's confidence at the time is not known.

6.2 Japan and Caucasian Émigré Forces

Japan's aggression in China heightened the war scare in the Far East. At the time the world press "was filled with reports of the possibility of war between the Soviet Union and Japan. In 1932–33, the mood in the Soviet Far East escalated to one of panic over expectations of war with Japan, as Soviet defectors to Manchukuo at the time testified."[35] In 1934 and 1935 the tense situation eased somewhat, as noted earlier, owing in part to the rapid Soviet buildup of military forces. Nevertheless, Moscow suspected that certain radical circles within the Japanese forces might stage war against the Soviet Union despite the prevailing wishes of the Japanese government against it. The threat of war in turn heightened Japan's prestige among the émigré population from the Soviet Union the world over.

---

32 See, for example, "Zenmō ni haru rokoku supaimō." *Tōkyō nichinichi shinbun* (evening edition) 4 October 1933, 1.

33 GGSK, S.9.4.5.

34 "Nam bylo by ochen' vygodno podrat'sia s Iaponiei i osnovatel'no pobit' ee." *Istoricheskii arkhiv* 2008, no. 6, 15–17.

35 See Hiroaki Kuromiya, "Stalin's Great Terror and the Asian Nexus." *Europe-Asia Studies*, 66, no. 5 (July 2014), 777. Japan shared the information it obtained from the defectors with Poland. Both Japanese and Polish archives contain the records of their interrogations. On the Polish records, see, for example, Centralne Archiwum Wojskowe (hereafter CAW), Warsaw, Poland, I.303.4.2015.

In the Caucasus, the prospect of a Soviet war with Japan encouraged the rebels, or at least so Moscow feared. In the spring of 1932, for example, there was yet another uprising organized by the "counter-revolutionary kulak-mullah underground" in Chechnia and Dagestan. The leaders allegedly went around the bazaars and mosques to agitate for insurrection. They declared that the "Soviet Union is fighting against Japan. Each nationality must establish its own government, and in Chechnia a government of shariah and imam."[36] The uprising was subsequently crushed with the help of Red Army soldiers. Rumors of war with Japan thus provided a powerful incentive for insurrection in the Caucasus in 1932.[37]

Soon after the foundation of Manchukuo, Japan's military, expecting conflict with the Soviet Union and sensing opportunity, began expanding and strengthening anti-Soviet intelligence.[38] In October 1932, the General Staff in Tokyo and Japan's military attaché in Moscow issued a special instruction to the Japanese military attachés in Paris and Warsaw on subversion against the Soviet Union. The attaché in Paris, put in charge of Europe and Turkey, was to draw up detailed plans for Tokyo by April 1933. The instruction noted that the importance of Japan's position against the export of Communism by the Soviet Union and the Third International (also known as the Communist International or Comintern, an international organization promoting world communism) and the justness of war against the Soviet Union should be understood widely in the world. It further gave instructions on the following three points "as preparations": (1) to carry out measures that would destroy the fighting capacity of the Soviet Union as soon as possible after the outbreak of war; (2) to assist the independence movements of Ukraine, Georgia, and Azerbaijan and "disturb" (*kakuran*) these areas; and (3) to link the anti-Soviet émigré Russian organizations to their comrades within the Soviet Union, call up rebellions in the country, agitate for "pacifism [defeatism?]" (one word after was deliberately not spelled out in the instruction), and scheme for the overthrow of the Soviet government. In addition, the instruction urged that a friendly relationship be maintained with France, Poland, the Little Entente (that is, Czechoslovakia, Romania, and Yugoslavia), the Baltic states, and Turkey (which would help carry out the diversionary plans already mentioned). And it further dictated the expansion of diversionary and intelligence organs in Europe and Turkey

---

36 Quoted in "Vtoroe pokorenie Kavkaza: Bol'sheviki i chechenskie povstantsy." *Rodina* 1995, no. 6, 46. The impact of the international situation on the uprisings, see also G.V. Marchenko, "Antisovetskoe dvizhenie v Chechne v 1920–1930-e gody." *Voprosy istorii* 2003, no. 1, 136.

37 See N.E. Eliseeva, "Chechnia: vooruzhennaia bor'ba v 20-30-e gody." *Voenno-istoricheskii arkhiv* no. 2 (1997), 162.

38 Earlier, in February 1932, Jan Kowalewski, a Pole who had trained the Japanese in cryptography in Tokyo and was now based in Moscow as Poland's military attaché, was deeply disappointed by Japan's weak intelligence in the Soviet Union. Although military units were being sent to the Far East, Japan had not even actively organized intelligence on the Trans-Siberian Railway. See RGVA, f. 308k, op. 12, d. 120, ll. 8-8ob. Subsequently Japan addressed this problem with Poland's support.

once an opportunity for war had been recognized: in London, Paris, Berlin, Vienna, Helsinki, Tallin, Kowno, Warsaw, Bucharest, Istanbul, and Ankara, as well as Tehran and Kabul. Ironically, this instruction fell into Soviet hands and was subsequently submitted by Moscow at the Tokyo War Crimes tribunal following World War II.[39]

Japan's intensified intelligence activity in Europe, the Middle East, and the Balkan peninsula (particularly Romania and Yugoslavia) as well as the Baltic states was immediately noticed by the Poles, who were operating the rival movement of Prometheanism. The Poles described Japan's activity as relying on the "Turan Society" of émigrés from Turkestan and the Caucasus, an intelligence organization that was "naively conspiratorial." The Poles reported that Japan and its intelligence were pursuing "practical avenues," using, for example, commercial firms in Persia.[40] Furthermore, some Polish intelligence officials suspected, almost certainly wrongly, that Japanese and British intelligence services were working together in Turkey and Persia for technical and tactical reasons, that Japan was closely collaborating with Estonian intelligence with Britain's approval, and that Japan possessed "very fine intelligence elements in Soviet territory."[41] In December 1933, Japan also set up special operation stations in Paris and Berlin, which worked independently of the diplomatic legations. Unlike Britain and the United States, and conscious of competition with them, France had some ardent defenders of Japan's policy toward China, which they considered an ungoverned and ungovernable place unworthy of a nation. Paris, fearing the contagious effects of disorder in China on its Indochinese colonies, saw in Japan a strong hand that could ensure stability in China.[42] Probably for this reason, Japan was able to station special agents in Paris. Yet apparently responding to pressure from Moscow, France closed Japan's special station in Paris in December 1934, whereas the one in Berlin operated into the 1940s.[43]

Japan's striking blitzkrieg in Jehol, discussed above, also coincided with its withdrawal from the League of Nations (in February 1933). As an American reported from Geneva:

> The Japanese delegation, defying world opinion, withdrew from the League of Nations Assembly today after the assembly had adopted a report blaming Japan for events in Manchuria.

---

39 NARA, RG331, Evidentiary Document 2979.

40 Speaking in 1935, Noe Zhordania stated that Japan had received permission to build two naval bases in Bushehr and Mishach (?) in the Persian Gulf to surround the Caucasus. This cannot be confirmed by other sources. See Georges Mamoulia, ed., *Kavkazkaia Konfederatsiia v ofitsial'nykh deklaratsiiakh, tainoi perepiske i sekretnykh dokumentakh dvizheniia 'prometei'* (Moscow: Sotsial'no-politicheskaia mysl', 2012), 120.

41 RGVA, f. 308k, op. 19, d. 31, ll. 88-88ob, and CAW, I.303.4.1976 (18 November 1933 report)

42 See Patrick Beillevaire, "Apres *la Bataille*: L'egarement japonophile de Claude Farrere." *Les carnets de l'exotisme* v. 5 (2005), 243–45.

43 Ikuhiko Hata, ed., *Senzenki Nihon kanryōsei no seido soshiki jinji* (Tokyo: Tokyo University Press, 1981), 382.

> The stunned international conclave, representing almost every nation on earth, sat in silence while the delegation, led by the dapper Yosuke Matsuoka, clad in black, walked from the hall. The crowded galleries broke into mingled hisses and applause.
> (...)
> Matsuoka, usually typifying the placid oriental diplomat, was nervous before he began his speech, and abandoned the text before he finished. He shouted from the rostrum:
> "Japan will oppose any attempt at international control of Manchuria. It does not mean that we defy you, because Manchuria belongs to us by right."
> "Read your history. We recovered Manchuria from Russia. We made it what it is today."
> He referred to Russia, as well as China, as a cause for "deep and anxious concern" for Japan.
> "We look into the gloom of the future and can see no certain gleam of light before us," Matsuoka declared.
> He reiterated that Manchuria was a matter of life and death for Japan, and that no concession or compromise was possible, saying: "Japan has been and will always be the mainstay of peace, order and progress in the Far East."
> In objecting to proposed international control of Manchuria, he asked, "Would the American people agree to such control of the Panama Canal Zone; would the British permit it over Egypt?"
> "The Japanese people will oppose any such attempt in Manchuria. I beg of this body to realize the facts and see a vision of the future. I earnestly beg of you to deal with us on our terms, to give us your confidence."
> "To deny us this appeal will be a mistake. I ask you not to adopt this report," Matsuoka said earnestly.[44]

Matsuoka's defiance impressed some Germans. Whereas Germany's Reichswehr (military) and foreign ministry were sympathetic to the Chinese, the "brutal proceedings of the Japanese in Manchuria had favorably impressed Hitler deeply," a German diplomat noted subsequently. The diplomat, Eric Kordt, further noted:

> Matsuoka's "energetic" actions in Geneva influenced the German dictator to go to similar lengths. Though in his book "Mein Kampf" Hitler had judged the Japanese rather unfriendly, he suddenly discovered the "co-spirited nation of heroes." The "Japanese Army" became his favorite theme and soon he used to expend [*sic*, "expand"] on its values and force with as much vigor as ignorance.[45]

Japan's actions impressed the émigrés, raising their hopes for confrontation with the Soviet regime. Already in 1931–32 the Japanese military attaché in Warsaw, Hikosaburo Hata (1890–1959) was carring out "important work" with émigré Muslim leaders. Japan's agents implemented similar work elsewhere.[46] Among these leaders were undoubtedly those from the Caucasus. In February 1933 in Warsaw, Hata met with two Ukrainians – Roman Smal'-Stots'kyi (1893–1969, a former diplomat of the Ukrainian National Republic) and Volodymyr Sal's'kyi (1885–1940, former minster of war in the

44 See http://100years.upi.com/sta_1933-02-24.html (consulted 11 November 2012).
45 Dr. Eric Kordt, "German Political History in the Far East during the Hitler Regime," Hoover Institution Archive, E-1903, 4.
46 Kirichenko, "Kominterun to Nihon," 109.

Ukrainian National Republic), both prominent Promethean activists, along with two Georgians, Simon Mdivani (1876–1937) and "Zachariadze" (General Aleksander Zakhariadze [1884–1957], the former chief of the General Staff of the Georgian army). (It was reported that at this meeting the chief of the Polish Dwójka [second department, i.e., military intelligence], Teodor Frugalski, and Lieutenant Colonel Stefan Mayer were also present, a report later vehemently denied by the Poles.)[47] Clearly the Japanese were interested in the political-military issues of Ukraine and Georgia.

Although Poland did not officially recognize Manchukuo, a product of Japanese imperialism, the Polish-sponsored Promethean movement enthusiastically supported it. Its organ declared in the autumn of 1932: "In this time of anxiety, pessimism, perhaps even discouragement we are experiencing, Japan's official recognition of the independence of Manchukuo is an event that commands attention and does not fail to delight all friends of the liberty of peoples." China, torn by internecine wars, was neither a state nor a nation. There was little bond among its peoples regarding race, language, or religion. China was "chaos and anarchy." Under these circumstances, the "danger of Soviet Russia" was all important. It had already conquered Outer Mongolia and had Manchuria in its sights. The new state of Manchukuo, with a population of thirty million and supported morally and materially by a great power (Japan), was an "international personality." The most important issue was the "liberty of the Manchu people itself."[48]

Mukhamed-Gaiaz Iskhaki (Iskhakov, (Gayaz Isxaqiy, Ayaz Ishaki, Gaiaz Iskhakyi, 1878–1954), a leader of émigré Muslims from Kazan and Promethean activist, was even more enthusiastic about Manchukuo. In an essay published in Japan in 1934, he emphasized the historical struggle of Manchus and Mongols for liberation from Russia and China. He characterized Manchukuo as championing the culture of oriental peoples and Japan as providing spiritual and material support to ensure peace in the Far East. The peoples in Manchuria, according to Iskhaki, felt rejuvenated by the foundation of Manchukuo. Iskhaki added that there were approximately two million Muslims (and ten thousand Turco-Tatars) in the new state. His goal was to support the new country on all fronts and to become a happy witness to the "unification and fusion of our Islamic culture and Far Eastern culture." At the same time Iskhaki promoted the idea of independence for Idel-Ural (Volga-Ural): just as it was logical for non-Han

47 CAW, I.303.4.5515 (February 1933 report). See also Hiroaki Kuromiya and Paweł Libera, "Notatka Włodzimierza Bączkowskiego na temat współpracy polsko-japońskiej wobec ruchu prometejskiego (1938)." *Zeszyty historyczne*, v. 169 (Paris, 2009), 120.

48 Editorial: "L'indépendance de la Mandchourie," *Prométhée*, no. 71 (October 1932), 1–2. Speaking in 1935 at a conference of Caucasian political parties supporting the Promethean movement, Noe Zhordaniia was supportive of Japan's move, stating that the pressure of the 160-million strong country (the Soviet Union) was a "threat to the very survival of Japan as an independent country." Mamoulia, ed., *Kavkazkaia Konfederatsiia*, 118.

peoples to be liberated from the Chinese, so it was logical for non-Russian peoples to be freed from Russia, whose future would be dissolution into republics of nations.[49]

Against this background of support by émigré groups, Japan actively courted their leaders to take part in its schemes against the Soviet Union. Masatane Kanda (1890–1983), whose interest in the Caucasus was discussed in chapter 5 (see p. 123), was appointed as Japan's military attaché in Turkey where he worked from 1932 to 1934. The Caucasus occupied a special place in the projects of Kanda and the Japanese secret service. At the time about 80 percent of the crude oil of the Soviet Union came from the oil fields of Baku, Grozny and Maikop. In the event of war with the USSR, Japan hoped to paralyze the Soviet military machine by inciting a general uprising of Georgians, Azerbaijanis, and Northern Caucasians, whom Japan considered hostile to both Russian imperialism and Bolshevism. In Turkey, Kanda energetically carried out work with Caucasian émigrés. He detailed his activity there in a report he submitted after leaving his post in Turkey. This report, whose original does not seem to have survived World War II in Tokyo, was intercepted by Soviet intelligence. The content is known only from this intercepted version. According to the report,

> (1) In the Azerbaijan line, we've been able to win over [Hosrovbek] Sultanov [former minister of war of the Azerbaijan Democratic Republic]. It is desirable for him to work in Persia in the future. Presently we have him travel around . . . . His relatives and his former subordinates live in Persia near the Soviet-Persian borders. I consider that there is enough potential in him for actual work. We've given him a code-name "Doctor Polat [or Polatt]."[50]
> (2) In the Northern Caucasus line, we've won over [Muhammad Said] Shamil. We intend to entrust to him the task of carrying out anti-Soviet propaganda among the Muslims. I've ordered him to make such plans.[51]
> (3) In the line of Crimean Tatars, we've won over their representative Jafal Said Ahmed . . . . In case it becomes impossible to use him against the [Soviet] Black Sea Fleet, I have an alternative plan.[52]

---

49 See Hiroaki Kuromiya and Andrzej Pepłoński, "Between East and West: Gaiaz Iskhaki and Gabdulkhai Kurbangaliev." *Nowy Prometeusz* 2012, no. 2, 97.

50 Note, however, that Sultanov was a complex figure suspected of connections with the Soviet secret police and British secret services. Before and during World War II, according German sources, he also served as a particularly trusted German Abwehr agent in Turkey. Agabekov, *OGPU*, 183–84, and G. von Mende. "Die kaukasische Vertretungen in Deutschland während des Zweiten Weltkrieges," 21. Personal Archives of G. von Mende (Oslo).

51 In 1932 Shamil temporarily abandoned the Promethean movement, rejoining it only in 1938 and thus in 1934 was free to be contacted by Kanda. For his criticism of Poles and the Promethean movement and his contact with Germans, see a report by a Soviet agent in his entourage dated 11 January 1935 in Lev Sotskov, *Neizvestnyi separatizm na sluzhbe SD i Abvera. Iz sekretnykh dos'e razvedki* (Moscow: RIPOL KLASSIK, 2003), 284–88.

52 "Jafal Said Ahmed" refers, surely, to Dzhafer Seidamet [Kirimer] (1889–1960), one of the leaders of the Crimean People's Republic (1917–18). He later emigrated abroad and worked in the Promethean movement.

> (4) There are about one thousand armed forces we can dispatch to Soviet territory from Persia in the initial phase of our plan.[53]
> (5) In the Soviet-Turkish border areas we can organize about one thousand armed forces from Northern Caucasians living in Turkey . . .
> (6) At the present moment, the best chance to organize illegal communication networks within Soviet territory is by Azerbaijani groups across the Soviet-Persian borders.[54]

In February 1934, before his return to Tokyo, Kanda traveled in Iraq, Syria, Palestine, and Egypt for intelligence purposes. Kanda further wrote in his report:

> Our political and subversive activity should not be limited to Europe. We should consider all kinds of political and subversive activity against the Soviet Union using all means and from all aspects without limiting ourselves to Europe. One of the more or less desirable plans for us in this regard is to use Muslim states.
> In order to realize this plan, we need to create positions of trade and commerce in Afghanistan, Turkey, Persia, Arabia, Egypt and other countries. We have to dispatch sufficiently able officers to these countries under such disguise, because it is now very difficult to find appropriate diplomats for this work . . . .
> We need to conduct agitation among notable Muslim leaders in all these countries in order to create stations for combined political and subversive activity against the Soviet Union . . .
> If we follow the British example of using Arabic soldiers in Palestine during World War I, it is realizable. The Turkic race (in Azerbaijan) is by far the best of the Muslim groups in this regard. The Muslims are more militant than the Ukrainians. Furthermore, we have to emphasize that Chinese Muslims are incomparably militant.[55]

Grandiose though Kanda's scheme was, it appears to have become thoroughly known to Moscow through its intelligence operations. It is difficult to believe that the scheme achieved any significant success.

After World War II, Kanda wrote a memoir in which he stated that while working in Turkey, he sought to open a communication route to Azerbaijan from Persia, but that after a Japanese military attaché was appointed in Persia in 1933, he entrusted this work to him.[56]

---

53 According to Soviet sources and documents of the Promethean movement, in 1930–31 more than five thousand Azerbaijanis fled Soviet Azerbaijan because of the forced collectivization and repressions. Some of these refuges settled in the frontier zone on the territory of Persia and conducted partisan warfare against Russians. See L.S. Gatagova, L.P. Kosheleva, and L.A. Rogovaia, eds., *TsK RKP(B)-VKP(b) i natsional'nyi vopros*, kn. 1 (Moscow: ROSSPEN, 2005), 670 and 673, "Obzor politicheskoi raboty za 1932 g. organizatsii narodov, vhodiashchikh v ligu 'Prometei'," in Mamoulia, ed., *Kavkazskaia Konfederatsiia*, p. 34 and "Appel de Mir Yacoub (Président par interim de la délégation de la République d'Azerbaïdjan à Paris) à Son Excellence Monsieur le Président de l'Assemblée de la Société des Nations," 10 September 1930 (Personal archive of Georges Mamoulia).

54 Kirichenko, "Kominterun to Nihon," 108.

55 Kirichenko, "Kominterun to Nihon," 109.

56 Masatane Kanda, "Jōhō kinmu ni taisuru kaisō," available at Bōeishō Bōei Kenkyūjo Toshokan (hereafter BBKT), Tokyo, Japan.

The attaché in question, Masao Ueda, a Soviet specialist stationed in Persia in 1933–35,[57] also emphasized the importance of the Caucasus in Japan's strategy against Moscow. In his May 1935 report to Tokyo, Ueda wrote:

> The main groups in Transcaucasia are Georgians, Turkish people in Azerbaijan, and Armenians. They all have their own cultures, and, compared with other ethnic minorities, possess far stronger identities, occupy a core group of the population among the constituent republics of the Soviet Union, and play a very important role in the political and economic life of Transcaucasia.
> Most of the leaders of these groups live outside their states, that is Iran, Turkey, and other countries, causing political trouble of various kinds. Therefore all countries are deeply interested in subduing them politically. The importance of this situation has to be acknowledged from the point of view of planning subversion . . .
> It appears that now, instead of Muslim groups, there exist secret fascist groups of Azerbaijani Turks.
> In view of the distribution of the Azerbaijani Turks, their associations, and their tribal relations as well as their national characters, they present to us the best value for the purpose of subversion. The treasure of the Soviet Union, the Baku oil fields, is located in the area where they live. The outlook of these Turks is very similar to that of the Japanese. In view of all the points discussed above, they are the fittest for our work . . .
> In the western regions of Transcaucasia live also a small number of Greeks, Germans, and Persians. Of course, they don't like the Soviet regime, and probably are engaged in intelligence, subversion, and other activities [for foreign countries?].
> If we could identify able leaders from among the Caucasian peoples, they could become active forces at any moment of necessity.[58]

Ueda's report, like Kanda's, also became known to Moscow (almost certainly intercepted by the Soviet intelligence network). In any event, Ueda's grasp of Transcaucasia seems to have been somewhat shaky, and undoubtedly his plan did not go very far.

In his memoirs written after World War II, Ueda stated that he traveled to Tehran by way of the Soviet Union (by rail from Tokyo to Baku via Moscow, then by boat to a Caspian Sea port near Rasht, Persia, thence by car to Tehran). His assignment was to gather intelligence about the Soviet Union from south of the border. During his tenure in Tehran he traveled to the Soviet Caucasus, Turkey, Syria, and Iraq, and in July 1934, when attending a conference of Japanese military attachés in Berlin, he again traveled through the Soviet Caucasus. But he never discussed his clandestine operations in the Caucasus, perhaps because he achieved very little.[59]

Along with Japan's rise, Germany's transformation (from coexistence with the Soviet Union symbolized by the Rapallo Treaty in 1922 to Hitler's ascension to power in

---

57 Before Persia, Ueda had worked as the head of Japan's intelligence station in Manzhouli, on the Manchu-Soviet border, in 1930–31. From 1938 to 1939 (until forced to return to Tokyo when Poland was destroyed by Germany and the Soviet Union), he was Japan's military attaché in Warsaw.

58 Quoted in Kirichenko, "Kominterun to Nihon," 107–8.

59 "Ueda Masao ikō," 3 vols. available at Yasukuni kaikō bunko shitsu (Tokyo).

Fig. 6.1. A banquet of representatives of the Promethean movement in Paris, probably on the occasion of the signing of a pact on the Caucasian Confederation in July 1934.

1933) also stimulated émigré activities among the Caucasians. The rise of a man whose declared enemy was Bolshevism did not fail to raise the hopes of émigrés. Indeed, in 1933 Spiridon Kedia, Shalva Karumidze, Mikheil Tsereteli, and other rightists organized the "Union of Georgian Nationalists in Germany."[60] Yet Germany did not take the Caucasus question seriously until late 1936.

Meanwhile, the acceptance by the League of Nations of the Soviet Union as a member in September 1934 and the death of Józef Piłsudski, patron of the Promethean movement, in 1935 gave impetus to unification efforts among the Caucasian émigrés. A pact for a Caucasian Confederation was signed by representatives of the Promethean movement in July 1934. In 1935, the Committee for the Independence of the Caucasus was reconstituted as the Council of Caucasian Confederation.[61] Yet, like its predecessor, this council was unable to unite the anti-Bolshevik forces, with many rightists staying away.

60 Mamoulia, *Les combats indépendandistes des Caucasiens entre URSS et puissances occidentales*, 154–55.

61 Mamoulia, *Les combats indépendandistes des Caucasiens*, 147.

Another factor raised morale among the rightists: Italy's challenge to Britain and France by its invasion of Abyssinia in 1935. In 1936 Italy colonized and incorporated Abyssinia into Italian East Africa. Many Caucasian émigrés, particularly rightists, perceived Italy's actions as a manifestation of Italy's *national* rise and discipline.[62] (In fact, even the Promethean group reacted favorably to Italy's rise, arguing that Ethiopia was not a unified country but a small "empire," as it were, with its own oppressed peoples. Italy "brings liberty, order, and the benefits of civilization to the enslaved peoples of Ethiopia." It harshly criticized the League of Nations for condemning Italy's action while remaining silent about Moscow's subjugation of non-Russian nations.)[63] Italy's rising prestige also led to the creation in 1936 of an anti-Bolshevik and anti-Turkish Armenian-Georgian Union by sympathizers of Mussolini's Italy.[64] Like Germany, however, Italy did not regard the Caucasus as a region of priority until 1936.

6.3 The Caucasus Group and Japan

In view of possible war with the Soviet Union, Japan began earnestly looking for reliable allies among the émigré groups, including the Caucasians. Japan correctly saw Britain and France as being behind the Polish-sponsored Promethean movement. Even though Tokyo remained aloof, it did not entirely reject the Promethean movement since it did see in it political utility. In the Far East, for example, a Promethean Club was created in 1932 in Harbin by Poles, with Ivan Svit, a Ukrainian, as its head. Georgians and Tatars also joined the club.[65] But although Japan did not explicitly support the Promethean Ukrainians (who were inclined to support the social-democratic forces of the former Ukrainian National Republic) and was more inclined toward the monarchist supporters of Pavlo Skoropads'kyi and the more radical Ukrainian Organization of Nationalists, it did finance the publication of the club's organ *Man'dzhurs'kyi Vistnyk* under Svit's editorship.[66]

The Ukrainians, in turn, courted Japan. In 1931 the Ukrainian community in Manchuria had begun entertaining the idea of forming an independent Ukrainian state in the so-called Zelenyi Klin,[67] covering the regions of Transbaikal, Amur,

62 See G. Mamoulia, K-M. Donogo, and M. Vatchagaev, *Gaidar Bammat i zhurnal "Kavkaz"* (Makhachkala–Paris: Akhul'go, 2010), 208–209.

63 See, for example, the editorial "En marge du conflit." *Prométhée* no. 108 (November 1935), 1-4.

64 Mamoulia, *Les combats indépendandistes des Caucasiens*, 159–160.

65 On 26 May 1932, the Society of Georgians in Harbin, headed by Dr. Dzhishkariani, celebrated the Day of Independence and was joined by local Poles, Ukrainians, Azeris, and Mountaineers as well as the consuls of the United States, Poland, and Belgium. The tone of the speeches made emphasized the importance of the cooperation between the Caucasus and Ukraine and of a pact for a Caucasian Confederation. See *damoukidebeli sakartvelo* (Independent Georgia), Paris, 1932, no. 79, 15.

66 See Kuromiya and Libera, "Notatka Włodzimierza Bączkowskiego," 119–20.

67 See I. Kossenko, "L'Ukraine d'Extrême Orient." *Prométhée* no. 97 (December 1934), 4–8.

Khabarovsk, the Maritime Province, and Sakhalin. (The Zelenyi Klin, populated by up to half a million to one million ethnic Ukrainians who had emigrated or been deported there, was three times the size of Soviet Ukraine.) Also, in November 1934 those Ukrainians in Turkey (supporters of the Ukrainian National Republic) were disappointed by the Polish-Soviet nonaggression pact and so turned to Japan for support. They submitted to the Japanese military attaché in Istanbul an action plan in the event of war between Japan and the Soviet Union. The plan included creating special Ukrainian military units in the Far East as well as assassinating prominent Communists in Soviet Ukraine. Even if war did not break out, they hoped that Japan would support their independence movement as well as those by Caucasians and Central Asians.[68] In 1934 the Organization of Ukrainian Nationalists proposed a similar plan to Japanese diplomats in Paris.[69] What actually resulted from these proposals is not known.

Concerning the Caucasus, Japan ultimately chose the rightist groups. It never trusted those social-democratically minded elements in the Promethean movement. After Warsaw and Paris signed non-aggression pacts with Moscow in 1932, Japan saw a golden opportunity and sought to convert disillusioned activists from the Promethean movement. The foundation of Manchukuo, as discussed earlier, only enhanced Japan's prestige among them. When the Social Democratic Georgian government in Paris requested that Japan allow their representative to be charged with defending the interests of Georgian refugees stationed in Manchukuo, Japan seems not to have accepted the appeal. (In January 1933, Japan asked Paris whether the Georgian government was legitimate. Paris responded that after the French-Soviet pact, it no longer enjoyed the official status of diplomatic legation in France.)[70] In general, however, while avoiding the Georgian Social Democrats working for the Promethean movement (in other words, those oriented towards France, Britain and Poland), Japan courted the Georgian rightists, ideological adversaries of the Georgian socialists, and similarly minded Northern Caucasians, first in Istanbul, then in Berlin.

In the autumn of 1933, Kanda, Japan's military attaché in Turkey, asked the prior of the local Georgian Catholic Church, Father Shalva Vardidze, for contact with Georgian émigrés of rightist persuasion. Vardidze recommended to Kanda Spiridon Kedia, the leader of the Georgian National Democratic Party; General Giorgi Kvinitadze, a veteran of the Russo-Japanese War and World War I and former chief of the Georgian Army

68 Reproduced in *Trudy Obshchestva izucheniia istorii otechestvennykh spetssluzb*, v. 2 (Moscow: Kuchkovo pole, 2006), 122-126.

69 See Archives du ministère des Affaires étrangères (AMAE). Correspondance politique et commerciale 1914–1940. Z (Europe). Dossier Japon 1930-1940, no. 140, fol. 105-106.

70 See "Visite de Monsieur Matsoudaïra, attaché à l'ambassade du Japon," 12 January 1933. AMAE. Correspondance politique et commerciale 1914–1940. Z (Europe). Dossier Russie (Géorgie) 1919-1939, no. 653, fol. 312. In fact, Paris renounced its recognition of the Georgian government-in-exile and closed its legation in Paris.

(1918–1921); and Mikheil Tsereteli and Alexander Manvelishvili, leaders of the Georgian patriotic organization Thethri Giorgi. In view of the activity of the Soviet secret police in Istanbul, however, the Japanese transferred the matter to Berlin.[71] In Berlin, Shalva Karumidze, who, as noted earlier, was a founder of the Union of Georgian Nationalists in Germany, assembled Georgian rightist émigrés under the journal *Klde*. This journal came to be financed by Japan. In Berlin another link was made as well between Japan and the Caucasians: Roman Mkurnali (1887–1946), a Georgian National Democrat and former colonel in the Intelligence Department of the Georgian Army General Staff[72] who maintained contact with German intelligence, introduced Haidar Bammat and Karumidze to a Japanese intelligence officer named Matsui ("married to a Russian" who was close to Mkurnali's wife).[73] This event appears to have taken place in 1935, although it may have been the previous year.

In January 1934, Bammat (who had been given Afghanistan citizenship in 1925 by the Afghan king whom he had impressed with his erudition) began publishing in Paris the political monthly *Kavkaz* (Caucasus) in Russian, with an initial print run of seven hundred copies. Originally financed by wealthy Caucasian patrons (such as Georgian Alexis Mdivani married to the American millionaire Barbara Hutton, and the wealthy family of Tapa Chermoev, whose niece Bammat had married), by 1935 the monthly came to be financed exclusively by Japan; in fact, the Japanese embassy in Paris is said to have been the source of the finance.[74] The monthly became a pan-Caucasian political organ whose goal was to unite rightist Caucasian political groups under the idea of a Caucasian confederation.[75] Armenians, however, refused to cooperate with the Cau-

---

71 Mamoulia, *Les combats indépendandistes des Caucasiens*, 193–94.

72 G. Kvinitadze. Colonel-lieutenant Roman Mkurnali. Certificat. Kvinitadze Family Archive (Chatou, France).

73 In an earlier essay, Mamoulia concluded, based on Hiroaki Kuromiya's earlier suggestion, that this officer was Iwane Matsui. See Georges Mamoulia, "L'histoire du groupe Caucase (1934–1939)." *Cahiers du monde Russe* 48, no. 1 (January-March 2007), 46. Matsui indeed worked in Europe briefly in the first half of the 1930s. Subsequently we came to believe that "Matsui" was probably a code name and that the officer was likely to be Lieutenant Colonel Shigeki Usui. A Soviet specialist previously stationed in Moscow and Warsaw, Usui worked in Berlin in 1935–37, where he ran secret operations. Usui and Bammat maintained a close personal relationship. In December 1937 Usui left the Berlin subversion organ mentioned in the text to Colonel Takanobu Manaki. What Usui did in Europe thereafter is not known. After returning to Tokyo in July 1938, he headed the subversion department of the general staff. Strangely, however, he does seem to have had a Russian mistress in Moscow. See Hiroaki Kuromiya, "The Mystery of Nomonhan, 1939." *The Journal of Slavic Military Studies* 24, no. 4 (December 2011), 664. According to an émigré Russian medical doctor in Tokyo, Iwane Matsui was an Orthodox Christian, and "Iwane" derived from the Russian name "Ivan." (see Sergei Bunin, "Samyi znamenityi russkii v Tokio," http://www.sovsekretno.ru/magazines/article/2989, accessed 23 November 2012). If this is true, "Matsui" may well have been Iwane Matsui, but this story cannot be confirmed.

74 Patrick von zur Mühlen, *Zwischen Hakenkreuz und Sowjetstern. Der Nationalismus der sowjetischen Orientvölker im Zweiten Weltkrieg* (Düsseldorf: Droste Verlag, 1971), 29.

75 See Mamoulia, *Les combats indépendandistes des Caucasiens*, 194, 198, 200.

Fig. 6.2. Lieutenant Colonel Shigeki Usui, 1938.

casus group, while Azerbaijanis such as Sultanov (whom, as discussed above, Kanda reportedly had won over) and Khalil bey Khasmammadov (1873–1947, former minister of internal affairs and justice of the Azerbaijan Democratic Republic, subsequently ambassador of Azerbaijan to Ottoman Turkey) worked with the group around the journal. Both were bitterly opposed to the Musavat Party of Mammad Amin Rasulzade (who worked with the Promethean movement). Two Muslim Ossetians, Alikhan Kantemir (1886–1963, see p. 114) in Turkey and Tambi Elekhoti (1886–1952) in Paris, a lawyer and former president of the Revolutionary-Insurrectionary Committee of Ossetia who fought against the Whites and the Reds in the Civil War, worked closely with Bammat on the journal *Kavkaz*.[76] In early 1937, the journal began publication in the Turkish language under the title *Kafkas almanağı*, but in May it was banned under pressure from Moscow.[77] From June, the *Kavkaz* began publishing in Georgian

76 Mamoulia, *Les combats indépendandistes des Caucasiens*, 202–204.
77 *Kavkaz*, 1937, no. 5 (41), 38.

(*Kavkasia*) and French (*Le Caucase*) as well, and from autumn in English (*The Caucasian Quarterly*) and German (*Der Kaukasus*).[78]

It appears that not only Japan but also Germany and Italy financed the journal at some point.[79] In all likelihood, this was after Germany and Japan signed in November 1936 the Anti-Comintern Pact against Moscow, which Italy joined a year later.

In Riga, capital of Latvia, where Japan had stationed an intelligence center, its military attaché, who also served as military attaché for Estonia and Lithuania, employed two Georgians: Nina Shvangiradze, who subsequently married an American and moved to Cairo, and Mrs. Maria Maglakelidze, wife of the well-known Georgian emigrant leader Shalva Maglakelidze.[80] In his memoirs Maglakelidze notes that he was very close to Japan's master spy Makoto Onodera, who "spoke perfect Russian" and who in 1936 advised him to break with both the Georgian Social Democratic government in exile and the Promethean movement and create a right-wing Georgian monarchist organization. Maglakelidze immediately followed his advice, founding in February 1937 the Georgian monarchist group Kartlossi, which was politically oriented toward Japan and Germany.[81]

It is not at all surprising that the Caucasus group (assembled around the journal *Kavkaz*) joined forces with Japan. Their common interests against the Soviet Union united them, just as Poland and Japan closely collaborated in intelligence against Moscow throughout the 1930s.[82] But although the journal *Kavkaz* was clearly pro-Japanese and pro-Germany, it does not appear that it uncritically accepted Japanese imperialism or Nazism. In its first issue, *Kavkaz* declared that "our enemy today is the Soviet Union."[83] Yet the Caucasus group did not reject Russia as such. It would have been folly to ignore geography or deny the cultural and economic ties of the Caucasus to Russia.[84] It also took Turkophilism as politically more expedient than Russophilism because Turkey was the only neighboring power that could pose a counterweight to Russia.[85] The group was critical of the "political and social structure associated with classical capitalism that had gone bankrupt," but expected to utilize for a better world "all the experiences of political and economic creation in Europe and

78 Mamoulia, *Les combats indépendandistes des Caucasiens*, 211.

79 von zur Mühlen, *Zwischen Hakenkreuz und Sowjetstern*, 29, 40.

80 NARA RG263, 2002/A/10/3 (Makoto Onodera), v. 1, 3 (we are grateful to Professor Jeffrey Burds for providing us with a copy of this document). During the Second World War in 1942-43, Maglakelidze commanded the Georgian legion of the Wehrmacht. Bammat was in touch with the two Georgians.

81 See Shalva Maghlakelidze, "mogonebebi" [Memoirs], in V. Rtskhiladze, *kartvelebi meore msoplio omshi germanuli droshis kvesh* [Georgians in the Second World War under the German Banner] (Tbilisi: Ganatleba, 1994), 142.

82 See Hiroaki Kuromiya and Andrzej Pepłoński, *Między Warszawą a Tokio: Polsko-Japońska współpraca wywiadowcza 1904–1944* (Toruń: Adam Marszałek, 2009).

83 Mamoulia, Donogo, and Vatchagaev, *Gaidar Bammat i zhurnal "Kavkaz,"* 49.

84 Mamoulia, Donogo, and Vatchagaev, *Gaidar Bammat i zhurnal "Kavkaz,"*, 276, 558–59.

85 Mamoulia, Donogo, and Vatchagaev, *Gaidar Bammat i zhurnal "Kavkaz,"*, 277.

America."[86] Japan was a force that represented the "national" instead of the "international." Japan's historical mission was to liberate itself and Asia from European imperialism. The enslaved nationalities under Soviet Communism could see no danger from Japan or Germany. In fact, Japan was the "fortress of peace and order" in Asia, and Japan and Germany represented the forces against the Third International in the world.[87]

The Caucasus group, however, either underestimated or ignored Japan's imperial ambitions. While defending Japan in world public opinion, it vastly overestimated its military capability and believed, after Japan's military actions developed into full-fledged war in 1937, that eventually it would place China under control. China, according to the group, was in semianarchy and not a state, and its existence was supported by the Soviet Union. The Sino-Japanese war was thus in fact a war for the liberation of Asia from Russian imperialism.[88] Nothing was said of the atrocities Japan committed in China (the Nanjing massacre in 1937, for example). The group believed, or hoped, that Germany and Britain would draw together against the Soviet Union, praising Adolf Hitler as a "genius-leader [*genial'nyu vozhd'*]."[89] It was, however, silent on the imperialist nature of Nazism or its blatant racism or the Kristallnacht pogrom of 1938. Yet there is no indication that it subscribed to the political ideology of Nazism or Japanese militarism. In all likelihood, like statesmen all over the world, the Caucasus group thought and acted merely or mainly in the interests of its particular political goals. Japan and Germany supported the group out of their own strategic interests. The Caucasus group did unequivocally declare, however, that no external force should dictate its will in the Caucasus.[90]

This does not mean that there was no dissent within the Caucasus group. Vakhtang Tsitsishvili, a Francophile, for example, left the group in 1937 in opposition to its pro-Axis orientation.[91]

6.4 The Anti-Comintern Pact

The so-called Anti-Comintern Pact signed by Japan and Germany in November 1936 decisively set the course of events leading to World War II. Neither Japan nor Germany was united in this new step toward reconfigurating the international order. In conclud-

86 Mamoulia, Donogo, and Vatchagaev, *Gaidar Bammat i zhurnal "Kavkaz,"*, 147.

87 Mamoulia, Donogo, and Vatchagaev, *Gaidar Bammat i zhurnal "Kavkaz,"*, 145–56, 154–55, 179–81, and 73.

88 Mamoulia, Donogo, and Vatchagaev, *Gaidar Bammat i zhurnal "Kavkaz,"*, 348 and *Kavkaz*, 1937, no. 8, 1-3, 1938, no. 5, 21, and 1938, no. 10, 6–7.

89 Mamoulia, Donogo, and Vatchagaev, *Gaidar Bammat i zhurnal "Kavkaz,"*, 287, 412–13.

90 Mamoulia, Donogo, and Vatchagaev, *Gaidar Bammat i zhurnal "Kavkaz,"* 391.

91 Mamoulia, *Les combats indépendandistes des Caucasiens*, 252–53.

Fig. 6.3. General Giorgi Kvinitadze with his wife and daughters, the sons of Haidar Bammat, and Shigeki Usui, Chatou, France, 1936.

ing the pact, both hoped that other countries, especially Great Britain, Poland, and Italy, would join. Such proved not to be the case, however, except for Italy. Two events significantly influenced this turn of events. One, in Europe, was the Franco-Soviet Treaty of Mutual Assistance of May 1935. (This pact was concluded in response to Germany's rearmament, symbolized by the introduction of conscription, which violated the terms of the Versailles Treaty.) Indeed, its ratification by France in March 1936 was used by Hitler to justify his military advance into the demilitarized Rhineland, again in violation of the Versailles Treaty. In the East, the Soviet Union and the Mongolian People's Republic concluded in March 1936 a mutual assistance pact, which officially allowed Soviet military forces to be stationed in Mongolia in opposition to Manchukuo-Japanese forces across the border.[92] (Although this treaty violated Chinese sovereignty in Outer Mongolia, which Moscow acknowledged, Moscow and the international community ignored Chinese protests.) The Anti-Comintern Pact was concluded against this background of international alignment.

92 See Jakub Wojtkowiak, "Kontyngent Armii Czerwonej w Mongolii w latach 1936–1938." *Dzieje najnowsze* 40, no. 3 (2008), 3–13. In fact, already in 1935 Moscow had sent a military detachment to the Mongolian People's Republic. See Ts. Batbaiar, *Mongolia i Iaponiia v pervoi polovine xx veka* (Ulan-Ude: VSGAKI, 2002), 110.

Fig. 6.4. Shigeki Usui and the sons of Haidar Bammat, Chatou, France, 1936.

Disunity within Japan over the Anti-Comintern Pact appeared almost farcical. As in 1931, the civilian government failed to control the military, which had spearheaded the pact with Germany, and in any case the civilian government frequently changed hands. In March 1937, a little over three months after Japan signed the pact, Naotake Satō, the new minister of foreign affairs in a newly created cabinet, declared to the French press that "I was the first to regret the Japan-German Accord," that he intended to prevent the anti-Communist German-Japanese agreement from becoming a military alliance, and that there "should be no war between Japan and Russia during the next ten years."[93] Even before this political comedy took place, on 16 January 1937 Japan's ambassador to Great Britain, Shigeru Yoshida, visited Soviet ambassador Ivan Maiskii and frankly regretted Japan's pact with Germany, stating that he did not belong to the "aggressive school" of Japanese political thought. Criticizing the conduct of Japan's army and navy, he told Maiskii that the Japanese people would pay dearly for the army and navy's "stupidities" and that he hoped the pact with Germany would be the last "stupidity" of his government.[94]

In November 1937 Italy joined the pact, thus laying the foundation for the subsequent grouping of Axis powers. In July 1934, after Austrian Nazis assassinated the chancellor of Austria, Engelbert Dollfuss, Italian-German relations had become strained under Benito Mussolini. Fearing territorial dispute with an expansionist Nazi Germany, Mussolini openly protected Austria from Hitler's possible takeover attempt. Yet Mussolini's war in Ethiopia and his international isolation eventually drew the two dictators closer, ultimately leading Italy to join the pact. Japan, too, did not consider Italy particularly friendly. In Italy's war in Ethiopia, for example, Japan's unofficial sentiments were with the Africans fighting against the white European power,[95] although the Japanese government refused to assist Haile Selassie's empire. (According to a French source, in 1935 Japan placed Italy, along with Britain and the United States, as being hostile toward Japan.)[96] But in the end, like Germany, Japan came to recognize Italy's possession of Abyssinia in return for Italy's approval of Manchukuo. In both cases, Moscow had a strategic interest in keeping Italy pitted against both Germany and Japan, but its "rapprochement with fascism" failed,[97] paving the way for Italy to join the pact. Both Italy and Germany intervened militarily in the Spanish Civil War (which began in July 1936) to support the nationalist rebels led by General Francisco Franco. Fearing the expansion of anti-Communist forces to other parts of Europe, especially to France, Moscow intervened on the side of the Republicans.

The Anti-Comintern Pact, as the name implied, was aimed explicitly at the Moscow-based Comintern (Third International). Its general content – the public treaty with its supplementary protocol and the secret supplementary treaty – is well known. The actual content of these documents, however, is not. The public treaty's supplementary protocol, also signed on 25 November 1936, stipulated:

---

93 *Japan Chronicle*, 12 March 1937, 5. The minister added that French "Foreign Minister Delbos and ex-Premier Laval have given assurance that the French-Soviet Pact applied only to Europe and not to the Far East."

94 Ivan Mikhailovich Maiskii, *Dnevnik diplomata. London. 1934–1943* vol. 1 (Moscow: Nauka, 2006), 155.

95 See J. Calvitt Clarke III, *Alliance of the Colored Peoples: Ethiopia and Japan before World War II* (Woodbridge, Suffolk: James Currey Ltd, 2011).

96 See AMAE, CPC 1914–1940. Z. Dossier Japon 1930-1940, no. 142, fol. 239.

97 See Calvitt Clarke III, *Russia and Italy against Hitler: The Bolshevik-Fascist Rapprochement of the 1930s* (New York: Greenwood Press, 1991).

(a) The competent authorities of both High Contracting States will closely cooperate in the exchange of intelligence on the activities of the Communist International and on reconnaissance and defensive measures against the Communist International.
(b) The competent authorities of both High Contracting States will, within the framework of the existing law, take stringent measures against those who at home or abroad act in the direct or indirect employ of the Communist International or assist its subversive work.[98]

Although the public treaty and protocol spoke only of the Communist International, all those concerned (Germany, Japan, and the Soviet Union) understood that the protocol was directed against the Soviet Union. The secret supplementary treaty, however, called things by their names and referred explicitly to the Soviet Union. The following year, when the pact was expanded to include Italy, it stated: "Considering that the Communist International continues constantly to imperil the civilized world in the Occident and Orient, disturbing and destroying peace and order" and "that only close collaboration of all states interested in the maintenance of peace and order can limit and eliminate that peril."[99]

Virtually unknown in Western historiography is that after the Anti-Comintern Pact was signed, Hiroshi Ōshima, Japan's military attaché in Berlin who spearheaded the pact, further pursued an agreement with Germany to promote much closer collaboration in military intelligence against the Soviet Union. Despite the skepticism in Berlin and Tokyo, Ōshima convinced Wilhelm Canaris, head of the *Abwehr* (German military intelligence), of the utility of such an agreement. On 11 May 1937, Ōshima and Canaris signed in Berlin "An Additional German-Japanese Agreement on the Exchange of Intelligence concerning Soviet Russia."[100] The agreement stipulated that the two countries exchange intelligence in Berlin and in Tokyo "to be dispatched immediately to the home countries." It covered all important and unevaluated (i.e., raw) intelligence concerning the Soviet army and air force and the military industry as well as "pure counterintelligence" that each side obtained. In addition to supplying raw intel-

98 Here we have relied, with some changes, on an on-line translation available at the Yale University Avalon Project: http://avalon.law.yale.edu/wwii/tri2.asp. The original is found in Theo Sommer, *Deutschland und Japan zwischen den Mächten, 1935–1940: Vom Antikominternpakt zum Dreimächtepakt* (Tübingen: J.C.B. Mohr, 1962), 494.

99 http://avalon.law.yale.edu/wwii/tri3.asp (translation slightly modified), and the German original in Sommer, *Deutschland und Japan*, 499.

100 This is available at BBKT, Miyazaki Shūichi Bunko, 32: "Japanese-German Military Agreements concerning Intelligence Exchange and Subversion." The German text is reproduced below as Appendix (pp. 203–07). The Japanese version is reprinted in Nobuo Tajima, *Nachizumu kyokutō senryaku: nichi-doku bōkyō kyōtei o meguru chōhōsen* (Tokyo: Kōdansha, 1997), 197–99, 246–47. We have not examined the German archive carefully, but see John P. Fox, *Germany and the Far Eastern Crisis 1931–1938* (Oxford: Clarendon, 1982), 221, 380. The source Fox cites is Oberkommando der Wehrmacht, Ausland, Nr. 51/37, Chefs, Aus., 8 July 1937, which used to be held in the Foreign and Commonwealth Office of the Library and Records Department in London. Some time after Fox used it, it was removed from the library. Kuromiya's extensive research in London in 2007 and 2008 failed to locate the document.

ligence to each other, Germany and Japan were also to exchange their views of the intelligence shared. This secret agreement was officially approved by the Japanese army and the German Wehrmacht (armed forces) on 7 October 1937, with additional clauses on conducting joint anti-Soviet counterintelligence and holding an annual meeting to exchange and evaluate the intelligence shared between the two countries.[101]

The most interesting part of the agreement is the "Additional Protocol concerning 'Anti-Soviet' Plotting and Subversion (*bōryaku, Zersetzungsarbeit*)." In it, Germany and Japan agreed to collaborate in encouraging all national minority movements within the Soviet Union, promoting anti-Bolshevik propaganda, and instigating revolutionary activities, terrorist acts and sabotage activities at the outbreak of war. Further, the additional protocol specified that the main spheres of action be divided between the two countries: (1) the western borderlands (from Finland to Bulgaria) would belong mainly to Germany, (2) the southwestern borderlands (Turkey and Iran) to both, and (3) the eastern Asiatic front primarily to Japan. Clause Seven of the protocol, for example, stated that in case one party was drawn into war with the Soviet Union, the other would be obliged to escalate diversionary tactics by "all means possible" in the areas of primary interest (the western borderlands for Germany and the eastern, Asiatic front for Japan) as well as the area of mutual interest (the southwestern borderlands). The action plan of the protocol covered five years, from 1937–1941.[102]

The Ōshima-Canaris agreement also included as an appendix an intriguing five-year plan of joint action in the Caucasus area. For 1937, for instance, it included the following to be accomplished in Turkey: contacting and bribing important political figures, establishing contacts with "military sites" (the general staff), and building secret stations at several points near the Soviet borders (under the guise of commercial ventures).[103] The 1937 plan for Europe included training cadres recruited from the Soviet Caucasus and dispatching them back into Soviet territory. The 1938 plan for Turkey envisaged strengthening and increasing border stations, founding communication links through Black Sea boats, setting up courier routes, training and placing border crossers, and establishing cells in the Caucasus area and links with them.[104] Similar plans for Iran were drawn up for 1938. The 1939 plan for Turkey included establishing radio communication, studying airport construction, and training a core group for the creation of a Caucasian Army; the plan for Iran included establishing

101 Tajima, *Nachizumu kyokutō senryaku*, 208–09. Julius Mader, *Hitlers Spionagegenerale sagen aus: Ein Dokumentarbericht über Aufbau, Struktur und Operationen des OKW-Geheimdienstamtes Ausland/Abwehr mit einer Chronologie seiner Einsätze von 1933 bis 1944* (Berlin: Verlag der Nation, 1971), 197–98 and 314–15 discusses this agreement, which dates it to June 1938, which seems to be a mistake, although possibly an additional agreement was signed at that time.

102 See Hiroaki Kuromiya and Georges Mamoulia, "Anti-Russian and Anti-Soviet Subversion: The Caucasian-Japanese Nexus." *Europe-Asia Studies* 61, no. 6 (2009), 1,427.

103 Kuromiya and Mamoulia, "Anti-Russian and Anti-Soviet Subversion," 1,427–1,428.

104 Kuromiya and Mamoulia, "Anti-Russian and Anti-Soviet Subversion," 1,428.

links by Caspian boats and setting up radio communication. The plan for the Caucasus for the same year envisaged setting up cells in Baku, Grozny, Tbilisi, Vladikavkaz, and Batumi as well as along the oil transport lines. In 1940, the goals were carrying out a detailed study of military objects for air attack, importing weapons for Turkey and Iran, and preparing for a general uprising for the Caucasus. Finally, for 1941, the plan envisaged completing military preparations and organizing cadres of the Caucasian Army in Turkey.[105]

The Caucasus group, based in Europe and Turkey with financial and logistical support from Germany and Japan, was to be the action group for these operations. According to a German account, to avoid any conflict between Japan and Germany, it was agreed that Haidar Bammat, who headed the group, was to be considered a German agent, but that Japan retained the right to instruct Bammat directly concerning his tactical stand.[106]

Clearly, Turkey played the central role in the Japanese-German plan for the Caucasus. According to a postwar American investigation, in 1937 Japan sought to establish a "Turkish-Japanese Intelligence Association for the purpose of gathering information concerning Russian activities."[107] According to master spy Makoto Onodera, who was stationed in Riga as Japan's military attaché, subversive political activities, later to be "used for fifth column purposes," were planned at the time for Ukraine and the Caucasus. The Caucasus operation was "headed by a non-German agent of the Abwehr [almost certainly Bammat] but was entirely under Japanese control."[108] This Japanese control was exercised by the afore-mentioned special intelligence/subversion organ based in Berlin[109].

In view of its 1925 neutrality treaty with the Soviet Union, however, Turkey made every effort to appear friendly to Moscow. Certainly, Ankara did not officially work with Japan's intelligence. In May 1937, as noted earlier, just before the Ōshima-Canaris agreement, Turkey shut down the Turkish edition of *Kavkaz* which had just begun publication in the country, under pressure from the Soviet government. Yet Turkey appears to have condoned to some extent Japan's work in Turkey.[110] Some elements of the Ōshima-Canaris agreement were implemented immediately. In June 1937, as noted, *Kavkaz* began publication in Georgian and French and in the autumn in English and German.

---

105 Kuromiya and Mamoulia, "Anti-Russian and Anti-Soviet Subversion," 1,428.

106 Mader, *Hitlers Spionagegenerale sagen aus*, 197–98.

107 NARA RG263, Entry A1-86, Box 22 (Michael Kedia), 319. We are grateful to Professor Jeffrey Burds for supplying this information to us.

108 NARA RG263, 2002/A/10/3 (Makoto Onodera), v. 1, 3.

109 See Yuriko Onodera, *Barutokai no hotori nite: Bukan no tsuma no daitōa sensō* (Tokyo: Kyōdō tsūshin, 1985), 74.

110 Sotskov, *Neizvestnyi separatizm*, 100.

Using its extensive intelligence network, Moscow was well versed in the Japanese-German negotiations leading to the conclusion of the pact and was well aware of its content and secret supplementary protocol.[111] Moscow also certainly understood that the Anti-Comintern Pact was in fact an anti-Soviet pact. Given the supposition, as discussed earlier, that Moscow was in possession of the Japanese codebook stolen from the Japanese embassy in Turkey, there is little doubt that the Ōshima-Canaris agreement quickly became known to Moscow.

In 1937, just as Germany and Japan began collaborating, Poland and Japan also started working together more closely in anti-Soviet intelligence. The two countries, united by common interests, had already been working closely for some time, although unofficially. In 1937 Japan began to work, if tentatively, with the Poland-sponsored Promethean movement. From Stalin's point of view, this almost certainly signified a grand espionage alliance of Germany, Japan, and Poland (even though, as far as can be judged, at the time Germany and Poland did not officially collaborate in intelligence against the Soviet Union). At least, this is the picture Stalin presented to the Soviet nation.[112]

6.5 The Great Terror

Moscow used the German-Polish-Japanese nexus to justify the Great Terror in 1937. The Anti-Comintern Pact of November 1936 and the Ōshima–Canaris agreement of May 1937 appear to have been important factors. Another was Japan's threat in the East, combined with renewed Muslim rebellions in Xinjiang.[113] The Caucasus, ethnically complex to an extraordinary degree, was probably the most politically unstable border area in the Soviet Union. It was there that all the major powers schemed against the Soviet Union – Germany, Poland, Italy, Britain, France and, of all countries, Japan. It was in the summer of 1937, precisely at the onset of the Great Terror's mass operations, that Japan and Germany began cooperating in the Caucasus in anti-Soviet subversion. The Soviet Union thus saw Japanese hands all over the eastern and southern Soviet border areas.

As early as February 1937, "Turko-Tatar peasants" were deported from the Azerbaijan–Iranian borderlands, as witnessed by an English diplomat who happened to

---

111 Moscow's acquisition of the content of the pact and its secret protocol is explained in W.G. Krivitsky, *I was Stalin's Agent* (London: Hamish Hamilton, 1939), 32–36.

112 See Hiroaki Kuromiya and Andrzej Pepłoński, "Stalin, Espionage, and Counter-espionage," in *Stalinism and Europe: Terror, War, Domination, 1937-1947*, ed. by Timothy Snyder and Ray Brandon (Oxford University Press, 2014).

113 See Hiroaki Kuromiya, "Stalin's Great Terror and the Asian Nexus." *Europe-Asia Studies* 66, no. 5 (July 2014), 775–793.

be there illegally.[114] In fact, more than five thousand Kurds, Muslim Armenians, and Turks in Azerbaijan were deported from the southern borderlands.[115] "Mountain Jews" were also resettled from Kuba (Quba) in Azerbaijan to the Crimea.[116] Harsh repression in Georgia led to rebellions and massive border crossings into Turkey from Adjara.[117] In Chechnia and Ingushetia, from mid-1937 onward, people began fleeing and taking refuge in the mountains, where they organized small bands of insurgents.[118] Just as ethnic Koreans were deported en masse from the Soviet Far East in the autumn of 1937, so Kurds, Muslim Armenians, Turks and others were deported in 1937 and 1938 from the Caucasian border areas.[119].

The brutal repression of ethnic Greeks in the Black Sea coastal area (including the Northern Caucasus) was related to the Caucasian–Japanese subversion scheme: Kanda mentioned ethnic Greeks in his subversion plan, and Stalin did not forget that Greece had intervened twenty years earlier in the Civil War against the Soviet government with more than twenty thousand soldiers. Indeed, the secret order of the Soviet secret police on the Greek operation (No. 50215 dated 11 December 1937) explicitly stated: "Greek intelligence is actively engaged in espionage and insurgency in the USSR, carrying out tasks of British, German, and Japanese intelligence."[120]

It is not an easy task to determine the scale of terror in the Caucasus, given that there were many mass operations, such as the "kulak operation," the "Polish operation," and the "Latvian operation." Broad pictures do, however, emerge from available statistical data. In Georgia, for instance, from October 1936 to 1937 more than 12,000 persons were arrested for political crimes, of whom 7,374 were indicted.[121] Because the terror continued until late 1938, this is far from comprehensive data. Regarding the kulak operation, which targeted mainly formerly repressed peasants and other "socially alien" elements, 4,975 were executed and 6,229 were sent to the Gulag, although the

114 See Terry Martin, "The Origins of Soviet Ethnic Cleansing." *The Journal of Modern History* 70, no. 4 (1998), 813–14.

115 See *Stalinskie deportatsii 1928–1953* (Moscow: MFD, Materik, 2005), 75–80.

116 Jörg Baberowski, *Der Feind ist überall: Stalinismus im Kaukasus* (Munich: Deutsche Verlags-Anstalt, 2003), 771.

117 See CAW, I.303.4.1964 (December 1937 report).

118 S.S. Magamadov and S.A. Kislitsyn, *Politicheskaia vlast' i povstancheskoe dvizhenie na Severnom Kavkaze. Ocherki istorii 1920–1930-kh gg.* (Rostov-na-Donu: Iuzhno-Rossiiskii institut-filial RANKh i GS pri Prezidente RF, 2011), 298.

119 See A.N. Iakovlev, *Stalinskie deportatsii 1928–1953* (Moscow: Materik, 2005), 75–80. The deportation of Kurds from the Azerbaijan-Iranian borderlands began as early as December 1936. See N.F. Bugai, *L. Beriia – I. Stalinu: 'Posle Vashikh ukazanii provedeno sleduiushchee . . .'* (Moscow: Grif i K, 2011), 112.

120 Ivan Dzhukha, *Grecheskaia operatsiia. Istoriia repressii protiv grekov v SSSR* (St. Petersburg: Aleteiia, 2006), p. 52.

121 See *Lubianka: Stalin i Glavnoe upravlenie gosbezopasnosti NKVD 1937–1938* (Moscow: MFD, 2004), 415.

initial limits given by Moscow were 2,000 and 3,000, respectively.[122] To be exact, the order on the kulak operation included "Georgian Mensheviks, Musavats, Ittihads, and Dashnaks" as well as "bandits" as targets.[123] A considerable number appear to have been arrested and executed as part of this operation. Indeed, already at the February-March 1937 plenum of the Communist Party Central Committee in Moscow, Lavrenti Beria, at the time first secretary of the Party Central Committee in Georgia, stated that in the Caucasus there used to be strong anti-Soviet parties and that their remnants had turned into "our cursed enemies," "Fascist agents," and "agents of foreign intelligence services," now were "beating down the door of the headquarters of foreign military forces."[124] In April 1938 Beria asked Moscow to allow him to execute one thousand "Mensheviks, SRs [Socialist Revolutionaries], Socialist Federalists, and National Democrats" who had returned from abroad and formed illegal organizations and to dispatch an additional five hundred to the Gulag. Moscow approved Beria's request.[125]

Most tellingly, Stalin approved 3,483 executions in Georgia from the lists submitted to him in 1937–38. Georgia was slightly behind Ukraine (4,132). Given the size of Georgia's population (only 12 percent of Ukraine's), the terror in Georgia was far more intense than the one in Ukraine. Indeed, proportionately speaking, as far as the Stalin lists were concerned, Georgia was clearly the hardest hit of all the constituent republics of the country.[126]

Data on other parts of the Caucasus are less complete. Judging from the Stalin lists and the national operations, the terror in Georgia was more intense than that in Azerbaijan, which in turn was more intense than that in Armenia.[127] In all these lands, former Mensheviks, Musavats, and Dashnaks who had returned from abroad with amnesty were denounced as "saboteurs" and "spies" who had returned home specifically to destroy the Soviet Union. In 1936 there were more than fifteen hun-

---

122 See Mark Iunge, Gennadii Bordiugov, and Rol'f Binner, *Vertikal' bol'shogo terrora: Istoriia operatsii po prikazu NKVD no. 00447* (Moscow: Novyi Khronograf, 2008), 522–23. The initial figures were later raised to 9,000 and 10,530, respectively, although these limits were not actually reached.

123 *Lubianka: Stalin i Glavnoe upravlenie gosbezopasnosti NKVD 1937–1938*, 274. On "Ittihads," see p. 81 of the present book.

124 *Voprosy istorii*, 1995, no. 5-6, 13.

125 Iunge, Bordiugov, and Binner, *Vertikal' bol'shogo terrora*, 322.

126 See Leonid Naumov, *Stalin i NKVD* (Moscow: Iauza-EKSMO, 2007), 252, 257. As early as July 1937, Beria reported to Moscow that two hundred "counter-revolutionary elements" had been executed in Georgia and requested that no fewer than one thousand people (counter-revolutionary Rightists, Trotskyites, spies, diversionists, wreckers, and the like), excluding kulaks and criminals, be shot. See *Lubianka: Stalin i Glavnoe upravlenie gosbezopasnosti NKVD 1937–1938*, 255. For the Great Terror in Georgia, see also Georges Mamoulia, "Osobaia troika NKVD Gruzinskoi SSR (1937–1938). Mestnaia specifika i mekhanizm funktsionirovaniia," available http://www.chechen.org/prometheus13.html (accessed 26 December 2012).

127 Naumov, *Stalin i NKVD*, 253, 307. For the Great Terror in the three areas, see also "Stalinist Terror in the South Caucasus," *Caucasus Analytical Digest*, no. 22 (1 December 2010), 2–16.

dred of them.[128] Little reliable aggregate data are available on the other regions of the Caucasus. In the kulak operation, Chechnia, Ingushetia, Dagestan, and Kabardino-Balkaria appear to have experienced harsher waves of terror,[129] likely owing to the persistence of peasant insurgencies. Altogether, according to official data, in Chechnia and Ingushetia, 9,410 people were arrested in 1937 and 1938.[130] This included all major Communist leaders and government officials (including village Soviet chairmen) who were ethnic Chechens and Ingush. As a result, Soviet-educated local elites also joined the ranks of insurgents in the mountainous areas.[131] In Dagestan, in the 1930s–1950s (during the Stalin era), fourteen thousand people were repressed, seven thousand five hundred of them for political reasons.[132] One Dagestani political leader was accused of having proposed in 1926 that Haidar Bammat be invited back from abroad to help develop the Dagestani economy. He was executed in 1937.[133]

In the Caucasus as elsewhere, foreign connections were the leitmotif of the Great Terror.[134] In the sense that it meant to eliminate any and all potential internal threats, the Great Terror functioned as "total counterespionage."[135] Germany, Poland, and Japan were singled out as the most dangerous states intent on destroying the Soviet Union by encouraging nationalism and separatism. Significantly, Moscow denounced Muslim clergy in the Caucasus as in the Crimea, Central Asia, and Bashkiria for harboring Japanese spies among themselves.[136] Furthermore, in the case of the Caucasus, Turkey, ostensibly on friendly terms with the Soviet Union, was also added to this list of anti-Soviet powers. Alleged connections with Turkish intelligence were widely used against individuals and groups.[137] Similarly, an "important part of the standard accusation of nationalism in Armenia was cooperation with the 'anti-Soviet' organizations of the Armenian Diaspora."[138] Nationalists in the Caucasus would, according

---

128 Baberowski, *Der Feind ist überall*, 763.

129 See Iunge, Bordiugov, and Binner, *Vertikal' bol'shogo terrora*, 520, 521, 522–23, 556–58, 562, 564. For some additional details, see Alex Marshall, *The Caucasus under Soviet Rule* (London-New York: Routledge, 2006), 237–38.

130 O.B. Mozokhin, *Pravo na repressii. Vnesudebnye polnomochiia organov gosudarstvennoi bezopasnosti. Statisticheskie svedeniia o deiatel'nosti VChK-OGPU-NKVD-MGB SSSR (1918–1953)* 2nd ed. (Moscow: Kuchkovo pole, 2011), 459, 463.

131 Magamadov and Kislitsyn, *Politicheskaia vlast' i povstancheskoe dvizhenie na Severnom Kavkaze*, 297–99.

132 See *Repressii 30-kh godov v Dagestane. Dokumenty i materialy* (Makhachkala: Iupiter, 1997), 40.

133 *Repressii 30-kh godov v Dagestane*, 325.

134 On foreign connections, see Hiroaki Kuromiya, "Stalin's Great Terror and International Espionage." *The Journal of Slavic Military Studies*, 24, no. 2 (2011), 238–52.

135 See Kuromiya and Pepłoński, "Stalin, Espionage, and Counterespionage," 73–91.

136 See "Iaponskie shpiony sredi musul'manskogo dukhovenstva." *Antireligioznik*, 1938, nos. 8–9, 66–67.

137 See, for example, *Lubianka: Stalin i Glavnoe upravlenie gosbezopasnosti NKVD 1937–1938*, 250.

138 Eduard Melkonian, "Repressions in the 1930s Soviet Armenia," *Caucasus Analytical Digest*, no. 22 (1 December 2010), 7.

to Beria, staged armed uprisings to be coordinated with military intervention by a foreign power or powers. In Georgia, according to confessions by a Georgian accused as a "foreign spy," "the number of insurgent organizations that are willing to speak out at the request of the nationalist center reached approximately 10,000 people." According to another, "the rebel organization recruited 3,124 people."[139]

An explicitly Japanese nexus was seen in some cases. It is well known that the so-called *kharbintsy* (people from Harbin, or Soviet citizens who had been repatriated from China after the 1935 sale of Chinese Eastern Railway to Manchukuo), were extensively terrorized. As with the rest of the country, any connection to Japan and Manchukuo proved almost fatal in the Caucasus as well. At the time of the Great Terror Moscow claimed that "almost all Georgian colonists" in the Far East had been recruited by Japan into intelligence work, and that the Society of Georgians in Harbin, founded in 1906, along with its branches elsewhere in the Far East, was a cover for Japanese intelligence.[140] Moreover, it was alleged that Japan targeted Georgians who owned restaurant cars and the waiters who worked in them and travelled between China and Russia. This kind of intelligence was called *marshrutnaia agentura* (literally "routing intelligence"). Under Soviet captivity in 1937, Giorgi Pitskhelauri, for example, testified that he was recruited by Japan as early as 1906. To penetrate the Soviet Union, Pitskhelauri was urged by Japan to take up Soviet citizenship. Japan allegedly sent him in 1926 from Harbin to Georgia, where he engaged in "counterrevolutionary" activity. Arrested in 1937, he was executed in 1938 as a "Japanese spy."[141] Other similar cases were already discussed in chapter 5.

It is impossible to confirm now whether these individuals actually spied for Japan. Such accusations were standard at the time. Their past association with Japan in the Far East alone was enough to have them arrested in 1937–38. These cases, in turn, suggest that Moscow suspected Japan's long reach in the Caucasus throughout the 1920s and beyond.

Of course, it was most likely the case that many of these people were in fact Moscow's secret agents. It is easy to understand why they were executed in view of the fact that Moscow was killing many of its own officials of foreign intelligence at

---

139 Quoted in Levan Avalishvili, "The 'Great Terror' of 1937–1938 in Georgia: Between the Two Reports of Lavrentiy Beria," *Caucasus Analytical Digest*, no. 22 (1 December 2010), 5. For the nationalist center, see Beria's report to Moscow reproduced in Vakhtang Guruli and Omar Tushurasvili, "Correspondence between Lavrenty Beria and Joseph Stalin (1937)," Appendix to *The Archival Bulletin* (Tbilisi), no. 3 (Fall 2008), 49–52. On Abkhaziia, see the case of Nestor Lakoba as accounted by Beria's son in Sergo Beria, *Moi otets Beriia: v koridorakh stalinskoi vlasti* (Moscow: OLMA-PRESS, 2002), 49–43. For an account by Lakoba's relative, see Stanislav Lakoba, *Abkhaziia posle dvukh imperii. XIX–XXI vv.* (Sapporo, Japan: Slavic Research Center, 2004), ch. 4.

140 As late as 1941, the Georgian National Association in Harbin had about four hundred members and operated a Georgian-language school. Also in Harbin was the Armenian National Society which also ran an Armenian-language school. See *Rubezh* (Harbin-Shanghai), 4 October 1941, 14.

141 File of K.O. Gelovani, Archive of the Ministry of Internal Affairs of Georgia (Tbilisi), 7—107.

Fig. 6.5. Kapiton Kvaratskhelia (seated on the right) and his daughter Susanna (standing).

the time: 275 (or 68 percent) of the 450 Soviet foreign intelligence officials in Moscow and abroad were repressed.[142] Among those who escaped repression were some relatives of Beria (see p. 122). Beria's maternal uncle, Kapiton Kvaratskhelia, ran a station bar (restaurant) in Harbin, which he had done with the approval of the Soviet government. The Manchukuo/Japanese police repeatedly summoned him to report on who visited his restaurant. In 1937 he returned to Georgia from Harbin with Beria's help. His daughter Susanna, who had joined him in Harbin, and her husband, Petr Kozliakovskii, returned to Georgia earlier, probably in 1934. Subsequently Susanna was accused of having had contact with White Russian émigrés, and her husband of having been a White Army official. Her flat in Harbin was said to have been visited constantly by Japanese intelligence officials. Yet they (at least Susanna and Kapiton)

142 I.A. Damaskin, *Stalin i razvedka* (Moscow: Veche, 2004), 205. More generally, for the purpose of protecting clandestine operations, the Soviet secret police often killed its undercover agents when their utility expired. See Aleksei Tepliakov, " 'Otrabotannyi material': massovaia likvidatsiia sekretnoi agentury sovetskikh spetssluzhb v 1920–1930-e gody." *Rossiiskaia istoriia*, 2013, no. 4, 101–115.

were not repressed. Bogdan Z. Kabulov, then working in the secret police in Tbilisi, issued an order not to touch her. (Whether a similar order was issued regarding Kapiton and Kozliakovskii is unknown.) This almost certainly suggests that she performed special operations in Harbin on behalf of the Soviet government, for neither Beria nor Kabulov could have protected her simply because she was Beria's blood relative. Stalin did not save his own relations. Another relative of Beria's, Giorgi Dzhakeli, son of Egor Dzhakeli who ran a restaurant in Harbin, was said to have been recruited to spy for Japan as early as 1910 (see p. 67). Dzhakeli also worked in Harbin and returned to Georgia (probably in 1934 with Susanna). Like Susanna, he was accused of being a Japanese spy, and in 1937–1938, like her, he was protected by Kabulov. In 1938, he bounced back to Harbin, where he worked for the Japanese railway police and served in the military units of White Russian émigrés under Japanese command (the so-called "Asano brigades"). In 1945, he was arrested by the Soviet forces occupying Manchuria, accused of treachery, and sentenced to twenty-five years in the Gulag, even though he almost certainly acted in Harbin by the order of Moscow. Subsequently, after Beria's arrest in 1953, Giorgi Dzhakeli "confessed" to having spied for Britain by Beria's order! Under arrest, Beria denied such absurd charges.[143]

How did Bammat and the Caucasus group react to the waves of terror that had eliminated many of those who had worked with them before 1921, and those who may have maintained some clandestine links to them? Their public statements do not reveal much, but they may have misunderstood the events. Bammat, for example, commented on the destruction of the Red Army High Command that it was an "agony of the regime": it reflected the "absence of real government" – "a doomed regime and a doomed country."[144] In any case, one sees no sign of their being intimidated by the Great Terror or seeking any political accommodation with Moscow. On the contrary, in 1937–38 they seem to have had "no doubt about the collapse of the Soviet Union in the impending war":

> While the [émigré] Armenians and Georgians were dealing with their republics' borders with Turkey, the fantasy of Greater Azerbaijan, encompassing Iranian Azerbaijan, found adherents among the Azeri groups. Haydar Bammat criticized this idea severely. The second chance for the Caucasians (after 1918) was *knocking on the door*, and the Caucasian intellectuals had to be awake and organized. The mistakes of the past could not be repeated.[145]

---

143 See O.B. Mozokhin, ed., *Politbiuro i delo Beriia. Sbornik dokumentov* (Moscow: Kuchkovo pole, 2012), 183–84, 234–35, 482–83. This does not mean that in deploying his relatives and agents abroad, Beria did not pursue his personal political goals; in fact, he did. See Françoise Thom, *Beria: Le Janus du Kremlin* (Paris: Les Éditions du Cerf, 2013).

144 Mamoulia, Donogo, and Vatchagaev, *Gaidar Bammat i zhurnal "Kavkaz"*, 319–21.

145 Mitat Çelikpala, "The North Caucasian émigrés between the World Wars." *International Journal of Turkish Studies* 9, nos. 1–2 (2003), 312.

By contrast, Pavel Miliukov, a liberal Russian leader in exile, reached the curious conclusion that in the last analysis, Stalin was a defender of Russia's (not the Soviet Union's) national interests, and so came to terms with the Soviet government. He even implicitly supported the Moscow show trials.[146] In fact, as early as 1934 Bammat had criticized Miliukov and like-minded Russians of morally no longer being émigrés.[147] Others, such as Mustafa Chokai (Chokaev, Shokai, Chokai-ogly, 1890–1941), a Kazakh émigré who was also a leader of the Promethean movement, denounced Japan for "empty propaganda" directed at the Soviet Muslim population.[148] In 1938 Chokai went so far as to criticize Japan's support of pan-Islamism as anachronistic: it only aroused the suspicions of Britain, France, and "Russia" (the Soviet Union)![149] Such a statement, extraordinarily strange coming from a Promethean leader, no doubt reflected the fear created by the Great Terror in their homelands. At the time Japan was forcefully courting Chokai away from the Promethean movement to join Bammat's Caucasus group;[150] it is unlikely that Japan succeeded.

According to official Soviet statistics, in 1937 and 1938 more than 1.3 million people were arrested for political crimes. Of them, more than 680,000 were sentenced to death. Almost certainly the number of executions is underestimated: the real figure may be closer to 1 million.[151] This monumental scale of terror was meted out to a powerless population who were undoubtedly intimidated. At the time Polish intelligence reported "a massive border crossing in Adjara (in today's Georgia) in 1937 as a result of rebellions caused by intensifying political repression in 1936 and 1937. In turn, the Soviet Union was said to have sent its own agents to Kurdistan to incite anti-Turkish rebellions. Two Soviet agents were caught and executed by Turkey in 1937."[152] The Terror caused, according to its executioner, secret police chief Nikolai Ezhov himself, "great anxiety, incomprehension," "dissatisfaction with the Soviet government, conversations about the proximity of war, and a strong desire for emigration." Poland, Germany, Iran, Greece and other governments filed protests against Moscow. The strongest protest came from Iran (as Persia was renamed in 1935), which complained about the repression (arrest, exile, and confiscation of property) of Iranian citizens in the Soviet Union. (Among the deported were former Iranian members

---

146 See Jens Petter Nielsen's revealing book: *Miliukov i Stalin: O politicheskoi evoliutsii Miliukova v emigratsii (1918-1943)* (Oslo: Universitetet i Oslo, Slavisk-Baltisk Institutt, 1983).

147 See Mamoulia, Donogo, and Vatchagaev, *Gaidar Bammat i zhurnal "Kavkaz"*, 54.

148 See, for instance, Mustafa Chokai's bitter denunciation of Japan: CAW, I.303.4.5500 (5 November 1937).

149 JACAR, reference code: B02031852300 (Japanese diplomatic telegram of 1 June 1938 from Geneva to Tokyo).

150 See Chokaev's letter to A.I. Chkhenkeli dated 21 April 1939: BDIC, Microfilm 881, roll 123.

151 See Michael Ellman, "Soviet Repression Statistics: Some Comments." *Europe–Asia Studies* 54, no. 7 (November 2002), 1151-1172.

152 See Hiroaki Kuromiya, *The Voices of the Dead: Stalin's Great Terror in the 1930s* (New Haven: Yale University Press, 2007), 94–95.

of the Soviet Communist Party.) Iran, in turn, according to Ezhov, retaliated against Soviet citizens in its own country.[153]

Needless to say, the Soviet people could not openly express their dissatisfaction with the Soviet government. A Pole who visited Georgia in 1934, however, left interesting remarks: there were virtually no street signs in Russian, nor did he hear much Russian spoken in Tbilisi. Professors, most of whom were survivors from the prerevolutionary period, lectured only in Georgian. Collectivization progressed more slowly than elsewhere in the Soviet Union.[154] At the time of the Great Terror a foreign visitor to the Caucasus recorded the following stories. Fitzroy Maclean, a British diplomat, visited, without permission, the Caucasus in the middle of the Great Terror in 1937. In Lencoran (Lankaran), Azerbaijan, a port city just north of the Iranian border, he witnessed the deportation of "Turco-Tartar peasants." Then he noted:

> As we watched the lorries [with deportees] rolling down to the shore a youngish nondescript man, with nothing to distinguish him from any other Soviet citizen, came up to me with a copy of *Krokodil*, the official comic weekly. I saw that he was pointing at an elaborate cartoon, depicting the horrors of British rule in India. A khaki-clad officer, with side whiskers and projecting teeth, smoking a pipe and carrying a whip, was herding some sad-looking Indians behind some barbed wire. "Not so different here," the man said, and was gone. It had been a glimpse, if only a brief one, at that unknown quantity: Soviet public opinion.[155]

Later he managed to reach Tbilisi, Georgia, where he saw

> a historical film in Georgian depicting a rising of the Georgians against their Russian oppressors. It was received with enthusiasm by the Georgian audience and I could not help wondering if in their applause there was not perhaps a note of wishful thinking. The uniforms of the Tsarist troops, who fell such easy victims to the fusillades of the Georgian patriots, did not somehow look so very different from those of the N.K.V.D. [Soviet secret police] Special Troops who were to be seen walking about the streets of Tiflis [Tbilisi].[156]

However frightened they may have been, the peoples of the Caucasus had not lost their critical sense.

---

153 N. Petrov and M. Iansen, *"Stalinskii pitomets" – Nikolai Ezhov* (Moscow: ROSSPEN, 2008), 375 (statement of 4 August 1939 given under arrest). In 1937, there were approximately forty thousand Iranians (of whom fifteen thousand Iranian citizens) in Soviet Azerbaijan. See *Stalinskie deportatsii 1928–1953*, 100. Already in the 1920s, the Soviet secret police envisaged the expulsion of all Persian (Iranian) citizens from the border regions. Clearly this measure was not implemented in full at the time. See Baberowski, *Der Feind ist überall*, 400.

154 See Jan Otmar Berson, *Minus Moskwa (Wołga - Kaukaz -Krym)* (Warsaw: Rój, 1935), 104, 113, 124. It was only in 1933 that Georgia began training Russian language teachers. See Stephen Jones, "The Establishment of Soviet Power in Transcaucasia: The Case of Georgia 1921–1928." *Soviet Studies*, 40, no. 4 (1988), 629.

155 Fitzroy Maclean, *Eastern Approaches*, with a new introduction by Charles W. Thayer (New York: Time Incorporated, 1964), 34.

156 Maclean, *Eastern Approaches*, 42.

6.6 Clandestine Operations

In line with the Ōshima-Canaris agreement of May 1937, Japan soon implemented its intelligence operations in the Caucasus. Several cross-border links were attempted by the Caucasus group with Japan's support. Iran served as a bridgehead, where the Georgian patriotic organization Thethri Giorgi was active and collaborated with the Caucasus group. In Tehran, Bammat's representative (former general of the Tsarist, Georgian, and Azerbaijani armies V.D. Kargareteli, one of whose daughters worked as a dragoman at the Japanese embassy in Tehran) and Japan's military attaché worked together to organize clandestine activities. Moscow suspected that Japan was transporting weapons secretly to the region using freight boats in the Persian Gulf. One of the purported aims of the clandestine missions to the Caucasus was to explore ways to deliver these weapons to the region. In July 1938, for example, three Georgians and members of Thethri Giorgi, Bezhan Giorgadze, G. Vardiashvili, and M. Nikolaishvili, crossed from Iran along the Soviet border to link up with Soviet Georgia. This was not the first time Nikolaishvili had done so, since he had entered Soviet Georgia successfully in 1929. This time, however, the three were arrested soon after crossing the border.[157] In August and September 1938, shortly after Japan and the Soviet Union engaged in a small war in the Far East (the battle of Lake Khasan), Samson Kruashvili and Elizbar Vachnadze (old members of Georgian fighting forces), along with someone named "Kazim Bey," tried in vain to cross the Turkish-Soviet border into Georgia. But they did manage to dispatch emissaries, who then contacted a clandestine organization in Batumi, collected military and other intelligence, returned to Turkey, and reported back to Bammat.[158] In November 1938, Bammat and the Caucasus group succeeded in dispatching a mission (headed by Kruashvili) from Turkey to Batumi, where they met with members of the clandestine organization. Kruashvili instructed them to create secret cells elsewhere in the Caucasus (Kutaisi, Tbilisi, and Vladikavkaz) as well as one on a passenger liner in Batumi in order to maintain contact with the outside world. The expedition was successfully completed.[159]

Perhaps owing to these operations (which relied on cross-border family connections), in December 1938 Tbilisi asked Moscow to expel 180 families from the border regions of Georgia who had family links with those living on the other side of the bor-

---

157 The file of B.G. Giorgadze, Archive of the Ministry of Internal Affairs of Georgia (Tbilisi), 47–48, 150–165, 321. See also Sotskov, *Neizvestnyi separatizm*, 102–103, and Gela Suladze, *kartuli ant'isabch'ota emigratsia da sp'etssamsakhurebi (1918–1953 ts'.ts')* (Georgian Antibolshevik Emigration and the Secret Services) (Tbilisi: "erovnuli mtserloba," 2010), 269. Before fleing Georgia in 1930, Vardiashvili was said to have organized "armed bands" who terrorized Soviet officials.

158 Reports to Bammat by E. Vachnadze and S. Kruashvili (September 1938) from the Bammat family archive in Paris. This and other reports are reproduced in Mamoulia, *Les combats indépendandistes des Caucasiens*, 376–80.

159 Mamoulia, *Les combats indépendandistes des Caucasiens*, 228, 381–84.

Fig. 6.6. Haidar Bammat, his wife, Shigeki Usui, and two unidentified individuals, Lausanne, Switzerland, July 1938, just before Usui's departure to Tokyo.

der. They were said to be reserve forces for "Turkish intelligence" and foreign spies. Moscow approved the request.[160]

Turkey appeared to overlook Japanese-supported operations from its territory. In the spring of 1938, *Kafdağı*, a new version in Turkish of the closed journal *Kavkaz*, began publication in Turkey.[161] Ultimately, however, in view of its relations with the Soviet Union, Turkey considered it politically expedient to expel Alikhan Kantemir's group operating with Bammat from Turkey. This move was prompted by a meeting, held in Turkey between 6 and 10 August 1938, of Japanese military attachés from the Soviet Union, Turkey, Egypt, Romania, Syria, and Afghanistan, as well as other Japanese diplomats from the region. Bammat was invited to attend this conference. Under the cover of an economic conference, the meeting was convened to launch intelligence and subversion in the Caucasus and Central Asia, evidently to divert Soviet efforts from the Far East. Soviet intelligence knew in advance about the meeting and its true purposes, however, and lodged complaints with the Turkish government,

160 L.S. Gatagova, comp., *Sovetskaia etnopolitika, 1930–1940-e gody. Sbornik dokumentov* (Moscow: Institut rossiiskoi istorii, 2012), 207–208.

161 Mamoulia, *Les combats indépendandistes des Caucasiens*, 219.

Fig. 6.7. From left: Alikhan Kantemir, Khalil bey Khasmammadov, and Haidar Bammat, Istanbul, 1938.

so on 10 August Turkey was obliged to file a protest to the Japanese ambassador in Ankara. As a consequence, Bammat, Kantemir and their supporters were expelled from Turkey.[162] Many of them settled in Berlin for the time being, while Bammat found residence in Switzerland. Their expulsion in turn eliminated the suspicion of some émigré Armenians toward the Bammat group (which Armenians suspected of being pro-Turkish). Consequently, a small Armenian group joined the Caucasus group in 1939.[163]

In France, as in Turkey, Moscow made every effort to suppress émigré political activity. "The importance which Stalin attached to the activities of the Georgian émigrés," as one historian has noted, was "displayed in 1938, when the Soviet embassy in Paris brought effectual pressure to bear on a pusillanimous French government to ban

162 See top-secret Soviet references on Bammat and Kantemir in RGASPI, f. 82, op. 2, d. 1090, ll. 138–41, and the particularly illuminating report, dated 15 August 1938, by Captain Leleu of the French military attaché's office in Istanbul: Service historique de l'armeé de Terre (Château de Vincennes), Series 7 N-3227. Leleu correctly pointed out that Turkey also feared losing hegemony among the Muslims in Eurasia.

163 Mamoulia, *Les combats indépendandistes des Caucasiens*, 226.

a celebration of the 750th anniversary of the Georgian national poet Shota Rustaveli, which was to have been held at the Sorbonne."[164]

In fact, it is unlikely that foreign subversion was very effective or widespread within the Soviet Union in the 1930s, although Stalin's suspicions knew no limits. After all, Stalin was well acquainted with foreign machinations against his country, and as he famously said, even if 5 percent of the suspicions were true, it was still a serious matter.[165] As far as can be ascertained, the Caucasus group, for instance, had only a very limited link with its sympathizers in Georgia. Meanwhile, untold Soviet citizens were executed as "Japanese spies" during the Great Terror.

Foreign espionage and subversion were facts of international life. Soviet operations abroad were incomparably more extensive and effective than those of Japan, Germany, or Poland in the Soviet Union. In Britain, Japan, Manchukuo, and elsewhere Soviet espionage far surpassed the wildest imagination of the counterintelligence organs involved. For instance, Sorge penetrated the highest political establishment in Japan. Soviet agents literally filled Manchukuo, which could not control its long border with the Soviet Union. Ataman Grigorii Semenov, widely regarded as an anti-Soviet leader of the émigrés in the Far East in Tokyo's employ, was in fact working secretly for Moscow.[166] Likewise, the Soviet Union dispatched its agents through the Caucasus to its southern neighboring countries. As mentioned, according to a Polish intelligence report of December 1937, the Soviet Union sent its agents to Kurdistan to incite rebellions against the Turks, though they were caught and executed by Turkey. In the mid-1930s, Poland was catching approximately eighteen hundred people every year illegally crossing the Polish–Soviet borders; of these, Poland concluded that 85 percent were Soviet spies.[167] Bammat's Caucasus group, too, was penetrated by Soviet agents. Giorgi Gegelia, for instance, who once served as Spiridon Kedia's secretary, continued working with the Caucasus group at least until late 1938. It appears the group failed to suspect Gegelia's involvement in the assassination of Noe Ramishvili in Paris in 1930, even though he was kicked out of Kedia's group afterward. In 1947 Gegelia returned to the Soviet Union, along with other Georgian repatriates.[168]

---

164 David Marshall Lang, *A Modern History of Soviet Georgia* (New York: Grove Press, 1962), 258.

165 He said: "*esli budet pravda khotia by na 5%, to i eto khleb.*" His 2 June 1937 speech in *Istochnik*, 1994, no. 3, 79–80.

166 See Hiroaki Kuromiya, "Ataman Semenov's Secret Life." *Przegląd Wschodni*, 2014, no. 2, 535–556.

167 Information given by Polish to Japanese authorities: "Soren no chōhō hanchō ni tsuite" marked "Secret" and dated September 1936, BBKT, 14.

168 See Józef Piłsudski Institute of America Archive, New York, Papers of Edmund Charaszkiewicz, sygnatura 3-1, fol. 25; Mamoulia, *Les combats indépendandistes des Caucasiens*, 227; Sotskov, *Neizvestnyi separatizm*, pp. 101–02; and Thom, *Beria*, 78, 506, 512, and 774.

7 War and Dénouement

The events leading up to the beginning of World War II in Europe are well known, and yet much remains to be uncovered and analyzed. Japan's clandestine activity in Europe and the Caucasus is one example. Another is the conduct of the Soviet intelligence and counterintelligence network. These and other subjects remain to be elucidated precisely because the materials on them were either destroyed or are still held in confidence from researchers. Nevertheless, certain outlines of the hidden world of intelligence do emerge from the sources available to us. War had heightened expectations for the liberation of the Caucasus from Soviet domination. Ultimately, however, the vicissitudes of the times shattered those dreams. Significantly, the war also ended Japan's long relationship with Caucasian émigré leaders.

7.1 The Realignment of Forces

The rise of rightist groups (particularly the Caucasus group) caused a serious crisis among other émigré Caucasian political groups. Most importantly, the Polish-sponsored Promethean movement, based on a liberal-democratic notion of national liberation to which the Georgian Social Democrats, among others, subscribed, found itself in a serious crisis in face of the ascendant rightists. In 1937, the Caucasus group, financially supported by Japan (and Germany), became the envy of other groups. As discussed in chapter 6, the group did not subscribe to the racist ideology of Nazism and was not dependent on it, nor did it subscribe to narrowly nationalistic ideologies (such as Georgian, Azerbaijani, or Northern Caucasian nationalism). Instead it advocated the common regional and federalist interests of the Caucasus. It is not clear whether the Promethean movement understood this important yet subtle point. Bammat himself had long criticized the Promethean movement, both in his writings directly to its Polish sponsor and in his own journal, for relying on, among others, the Georgian Social Democrats, whom he characterized, somewhat unfairly, as "unpatriotic" and "pro-Russian."[1] By 1937, however, the Poles had come to recognize the advantages of the Caucasus group and the disadvantages of the Promethean movement. They recommended that émigré youth be detached from the Bammat group to make them "spiritually independent of Nazism and fascism" and to direct them toward a nationalism in the style of Józef Piłsudski (by which was meant Piłsudski's "realist" diplomacy and federalism).[2] Clearly, however, the Promethean movement

1 See Sergiusz Mikulicz, *Prometeizm w polityce II Rzeczypospolitej* (Warsaw, Książka i Wiedza, 1971), 180–83 and Andrzej Grzywacz and Grzegorz Mazur, "Ruch Prometejski w Polsce." *Zeszyty historyczne*, v. 110 (1994), 83.

2 Cited in Lev Sotskov, *Neizvestnyi separatizm na sluzhbe SD i Abvera. Iz sekretnykh dos'e razvedki* (Moscow: RIPOL KLASSIK, 2003), 313–14.

had steadily declined after the death of Piłsudski, its political sponsor, in 1935, and the new orientation did not stop its slide.

Despite these circumstances and differences in political orientation, Poland and Japan appear to have moved even closer than before in intelligence collaboration. This was all the more surprising in view of the Anti-Comintern Pact, in which Japan and Germany, Poland's potential foe, joined forces and treated the Promethean movement as something to be watchful over. Simultaneously, the German-Japanese press agency (Agence Telepress) based in Geneva was also trying to outdo the Promethean press agency (Ofinor).[3] Japan tried courting some Promethean activists at the time (see p. 163), but it did not succeed in the end. Although Japan began working, if tentatively, with the Promethean movement, its offers of financial assistance were rejected by Poland on the grounds that, in the Polish government's view, Japan was more interested in using the movement for political subversion and espionage than in supporting its political goals.[4] Poland had every reason to discuss the Promethean movement with Japan in order to prevent the latter from usurping it and, if possible, to detach Japan from Germany and draw it closer. At the same time, Japan had its own interests in the Promethean movement as an intelligence tool. In the autumn of 1937, Japanese foreign minister Kōki Hirota (1878–1948) instructed the foreign ministry's legations in Europe to organize an extensive intelligence network against the Soviet Union. Although one can know the content of this instruction only indirectly, it appears that Hirota and the Japanese ambassador in Warsaw, Shūichi Sakō (1887–1949), exchanged views on Japan's political use of the Promethean movement. Sakō cautioned Hirota that although Poland was extraordinarily friendly toward Japan (and that if war broke out between Japan and the USSR, Poland would use the Promethean movement to its full capacity to dismember the Soviet Union), Poland's friendly attitudes toward Japan would not be guaranteed in the event of a Soviet-Japanese rapprochement. In the end, Hirota urged the Japanese legations to use cultural organizations and exchanges as a cover for intelligence.[5]

This secret instruction appears to have been intercepted, or at least its content became known to Moscow. On 26 October 1937, the Soviet ambassador to Poland complained that Japan and Poland were forming an anti-Soviet bloc under the guise of cultural conventions.[6] In any event, Ambassador Sakō appears to have soon concluded that cultural conventions were too limited for Japan's purposes. Therefore, according to his 11 May 1938 telegram to Hirota, Sakō sent his assistant, Masutarō Inoue, on a "strictly personal basis," to the representatives of the Promethean movement

3 CAW I.303.4.5707 (February-March 1938 reports).

4 See Mikulicz, *Prometeizm*, 266–68.

5 GGSK, B.1.0.0.Po/R (11 May 1938 secret dispatch from Warsaw to Tokyo in four parts). See also Hiroaki Kuromiya and Paweł Libera, "Notatka Włodzimierza Bączkowskiego na temat współpracy polsko-japońskiej wobec ruchu prometejskiego (1938)." *Zeszyty historyczne*, v. 169 (2009), 127.

6 Archiwum Akt Nowych, Warsaw, Poland, MSZ, syg. 6653, 20.

to conclude some form of formal agreement with Poland. The Polish representatives responded to the proposal a few days later. The response was quite instructive. Although Poland's goal was to isolate the Soviet Union, it was not strong enough to break the "Soviet-French alliance"; therefore Poland strove to "disturb" Soviet-French and Soviet-British relations as much as possible. Poland explained that the Promethean movement was friendly toward Japan, that it was willing to share its most secret operations with Japan, and that Japan was welcome to utilize it fully. At the present moment, however, Poland was not willing to formalize its work with Japan; instead it wished to have "substantive cooperation". The *dépêche* went on to explain what Poland meant by operation, but unfortunately this section was erased (whited out), and there is no way to know what it said.[7] As far as the Caucasus was concerned, Japan's collaboration with the Caucasian activists of the Promethean movement appeared to remain rather limited,[8] although Japan seems to have broadened its contact with émigré activists from the Caucasus in general.

In contrast, Japanese-German collaboration in the realm of intelligence does not seem to have gone so smoothly. Although routine exchanges of information did take place in Berlin, Moscow, and elsewhere,[9] no "annual meeting to exchange and evaluate the intelligence shared," stipulated in the May 1937 agreement between Hiroshi Ōshima and Wilhelm Canaris ever took place. Nor did the two countries work together at all in the field of diversion, according to Ōshima's testimony after World War II. Furthermore, even though a German intelligence instructor was due to teach at a Japanese intelligence school, no one went from Germany to Tokyo for this purpose.[10] This awkward relationship had in fact to do with the sympathy that many Germans entertained toward the Chinese against whom Japan was fighting. German diplomat Hans von Herwarth, stationed in Moscow from 1931 to 1939, recalled the atmosphere of the time: "In spite of the German-Japanese alliance, my own sympathies and those of practically everyone in the Embassy were with the Chinese. . . . Later, during the battle of Shanghai [in 1937], we all cheered for the Chinese, because their forces had been trained by German officers. Everyone at the Embassy exulted over the stiff resistance the Chinese put up."[11] But in the end, Hitler forced the German military advisers to withdraw from China.

---

7 Kuromiya and Libera, "Notatka Włodzimierza Bączkowskiego," 128.

8 Kuromiya and Libera, "Notatka Włodzimierza Bączkowskiego," 129.

9 In Moscow, for example, a three-day meeting to exchange information about the Soviet Union took place in 1937 between Japanese and German military intelligence. See a report of 25 May 1943 from Berlin to Tokyo by Japan's former assistant military attaché in Moscow Etsuo Kōmoto, in The National Archives, Kew, UK (hereafter NA), HW35.10.2 (intercepted and decoded by Allied forces during World War II).

10 November 1959 interview given to Kenichirō Kōmura in "Bōchō ni kansuru kaisōroku chōshu roku' [Records of recollections concerning counter-intelligence] in Bōeishō Bōei Kenkyūjo Toshokan (BBKT).

11 Hans von Herwarth (with S. Frederick Starr), *Against Two Evils* (New York: Rawson, Wade Publishers, 1981), 113.

Meanwhile, the international situation began changing dramatically in both East and West. With the Anschluss in March 1938, Austria was absorbed into the Third Reich. From July to August of that year, fighting erupted between Japan and the Soviet Union along the Korean-Russian border (the Battle of Lake Khasan/Changkufeng/-Chōkohō). Both sides disagreed sharply on who was responsible for the battle and who had won. Until recently, the Soviet claim that Japan was the aggressor and that the Soviet side won the battle has been generally accepted in the field. But newly declassified Soviet military sources have suggested that Moscow in fact provoked the battle (to test Japan's knowledge of Soviet military forces in the wake of the defection to Japan's side of Genrikh S. Liushkov, the Soviet secret police chief in the Far East, who Moscow suspected had revealed vital information to Japan), and that Marshall V.K. Bliukher, the Red Army commander in the Far East, had resisted it, for which he was severely attacked by Stalin.[12] It has also become known that in the battle, more Soviet fighters were killed (759, plus 95 missing and 100 who died in hospitals) than Japanese (525 by Japanese accounts, and approximately 650 by a Soviet account).[13] This battle was followed in September 1938 by the Munich Agreement, which permitted Germany to occupy the Sudetenland of Czechoslovakia. This compromise was worked out jointly by Europe's major powers – Germany, Britain, France, and Italy – without Moscow's participation, prompting the Caucasus group to rejoice that the Soviet Union had now been marginalized in the event of peace or war in Europe.[14] The celebration was, however, premature.

The Munich Agreement also prompted Bammat, the leader of the Caucasus group, to reach beyond the Caucasus and create a Ukrainian-Caucasian committee in Europe.[15] Simultaneously he attempted to make the journal *Kavkaz* into this committee's organ.[16] Following Prague's loss of the Sudetenland, both Slovakia and Carpathian Ruthenia (Rus') declared autonomy within Czechoslovakia. The latter was soon taken over by Ukrainian nationalists, declaring itself "Carpatho-Ukraine." Japan is known

12 See *Glavnyi voennyi sovet RKKA. 13 marta 1938 g.–20 iiunia 1941 g.: Dokumenty i materialy* (Moscow: ROSSPEN, 2004), 138, *Voennyi sovet pri narodnom komissare oborony SSSR: Dokumenty i materialy. 1938, 1940 gg.* (Moscow: ROSSPEN, 2006), 211, 213, 255–56; and Nikolai Velikanov, *Bliukher* (Moscow: Molodaia gvardiia, 2010), 266. Bliukher was soon arrested, tortured, and died in prison on 9 November 1938. For more detail, see Hiroaki Kuromiya, "The Battle of Lake Khasan Reconsidered." *The Journal of Slavic Military Studies* 29, no. 1 (2016), 99–109.

13 G.F. Krivosheev, *Rossiia i SSSR v voinakh XX veka: Poteri vooruzhennykh sil. Statisticheskoe issledovanie* (Moscow: OLMA-PRESS, 2001), 173.

14 *Kavkaz*, 1938, no. 7, 4, and G. Mamoulia, K.M. Donogo, and M. Vatchagaev, *Gaidar Bammat i zhurnal "Kavkaz"* (Makhachkala–Paris: Akhul'go, 2010), 399–401.

15 See the French police report: Service historique de l'armée de Terre (Château de Vincennes) Series 7 N-3086. For Bammat's contact with the Ukrainians, see also NARA RG263, Entry A1-86, Box 22 (Michael Kedia, 22 March 1948 intelligence report).

16 H. Bammat, Letter to O. Tokarzewski-Karaszewicz, 8 February 1939. Jan Tokarzewski-Karaszewicz Papers, Ukrainian Research Institute, Harvard University, Cambridge, Massachusetts.

to have been in touch with Carpatho-Ruthenian activists and to have encouraged Bammat and his group to cooperate with Ukrainian nationalists.[17] But it is unclear whether Japan and the Caucasus group played any substantive role in the rise of Carpatho-Ukraine, which raised hopes for a new world order among those striving to achieve the independence of their homelands from the Soviet Union. Of course, the future of Carpatho-Ukraine was to prove disappointing to many: forced to give up part of its territory to Hungary (the First Vienna Award), and in March 1939, when it declared its independence from Czechoslovakia, it was immediately occupied by Hungary.

7.2 An Attempt on Stalin's Life?

In turning down Japan's offer of financial aid to the Promethean movement, the Poles were not mistaken that in Europe Japan was given more to subversion and espionage than constructive political activity. Japan's apparent attempt on Stalin's life is symbolic of its true interests.

Japan's goal in assassinating Stalin is not at all clear. Possibly it hoped to plunge the country into chaos and crisis. In 1938–39, Japan's special subversion organ in Berlin appears to have hatched the scheme to dispatch an armed squad to the Soviet Union to assassinate its leader. Exactly when the squad crossed the Soviet border from Turkey, if it did at all, is unknown, but it is likely to have been in late 1938 or early 1939. On 31 January 1939 Heinrich Himmler, head of the Nazi Schutzstaffel (SS), visited Ōshima in his Berlin office. According to Himmler:

> We discussed conclusion of a treaty to consolidate the triangle Germany/Italy/Japan into an even firmer mold. He also told me that, together with German counter-espionage [the Abwehr], he was undertaking long-range projects aimed at the disintegration of Russia and emanating from the Caucasus and the Ukraine. However, this organization was to become effective only in case of war.
>
> Furthermore he had succeeded up to now to send 10 Russians with bombs across the Caucasian frontier. These Russians had the mission to kill Stalin. A number of additional Russians, whom he had also sent across, had been shot at the frontier.[18]

If the squad had indeed crossed the Caucasian border into the Soviet Union, these "Russians" (or at least some of them) were almost certainly people from the Caucasus. Interrogated after World War II, Ōshima did not recall meeting with Himmler on

17 Japan's role in Bammat's courting of the Ukrainian nationalists, see NARA RG263, 2002/A/10/3 (Makoto Onodera), v. 1, 3; Kenji Suzuki, *Chūdoku taishi Ōshima Hiroshi* (Tokyo, Fuō shobō, 1979), 93, discusses the work of Japan's special intelligence/subversion organ in Berlin with Carpatho-Ukrainians as directed by Takanobu Manaki (see p. 146).

18 Here we have relied on the English translation at the Yale Avalon Project: http://www.yale.edu/lawweb/avalon/imt/document/nca_vol4/2195-ps.htm, accessed October 2008.

that date and firmly and consistently denied knowledge of the matters described in Himmler's notes, attributing them to the secret activities of Usui, Manaki, and Bammat which he had not overseen. He then added: "I just want to say that this matter of using espionage agents is something that every General Staff does and, therefore, I did not consider it important enough to tell you about it in detail."[19]

It is difficult to confirm whether any attempt on Stalin's life actually took place. Had an attempt of this significance actually occurred (and been thwarted), it would have been celebrated as a great success for Soviet counterintelligence activity. Yet no such record has surfaced. The archive of the former NKVD in Georgia has no record on such an attempt. In an interview Ōshima gave in Tokyo in 1959, he stated that the case of the Stalin assassination squad was revealed at the Tokyo trial.[20] What is certain is that many schemes and conspiracies were hatched by the Japanese and their agents. According to one account, Japan's subversion organ in Berlin managed to dispatch about thirty agents each year to the Soviet Union through Finland, Estonia, Lithuania, Poland, Turkey, and elsewhere.[21] Yuriko Onodera, wife of Makoto Onodera (Japan's military attaché in the Baltic states at the time) said that the "Manaki organ" in Berlin worked on a plan to assassinate Stalin, and that her husband himself once transported small bombs from Berlin to Estonia to be given to his agents.[22]

What is equally clear is that Soviet agents had also penetrated Japan's diversionary organs. Again according to Yuriko Onodera, while working with émigré activists in Europe, her husband came to realize that Manaki's activities were an open secret in Europe and immediately alerted his friend Usui to this problem.[23] It appears that Manaki's Russian mistress in Paris was a Soviet double agent.[24] Within the Bammat group there was also a Soviet agent.[25] Ōshima's office, too, was penetrated by a Soviet double

---

19 NARA, RG331, Numerical Case Files Relating to Particular Incidents and Suspected War Criminals, Case 247 (interrogations of 5 and 6 March 1946). At the time (1946), Usui was dead (killed in the war), and Manaki, held in Vietnam, was never interrogated by the Tokyo War Crimes Tribunal. It was Manaki who had led Japan's subversion organ in Berlin in 1938–39.

20 His November 1959 interview given to Kenichirō Kōmura cited above. The Himmler statement was presented as Exhibit No. 489. The Soviet prosecutors were of course familiar with it. See GARF, f. 7867, op. 377, d. 460, l. 2.

21 Suzuki, *Chūdoku taishi Ōshima Hiroshi*, 93.

22 Yuriko Onodera, "Onodera Makoto Rikugun shōshō no jōhō katsudō 1935–1946" [The Intelligence Work of Major General Makoto Onodera], 33 (a manuscript available at the Tokyo University Historiographical Institute, Tokyo). The sentence about planning to assassinate Stalin was marked by someone (evidently as a politically inconvenient revelation) and covered over with a thin piece of paper on which a different sentence was written, One can still read the original sentence through the paper.

23 Yuriko Onodera, "Onodera Makoto," 34–35.

24 Suzuki, *Chūdoku taishi Ōshima Hiroshi*, 94–95.

25 See Georges Mamoulia, *Les combats indépendandistes des Caucasiens entre URSS et puissances occidentales: Le cas de la Géorgie (1921–1945)* (Paris: L'Harmattan, 2009), 227.

agent.[26] It is also possible that an Azerbaijani agent used by Japan in Paris in 1937–38 was also a Soviet double agent.[27] More generally, the famous Soviet spy Richard Sorge, having deeply penetrated the German embassy in Tokyo and the Japanese political establishment, supplied invaluable information to Moscow. (Sorge and Manaki knew each other in Tokyo.) As a result, Ōshima's and Manaki's activities were closely watched by Soviet agents in Berlin. It is therefore likely that some of these "assassins" sent into Soviet territory were in fact Soviet agents.

If this was the case, then Japan's attempt at Stalin's life would have been used by Soviet counterintelligence to capture and liquidate the most active Caucasian émigré elements. This would have literally been an exercise in futility and, even worse, self-destructive. In any event, by 1938–39 Moscow had gained full knowledge of the cipher codes of Japanese diplomatic correspondence through a Japanese diplomat based in Prague.[28] The activities of the Caucasus group supported by Japan were also likely to have been thwarted effectively by Soviet counterintelligence.

7.3 The Molotov-Ribbentrop Pact and World War II

As the cloud of war hovered, each country was maneuvering furiously. In March 1939 Hitler defied the Munich Agreement and occupied and destroyed Czechoslovakia. A week later France and Britain reacted by pledging to guarantee Polish independence. The following day, on 7 April 1939, Mussolini's Italy invaded and annexed Albania. In return, Britain and France extended their guarantee of support to Greece and Romania. In May and June, in the face of the German threat, Britain and France each concluded a mutual assistance pact with Turkey, which feared Italy's further advance into the Balkans. These treaties, in turn, resulted in a more elaborate three-power (Franco-Anglo-Turkish) mutual assistance pact in October 1939.[29] These moves by Turkey in turn led Germany to terminate collaboration with Haidar Bammat and his associates, whom Berlin did not trust, considering them pro-Turkish.[30] On 22 May 1939, Hitler and Mussolini further signed the Pact of Steel (a pact of friendship and alliance) aimed against Britain and France. (Japan did not join them, considering the Soviet Union, rather than Britain or France, its main enemy.)

---

26 See Jeffrey Burds, "The Soviet War against 'Fifth Columnists': The Case of Chechnya, 1942–4." *Journal of Contemporary History* 42, no. 2 (2007), 281.

27 See Takeyasu Tsuchihashi, *Gunpuku seikatsu shijūnen no omoide* (Tokyo, Keisō shuppan, 1985), 326–27.

28 See Hiroaki Kuromiya and Andrzej Pepłoński, "Kōzō Izumi and the Soviet Breach of Imperial Japanese Diplomatic Codes." *Intelligence and National Security* 28, no. 6 (2013), 769–84.

29 Zehra Önder, *Die türkische Außenpolitik im Zweiten Weltkrieg* (München: Oldenbourg, 1977), 11, 19–20, 33.

30 Mamoulia, *Les combats indépendandistes des Caucasiens*, 209, 230.

Fig. 7.1. The Caucasus on the eve of World War II.

Bammat and the Caucasus group found their own reasons for not working with the Germans: on 23 August 1939, Germany and the Soviet Union signed a nonaggression pact (the Molotov-Ribbentrop Pact), which among other stipulations obliged Germany to ban all anti-Soviet émigré activity. This dramatic turn of events drawing together two mortal enemies surprised the entire world. It violated the Anti-Comintern Pact (on the German side) as well as the mutual assistance pact with France (on the Soviet side). The political impact was such that the cabinet of the Japanese government, a party to the Anti-Comintern Pact, was forced to resign, declaring that the new “anti-Anti-Comintern pact” between Berlin and Moscow was so bizarre as to be incomprehensible. The pact, moreover, left Japan alone in charge of anti-Soviet intelligence in the Caucasus, an area of “mutual interest” to Germany and Japan as stipulated in the Ōshima-Canaris agreement of May 1937.[31]

31 For the transition to Japan of the hegemony among the anti-Soviet émigré groups in general at this time, see Paul Leverkuehn, *Der geheime Nachrichtendienst der deutschen Wehrmacht im Kriege* (Frankfurt a.M.: Bernard & Graefe, 1957), 132.

It was probably for this reason that in November or December 1939, Shalva Berishvili (1901–89), a professional spy and nephew of the former Promethean leader and Georgian Social Democrat Noe Ramishvili, became acquainted ("accidentally," according to Berishvili) with the Japanese military attaché in Turkey, Hōryō Tateishi. Berishvili, who in 1930 had successfully accomplished a secret mission to the Soviet Caucasus and repeated another mission in October 1939, was charged by the Georgian Menshevik (Social Democratic) government in exile with coordinating intelligence operations in Turkey. (By this time, after expelling the Caucasian political émigrés in 1938, Turkey was now compelled to use Caucasian émigrés again for intelligence in view of the German-Soviet rapprochement in August 1939.) Tateishi, a Russian hand (it is known that he was stationed in Poland and the Soviet Union in 1935), worked in Turkey as an attaché from 1938 to 1945, an extraordinarily long tenure by Japanese standards of the time, a testimony to his competence as an intelligence officer. Berishvili's clandestine trip to Georgia in 1939 yielded much valuable information, including Soviet secret plans to occupy Turkey and annex Iranian Azerbaijan at a propitious moment.[32] In the summer of 1940, Berishvili, working with French, British, and Turkish intelligence services, made another secret mission to Georgia (he later claimed that he had received no special assignment from Tateishi. During this mission, however, Berishvili switched sides and offered his services to Moscow (under the code name "Omeri"). Briefed in Moscow and placed under Lavrenti Beria's direct control, he was sent back to Turkey. Moscow authorized him to meet with Tateishi, which he did in Turkey in late 1940. Subsequently arrested in the Soviet Union, Berishvili "confessed," according to Soviet records, that in that meeting he provided to the Japanese military attaché information about the Red Army.[33]

Independently of Berishvili and his group, Bammat's Caucasus group, supported by Japan, also carried out a secret mission to the Caucasus in September-October 1939, shortly after the Soviet Union and Japan had engaged in a serious battle in Khalkhin Gol on the Mongolian-Manchukuo border (ending in Japan's decisive defeat).[34] Samson Kruashvili (who had successfully returned from an August-September 1938 mission to Soviet Georgia) and Osman Tedoradze crossed the Soviet border from Turkey and reached Batumi. Their comrades in Batumi were astonished to see them, prompting them to ask questions such as "How can you fight against the Bolsheviks now that an accord with the Germans has been concluded?" The two reassured them that the new situation did not change their fight against the Communists at all and that they

32 Mamoulia, *Les combats indépendandistes des Caucasiens*, 241–43, 259–60.

33 File of Sh.N. Berishvili, Archive of the Ministry of Internal Affairs of Georgia (Tbilisi), 78–79, and Gela Suladze, *kartuli ant'isabch'ota emigratsia da sp'etssamsakhurebi (1918–1953 ts'.ts')* (Georgian Antibolshevik Emigration and the Secret Services) (Tbilisi: "erovnuli mts'erloba," 2010), 275–309.

34 As it turned out, Japan's defeat was not as decisive as it appeared; also, the commander of the Japanese fighting forces may have been a Soviet agent. See Hiroaki Kuromiya, "The Mystery of Nomonhan, 1939." *The Journal of Slavic Military Studies* 24, no. 4 (December 2011), 659–77.

would fight with the same vigor as before and with the same support as before. (Clearly the reference to the "same support as before" implied Japan's support.) It turned out, according to Kruashvili's report to Bammat, that their comrades in Georgia had established links in all of Georgia (and in Armenia as well), and that everywhere people were interested in their movement. But the Kruashvili-Tedoradze mission was cut short: their arrival coincided with the uncovering by the Soviet police of a clandestine "Turkish" organization in Ajaria. Sensing danger, they returned to Turkey. Fired on at the border, the two managed to return to Turkey, although Tedoradze was wounded.[35]

Germany having withdrawn (only for the time being, as it turned out), Britain and France came decisively onto the Caucasian scene. Both countries had maneuvered to turn Germany and the Soviet Union against each other to their mutual destruction, but the maneuver failed, resulting in the Molotov-Ribbentrop Pact. They now had to face the dire consequences. On 1 September 1939, Germany invaded Poland, to which Britain and France responded militarily, albeit feebly. World War II thus began. Along with the Polish army, Caucasian émigré groups fought against the German invaders.[36] In accordance with the secret protocol of the Molotov-Ribbentrop Pact, the Soviet Union invaded eastern Poland and annexed it to Ukraine and Belarus. Poland was thus destroyed by Germany and the Soviet Union. Following its agreement with Germany, the Soviet Union duly provided oil, grain, and other vitally needed materials to the Nazis. In November 1939, the Soviet Union further invaded Finland, demanding the concession of border territory. By default, Moscow thus became a de facto enemy of Britain and France. This prompted the two countries to target the oil fields in the Caucasus for destruction, for they accounted for approximately 80 percent of the oil supply in the Soviet Union, by means of which Moscow was assisting Germany's war efforts.

In the end Operation Pike, as the British-French scheme became known,[37] was never carried out, just as the earlier scheme of the two countries to intervene in the Winter War between Finland and the Soviet Union in support of the former never came to fruition, owing to Finland's capitulation in March 1940. Considering that an attack on the Caucasian oil fields would lead to war with the Soviet Union, Britain even entertained the idea of encouraging Japan into battle against the Soviet Union in the Far East to distract it from the West. Japan had its own scheme of attacking the Caucasian oil fields as part of its strategy against the Soviet Union. Japan's taking of Xinjiang, or Chinese Turkestan, would have placed the oil fields of the Caucasus within the direct reach of long-range bombers taking off from Xinjiang. Even without Xinjiang, Japan

---

35 Report by Kruashvili to Bammat (November 1939) from the Bammat family archive in Paris. See also Mamoulia, *Les combats indépendandistes des Caucasiens*, 385–88.

36 See Mitat Çelikpala, "The North Caucasian Émigrés between the World Wars." *International Journal of Turkish Studies* 9, nos. 1–2 (2003), 313.

37 See Patrick Osborn, *Operation Pike: Britain versus the Soviet Union, 1939-1941* (Westport, Conn.: Greenwood Press, 2000).

was suspected of providing financial support to Bammat and the Caucasus group to organize sabotage in the oil operations of Baku and Grozny.[38] As it was, the British-French scheme had its own danger of cementing the German-Soviet alliance against them. Nevertheless, supported by all stripes of Caucasian émigré political groups,[39] elaborate preparations went ahead, only to fail owing to the unexpectedly swift fall of Paris in June 1940.[40]

Although Moscow was familiar with the British-French scheme and took appropriate military preparations in the Caucasus, it was as much disappointed by the French capitulation as it gloated, for it meant that, with only Britain standing against Germany in the West, Hitler's attention now might turn to the East – to the Soviet Union. Stalin knew that confrontation with Nazi Germany was inevitable, but he wanted to delay it as long as possible while strengthening the Soviet Union's fighting capacity. Stalin was at times overconfident that he could outsmart Hitler. Nevertheless, the fall of France prompted the Soviet Union to expand what it considered a vital security zone: it occupied and then incorporated into itself the three Baltic states (Estonia, Latvia, and Lithuania) as well as Bessarabia and Northern Bukovyna (both of which had been under Romania until then).

These events were extremely disappointing to the Caucasus group and many other émigré groups. To them, Japan's defeat at Khalkhin Gol, the destruction of Poland, Hungary's elimination of Carpatho-Ukraine, Finland's capitulation and territorial concession to the Soviet Union, the disappearance of the Baltic states, and the forceful incorporation of Bessarabia and Northern Bukovyna into the Soviet Union – all were bad omens. The Caucasus group thereupon dissolved and publication of its journal *Kavkaz* ceased (as did, in the wake of Paris's fall, publication of *La Revue de Promethée*, which had replaced *Promethée* in 1938).[41]

Even so, Bammat and his group did not abandon their fight or hope for ultimate victory. According to a report sent by Berishvili, now working for Moscow, to Beria in September 1940, even though for now the Soviet Union was on friendly terms with Germany, the Caucasus group was continuing their activity and propaganda, "hoping that after the defeat of Britain, Germany would start war on the Soviet Union and

---

38 See French counterintelligence information in "Note de l'inspecteur général de la surveillance du territoire," 29 September 1939, Centre d'archives contemporaines (Fontainebleau), box no. 19940501; also, Mamoulia, *Les combats indépendandistes des Caucasiens*, 223.

39 See Mamoulia, *Les combats indépendandistes des Caucasiens*, 271; also Burds, "The Soviet War against 'Fifth Columnists'," 285.

40 Britain still did not, however, completely abandon the possibilities of the operation until Hitler's attack against the Soviet Union in June 1941. See Günter Kahle, *Das Kaukasusprojekt der Alliierten vom Jahre 1940* (Opladen: Westdeutscher Verlag, 1973).

41 Ironically, it was just before the fall of Paris that the Armenians, fearing the repetition of 1918, abandoned the territorial issues with Turkey and decided to join the council of the Caucasian Federation (see p. 143) led by the Prometheans. See Mamoulia, *Les combats indépendandistes des Caucasiens*, 259, 389–90.

Fig. 7.2. Mikheil Kedia in the 1930s, France.

liberate the peoples of the Caucasus." The group, Berishvili emphasized, "has a lot of money at its disposal, and Bammat in particular."[42] Clearly the money came from the Japanese. According to Berishvili, however, Bammat refused to cooperate with "Georgian fascist organizations" (namely rightists, united in January 1940 in Paris under the name of the Georgian National Committee), which demanded that a Georgian, not Bammat, lead the common front against Moscow.[43] These Georgians, however, did not blindly follow the Nazis. For example, Mikheil Kedia (see p. 120), who worked closely with German intelligence, protected from Nazi pursuit in occupied Paris the Georgian Social Democrats who were very critical of Nazi Germany. Kedia also used his relations with the German Sicherheitsdienst (security service) to prevent the deportation of eighty Georgian Jews living in occupied Paris.[44]

42 See Mamoulia, *Les combats indépendandistes des Caucasiens*, 232.

43 See *Organy gosudarstvennoi bezopasnosti SSSR v Velikoi otechestvennoi voine*, vol. 1, part 1 (Moscow: Kniga i biznes, 1995), 275.

44 Mamoulia, *Les combats indépendandistes des Caucasiens*, 295.

Moscow suspected that, while supporting Bammat and other Caucasian rightist groups, Japan was pressing ahead with its own clandestine operations without German support. Captured "Japanese agents" interrogated by the Soviets reveal that specially trained sabotage groups "were to commence their activity with the launch by Japan of military operations against the Soviet Union. [They were] to operate in the rear of the Red Army with objectives of destroying telephone and telegraph lines, bridges, storehouses, transport routes, with the assassination of Soviet-Party administrative personnel, as well as with robberies, acts of arson and other activities directed at the weakening of the [Soviet] rear."[45] This was a political fabrication typical of the Stalin era, prompted by Japan's shadow in the Caucasus.

In view of the dangers posed by these "sabotage groups," Stalin intensified the protection of those areas (i.e. periphery) deemed weak links in Soviet security by establishing in February 1941 a special Department for the Struggle against Banditry in the NKVD. Its head was Sh.O. Tsereteli, a Georgian, and its First Section was charged with the Caucasians.[46] (The term "banditry" is reminiscent of the time during and after the Civil War of 1918–21, when the Soviet periphery, including the Caucasus, was plagued with anti-Soviet "bandits.")

Meanwhile, the international situation continued to change rapidly. The defeat of France made it attractive for both Italy and Japan to strengthen (or restrengthen in the case of Japan in the wake of the fall-out from the Molotov-Ribbentrop pact) their ties to Germany. Japan's political and military leaders were deeply divided on this matter. In the end, however, Japan chose Germany in hopes it would help Japan in dealing with the United States, with which Japan was drawing ever closer to military confrontation. As the Tripartite Pact of 27 September 1940 stipulated: "Germany, Italy and Japan agree to co-operate in their efforts on aforesaid lines [affirming and respecting the leadership of Germany and Italy "in establishment of a new order in Europe" and the leadership of Japan "in the establishment of a new order in greater East Asia"]. They further undertake to assist one another with all political, economic and military means when one of the three contracting powers is attacked by a power at present not involved in the European war or in the Chinese-Japanese conflict." Further, the pact declared: "Germany, Italy and Japan affirm that the aforesaid terms do not in any way affect the political status which exists at present as between each of the three contracting powers and Soviet Russia."[47] This last clause left open the possibility of including the Soviet Union into this Axis Pact. Indeed, the Japanese government pursued this possibility as a leverage against the United States. Germany was

45 Burds, "The Soviet War against 'Fifth Columnists'," 273–74.

46 *NKVD-MVD SSSR v bor'be s banditizmom i vooruzhennym natsionalisticheskim podpol'em na zapadnoi Ukraine, v zapadnoi Belorossii i Pribaltike (1918–1956)* (Moscow: Ob'edinennaia redaktsiia MVD Rossii, 2008), 419, 473, 583. See also Burds, "The Soviet War against 'Fifth Columnists'," 289.

47 Translation by the Avalon project: http://avalon.law.yale.edu/wwii/triparti.asp (accessed February 2013).

less sincere in this matter. Berlin did invite Moscow to join the three countries, and in November 1940 Moscow did respond by sending for negotiation Commissar of Foreign Affairs Viacheslav Molotov to Berlin. Yet both sides understood that this would be an impossible alliance, and nothing came of it. Japan still clung to the illusion, however, thus concluding on 13 April 1941 a neutrality pact with the Soviet Union, ignorant that four months earlier Hitler had already decided to start war against the Soviet Union by mid-1941. Moscow benefitted enormously from the fact that the alliance between Japan and Germany was an "inoperative alliance."[48] At the same time, the Soviet-Japanese neutrality pact was a huge blow to those Caucasians and other émigrés who had long worked with Japan against Moscow.

Turkey, which cautiously kept all options open regarding the Soviet Union even when it concluded a pact of mutual assistance with Britain and France, also concluded a neutrality pact with the Soviet Union (on 24 March 1941). Preceding Japan's neutrality pact with the Soviet Union by three weeks, it signified another serious blow to the anti-Soviet forces working within and outside Turkey. Thus, to be safe, Turkey signed a non-aggression treaty with Germany as well. This was 18 June 1941, four days before the Germans invaded the Soviet Union.

7.4 The Expansion of War

Hitler launched Operation Barbarossa against his life-time enemy, Soviet Bolshevism, on 22 June 1941, having kept his allies, Italy and Japan, in the dark about his secret plan. Within Japan's political and military establishment, there were those who, opposing the Soviet-Japanese neutrality treaty, wished to join the Germans in launching war against the Soviet Union in the East. Ultimately, however, Japan chose to go southward to attack American, British, and Dutch interests in order to secure its oil supply. In September 1940, Japan's quagmire in China led to its invasion of northern Indochina (now under the control of Vichy France) to cut the supply line of arms to Chinese forces. But this only strengthened American military and financial aid to China and hardened Washington's resolve against Japan. In July 1941, Japan invaded and occupied southern Indochina to secure the raw materials of Southeast Asia. In response, the following month the United States, Britain, and the Netherlands imposed an oil embargo on Japan. This was a crucial move jeopardizing Japan's war machine because Japan depended on the United States for more than 80 percent of its oil supply. This is the immediate background to Japan's decision to launch war against the United States and its allies instead of going northward to attack the Soviet Union. This

48 The expression "inoperative alliance" (*die wirkungslose Allianz*) is taken from Theo Sommer, *Deutschland und Japan zwischen den Mächten 1935–1940: Vom Antikominternpakt zum Dreimächtepakt* (Tübingen: J.C.B. Mohr, 1962), 450.

decision had its rationale: compared with the south, the Soviet Far East appeared too barren to secure the life-lines of the Japanese war machine.

By mid-October 1941, Stalin came to be reasonably certain that Japan, planning to strike the United States, would not attack the Soviet Union in the near future. Moscow had received a number of confidential reports from spies placed high in the Japanese establishment. This allowed Stalin to transfer from the Far East eight divisions of Soviet military forces to fight against the Germans in the West. Such transfers had taken place before, but this was the largest and most decisive.[49] These forces helped Stalin defend Moscow from the German onslaught. Of course, there was no guarantee that Japan would not attack the Soviet Union in case the situation changed, and indeed Japan retained such plans. Moscow was therefore forced to continue to maintain considerable forces in the Far East even at the direst moment of the war against Germany in the West. Meanwhile, Japan attacked the United States on 7/8 December 1941 (Pearl Harbor), and the war thus spread to the Pacific.

Clearly Germany's war against the Soviet Union emboldened the Caucasian émigrés, whereas Japan's war against the United States mattered little to them. The situation had altered dramatically from that of the period after the Molotov-Ribbentrop Pact: for the Caucasian émigré groups Japan was virtually out and Germany was definitely in.

In the Soviet Caucasus, the specter of armed uprising was already present even before the German attack. In 1940, for example, Hasan Israilov ("Terloev"), a Chechen barrister, openly broke with Soviet power and took control of parts of Southern Chechnia. In February of that year, the insurgents set up the Provisional People's Revolutionary State of Chechnia-Ingushetia. Although by the beginning of 1941, the area had been retaken by Soviet forces,[50] between January and 22 June 1941, there were thirty-one cases of insurgencies in Chechnia and Ingushetia.[51]

After the German attack in June 1941, the specter of insurgency in the Caucasus became a nightmare for the Soviet government. The day the war broke out, Chechen insurgents declared war against the Soviet government in the name of the Chechen people.[52] It appears that in Chechnia and Ingushetia, roughly ninety percent of men

49 See V.M. Petrenko, "Dal'nevostochnyi front nakanune i v period Velikoi Otechestvennoi voiny 1941–1945 gg." *Voenno-istoricheskii zhurnal* 2010, no. 10, 21.

50 S.S. Magamadov and S.A. Kislitsyn, *Politicheskaia vlast' i povstancheskoe dvizhenie na Severnom Kavkaze. Ocherki istorii 1920–1930-kh gg.* (Rostov-na-Donu: Iuzhno-Rossiiskii institut-filial RANKh i GS pri Prezidente RF, 2011), 301 and Burds, "The Soviet War against 'Fifth Columnists'," 293–94. For the political situation in the Caucasus at the time, see a firsthand account by a Chechen who defected to the West, though an account not always reliable: Aleksandr Uralov (A. Avtorkhanov), *Narodoubiistvo v SSSR. Ubiistvo chechenskogo naroda* (Munich, Svobodnyi Kavkaz, 1952).

51 See V.P. Galitskii, "Velikaia otechestvennaia voina 1941–1945 gg. '. . . dlia aktivnoi podryvnoi diversionnoi deiatel'nosti v tylu u Krasnoi Armii'." *Voenno-istoricheskii zhurnal* 2001, no. 1, 18.

52 See Georges Mamoulia, *Gruzinskii legion v bor'be za svobodu i nezavisimost' Gruzii v gody Vtoroi mirovoi voiny* (Tbilisi: private publication, 2007), 277.

of military service age dodged the military draft or deserted the army. (Of 80,000 or so men who should have served in the Red Army, only about 10,000 Chechen and Ingush men did serve; of these, 2,300 were killed or missing in action.) In March 1942, for example, 14,576 were called up, but 13,560, or 93 percent, deserted and joined the insurgents in the mountainous areas.[53] Because Moscow no longer trusted the Chechens and other Northern Caucasians, in that month all serving Chechens and Ingush were "recalled to the reserve" from active duty; moreover, the summons in July 1942 of those born in 1924–25 came "accompanied by explicit secret instructions to exclude from this cadre men of Chechen, Ingush, Kabard, Balkar and Dagestani nationality."[54] In Karachay, too, "hundreds and thousands" of men deserted to the mountains to join the insurgents and fight against the Soviet forces.[55] In Georgia, 5,686 men were detained for desertion and draft-dodging in 1942; in 1943 the number climbed to 12,958.[56] Local party leaders were no more reliable. In August-September 1942, for example, when German forces were drawing closer to Chechnia toward the oil city of Grozny (and further onto Baku in Azerbaijan), sixteen of twenty-four (two thirds) of the district party committee secretaries in Chechnia deserted their posts.[57] But the German military forces stalled just short of Chechnia (and far from the oil wells of Baku).

With respect to German occupation policy, despite its harshness and brutality, "German rule in the North Caucasus did not evoke the violent popular disillusionment and eventual hostility which it had farther north"; indeed, the Northern Caucasus suffered the least of all areas of the Soviet Union occupied by Germany.[58] In part this was because the region, unlike Ukraine and Russia, was not in the German settlement plans, and in part because the occupation was brief. Yet it also reflected German thinking about the Caucasus's disloyalty to Moscow. By comparison, Georgia remained under stricter Soviet control. Yet even there unrest manifested itself. For example, at a meeting held at the Tbilisi Opera House in 1942, "leaflets were distributed calling on the people to overthrow Russian Communist rule and proclaim Georgia's independence."[59] As it was, as far as political security was concerned, excluding the territory recently annexed by the Soviet Union (Western Ukraine and Western Belarus, the Baltic states, parts of former Finland, and Bessarabia), no other parts of the country proved as disruptive as the Caucasus during the war.

---

53 See Igor' Pykhalov, "Severnyi Kavkaz. Prichiny deportatsii 1943–1945 gg." *Molodaia gvardiia* 2002, no. 10, 87.

54 Alex Marshall, *The Caucasus under Soviet Rule* (London-New York: Routledge, 2010), 263.

55 Magamadov and Kislitsyn, *Politicheskaia vlast' i povstancheskoe dvizhenie na Severnom Kavkaze*, 301.

56 Mamoulia, *Gruzinskii legion*, 283.

57 See Pykhalov, "Severnyi Kavkaz," 97.

58 Alexander Dallin, *German Rule in Russia 1941–1945: A Study of Occupation Policies*, 2nd ed. (Boulder, Colorado: Westview Press, 1981), 238, 248.

59 David Marshall Lang, *A Modern History of Soviet Georgia* (New York: Grove Press, 1962), 259.

There, popular expectations of Japan's entry into war against the Soviet Union persisted, although Japan itself was too busy fighting in the Pacific. According to German sources, certain Japanese circles suspected in 1942 that the nationalities question in the Soviet Union had "diminished in relevance" in war[60] Also, insurgency and rebellion had failed to pose a substantial challenge to the Soviet government. From Georgia, for example, where insurgent groups stood up against the Soviet government, it was reported that the younger generation in particular, raised under the Soviet regime, had come to identify with it.[61] Among casualties in the fight against Germany, 7.7 times more Georgian were killed or went missing in action than Chechens or Ingush (based on 1939 population data).[62] (Many of these men served in the national units of the Red Army created during the war in a token nod to their national sentiments.)

But whatever "certain Japanese circles" might have thought, Japan's operatives in Europe and elsewhere never ceased to regard the Soviet Union as a potential enemy. In 1941, even after the Soviet-Japanese neutrality pact was signed, Tateishi, Japan's military attaché in Turkey, was in touch with Bammat's group. Bammat's representative in Turkey, an Azeri, Fuad Emirdzhan (Emirdzhanov) – according to Soviet sources working with Tateishi – was recruiting agents from the Caucasian Mountaineers in Turkey. Fuad's brother, Mamed Emirdzhan, moved to Kars in Turkey, close to the Turkish-Georgian-Armenia borders, for intelligence purposes.[63] Ōshima, now Japan's ambassador to Germany, remained loyal in spirit to the Anti-Comintern Pact and maintained very close ties to the German government throughout the war. After the war, Moscow used Japan's alleged violation of the neutrality pact to cover the fact that it was ultimately the Soviet Union that actually violated it and staged war against Japan in 1945.[64] In the Far East, too, Japan continued to monitor the Soviet Union intensely as a potential foe to fight.[65]

Throughout the war it appears that clandestine links between the Caucasian émigré groups and underground groups in the Caucasus were maintained, however tenuous they may have been. This was certainly the case with both the Georgian rightist groups and the Georgian Social Democrats (Mensheviks).[66] The Georgian-German operation in October 1943, known as *Aktion Mainz*, was especially successful owing to the contact the Georgian groups had kept with their underground groups in Batumi:

---

60 See Patrik von zur Mühlen, *Zwischen Hakenkreuz und Sowjetstern: Der Nationalismus der sowjetischen Orientvölker im Zweiten Weltkrieg* (Düsseldorf: Droste Verlag, 1971), 200.

61 von zur Mühlen, *Zwischen Hakenkreuz und Sowjetstern*, 206.

62 Marshall, *The Caucasus under Soviet Rule*, 246.

63 See *Organy gosudarstvennoi bezopasnosti SSSR v Velikoi otechestvennoi voine*, vol. 2, part 2 (Moscow: Rus', 2000), 9.

64 See Ōshima's assistant's testimony given after the war: International Military Tribunal for the Far East (1946–1948) Exhibit 811 (Harvard University Law School Library).

65 See NA, HW40.208 (1946 interrogation of Yukio Nishihara).

66 See Mamoulia, *Les combats indépendandistes des Caucasiens*, 296, 299, and Mamoulia, *Gruzinskii legion*, 324, 328.

groups of Georgian émigrés headed by David Erkomaishvili crossed the Georgian border, reached Batumi, contacted underground groups, and returned with much political, economic, and military information, which was then handed to the Germans. The operation was repeated in May and June 1944.[67] At the time, "a steady stream of weapons, sabotage material and propaganda" was being smuggled in the other direction to sympathizers in Georgia.[68]

With or without direct contact with their lands, the Caucasian émigré groups responded positively to the new situation of Germany's war against the Soviet Union. In October 1941, for example, General Giorgi Kvinitadze, who belonged to Bammat's Caucasus group, turned directly to Hitler, hoping that Germany would liberate Georgia. Said Shamil had similarly turned to Germany even earlier, in August 1941.[69] Soon afterward, the former Georgian envoy to Germany, Vladimir (Lado) Akhmeteli, who had abandoned the Social Democratic camp for the Caucasus group in the mid-1930s, offered to the German Foreign Ministry a plan for a Great Caucasian Federation. Two months later he proposed to Hitler creating a Georgian Legion out of thirty thousand to fifty thousand Soviet Georgian prisoners of war, which his friend General Kvinitadze could command. (There were numerous cases of Soviet Georgian soldiers surrendering voluntarily to the German side.)[70] Akhmeteli suggested to the Germans that the Caucasus could live, for the time being, under a German protectorate, although, as far as Georgia was concerned, an independent monarchy would be installed in due course.[71]

Visions of a free Caucasus, however, were never supported by Nazi ideology. Some Germans, such as Friedrich Werner von der Schulenburg, the last German ambassador to the Soviet Union before the war and previously chief of the German mission in the Caucasus at the time Georgia declared its independence in May 1918, were supporters of Caucasian national sentiments. Schulenberg went so far as to unite the Georgian political groups, who chose the Georgian prince Irakli Bagrationi of Mukhrani (in exile in France, Italy, and then in Spain) as a candidate for the throne. In April 1942, Schulenberg also invited a number of Caucasian émigré leaders to a conference in Berlin. This so-called Adlon meeting (after the name of the luxury hotel in Berlin where it took place) was attended by members of the former Caucasus group and other rightist parties, as well as some former Promethean group leaders: Haidar Bammat, Alikhan Kantemir, Vassan-Giray Dzhabagi, Spiridon Kedia,

67 See von zur Mühlen, *Zwischen Hakenkreuz und Sowjetstern*, 174–175.

68 See Perry Biddiscombe, "Unternehmen Zeppelin: The Deployment of SS Saboteurs and Spies in the Soviet Union, 1942–1945." *Europe-Asia Studies* 52, no. 6 (2000), 1132–33. The author states that the Soviet claim that Soviet agents had penetrated these groups and crippled the Georgian underground is unconvincing.

69 See von zur Mühlen, *Zwischen Hakenkreuz und Sowjetstern*, 105, 121.

70 See Mamoulia, *Gruzinskii legion*, 61–62, 323.

71 Von zur Mühlen, *Zwischen Hakenkreuz und Sowjetstern*, 105–106.

Prince Shalva Amiredzhibi, Mikheil Tsereteli, General Leo Kereselidze, Irakli Bagrationi, Zurab Avalishvili, Shalva Maglakelidze, Davit Vachnadze, Hosrovbek Sultanov, Khalil bey Khasmammadov and his collaborator Fuad Emirdzhan, Mammad Amin Rasulzade, Mustafa Vekilli, Mir Yakub Mekhtiev, and Nazhde, an Armenian general (thus representing Georgia, the Northern Caucasus, Azerbaijan, and Armenia). Yet the *Ostministerium*, the German civil administration of occupied territory headed by chief Nazi ideologist Alfred Rosenberg, was adamantly opposed to imparting any promise of independence to the Caucasian political leaders.[72]

Bammat for his part demanded Germany's immediate recognition of the Caucasus's independence as a precondition for collaboration. He told his Georgian colleague Spiridon Kedia at this conference: "I'm surprised by the silence of [our] Caucasians. Why don't they demand more forcefully the independence of the Caucasus from the Germans? We need to demand categorically the recognition of the independence of the Caucasus from the Germans .... Otherwise we cannot cooperate with them."[73] Bammat still dreamed of a Caucasian Federation living in the international equilibrium of the Western (German) and Eastern (Japanese) powers. Rosenberg, however, was greatly offended by Bammat's "ingratitude," and Bammat returned to Switzerland deeply disillusioned by the Germans. But judging by his private correspondence in the wake of the conference, he still had not given up his hopes entirely, noting the possibility that the *Ostministerium* might adopt "a more reasonable direction in the future" (*une direction plus raisonnable dans l'avenir*) and expecting the "last word" that would come from a "very higher instance."[74] No encouraging last word followed, however. His hopes dashed, Bammat thereafter resigned from active political life. Rasulzade, too, understood in the end that Nazi policy and the independence of Azerbaijan were incompatible, and in August 1943 he left Berlin for Romania. By that time, Said Shamil had also stopped even speaking with the Germans and returned to Turkey.[75] Nonetheless, in the summer of 1942, as the Wehrmacht was pushing toward the Caucasus, Bammat returned briefly to politics: along with Shamil and Vassan-Giray Dzhabagi (see p. 186), an Ingush who had belonged to the Promethean movement, Bammat negotiated with the Germans in Berlin regarding the political future of the Northern Caucasus. The negotiation got nowhere.[76]

---

72 See G. von Mende, "Die kaukasischen Nationalkomitées," 1. Personal Archives of G. von Mende (Oslo). See also Mamoulia, *Les combats indépendandistes des Caucasiens*, 287–91, and von zur Mühlen, *Zwischen Hakenkreuz und Sowjetstern*. 71, 107.

73 Mamoulia, *Les combats indépendandistes des Caucasiens*, 233–34.

74 H. Bammat, Letter to O. Tokarzewski-Karaszewicz, 14 June 1939. Jan Tokarzewski-Karaszewicz Papers, Ukrainian Research Institute, Harvard University, Cambridge, Massachusetts.

75 Georges Mamoulia and Ramiz Abutalybov, *Strana ognei. V bor'be za svobodu i nezavisimost'. Politicheskaia istoriia azerbaidzhanskoi emigratsii 1920–1945 gg.*, (Paris-Baku: CBS, 2014), 508-517.

76 See Joachim Hoffmann, *Kaukasien 1942/43: Das deutsche Heer und die Orientvölker der Sowjetunion* (Freiburg: Rombach Verlag, 1991), 186.

Others continued working with the Germans, however, because Germany appeared to them the only hope for their dream of a free Caucasus. Although the center of the Armenian Dashnak party refused to work with them and supported the Allies, some groups of Dashnaks, as well as right-wing Armenian groups, supported the German war against the Soviet Union.[77] Even the Georgian Mensheviks, who were firmly against Nazi ideology, were willing to work indirectly with the Germans out of political expediency. Their intermediary was Mikheil Kedia, who, as discussed earlier, worked closely with German intelligence. Yet he respected the Georgian government in exile headed by Noe Zhordania, a Menshevik (Social Democrat), as the symbol of the Georgian nation. According to Gerhard von Mende, who was closely involved with the Caucasian émigré groups, the Mensheviks accepted Kedia as the representative of all Georgian political forces in exile and worked with him, even providing him with information on their underground organizations in Georgia.[78] Without the German authorities' knowledge, the Georgians adopted a secret plan to dispatch groups to Georgia, proclaim its independence, and present a fait accompli to the Germans when they conquered Soviet Georgia.[79] Of course this plan did not materialize. Some historians suspect that Kedia was a Soviet double agent,[80] although documents we have examined at the Georgian NKVD archive do not support their view.

More generally, numerous Caucasians, both émigrés and prisoners of war/deserters from the Red Army, consented to fight on the German side against the Soviet Union. Along with Georgians, Northern Caucasians (Chechens, Dagestanis, Ingush, and others), and Azeris, Armenians also joined in these *Ostlegionen* (Eastern Legions). In 1942, unlike similar formations of Russians and other Slavic peoples (such as A.A. Vlasov's Russian Liberation Army), they were widely deployed on the battlefield, including during the Caucasus campaign of 1942 (Operation Edelweiss). Altogether tens of thousands of people served in the Caucasian legions.[81] Many Caucasians also worked for German intelligence, whether military intelligence (the Abwehr) or state/party intelligence (the Sicherheitsdienst). Haidar Bammat's former collaborator, Osman Saidurov ("Gube"), originally from Dagestan, worked for the Abwehr and took part in a special operation in Chechnia where he and his team were parachuted in August 1942. But they were more successful in sabotage operations

77 Von zur Mühlen, *Zwischen Hakenkreuz und Sowjetstern*, 109.

78 See von zur Mühlen, *Zwischen Hakenkreuz und Sowjetstern*, 114, and Mamoulia, *Les combats indépendandistes des Caucasiens*, 294–96.

79 See Mamoulia, *Les combats indépendandistes des Caucasiens*, 298–99.

80 See Burds, "The Soviet War against 'Fifth Columnists'," 287, 302, 312.

81 See Joachim Hoffmann, *Ostlegionen 1941–1943: Turkotataren, Kaukasier und Wolgafinnen im deutschen Heer* (Freiburg: Rombach, 1976). For Georgian legions, see Mamoulia, *Gruzinskii legion.* General John Shalikashvili, who became Chairman of the US Joint Chiefs of Staff in 1993, was born in Poland in 1936, where his father, Prince Dimitri Shalikashvili, was a Georgian émigré. After fighting alongside the Poles against the invading Germans, Dmitri Shalikashvili subsequently fought against Moscow in the Georgian legion.

Fig. 7.3. Fighters of the Caucasian special military unit *Sonderverband Bergmann* in a military position near Terek, Northern Caucasus, 1942.

than in organizing a German-Chechen alliance (owing in part to Germany's refusal to recognize autonomous insurrectionary movements). Four months later Saidurov was arrested in Chechnia by the Soviets.[82] Hundreds of Caucasians also formed the so-called *Sonderverband Bergmann* (Special Assignment Unit Mountaineer) and were widely deployed in the Caucasus for reconnaissance, sabotage, subversion, and actual fighting. Some worked quite successfully. In addition, the Caucasians also joined the Unternehmen Zeppelin, the deployment of SS saboteurs and spies in the Soviet Union undertaken from 1942 to 1945. As Perry Biddiscombe has noted, "Of all the Zeppelin agents dispatched behind the Soviet front, only the Moslem Caucasians seem to have had more success in spreading propaganda and organising partisan warfare than in simply gathering information."[83] All this added to Moscow's wholesale suspicions of the Caucasians, even though it succeeded in penetrating some of these groups.

By that time, however, the prospect of defeat was looming ever larger for Nazi Germany, and those who fought with the Germans had to ponder their own fate af-

82 See Burds, "The Soviet War against 'Fifth Columnists'," 397–300.
83 Biddiscombe, "Unternehmen Zeppelin," 1137.

ter Germany's inevitable loss. Among them, Mikheil Kedia and other émigré leaders needed to protect themselves and those who had fought on the German side against the Soviet Union. Fortunately, their interests and those of the United States now coincided, and thus already in 1944 Kedia offered his services ("the use of his Georgian intelligence network, with it's [*sic*] outposts allegedly reaching as far as Moscow") to the US Office of Strategic Services (OSS, the CIA's predecessor). By this time, US intelligence was keenly interested in the Soviet Union as a potential rival and enemy. Under possible threat from the Soviet Union, Turkey, in turn, was "pushing hard for close Turkish-American relations, for substantial American economic and military aid, and for a solid American defence commitment." Turkey thus appeared to Americans as "the perfect base for 'JE-Land [Soviet Union] Operations'."[84] Like many Muslim leaders from Azerbaijan and the Northern Caucasus, Kedia had maintained amicable relations with key figures in the Turkish government, and so was a valuable asset to the United States and Turkey. Thus Kedia, Alikhan Kantemir, A. Atamalibekov (Azeri), and A. Dzhamalian (Armenian), as well as Gerhard von Mende came to be recruited by the OSS (Operation Ruppert), and US-Turkish cooperation came into being by the beginning of 1945.[85] Sensing the victory of the Allied forces, Turkey had already severed diplomatic ties with Germany in August 1944, and on 5 January 1945, it also broke off diplomatic relations with Japan. On 23 February, Turkey declared war on both countries.[86]

It was only in March that the German government, urged by Kedia and others, was forced to acknowledge, de facto, the independence of the Caucasus.[87] Needless to say, this acknowledgment came too late and was of no practical significance. From February 1945, Kedia and other Caucasian leaders negotiated in Geneva with the International Red Cross and the Allies to secure for former Soviet citizens (many of whom fought in the *Ostlegionen* and other military units against the Soviet Union) the right to remain in the West if they so wished. Yet this led nowhere, for their fate had already been sealed at the Yalta Conference in February of that year. Gerhard von Mende, the German expert who worked with these Caucasians, estimated very roughly that one hundred thousand Caucasians were repatriated to the Soviet Union, though some reckon this figure is too low.[88]

84 Burds, "The Soviet War against 'Fifth Columnists'," 309–10. See also Mamoulia, *Les combats indépendandistes des Caucasiens*, 327–38.

85 Burds, "The Soviet War against 'Fifth Columnists'," 311.

86 See Önder, *Die türkische Außenpolitik im Zweiten Weltkrieg*, 240 and Johannes Glasneck and Inge Kircheisen, *Türkei und Afghanistan – Brennpunkte der Orientpolitik im Zweiten Weltkrieg* (Berlin: Deutscher Verlag der Wissenschaften, 1968), 156–57.

87 See Mamoulia, *Les combats indépendandistes des Caucasiens*, 325. Kedia and others sent a number of ultimatums to Rosenberg, demanding that "the Reich recognize the [Caucasian] separatists as 'equivalent partners and allies' " and that unless this was done, "we can no longer assume any responsibility before our peoples or Germany." See Dallin, *German Rule in Russia*, 629.

88 See von zur Mühlen, *Zwischen Hakenkreuz und Sowjetstern*, 227.

In all these events, Japan appeared to remain marginal owing to the neutrality pact concluded with Moscow in April 1941. Bammat lived in Switzerland aloof from international politics, although from 1943 he served as Afghanistan's diplomatic representative in Switzerland. After the Hotel Adlon meeting in Berlin, Bammat entertained more sympathy with Japan (which was not fighting against the Soviet Union) than with Germany (which actually was). Bammat also maintained close contact with Japan's ambassador to Germany, Ōshima, and Japan's military attaché in Turkey, Tateishi. After January 1945, Turkey broke relations with Japan, Tateishi faced the possibility of detention by Turkish authorities. He thus instructed his colleagues in Europe that Bammat be used as his intermediary for communication and gave them Bammat's address in Lausanne, Switzerland: Bammat in turn was to forward all communication to Japan's legation in Bern. Tateishi added: "I think you know BAMATE [Bammat]. He has cooperated with Japan for many years, and has particularly close connections with Lt. General Ōshima. I have not gotten in touch with him about these letters [which Tateishi was to write in plain text in English or French and send from Turkey], but I think he will gladly undertake the business."[89]

During the war, although clearly Japan did not play a critical role, it nevertheless appeared to support the national aspirations of the Caucasian émigrés. After Hitler's attack on the Soviet Union, Moscow pressured Afghanistan, a neutral country, to expel the nondiplomatic personnel of Germany and Italy. Japan, on the other hand, expanded its intelligence activity in this neutral state, despite the Afghan government attempt to restrict these endeavors. Japan persisted, and, with the implicit support of Turkish intelligence, it continued working with leaders from among émigré Muslims of the Soviet Union.[90] Bammat's status as the Afghan government representative in Switzerland no doubt helped Japan keep its options open against the Soviet Union in the Caucasus and Central Asia.

In his last political publication released in July 1943 under a pen name, Bammat continued urging Germany to recognize the independence of the Caucasus and help liberate it from the Russian yoke. He also expressed hope that Turkey would contribute to liberating not only the Caucasus but also Turkestan and Idel-Ural (Volga-Ural). Although Bammat's hopes were to be dashed, his views proved prescient: the "total victory" of Britain and the United States over the Third Reich, achieved with the help of Moscow, exposed Turkey to great danger from the Soviet Union. Already in 1943 he

---

89 NARA RG457, Japanese Attaché Messages 1943–1945, SRA 15,001–15,800, Box. 20 (SRA 15687, 23 January 1945).

90 See Patrick von zur Mühlen, "Japan und die Sowjetische Nationalitätenfrage am Vorabend und während des Zweiten Weltkrieges" *Vierteiljahrshefte für Zeitgeschichte* 21, no. 3 (1973), 330–31, and Glasneck and Kircheisen, *Türkei und Afghanistan*, 259–60.

Fig. 7.4. Haidar Bammat and Alikhan Kantemir, behind whom stands a portrait of Shigeki Usui, Lausanne, Switzerland, August 1945.

had warned the Balkans of domination by Moscow after the war and predicted the Allies would solicit Moscow's participation in annihilating Japan.[91]

Although Japan, and particularly its army, never abandoned the possibility of war against the Soviet Union, that prospect was becoming ever more remote as the Pacific War turned decisively against it by 1943. Whatever plans Japan may have had in store for the Caucasus were likely known to Moscow in any event for two reasons. First, some Caucasian émigré groups had been penetrated by Soviet agents (including "Omeri," who in fact was Berishvili). And second, Japan's diplomatic cipher correspondence had been broken by Moscow, thanks to Kōzō Izumi, a Japanese diplomat turned Soviet agent stationed in Sofia in Bulgaria and Istanbul during the war.[92]

91 Georges Rivoire (H. Bammat), "La position de la Turquie." *Le mois suisse: Littéraire et politique. Revue nationale et Européenne* (Montreux), no. 52 (1943), 34–37, 45, 49. See also Mamoulia, *Les combats indépendandistes des Caucasiens*, 234–35.
92 See Kuromiya and Pepłoński, "Kōzō Izumi."

7.5 Dénouement

The fate of the Soviet Caucasus was sealed, for the time being, by the triumph of the Soviet Union over Germany. Well before Soviet forces took Berlin in May 1945, Moscow was hard at work on Caucasian strategies, going so far as to implement ethnic cleansing in the Northern Caucasus. Already in late 1943, the Karachays were deported to Central Asia, and in the following February the Chechens and Ingush were deported wholesale to Kazakhstan and Kyrgysztan (Operation Chechevitsa). "No exceptions were allowed. Party leaders, war heroes, and famous writers and artists were sometimes sent separately under somewhat better circumstances, but everyone had to go."[93] With Karachays and Balkars (deported in March 1944), the deported Chechens and Ingush numbered more than six hundred thousand. During the brutal process of transport, roughly ten thousand perished and, according to one account, approximately one hundred thousand died in the first three years of exile.[94] Ostensibly, they were expelled because "many Chechens and Ingush were traitors to the homeland, changing over to the side of fascist occupiers, joining the ranks of diversionaries and spies left behind the lines of the red Army by the Germans. They formed armed bands at the behest of the Germans fighting against Soviet power."[95] The real reason, however, was likely to have been Moscow's suspicion "that sympathy for local insurgents was widespread, that problems with conscription and desertion reflected an endemic lack of Soviet patriotism, and that the local party apparatus was inefficient, infiltrated by potential traitors, and wholly unreliable."[96] Whatever the extent of treachery among Chechens and Ingush, and however many of them may have fought in the Red Army, entire nations ("bandit nations") were held collectively responsible and punished accordingly. This was a "Soviet-style final solution."[97] Furthermore, in the autumn of 1944, suspecting that Turkey had a secret plan to attack the Soviet Caucasus, Moscow deported more than ninety thousand "Meshkhetian Turks" (in fact, Georgian Muslims living in Meshketia), Kurds, Khemshins, and Greeks from Georgia's borderlands with Turkey to Central Asia.[98] In all these operations in the Caucasus, Moscow extensively used American trucks sent by Lend-Lease via Iran to transport deportees to rail stations and depots.

---

93 Norman M. Naimark, *Fires of Hatred: Ethnic Cleansing in Twentieth-Century Europe* (Cambridge, MA: Harvard University Press, 2001), 96.

94 Naimark, *Fires of Hatred*, 97.

95 Naimark, *Fires of Hatred*, 94.

96 Marshall, *The Caucasus under Soviet Rule*, 268.

97 Naimark, *Fires of Hatred*, 96. These deportations were followed in May 1944 by the expulsion of Crimean Tatars. The expression "bandit nation" is taken from Burds, "The Soviet War against 'Fifth Columnists'," 303.

98 These and other expulsions are detailed in *Stalinskie deportatsii 1928–1953* (Moscow: MFD-Materik, 2005).

These events deeply traumatized some émigrés, such as Bammat. Abandoning all political activity, he focused on the study of Islam in exile in Switzerland. Although his former comrades who continued fighting for the liberation of the Caucasus sought to persuade him to return to political life, Bammat refused, saying that he would not want his compatriots in the Caucasus to pay for his actions abroad.[99] Those who continued the fight did so under the completely different circumstances of the Cold War. Meanwhile, defeated in August 1945, Japan no longer harbored any strategic interests in the Caucasus, thus putting an end to its long relations with Caucasian fighters for liberation.

99 See Mamoulia, *Les combats indépendandistes des Caucasiens*, 235.

8 Conclusion

At first glance the Caucasus and Japan, separated by the vast Eurasian continent, were unlikely political partners. Yet it was no simple coincidence that brought them together. Just as Poland and Japan came together against their perceived common foe (initially the Russian Empire, then the Soviet Union),[1] the Caucasus and Japan found in each other allies in the common aim of dismembering first Russia and then the Soviet Union. Having fallen far short of their goal, their long-lasting relations are now almost completely forgotten. The secrecy of their collaboration has meant that many relevant documents have been lost. This history of Eurasian collaboration, however, should not be dismissed merely as a curious historical episode.

Caucasian national aspirations, like those of many other nations under Western colonial rule, were greatly stimulated by Japan's challenge to the Russian Empire. Japan's support for them contributed in one way or another to its victory over Russia in 1905. The victory of a small Asian constitutional state over the biggest autocratic empire in the world opened a new chapter in world history. In the Caucasus as elsewhere, numerous small nations now believed that liberation from their imperial masters was possible. World War I led to the collapse of the four empires in Central and Eastern Europe and the independence of many national groups, those in the Caucasus included. But the independence of the Caucasians proved short-lived, as they were then conquered by Moscow and incorporated as constituents into a reestablished empire in the form of the Soviet Union. The Caucasians repeatedly challenged Soviet power in the 1920s, 1930s, and 1940s. Their challenge was supported from abroad by émigrés, who were in turn assisted by countries whose interests coincided with those of the Caucasians: Poland and Japan in the 1920s and 1930s, and Germany during World War II. Japan's role in this history of the Caucasian struggle for liberation is the least known. Yet its strategy was probably the most extensive, encompassing bases from the Far East to the Middle East to Western Europe: it was, literally, a Eurasian operation.

The five-year plan of subversion in the Soviet Caucasus that Japan and Germany jointly devised in 1937 was the most significant of its kind. A number of operations, including clandestine missions into the Caucasus, were carried out. Yet ultimately the practical difficulties proved overwhelming. Germany and Japan distrusted each other, and political discord, commonplace among the émigré groups, made it difficult to act in unison. Moreover, sponsoring their subversion had to be done clandestinely, because, if revealed, it would have caused diplomatic crises. Communication and coordination on a Eurasian scale presented special difficulties of their own. Links with the Soviet Caucasus were hard to establish, and dangerous because Soviet provocation and counterespionage were ubiquitous. It is safe to assume that nearly all Cau-

1 See Hiroaki Kuromiya and Andrzej Pepłoński, *Między Warszawą a Tokio: Polsko-Japońska współpraca wywiadowcza 1904–1944* (Toruń: Adam Marszałek, 2009).

casian émigré groups, including the Caucasus group with which Japan worked in the 1930s, were penetrated by Soviet agents. Moreover, having learned a bitter lesson from Japan's "total espionage," Moscow refined its own version and matched it with "total counter-espionage" in the form of the Great Terror in the 1930s. Japan and the Caucasus group could do little more than maintain very tenuous links with the Caucasus. Although Japan ultimately decided not to fight against the Soviet Union, choosing to challenge the United States and other Western powers instead, Japan continued to consider the Soviet Union a potential foe and so maintained relations with the Caucasus group.

Even though their alliance was not constant (notably during World War I) and their collaboration failed to achieve its goal, relations between Japan and the Caucasus left no bitter taste. This, too, is very similar to the relationship between Japan and Poland from 1904 to 1945. Giorgi Dekanozishvili and Motojirō Akashi maintained cordial relations to the end, even though Japan's support was cut off halfway through their common struggle. Remarkably, both Haidar Bammat and Alikhan Kantemir had very fond memories of their work with the Japanese (especially Shigeki Usui), as the photograph of them taken in August 1945 in Lausanne, Switzerland, suggests (see Figure 7.4 on p. 192 with a photograph of Usui in the background). By then, Usui was dead (killed in action in December 1941 in Rangoon or Yangon, Burma).

There are paradoxes, however. The Caucasians must have been aware that Japan was at the same time a liberator and an oppressor. Japan's anticolonial, anti-Western rhetoric and its victory over Russia in 1905 galvanized those suffering under Russian and Western colonialism. Euphoria spread over Eurasia, including the Caucasus and the Balkans. The Ottomans were invigorated by the events of 1904–05, but so were those peoples living under the Ottoman Empire! What Dekanozishvili, had he lived long enough to observe Akashi's brutal role in Korea, might have thought is anyone's guess. As Japan found itself increasingly cornered politically by Western imperial powers in the wake of its invasion of Manchuria in 1931, Its imperialist ambitions came into clearer focus. In the name of uniting Asians against Western colonialism, Japan promoted its own imperialist agenda. This should have been clear to anyone after Japan annexed Korea in 1910 and exacted humiliating concessions from China during World War I (in both cases with Russia's implicit consent). Like Western colonial powers, Japan maintained extraterritoriality in China. In fact, Japan's colonial arrogance became abundantly clear to Turkey soon after the Russo-Japanese War, when there was much admiration for Japan's victory in the Sublime Porte: Japan demanded the same unequal status from the Ottomans as that enjoyed by Western colonial powers. Yet, in the 1930s, while Asians turned increasingly against the Japanese, the Caucasians, and the Caucasus group in particular, worked with them amicably. Why?

Here distance certainly mattered. Unlike Asia, where Japan had colonial ambitions, Japan was too far from the Caucasus to assert such claims. This proved both a strength and weakness in the Caucasian-Japanese nexus. Japan's support in 1905 was critical to the events of that year in the Caucasus. Yet Japan withdrew when it really mattered: once the war was over, Japan's interest in the Caucasus temporarily waned. (Akashi himself did not abandon his Caucasian friends, and the *Sirius* operation proved much more successful than the famous *John Grafton* affair.) And even though Japan was the strongest supporter of Caucasian interests against the Soviet Union in the 1930s, it did, and could do, little to nothing for the Caucasus during World War II. Poland was a more consistent supporter of the Caucasians' anti-Soviet interests. Yet Poland alone was too weak to protect them on its own, and indeed it was destroyed by Germany and the Soviet Union in 1939. By contrast, it was Germany that rendered critical support to the Caucasians during World Wars I and II. In both instances, however, Germany was defeated. In the latter war, the position of Caucasian émigrés was much more precarious because of the racist policy of Nazi Germany and its denial of the aspirations of Caucasians for political independence. People like Bammat harbored no illusions about German political goals. But they did retain illusions about Japan's "good will." Many Caucasians nevertheless worked with the Germans in hopes they would prevail in the end. Their hopes proved delusive.

There is no evidence that those who collaborated with Nazi Germany shared Nazi ideology. Many did share elements of fascist ideology (nationalism, skepticism of laissez-faire capitalism, and opposition to the Versailles settlement in the wake of World War I). They initially believed that Hitler was a "genius leader," and they greeted Japan as a liberator even as Japan was trying to destroy China. (One should add that at the beginning, even the liberally minded Prometheans also welcomed Japan's aggression in China, which they considered an empire.) Yet there is no evidence to suggest that Bammat and others shared the racist and anti-Semitic ideology of Nazism. In German-occupied Paris, Mikheil Kedia, who worked with the Germans, even took trouble to protect Jews and Social Democrats. One simply does not know how much they knew about the Nazi destruction of the European Jewry. It is possible they knew very little or knew but did little about it. In any event, there is much evidence that their collaboration was purely tactical, although this does not absolve them from having been party to the German war effort (if not necessarily Nazi war crimes).

Ideologically, Japan's emphasis on liberating oppressed nations was far more dangerous to Moscow than was Nazism or fascism. It had strong appeal for those living under colonial power (including the Soviet Empire and China).[2] Among the Inner Mongolians, for example, who feared China's imperial domination, Japan's conquest of Manchuria meant autonomy for Mongolians. Owen Lattimore, an American specialist of Mongolia and no friend of Japan, even stated in 1934 that

2 That was why Moscow fabricated (or was at least a party to the fabrication and spreading of) the infamous "Tanaka Memorial," purportedly laying out Japan's imperial conquest of Asia. See p. 68 of the present book.

> the autonomous province [of Xing'an or Hsingan or Barga] itself has a greater degree of freedom in its internal affairs than any other part of Manchukuo. The Mongols are ruled partly by their hereditary princes and partly by elective and appointed officials. They are even allowed to maintain their own troops.[3]

In 1936, Japan allowed the Inner Mongolians to have their own government, the Mongolian Military Government in Chahar with Prince De Wang (Demchugdongrub) as its head.[4] This was why Bammat and others continued to entertain illusions about Japan, and why Moscow regarded Japan as a mortal enemy whose influence it feared might spread into Outer Mongolia (under Moscow's control) and the Soviet Union (including Buryatia).

For this reason Stalin was much more obsessed, at least initially, with Japan's threat than with Nazi Germany's. Stalin suspected he could deal with the Nazi dictator. Indeed, he concluded the Molotov-Ribbentrop Pact and destroyed Poland with Hitler, erroneously believing he was outmaneuvering the latter. By comparison, Stalin could not find any leader in Japan with whom he could bargain, because there was no dictator in Japan. Moreover, unlike Germany, Japan had been working with Poland, the Caucasus, the Baltics, and others, encircling the Soviet Union on the Eurasian continent. This is why Moscow caught far more "Japanese spies" than "German spies" in 1937–38. Stalin thus resorted to numerous political and military provocations to weaken Japan. The Battle of Khalkhin Gol in 1939, in which Japan was routed, for example, was provoked by Moscow for this purpose because it had a superb secret weapon: the commander of the main Japanese fighting forces was a Soviet agent![5]

In the end, Moscow was saved by Japan's increasingly self-destructive imperialist war against the Chinese. The United States played a critical role in this. Washington saw Japan as a usurper of its own colonial interests in China and Asia in general. Japan's adventure in China led to what might be called an informal and virtual united front against Japan between the United States and the Soviet Union in the resumption of American-Soviet diplomatic relations in 1933. President Franklin D. Roosevelt used the *New York Times* correspondent in Moscow, Walter Duranty to present the Soviet Union in the best possible light to the American public in order to facilitate US recognition of the Soviet Union.[6] Duranty was an apologist for Stalin. When millions of people were dying from hunger in the Soviet Union in 1932, Duranty repeatedly de-

---

3 Owen Lattimore, *The Mongols of Manchuria* (New York: H. Fertig, 1934), 21.

4 The government was Japan's puppet government, however, and did not signify the independence of Inner Mongolians in Barga.

5 See Hiroaki Kuromiya, "The Mystery of Nomonhan, 1939." *The Journal of Slavic Military Studies* 24, no. 4 (December 2011), 659–77. There is little doubt that the 1938 battle of Lake Khasan was also provoked by Moscow against Japan. See Hiroaki Kuromiya, "The Battle of Lake Khasan Reconsidered." *The Journal of Slavic Military Studies* 29, no. 1 (2016), 99–109.

6 Tim Tzouliadis, *The Forsaken: An American Tragedy in Stalin's Russia* (New York: Penguin, 2008), 55–59.

nied the existence of famine.[7] There is also testimony that he regularly reported to the Soviet secret police in the 1930s.[8] Roosevelt also mobilized the services of Armand Hammer, who, it is now widely believed, was a Soviet agent, or at least an agent of influence for the Soviet government, working as its mouthpiece in the United States.[9]

Ostensibly Roosevelt's rationale was that recognizing the Soviet Union would boost trade and help improve an American economy still reeling from the Great Depression. Yet his real reason was to use the Soviet Union to offset Japan's growing power in the Far East.[10] In 1934, Karl Radek, who was serving as Stalin's personal diplomat, frankly stated that Moscow's intention was to sabotage US-Japanese relations.[11] Thus, Japan was at the center of the American-Soviet rapprochement, a point almost universally neglected by historians of the Soviet Union. After Japan started a full-scale war against China in 1937, Moscow and Washington secretly consulted with each other and together helped China against Japan.[12]

Confronted by a perceived "siege" by the Great Powers, Japan became disoriented. Stalin aptly noted in 1939:

> As a result of the now two-year-old war with China which hasn't been won, Japan has lost its balance and has begun to get nervous and act out of gear, now attacking Britain, now the Soviet Union, and now the People's Republic of Mongolia. Its action has no reason. This has revealed Japan's weakness. Its conduct may unite all others against it.[13]

Moscow made every effort to use the United States against Japan, and Washington did not betray Moscow's expectations.[14] Ultimately, Japan decided to engage militarily with the United States instead of the Soviet Union. It was a huge boon for Stalin and a big disappointment to Soviet émigrés and Germans alike.

---

7 See S.J. Taylor, *Stalin's Apologist: Walter Duranty, The New York Times's Man in Moscow* (New York: Oxford University Press, 1990).

8 Carl Blumay and Henry Edwards, *The Dark Side of Power: The Real Armand Hammer* (New York: Simon & Schunster, 1992), 48.

9 Blumay and Edwards, *The Dark Side of Power*, 48.

10 On the United States, see Beatrice Farnsworth, *William C. Bullitt and the Soviet Union* (Bloomington-Indianapolis: Indiana University Press, 1967), ch. 5; on the Soviet Union, see Stalin's coded telegram on Litvinov's visit to the United States, RGASPI, f. 558, op. 11, d. 82, l. 43, and the Politburo directive to Maksim Litvinov (25 October 1933), f. 17, op. 162, d. 15, l. 119.

11 RGASPI, f. 558, op. 11, d. 792, l. 1.

12 For the secret US-Soviet consultations over China and against Japan, see Pavel Sudoplatov, *Raznye dni tainoi voiny i diplomatii. 1941 god* (Moscow: OLMA-PRESS, 2001), 150.

13 *Zhonghua min guo zhong yao shi liao chu bian—dui Ri kang zhan shi qi. Di 3 bia, Zhan shi wai jiao* (Taipei: Jing xiao zhe Zhong yang wen wu gong ying she, 1981), 425.

14 For details, see Hiroaki Kuromiya, "The Promethean Movement and Japan's Diplomacy," in *Ruch Prometejski i walka o przebudowę Europy Wschodniej (1918–1940)*, ed. by Marek Kornat (Warsaw: In-t Historii PAN, 2012), 144–45.

Did Bammat and others who worked with the Japanese understand the essence of Great Power politics that hid American colonialism in Asia? One does not know for sure. The present work has shown that the United States was intricately embroiled in the trans-Pacific shadow triangle of Russia, Japan, and itself. Yet its hidden role in this embroilment, which began with Japan's victory in the Russo-Japanese War, has been almost completely omitted by Eurocentric or Americocentric works. Hence the importance of a Eurasian perspective.

In any event, deeply disappointed by the Germans but still hopeful of Japan, by 1943 Bammat had settled in Switzerland and abandoned politics to concentrate on his study of Islam. He died in Paris in 1965. Kantemir, like Mikheil Kedia and many others who had worked with the Japanese before 1941, collaborated from June 1941 to 1945 with the Germans and, foreseeing Hitler's defeat, quickly began working with the United States, in which they saw a new ally. Kantemir continued to be active in émigré politics, editing several journals devoted to the Caucasus,[15] and died in Munich in 1963. Takanobu Manaki, who, like Usui, worked closely with the Caucasus group in the 1930s, met the end of the war in Indochina and died in 1979. Even in private conversations after the war, he did not disclose his clandestine work in the 1930s with the Caucasians and others.[16] Hiroshi Ōshima, who, along with Manaki and Usui, collaborated closely with the Caucasus group, was arrested after the war. Tried as a war criminal for his role in Japan's wartime alliance with Germany, he was sentenced to life imprisonment. Released in 1955, he lived another twenty years. Like Manaki, however, Ōshima remained largely silent about Japan's secret work with the Caucasians, even though it was he who signed the May 1937 secret agreement with Germany on clandestine work in the Caucasus.

In 1937–38, in the Caucasus as elsewhere in the Soviet Union, countless people were destroyed by Moscow for their alleged Japanese connections. But Soviet agents who worked against the Caucasian-Japanese network did not fare any better. Numerous secret police agents were executed. Lavrenti Beria himself, who oversaw the Great Terror in the Caucasus by Stalin's order, was executed in 1953, charged with espionage for foreign countries. Some of his own relatives had had close connections with Japanese authorities in Manchuria, although they were almost certainly working for the Soviet government. Shalva Berishvili, a professional spy who had contact with Hōryō Tateishi, Japan's military attaché in Turkey, turned against his comrades and worked for Moscow as "Omeri." Yet he was also arrested in 1942 by the Soviet secret police on suspicion of working for Polish, British, French, German, Turkish, and Japanese intelligence and sentenced to twenty five years in the Gulag.[17] (Tateishi

15 See Patrik von zur Mühlen, *Zwischen Hakenkreuz und Sowjetstern: Der Nationalismus der sowjetischen Orientvölker im Zweiten Weltkrieg* (Düsseldorf: Droste Verlag, 1971), 229 and 231.

16 Private communication and interview records in Tokyo.

17 O.B. Mozokhin, ed., *Politbiuro i delo Beriia. Sbornik dokumentov* (Moscow: Kuchkovo pole, 2012), p. 314. His memoirs were published in 1993 in Georgian: *Tbilisi*, 30 June, 1, 5–7, 13–15, 19–20 July 1993.

served in Turkey until the end of the war and died in Japan in 1957.) Bezhan Giorgadze, working for the Caucasus group, was arrested crossing the Iranian-Azerbaijan border by Soviet border guards in July 1938. Although released from captivity in 1944 under an agreement with the Soviet secret police, he was not trusted by the police, and was arrested again in 1951, and sentenced the following year to twenty five years in the Gulag. Released in 1957 after Stalin's and Beria's deaths, he worked for the Institute of History at the Georgian Academy of Sciences in Tbilisi, where he translated many works from Latin, French, Italian, and Portuguese into Georgian. He died in Georgia in the 1980s.[18]

History is rife with irony. Poland's fate was much too familiar to the Caucasians. Even though Britain and France went to war against Nazi Germany to protect Poland, ultimately they sacrificed it. In October 1944 in Moscow, Stanisław Mikołajczyk, prime minister of the Polish government in exile (in London), was shocked to learn that Britain and the United States had let Stalin have his way over the future territory of Poland (the demarcation of Poland and the Soviet Union along the Curzon line). In response to Mikołajczyk's protest, British Prime Minister Winston Churchill said,

> If you think you can conquer Russia, well, you are crazy, you ought to be in a lunatic asylum. You would involve us in a war in which twenty-five million lives might be lost. You would be liquidated. You hate the Russians. I know you hate them. We are very friendly with them, more friendly than we have ever been. I mean to keep things like that. I tell you, we'll become sick and tired if you continue arguing. We shall tell the world how unreasonable you are. We shall not part friends.[19]

As an Englishman present at the exchange observed, "This was not diplomacy. Nor did it intimidate Mikolajczyk."[20] The Caucasus fared worse than Poland because its claims were not even considered by the Great Powers. István Deák once said of Hungary's experience of World War II: "In Hungary, at least, one of the things history teaches Hungarians is that it is a terrible mistake to be a small country in Central Europe."[21] This was also a lesson the Caucasians learned.

No small country itself, Japan was nonetheless small by comparison. Well before the Pacific War began, the Great Powers (particularly the Soviet Union and the United States) formed a united front covertly against a power (Japan) bent on subverting Western colonial rule in Asia. To preserve their interests, they contained the only Asian power capable of challenging them and ended up preserving the largest Asian empires (China and the Soviet Union) intact. It was only after China was taken over by

---

18 See the file of B.G. Giorgadze, Archive of the Ministry of Internal Affairs of Georgia (Tbilisi).

19 *Churchill Taken from the Diaries of Lord Moran: The Struggle for Survival 1940–1965* (Boston, 1966), 214–15.

20 *Churchill Taken from the Diaries of Lord Moran*, 215.

21 István Deák, Jan T. Gross, and Tony Judt, eds., *The Politics of Retribution in Europe: World War II and Its Aftermath* (Princeton: Princeton University Press, 2000), 68.

communists that the Western powers began questioning China's occupation of non-Han lands (particularly Tibet and Xinjiang).

There is another important irony in the outcome of Japan's long engagements against the Russian Empire and Soviet Union in which the Caucasus played a vital role. Once the Cold War started, the United States borrowed heavily from Japan's experience. In the 1930s Japan, Germany, and Poland, all seeing the Soviet Union as an enemy, devised strategies to dismember it. Of these, Japan's plan was the oldest and grandest. Nazi racist ideology prevented Germany from fully exploiting the Soviet Union's national minorities living on the periphery of the country. Poland, meanwhile, raised a serious political challenge to the Soviet Union in the form of the Promethean movement, and worked with Japan to devise plans to utilize the ethnic Ukrainians living in the Soviet Far East (see p. 144). Yet Poland could not cover all parts of the Soviet Union, especially in Asia. At the beginning of the twentieth century, Japan covered most of the Eurasian periphery more broadly, a truly Eurasian scheme. But while it must have expended enormous resources, both human and material, in the end it proved too small a match for its gigantic neighbor. The United States, on the other hand, a country with vast resources, adopted Japan's old Eurasian strategies during the succeeding years of the Cold War.

It is well known that after World War II the United States recruited many of the German spies and specialists of the Caucasus and Soviet Union.[22] Less known is that the United States also recruited many former Japanese intelligence officers after Japan's surrender.[23] During the war Washington had secretly studied Japan's work with the peoples of the Caucasus and Central Asia,[24] and after the war it sought Japanese expertise. Thus, the Americans emulated, refined, and expanded Japan's use of the Caucasus and the Muslim world as a "citadel against Communism" during the Cold War.[25]

---

22 See, for example, the classic work by Hermann Zolling and Heinz Höhne, *Pullach intern: General Gehlen und die Geschichte des Bundesnachrichtendienstes* (Hamburg: Hoffmann u. Campe, 1971), and Jeffrey Burds, "The Soviet War against 'Fifth Columnists': The Case of Chechnya, 1942–4." *Journal of Contemporary History* 42, no. 2 (2007), 309–313.

23 See, for example, Tetsuo Arima, *Daihonei sanbō ha sengo nani to tatakattanoka* (Tokyo: Shinchōsha, 2010) and Mikio Haruna, *Himitsu no fairu: CIA no tainichi kōsaku* (Tokyo: Kyōdō tsūshinsha, 2000).

24 See United States Office of Strategic Services, Research and Analysis Branch no. 890.2, *Japanese Attempts at Infiltration among Muslims in Russia and Her Borderlands* (Washington, D.C.: Dept. of State Office of Intelligence Research, 1944).

25 See Selçuk Esenbel, "Japan's Global Claim to Asia and the World of Islam: Transnational Nationalism and World Power, 1900–1945." *The American Historical Review* 109, no. 4 (2004), 1169.

Appendix

An Additional German-Japanese Agreement on the Exchange of Intelligence concerning Soviet Russia [USSR][26]

Berlin, den 11. 5. 1937.

Deutsch-Japanische Zusatzvereinbarungen betreffend Austausch der Nachrichteln über Sowjetrussland.

1. Der Austausch erfolgt in der Weise, dass das Reichskriegsministerium dem japanischen Militär-Attaché in Berlin die eingehenden Nachrichten übermittelt. Uebergabe des japanischen Materials erfolgt in Tokio an den deutschen Militär-Attaché zwecks sofortiger Weiterleitung auf dem Kurierwege an Abwehrabteilung.
2. Der Austausch erstreckt sich auf sämtliches bei den beiderseitigen nachrichtenbeschaffenden Stellen einlaufendes, unausgewertetes wichtiges Material, und zwar bezgl. Heer, Luftwaffe, Rüstungsindustrie sowie Nachrichten über reine Spionageabwehr.
3. Ferner werden von Zeit zu Zeit von beiden Stellen Fragebogen übermittelt. Beide Stellen bemühen sich, diese Fragen zu beantworten.
4. Nach Beurteilung des eingetroffenen unausgewerteten Materials gegen die Werturteile der auswertenden Stelle der anderen Stelle zu.
5. Die deutschen und die japanischen Wehrmachtdienststellen überlegen gemeinsam, inwieweit ein Austausch bestehender Erfahrungen auf dem Gebiet des Nachrichtendienstes möglich ist.

gez.: Canaris Oshima

Berlin, den 11. 5. 1937.

26 The original German version, reproduced here with the original punctuation preserved, is available at the BBKT, Miyazaki Shūichi Bunko, 32: "Japanese-German Military Agreements concerning Intelligence Exchange and Subversion." The attached "five-year plan" is in table format in the original. The Japanese version is reprinted in Nobuo Tajima, *Nachizumu kyokutō senryaku: nichidoku bōkyō kyōtei o meguru chōhōsen* (Tokyo, Kōdansha, 1997), 197–99 and 246–47.

Deutsch-japanische Zusatzvereinbarungen betreffend Zersetzungsarbeit gegen Sowjetrussland.

1. Die gemeinschaftliche Arbeit besteht im folgenden:
   (a) Aktivierung sämtlicher Minderheitenbewegungen.
   (b) Antibolschewistische Propaganda.
   (c) Vorbereitungen zum Einsatz von revolutionären Handlungen, terroristischen Akten und Sabotagehandlungen bei Kriegsausbruch.
2. Die zu treffenden Vorbereitungen haben innerhalb Gesamtsowjetrusslands zu erfolgen. Es werden drei Interessengebiete eingeteilt:
   (a) die europäische Westfront von Finnland bis Bulgarien als deutsches Hauptinteressengebiet.
   (b) die Südwestfront (Türkei und Persien) als gemeinschaftliches Interessengebiet.
   (c) die asiatische Ostfront als japanisches Hauptinteressengebiet.
3. Die Zusammenarbeit wird sich nach anliegendem Fünfjahrplan von 1937 – 1941 erstrecken.
4. Die Kosten im gemeinschaftlichen Interessengebiet werden von beiden Teilen je zur Hälfte getragen.
5. Beide Teile unterrichten sich laufend gegenseitig über den Stand der Zersetzungsarbeit in den jeweiligen Hauptinteressengebieten.
6. Ohne gegenseitiges Einverständnis werden andere Staaten in die Zusammenarbeit nicht mit hineingezogen.
7. Die militärischen Stellen sorgen für reibungslose Zusammenarbeit mit den politischen Stellen, soweit diese für eine Mitarbeit in Frage kommen, und sichern diese Arbeit vor Störungen unmaßgeblicher Stellen.
8. Im Falle einer der beiden Staaten in einen Krieg mit Sowjetrussland verwickelt wird, wird der andere Teil in seinem unter (2) bezeichneten Hauptinteressengebiet sowie in dem gemeinsamen Interessengebiet die Zersetzungsarbeit mit allen Mitteln steigern.
9. Bei der jährlich stattfindenden gemeinsamen Beratung wird der Erfolg auf allen Gebieten untersucht und der das gemeinschaftliche Interessengebiet betreffende Arbeitsplan für das kommende Jahr auf Grund des genannten Fünfjahresplans festgelegt.

gez.: Canaris Oshima

Vorbemerkungen:

1. Der 5-Jahres-Plan soll nur eine Richtlinie für die gemeinsame Arbeit geben. Es bleibt vorbehalten, ihn je nach der Lage und dem inzwischen Erreichten entsprechend zu ändern.
2. Der Plan erstrebt unter langsamer Verstärkung der Arbeit in sämtlichen in Frage kommenden Ländern, beim Abschluss die Vollendung der Kriegsvorbereitungen bis zu einem gewissen Grade zu gewährleisten.

Türkei

1937. (1) Verbindung u. U. unter Bestechung zu politischen Würdenträgern; (2) Verbindungen mit militärischen Stellen (Chef d. Genst. usw.); (3) Einrichtung v. einigen als Wirtschaftsunternehmen getarnten Stützpunkten an der Grenze; (4) Forschungsarbeit über Verhältnisse der politischen u. militärischen Lage; (5) Langsam beginnende Propaganda für Deutschland u. Japan gegen Russland; (6) Ausbildung v. V-Leuten[27] i. d. Türkei (bedürftige Schüler durch Geld getarnt als Stipendien gewinnen).

1938. (1) Verstärkung der bisherigen Arbeit; (2) Wenn mögl. nicht durch uns, sd. [sondern] entsprechende politische Stellen (Ri[bbentrop])[28] Aufname politischer Verbindungen mit d. Regierung zur Duldung einer antibolschew. Front; (3) Weiterer Ausbau von einigen Stützpunkten; (4) Schaffung einer Schiffsverbindung auf dem Schwarz. Meer; (5) Einrichtung v. Kurierwegen u. Ausbildung u. Einstellung v. Grenzgängern; (6) Einrichtung von Zellen im kauk. Gebiet u. Herstellung d. Verbind. zu ihnen.

1939. (1) Verstärkung der bisherigen Arbeit; (2) Schaffung von Radioverbindungen; (3) Erkundung von Landungsplätzen für Flugzeuge; (4) Ausbildung von Kaukas. für den Kern einer kaukas. Armee.

1940. (1) Verstärkung der bisherigen Arbeit; (2) Eingehende Vorbereitung für Fliegerangriffe auf militärisch wichtige Objekte; (3) Waffeneinfuhr.

1941. (1) Verstärkung der bisherigen Arbeit; (2) Vollendung der Kriegsvorbereitung; (3) Aufstellung d. Kaders für eine kaukas. Armee.

Iran (Persien)

---

27 Plural of *Verbindungsmann*/*Vertrauensmann*, or contact man/trusted representative.

28 The *Büro Ribbentrop*, subsequently *Dienststelle Ribbentrop*, was Hitler's private office for diplomacy, headed by Joachim von Ribbentrop, which worked alongside or sometimes against the German Foreign Ministry. Ribbentrop was a decisive force that supported the Anti-Comintern Pact with Tokyo. When the present agreement was signed in May 1937, Ribbentrop was Germany's Ambassador to Great Britain.

1937. (1) Forschungsarbeit über politische u. militärische Lage; (2) Verbindung mit Militärkreisen; (3) Wenn mögl. nicht durch uns, sdn. [sondern] entsprechende pol. Stellen (Büro Ri[bbentrop])[29] Einrichtung wirtschaftlicher Verbindungen.
1938. (1) Verstärkung der bisherigen Arbeit; (2) Schaffung von Stützpunkten an der Grenze; (3) Schulung u. Einsetzung von Kurieren und Grenzgängern; (4) Ausbildung v. V-Leuten.
1939. (1) Verstärkung der bisherigen Arbeit; (2) Schaffung v. Schiffsverbindungen auf d. Kaspischen Meer; (3) Schaffung v. Radioverbindungen mit dem Kaukasus.
1940. (1) Verstärkung der bisherigen Arbeit; (2) Eingehende Vorbereitungen für Fliegerangriffe auf militärisch wichtige Objekte; (3) Waffeneinfuhr;
1941. (1) Verstärkung der bisherigen Arbeit; (2) Vollendung der Kriegsvorbereitungen;

Kaukasus.

1937. (1) Forschungsarbeit über politische und militärische Lage.
1938. (1) Verstärkung der bisherigen Arbeit; (2) Schaffung ständiger Verbindungswege; (3) Beginn der Propaganda.
1939. (1) Verstärkung der bisherigen Arbeit; (2) Einrichtung von Zellen in Baku, Grosni, Tiflis, Wladikawkas, Batum und längs d. Ölleitung; (3) Aufname v. Verbindungen zur Roten u. Territorialarmee.
1940. (1) Verstärkung der bisherigen Arbeit; (2) Vorbereitung eines Volksaufstandes; (3) dto.

Europäische Länder.

1937. Wenn mögl. nicht durch uns sd. entsprechende pol. Stellen ((Büro Ri[bbentrop]). Politische Vorbereitung in den Grenzländern, bes. in Bulgarien u. Rumänien; (2) Ausbildung v. Kaukas., die aus den Ländern, in denen sie wohnen, herausgeholt u. wieder zurückgeschickt werden; (3) Ueberwachung der Arbeit, Englands, Italiens, Polens für den Kaukasus.
1938. (1) Verstärkung der bisherigen Arbeit.
1939. (1) Verstärkung der bisherigen Arbeit; (2) Schaffung einer Basis (Depots) im östlichen Mittelmeer; (3) Kaukas. Armee Kader.
1940. (1) Verstärkung der bisherigen Arbeit.
1941. dto.

Emigration.

1937. (1) Unterstützung der nationalen kaukas. Gruppen unter Leitung von Bammat zu Propagandazwecken: (a) Erweiterung der Zeitschrift Kaukasus; (b) Herausgabe

---

29 See note 3.

der Zeitschrift in den erforderlichen Sprachen; (c) Propaganda im Kaukasus und anderen Ländern; (2) Ueberwachung der Prometheus-Bewegung.

1938. (1) Verstärkung der bisherigen Arbeit; (2) Einleitung einer antibolschewistischen Propagandatätigkeit.

1939. (1) Verstärkung der bisherigen Arbeit.

1940. (1) Verstärkung der bisherigen Arbeit.

1941. (1) Verstärkung der bisherigen Arbeit; (2) Vollendung der Kriegsvorbereitung.

Bibliography

Archives and Private Papers

Archive of the Ministry of Internal Affairs of Georgia, Tbilisi, Georgia.
Archives du ministère des Affaires étrangères , Paris, France.
Archives de la préfecture de la police de Paris, France.
Arkhiv vneshnei politiki Rossiiskoi Federatsii, Moscow, Russia.
Archiwum Akt Nowych, Warsaw, Poland.
Bibliothèque de documentation internationale contemporaine, Nanterre, France.
Bōeishō Bōei Kenkyūjo Toshokan, Tokyo, Japan.
Centralne Archiwum Wojskowe, Warsaw, Poland.
Centre historique des archives nationales, Paris, France.
Centre d'archives contemporaines, Fontainebleau, France.
Gosudarstvennyi arkhiv Rossiiskoi Federatsii, Moscow, Russia.
Gaimushō Gaikō Shiryō Kan, Tokyo, Japan.
Georgian State Central Historical Archive, Tbilisi, Georgia.
Haus-, Hof- und Staatsarchiv, Politisches Archiv, Vienna, Austria.
Hoover Institution Archive, Stanford University, USA.
Japan Center for Asian Historical Records, National Archives of Japan, Tokyo, Japan.
Józef Piłsudski Institute of America Archive, New York, USA.
National Archives, Kew, UK.
National Archives and Records Administration, College Park, USA.
Rossiiskii gosudarstvennyi arkhiv sotsial'nopoliticheskoi istorii, Moscow, Russia.
Rossiiskii gosudartsvennyi voenno-istoricheskii arkhiv.
Rossiiskii gosudarstvennyi voennyi arkhiv, Moscow, Russia.
Ukrainian Research Institute, Harvard University, Cambridge, Massachusetts, USA.
Service historique de l'armée de Terre, Château de Vincennes, France.
N. Badual-Kereselidze Family Archive, Aix-en-Province, France.
M. Bammat Family Archive, Paris, France.
G. Kvinitadze Family, Chatou, France.
Personal Archives of G. von Mende, Oslo, Norway.
Personal archive of Georges Mamoulia, Paris, France.

Printed Books

Agabekov, Georges. *OGPU: The Russian Secret Terror.* New York: Brentano's, 1931.

Afary, Janet. *The Iranian Constitutional Revolution, 1906-1911.* New York: Columbia University Press, 1996.

Akashi, Motojirō. *Rakka ryūsui: Colonel Akashi's Report on His Secret Cooperation with the Russian Revolutionary Parties during the Russo-Japanese War.* Helsinki: Societas Historica Finlandiae, 1988.

Akmese, Handan Nezir. *The Birth of Modern Turkey: The Ottoman Military and the March to World War I.* London–New York: I. B. Tauris, 2005.

Altstadt, Audrey. *The Azerbaijani Turks: Power and Identity Under Russian Rule.* Stanford: Hoover Institution Press, 1992.

Arima, Tetsuo. *Daihonei sanbō ha sengo nani to tatakattanoka.* Tokyo: Shinchōsha, 2010.

Armstrong, H.C. *Unending Battle.* New York-London: Harper & Brothers, 1934.

Ascher, Abraham. *The Revolution of 1905: Russia in Disarray.* Stanford, Calif.: Stanford University Press, 1988.

Avalishvili, Zourab. *The Independence of Georgia in International Politics 1918–1921.* London: Headley Brothers, 1940.

Baberowski, Jörg. *Der Feind ist überall: Stalinismus im Kaukasus.* Munich: Deutsche Verlags-Anstalt, 2003.

Bagirova, I.S. *Politicheskie partii i organizatsii Azerbaidzhana v nachale XX veka (1900–1917).* Baku: Elm, 1997.

Balaev, Aidyn. *Azerbaidzhanskoe natsional'noe dvizhenie; ot "Musavata" do Narodnogo Fronta.* Baku: Elm, 1992.

Balaev, Aidyn. *Mamed Emin Rasulzade. Na chuzhikh beregakh 1922–1943.* Moscow: Maska, 2013.

Bammate, Haidar. *The Caucasus Problem: Questions concerning Circassia and Daghestan.* Berne: Staempfli & Cie, 1919.

Barrett, Thomas M. *At the Edge of Empire: The Terek Cossacks and the North Caucasus Frontier, 1700-1860* . Boulder: Westview Press, 1999.

Batbaiar, Ts. *Mongolia i Iaponiia v pervoi polovine xx veka.* Ulan-Ude: VSGAKI, 2002.

Baumgart, Winfried. *Deutsche Ostpolitik 1918. Von Brest-Litowsk bis zum Ende des Ersten Weltkrieges.* Vienna-Munich: Oldenbourg, 1966.

Bechhofer, C.E. *In Denikin's Russia and the Caucasus, 1919–1920.* London: W. Collins Sons, 1921.

Beria, Sergo. *Moi otets Beriia: v koridorakh stalinskoi vlasti.* Moscow: OLMA-PRESS, 2002.

Berson, Jan, Otmar. *Minus Moskwa (Wołga - Kaukaz -Krym).* Warsaw: Rój, 1935.

Berton, Peter. *Russo-Japanese Relations, 1905–1917: From Enemies to Allies.* Milton Park, Abingdon–New York: Routledge, 2012.

Bihl, Wolfdieter. *Die Kaukasus-Politik der Mittelmächte. Teil I: Ihre Basis in der Orient-Politik und ihre Aktionen 1914–1917.* Wien-Köln-Graz: Böhlaus, 1975.

Bihl, Wolfdieter. *Die Kaukasus-Politik der Mittelmächte. Teil II. Die Zeit der versuchten kaukasischen Staatlichkeit (1917–1918).* Vienna-Köln-Graz: Böhlau, 1992.

Black, Cyril E. *et al.*, eds., *The Modernization of Japan and Russia: A Comparative Study.* New York: Free Press, 1975.

Blumay, Carl, and Henry Edwards. *The Dark Side of Power: The Real Armand Hammer.* New York: Simon & Schunster, 1992.

Bugai, N.F. *L. Beriia – I. Stalinu: 'Posle Vashikh ukazanii provedeno sleduiushchee . . .'* Moscow: Grif i K, 2011.

Burdett, Anita L.P., ed., *Caucasian Boundaries: Documents and Maps 1802–1946*, v. 1. London: Archive Editions, 1996.

Burleigh, Bennet, *Empire of the East or Japan and Russia at War, 1904–5*. London: Chapman & Hall, 1905.

Chaqueri, Cosroe. *The Soviet Socialist Republic of Iran: Birth of the Trauma*. Pittsburgh, PA: University of Pittsburgh Press, 1995.

Churchill Taken from the Diaries of Lord Moran: The Struggle for Survival 1940–1965. Boston: Houghton, 1966.

Clarke III, J. Calvitt. *Alliance of the Colored Peoples: Ethiopia and Japan before World War II*. Woodbridge, Suffolk: James Currey Ltd, 2011.

Clarke III, Calvitt. *Russia and Italy Against Hitler: The Bolshevik-Fascist Rapprochement of the 1930s*. New York: Greenwood Press, 1991.

Dallin, Alexander. *German Rule in Russia 1941–1945: A Study of Occupation Policies*, 2nd ed. Boulder, Colorado: Westview Press, 1981.

Damaskin, I.A. *Stalin i razvedka*. Moscow: Veche, 2004.

Deák, István, Jan, T. Gross and Tony Judt, eds., *The Politics of Retribution in Europe: World War II and Its Aftermath*. Princeton: Princeton University Press, 2000.

Dickinson, Frederick R. *World War I and the Triumph of a New Japan, 1919-1930*. Cambridge-New York: Cambridge University Press, 2013.

Dokumenty i mater'ialy po vneshnei politike Zakavakz'ia i Gruzii (Tiflis: Tipografiia Pravitel'stva Gruzinskoi Respubliki, 1919.

Dokumenty vneshnei politiki SSSR, vol. 1. Moscow: Politizdat, 1959.

Dokumenty vneshnei politiki SSSR, vol. 3. Moscow: Politizdat, 1959.

Dornheim, Andreas. *Röhms Mann fürs Ausland. Politik und Ermordung des SA-Agenten Georg Bell*. Münster: Lit Verlag, 1998.

Durland, Kellogg. *The Red Reign: The True History of an Adventurous Year in Russia*. New York: The Century Co., 1908.

Dzhukha, Ivan. *Grecheskaia operatsiia. Istoriia repressii protiv grekov v SSSR*. St. Petersburg: Aleteiia, 2006.

Eklof Ben, John Bushnell, and Larissa Zakharova, eds., *Russia's Great Reforms, 1855-1881*. Bloomington-Indianapolis: Indiana University Press, 1994.

Esenbel, Selçuk, and Chiharu Inaba, eds., *The Rising Sun and the Turkish Crescent: New Perspectives on the History of Japanese Turkish Relations*. Istanbul: Boğaiçi University Press, 2003.

Farnsworth, Beatrice. *William C. Bullitt and the Soviet Union*. Bloomington-Indianapolis:Indiana University Press, 1967.

Figes, Orlando. *The Crimean War: A History*. New York: Metropolitan Books, 2010.

Fischer, Louis. *Russia's Road from Peace to War: Soviet Foreign Relations 1917–1941*. New York: Harper & Row, 1969.

Foreign Relations of the United States. The Soviet Union, 1933–1939. Washington DC: U.S. Government Printing Office, 1952.

Fox, John P. *Germany and the Far Eastern Crisis 1931–1938*. Oxford: Clarendon, 1982.

Fuller, Jr., William C. *The Foe Within: Fantasies of Treason and the End of Imperial Russia*. Ithaca–London: Cornell University Press, 2006.

Furukawa, Kaoru. *Yume harukanaru: kindai nihon no kyojin Kuhara Fusanosuke*. Tokyo: PHP Kenkyūjo, 2009.

Futrell, Michael. *Northern Underground: Episodes of Russian Revolutionary Transport and Communications through Scandinavia and Finland, 1863–1917*. New York: Frederick A. Praeger, 1963.

Gasanly, Dzhamil'. *Russkaia revoliutsia i Azerbaidzhan. Trudnyi put' k nezavisimosti 1917–1920*. Moscow: Flinta, 2011.

Gasparian, A.S. *Operatsiia "Trest." Sovetskaia razvedka protiv russkoi emigratsii. 1921–1937 gg.* Moscow: Veche, 2008.

Gatagova, L.S., L.P. Kosheleva and L.A. Rogovaia, eds., *TsK RKP(B)-VKP(b) i natsional'nyi vopros*, kn. 1. Moscow: ROSSPEN, 2005.

Gatagova, L.S., comp., *Sovetskaia etnopolitika, 1930–1940-e gody. Sbornik dokumentov.* Moscow: Institut rossiiskoi istorii, 2012.

Geifman, Anna. *Thou Shalt Kill: Revolutionary Terrorism in Russia, 1894–1917.* Princeton: Princeton University Press, 1993.

Gellner, Ernest. *Nations and Nationalism.* Oxford: Blackwell, 1983.

Genis, Vladimir. *Krasnaia Persiia: bol'sheviki v Giliane 1920–1921.* Moscow: MNPI, 2000.

Georgien, eine sozialdemokratische Bauernrepublik: Eindrücke und Beobachtungen von Karl Kautsky. Wien: Verlag der Wiener Volksbuchhandlung, 1921.

Glasneck, Johannes and Inge Kircheisen. *Türkei und Afghanistan – Brennpunkte der Orientpolitik im Zweiten Weltkrieg.* Berlin: Deutscher Verlag der Wissenschaften, 1968.

Glavnyi voennyi sovet RKKA. 13 marta 1938 g.–20 iiunia 1941 g.: Dokumenty i materialy. Moscow: ROSSPEN, 2004.

Grekov, N.V. *Russkaia kontrrazvedka v 1905–1917 gg.: shpionomaniia i real'nye problemy.* Moscow: Mosk. obshch. nauch. fond, 2000.

Gronskii, Ivan. *Iz proshlogo. Vospominaniia.* Moscow: Izvestiia, 1991.

Grzywacz, Andrzej, Marcin Kwiecień, and Grzegorz Mazur, eds., *Zbiór dokumentów ppłk. Edmunda Charaszkiewicza.* Kraków: Fundacja CDCN and Księg. Akademicka, 2000.

Hara, Teruyuki. *Shiberia shuppei: kaukemi to kanshō, 1917–1922.* Tokyo: Chikuma shobō, 1989.

Haruna, Mikio. *Himitsu no fairu: CIA no tainichi kōsaku.* Tokyo: Kyōdō tsūshinsha, 2000.

Haslam, Jonathan. *The Soviet Union and the Threat from the East, 1933–41: Moscow, Tokyo and the Prelude to the Pacific War.* Pittsburgh, PA: University of Pittsburgh Press, 1992.

Hata, Ikuhiko, ed., *Senzenki Nihon kanryōsei no seido soshiki jinji.* Tokyo: Tokyo University Press, 1981.

Hatano, Masaru. *Manmō dokuritsu undō.* Tokyo: PHP Kenkyūjo, 2001.

Hayashi, Saburō. *Kantōgun to kyokutō sorengun.* Tokyo: Fuyō shobō, 1974.

Heretz, Leonid. *Russia on the Eve of Modernity: Popular Religion and Traditional Culture under the Last tsars.* Cambridge: Cambridge University Press, 2008.

Herwarth, Hans von. (with S. Frederick Starr.), *Against Two Evils.* New York: Rawson, Wade Publishers, 1981.

Hipler, Bruno. *Hitlers Lehrmeister: Karl Haushofer als Vater der NS-Ideologie.* St. Ottilien: EOS Verlag, 1996.

Hoffmann, Joachim. *Ostlegionen 1941–1943: Turkotataren, Kaukasier und Wolgafinnen im deutschen Heer.*Freiburg: Rombach, 1976.

Hoffmann, Joachim. *Kaukasien 1942/43: Das deutsche Heer und die Orientvölker der Sowjetunion.* Freiburg: Rombach Verlag, 1991.

Hovannisian, Richard G. *Armenia on the Road to Independence, 1918.* Berkeley-Los Angeles, CA: University of California Press, 1967.

Hovannisian, Richard G. *The Republic of Armenia. Vol. 1: The First Year, 1918–1919.* Berkeley-Los Angeles, CA: The University of California Press, 1971.

Hovannisian, Richard G. *The Republic of Armenia. Vol. II: from Versailles to London, 1919–1920.* Berkeley-Los Angeles: University of California Press, 1982.

Hovannisian, Richard G. *The Republic of Armenia: Vol. III: From London to Sévres February – August 1920.* Berkeley-Los Angeles: University of California Press, 1996.

Hovannisian, Richard G. *The Republic of Armenia. Vol. IV: Between Crescent and Sickle: Partition and Sovietization.* Berkeley-Los Angeles: University of California Press, 1996.

Ibrahim, Abdürrechid. *Un Tatar au Japon – voyage en Asie (1908–1910)*, tr. and ed. Georgeon, François. Arles: Actes Sud, 2004.

Inaba, Chiharu. *Akashi kōsaku: bōryaku no nichiro sensō.* Tokyo: Maruzen, 1995.

Iremaschwili, Joseph. *Stalin und die Tragödie Georgiens.* Berlin: Verfasser, 1931.

Iskhakov, S.M., ed., *Iz istorii azerbaidzhanskoi emigratsii. Sbornik dokumentov, proizvedenii, pisem.* Moscow: Izd-vo Sotsial'no-politicheskaia mysl', 2011.

Ishimitsu, Masato. ed., *Ishimitsu Makiyo no shuki.* Tokyo: Chūō kōron, 1988.

Iunge, Mark, Gennadii Bordiugov and Rol'f Binner. *Vertikal' bol'shogo terrora: Istoriia operatsii po prikazu NKVD no. 00447.* Moscow: Novyi Khronograf, 2008.

Iznanka revoliutsii. Vooruzhennoe vozstanie v Rossii na iaposnkiia sredstva. St. Petersburg: Tip. A.S. Suvorina, [1906].

Jersild, Austin. *Orientalism and Empire: North Caucasus Mountain Peoples and the Georgian Frontier, 1845–1917.* Montreal: McGill-Queen's University Press, 2002.

Jones, Stephen F. *Socialism in Georgian Colors: The European Road to Social Democracy, 1883–1917.* Cambridge: Harvard University Press, 2005.

Kahle, Günter. *Das Kaukasusprojekt der Alliierten vom Jahre 1940.* Opladen: Westdeutscher Verlag, 1973.

Kazemzadeh, Firuz. *The Struggle for Transcaucasia (1917–1921).* New York: Philosophical Library, 1951.

Khodarkovsky, Michael. *Bitter Choices: Loyalty and Betrayal in the Russian Conquest of the North Caucasus.* Ithaca-London: Cornell University Press, 2011.

Kikkawa, Manabu. *Hiroku Rikugun rimenshi: shōgun Araki no shichijūnen.* Tokyo: Yamato Shobō, 1954.

King, Charles. *The Ghost of Freedom: A History of the Caucasus.* Oxford-New York: Oxford University Press, 2008.

Knight, Amy. *Beria: Stalin's First Lieutenant.* Princeton, NJ: Princeton University Press, 1993.

Komori, T. *Akashi Motojirō*, 2 vols. Tokyo: Hara Shobō, 1968.

Komura, Fujio. *Nihon isrāmu shi.* Tokyo: Nihon isrāmu yūkō renmei, 1988.

Kowner, Rotem, ed., *The Impact of the Russo-Japanese War.* London–New York: Routledge, 2007.

Kravtsev, I.N. *Tainye sluzhby imperii.* Moscow: Izd-vo RAGC, 1999.

Krivitsky, W.G. *I was Stalin's Agent.* London: Hamish Hamilton, 1939.

Krivosheev, G.F. *Rossiia i SSSR v voinakh XX veka: Poteri vooruzhennykh sil. Statisticheskoe issledovanie.* Moscow: OLMA-PRESS, 2001.

Kuromiya, Hiroaki. *Stalin: Profiles in Power.* Harlow, UK: Longman, 2005.

Kuromiya, Hiroaki. *The Voices of the Dead: Stalin's Great Terror in the 1930s.* New Haven: Yale University Press, 2007.

Kuromiya, Hiroaki and Andrzej Pepłoński. *Między Warszawą a Tokio: Polsko-Japońska współpraca wywiadowcza 1904-1944* . Toruń: Adam Marszałek, 2009.

Kvashonkin, A.V., O.V. Khlevniuk., L.P. Kosheleva et al., eds., *Bolshevistskoe rukovodstvo. Perepiska. 1912-1927. Sbornik dokumentov.* Moscow: POSSPEN, 1996.

Kvinitadze, G.I. *Moi vospominaniia v gody nezavisimosti Gruzii, 1917–1921.* Paris: YMCA Press, 1985.

Lakoba, Stanislav. *Abkhaziia posle dvukh imperii. XIX–XXI vv.* Sapporo, Japan: Slavic Research Center, 2004.

Lang, David, Marshall. *A Modern History of Soviet Georgia.* New York: Grove Press, 1962.

Laskhishvili, Giorgi. *memuarebi [Memoirs] (1885–1915).* Tbilisi: [n.p.], 1934.

Lattimore, Owen. *The Mongols of Manchuria.* New York: H. Fertig, 1934.

Lattimore, Owen. *Pivot of Asia: Sinkiang and the Inner Asian Frontiers of China and Russia.* Boston: Little Brown, 1950.

Layton, Susan. *Russian Literature and Empire: Conquest of the Caucasus from Pushkin to Tolstoy.* Cambridge: Cambridge University Press, 1994.
Lenin, V.I. *Polnoe sobranie sochinenii*, vol. 42. Moscow: Politizdat, 1970.
Lensen, George Alexander, ed., *Revelations of a Russian Diplomat: The Memoirs of Dmitrii I. Abrikossow.* Seattle: University of Washington Press, 1964.
Leverkuehn, Paul. *Der geheime Nachrichtendienst der deutschen Wehrmacht im Kriege.* Frankfurt am M.: Bernard & Graefe, 1957.
Lohr, Eric. *Nationalizing the Russian Empire: The Campaign against Enemy Aliens during Word War I.* Cambridge, MA: Harvard University Press, 2003.
Loris-Melicof, Jean. *La Révolution Russe et les nouvelles républiques transcaucasiennes.* Paris: Librairie Félix Alca, 1920.
Lubianka: Stalin i Glavnoe upravlenie gosbezopasnosti NKVD 1937–1938. Moscow: MFD, 2004.
Lubianka: Stalin i VChK-GPU-OGPU-NKVD. Arkhiv Stalina. Dokumenty vyschikh organov partiinoi i gosudarstvennoi vlasti. Ianvar' 1922–dekabr' 1936. Moscow: Mezhdunarodnyi fond Demokratiia, 2003.
Luke, Harry. *Cities and Men: An Autobiography*, vol. 2. London: Geoffrey Bles, 1953.
Maclean, Fitzroy. *Eastern Approaches*, with a new introduction by Charles W. Thayer. New York: Time Incorporated, 1964.
Mader, Julius. *Hitlers Spionagegenerale sagen aus: Ein Dokumentarbericht über Aufbau, Struktur und Operationen des OKW-Geheimdienstamtes Ausland/Abwehr mit einer Chronologie seiner Einsätze von 1933 bis 1944.* Berlin: Verlag der Nation, 1971.
Magamadov, S.S. and S.A. Kislitsyn. *Politicheskaia vlast' i povstancheskoe dvizhenie na Severnom Kavkaze. Ocherki istorii 1920–1930-kh gg.* Rostov-na-Donu: Iuzhno-Rossiiskii institut-filial RANKh i GS pri Prezidente RF, 2011.
Maiskii, Ivan Mikhailovich. *Dnevnik diplomata. London. 1934–1943* vol. 1. Moscow: Nauka, 2006.
Maj, Ireneusz Piotr. *Działalność Instytutu Wschodniego w Warszawie 1926–1939.* Warsaw: Instytut Studiów Politycznych PAN, 2007.
Mamoulia, Georges. *Gruzinskii legion v bor'be za svobodu i nezavisimost' Gruzii v gody Vtoroi mirovoi voiny.* Tbilisi: private publication, 2007.
Mamoulia, Georges. *Les combats indépendandistes des Caucasiens entre URSS et puissances occidentales: Le cas de la Géorgie (1921–1945).* Paris: L'Harmattan, 2009.
Mamoulia, Georges. *Bor'ba za svobodu i nezavisimost' Kavkaza (1921–1945).* Tbilisi-Paris: Meridiani, 2012.
Mamoulia, Georges, ed., *Kavkazskaia Konfederatsiia v ofitsialnykh deklaratsiiakh, tainoi perepiske i sekrethykh dokumentakh dvizheniia "Prometei." Sbornik dokumentov.* Moscow: Sotsial'no-politicheskaia mysl', 2012.
Mamoulia, Georges and Ramiz Abutalybov. *Strana ognei. V bor'be za svobodu i nezavisimost'. Politicheskaia istoriia azerbaidzhanskoi emigratsii 1920–1945 gg.* Paris-Baku: CBS, 2014.
Mamoulia, Goerges, Mairbek Vatchagaev and Khadzhi Murad Donogo, eds, *Gaidar Bammat - izevestnyi i neizvestnyi. Sbornik dokumentov i materialov.* Baku: Azerbaijanskoe istoricheskoe obshchestvo, 2015.
Mamoulia, Georges, Khadzhi Murad Donogo, and Mairbek Vatchagaev et al., eds, *Gaidar Bammat i zhurnal "Kavkaz". Sbornik dokumentov i materialov.* Makhachkala-Paris: Akhul'go, 2015.
Marshall, Alex. *The Russian General Staff and Asia, 1800–1917.* London-New York: Routledge, 2006.
Marshall, Alex. *The Caucasus under Soviet Rule.* London-New York: Routledge, 2006.
Materski, Wojciech. *Georgia rediviva: Republika Gruzińska w stosunkakh międzynarodowych 1918–1921.* Warsaw: Instytut Studiów Politycznych PAN, 1994.
McDonald, David MacLaren. *United Government and Foreign Policy in Russia 1900–1914.* Cambridge, MA: Harvard University Press, 1992.

McMeekin, Sean. *The Berlin-Baghdad Express: The Ottoman Empire and Germany's Bid for World Power.* Cambridge, MA: Harvard University Press, 2010.

Meijer, Jan M., ed., *The Trotsky Papers, 1917–1922*, Pt. One. The Hague: Mouton & Co., 1964.

Menteshashvili, I.Sh. *Zakavkaz'e v anglo-russkikh protivorechiiakh v 1880–1914 gg.* Tbilisi: [n.p.], 2001.

Mémoire sur l'invasion de la Géorgie par les Armées de la Russie des Soviets. Paris: A. Simon, 1921.

Mikulicz, Sergiusz. *Prometeizm w polityce II Rzeczypospolitej.* Warsaw: Książka i Wiedza, 1971.

Morley, James W. *The Japanese Thrust into Siberia, 1918.* New York: Columbia University Press, 1957.

Montefiore, Simon Sebag. *Young Stalin.* London: Weidenfeld & Nicolson, 2007.

Mostashari, Firouzeh. *On the Religious Frontier: Tsarist Russia and Islam in the Caucasus.* London-New York: I.B. Tauris, 2006.

Mozokhin, Oleg. *VChK-OGPU na zashchite ekonomicheskoi bezopasnosti gosudarstva i v bor'be s terrorizmom.* Moscow: Iauza-Eksmo, 2004.

Mozokhin O.B. ed., *Politbiuro i delo Beriia. Sbornik dokumentov.* Moscow: Kuchkovo pole, 2012.

Mozokhin, O.B. *Pravo na repressii. Vnesudebnye polnomochiia organov gosudarstvennoi bezopasnosti. Statisticheskie svedeniia o deiatel'nosti VChK-OGPU-NKVD-MGB SSSR (1918–1953)* 2nd ed. Moscow: Kuchkovo pole, 2011.

Mühlen, Patrick von zur. *Zwischen Hakenkreuz und Sowjetstern. Der Nationalismus der sowjetischen Orientvölker in Zweiten Weltkrieg.* Düsseldorf: Droste Verlag, 1971.

Naimark, Norman M. *Fires of Hatred: Ethnic Cleansing in Twentieth-Century Europe.* Cambridge, MA: Harvard University Press, 2001.

National Republic of Georgia: Hearings before the Committee on Foreign Affairs, House of Representatives, Sixty-ninth Congress, first session, on H.J. Res. 195, Providing for the Appointment of a Diplomatic Representative to the National Republic of Georgia, April 1 and 2, 1926. Washington: Govt. Print. Office, 1926.

Naumov, Leonid. *Stalin i NKVD.* Moscow: Iauza-EKSMO, 2007.

Newman, Robert P. *Owen Lattimore and the 'Loss' of China.* University of California Press, 1992.

NKVD-MVD SSSR v bor'be s banditizmom i vooruzhennym natsionalisticheskim podpol'em na zapadnoi Ukraine, v zapadnoi Belorossii i Pribaltike (1918–1956). Moscow: Ob'edinennaia redaktsiia MVD Rossii, 2008.

Nihon rikugun to Ajia seisaku: rikugun taishō Utsunomiya Tarō nikki, vol. 1. Tokyo: Iwanami, 2007 and vol. 2. Tokyo: Iwanami, 2007.

Nielsen, Petter. *Miliukov i Stalin: O politicheskoi evoliutsii Miliukova v emigratsii (1918-1943).* Oslo: Universitetet i Oslo, Slavisk-Baltisk Institutt, 1983.

Norden, A. *Fälscher: Zur Geschichte der deutsch-sowjetischen Beziehungen.* Berlin: Dietz Verlag, 1960.

O'Brien, Phillips Payson. ed., *The Anglo-Japanese Alliance, 1902–1922.* London-New York: Routledge Curzon, 2004.

okmebi kartvel revolutsionerta p'irveli konperentsiisa [Minutes of the first conference of the Georgian revolutionaries]. Paris: "Sakartvelo," 1904.

Onodera, Yuriko. *Barutokai no hotori nite: Bukan no tsuma no daitōa sensō.* Tokyo: Kyōdō tsūshin, 1985.

Organy gosudarstvennoi bezopasnosti SSSR v Velikoi otechestvennoi voine, vol. 1, part 1. Moscow: Kniga i biznes, 1995.

Organy gosudarstvennoi bezopasnosti SSSR v Velikoi otechestvennoi voine, vol. 2, part 2. Moscow: Rus', 2000.

Osborn, Patrick R. *Operation Pike: Britain versus the Soviet Union, 1939–1941.* Westport, CT-London: Greenwood Press, 2000.

Osmanov, E.M., comp., *Iz istorii russko-iaponskoi voiny 1904–1905 gg.* Spb: Izd-vo S-Peterb. un-ta, 2005.
Önder, Zehra. *Die türkische Außenpolitik im Zweiten Weltkrieg.* München: Oldenbourg, 1977.
Padalko, P.E. *Iaponiia v sud'bakh Rossiian: Ocherki istorii tsarskoj diplomatii i rossiiskoi diaspory v Iaponii.* Moscow: Kraft+, 2004.
Pavlov, D.B. *Iaponskie den'gi i pervaia russkaia revoliutsiia.* Moscow: Veche, 2011.
Persidskii front mirovoi revoliutsii: dokumenty o sovetskom vtorzhenii v Gilian (1920–1921). Moscow: Kvadriga, 2009).
Persits, M. A. *Zastenchivaia interventsiia: O sovetskom vtorzhenii v Iran i Bukharu v 1920–1921 gg.* Moscow: Muravei-Gaid, 1999.
Petrov, N., and M. Iansen. *"Stalinskii pitomets" – Nikolai Ezhov.* Moscow: ROSSPEN, 2008.
Price, M. Philips. *War & Revolution in Asiatic Russia.* New York: The Macmillan company, 1918.
Rayfield, Donald. *Stalin and His Hangmen: Au Authoritative Portrait of a Tyrant and Those Who Served Him.* London: Viking, 2004.
Rayfield, Donald. *Edge of Empires: A History of Georgia.* London: Reaktion Books, 2012.
Repressii 30-kh godov v Dagestane. Dokumenty i materialy. Makhachkala: Iupiter, 1997.
Revoliutsiia 1905–07 gg v Gruzii. Sbornik dokumentov. Tbilisi: Sakhelgami, 1956.
Reynolds, Michael A. *Shattering Empires: The Clash and Collapse of the Ottoman and Russian Empires 1908–1918.* Cambridge: Cambridge University Press, 2011.
Riess, Curt. *Total Espionage.* New York, NY: G.P. Putnam's Sons, 1941.
Rossos, Andrew. *Russia and the Balkans: Inter-Balkan Rivalries and Russian Foreign Policy, 1908–1914.* Toronto: University of Toronto Press, 1981.
Sadykova, Bakhyt. *Mustafa Tchokay dans le mouvement prométhéen.* Paris: L'Harmattan, 2007.
Sakharov, V.A. *"Politicheskoe zaveshchanie" Lenina. Real'nost' istorii i mify politiki.* Moscow: Izd-vo Moskovskogo universiteta, 2003.
Sakhokia, Tedo. *tsimbirshi. mogonebani 1905 ts'lis revolutsiis droidan* [My exile in Siberia. Memoirs from the period of the 1905 revolution]. Tbilisi: literaturis muzeumi, 2011.
Sergeev, Evgeny. *Russian Military Intelligence in the War with Japan, 1904–05: Secret Operations on Land and at Sea.* London–New York: Routledge, 2007.
Seth, Ronald. *Secret Servants: A History of Japanese Espionage.* New York: Farrar, Straus and Cudahy, 1957.
Shalva Amiredzhibi (1886-1943), vol. 1. Tbilisi: [n.p.], 1997.
Shulatov, Ia. A. *Na puti k sotrudnichestvu: Rossiisko-iaponskie otnosheniia v 1905–1914 gg.* Khabarovsk-Moscow: Izd-vo Instituta vostokovedeniia RAN, 2008.
Shvelidze, D. *polit'ikuri part'iebis ts'armoshoba sakartveloshi. pederalist'ebi* [The origins of the political parties in Georgia. Federalists]. Tbilisi: "Arsi," 1993.
Shvelidze, Dimitri, and Giorgi Gaprindashvili. *giorgi dekanozishvili – mamulishvilis dabruneba* [Giorgi Dekanozishvili – the patriots return]. Tbilisi: Universali, 2010.
Siegel, Jennifer. *Endgame: Britain, Russia and the Final Struggle for Central Asia.* London–New York: I. B. Tauris, 2002.
Snyder, Timothy. *Sketches from a Secret War: A Polish Artist's Mission to Liberate Soviet Ukraine.* New Haven: Yale University Press, 2005.
Smith, Jeremy. *The Bolsheviks and the National Question, 1917–1923.* London: Macmillan, 1999.
Soiuz ob"edinennykh gortsev Severnogo Kavkaza i Dagestana (1917–1918 gg.), Gorskaia Respublika (1918–1920 gg.): dokumenty i materialy. Makhachkala: Institut istorii, arkhelogii i etnografii DNTs RAN, 1994.
Sokol, Edward Dennis. *The Revolt of 1916 in Russian Central Asia.* Baltimore, MD: The Johns Hopkins Press, 1954.

Sommer, Theo. *Deutschland und Japan zwischen den Mächten 1935–1940: Vom Antikominternpakt zum Dreimächtepakt.* Tübingen: J.C.B. Mohr, 1962.
Sotskov, Lev. *Neizvestnyi separatizm na sluzhbe SD i Abvera. Iz sekretnykh dos'e razvedki.* Moscow: RIPOL KLASSIK, 2003.
Stalin, I.V. *Sochineniia*, vols. 1-13. Moscow: Politizdat, 1946-1951.
Stalin i Kaganovich. Perepiska. 1931–1936 gg. Moscow: ROSSPEN, 2001.
Stalinskie deportatsii 1928–1953. Moscow: MFD, Materik, 2005.
Sudoplatov, Pavel. *Raznye dni tainoi voiny i diplomatii. 1941 god.* Moscow: Olma-PRESS, 2001.
Suladze, Gela. *kartuli ant'isabch'ota emigratsia da sp'etssamsakhurebi (1918–1953 ts'.ts')* [Georgian Antibolshevik Emigration and the Secret Services]. Tbilisi: "erovnuli mtserloba," 2010.
Suny, Ronald Grigor. *The Baku Commune 1917–1918: Class and Nationality in the Russian Revolution.* Princeton, NJ: Princeton University Press, 1972.
Suny, Ronald Grigor. *Armenia in the Twentieth Century.* Chico, CA: Scholarly Press, 1983.
Suny, Ronald Grigor. *The Making of the Georgian Nation.* Bloomington-Indianapolis: Indiana University Press, 1988.
Suny, Ronald Grigor. *Looking toward Ararat: Armenia in Modern History.* Bloomington-Indianapolis: Indiana University Press, 1993.
Suny, Ronald Grigor, Fatma Müge Göçek and Norman M. Naimark, eds., *A Question of Genocide: Armenians and Turks at the End of the Ottoman Empire.* Oxford-New York: Oxford University Press, 2011.
Suzuki, Kenji. *Chūdoku taishi Ōshima Hiroshi.* Tokyo, Fuō shobō, 1979.
Swietochowski, Tadeusz. *Russian Azerbaijan, 1905–1920: The Shaping of National Identity in a Muslim Community.* Cambridge: Cambridge University Press, 1985.
Tajima, Nobuo. *Nachizumu kyokutō senryaku: nichidoku bōkyō kyōtei o meguru chōhōsen.* Tokyo: Kōdansha, 1997.
Tanaka Giichi denki, vol. 1. Tokyo: Tanaka Giichi denki kankō kai, 1958.
Tani, Hisao. *Kimitsu nichiro senshi.* Tokyo: Hara shobō, 1966.
Taylor, S.J. *Stalin's Apologist: Walter Duranty, The New York Time's Man in Moscow.* New York: Oxford University Press, 1990.
Tatamiya, Eitarō. *Hashimoto Kingorō Ichidai.* Tokyo: Fuyō shobō, 1982.
Thom, Françoise. *Beria: Le Janus du Kremlin.* Paris: Les Éditions du Cerf, 2013.
Torma, Franziska. *Turkestan-Expeditionen. Zur Kulturgeschichte deutscher Forschunsgreisen nach Mittelasien (1890–1930).* Bielefeld: Transcript, 2011.
Trudy Obshchestva izucheniia istorii otechestvennykh spetssluzb, v. 2. Moscow: Kuchkovo pole, 2006.
TsK RKP(b)–VKP(b) i natsional'nyi vopros. Kniga 1. 1918–1933 gg. Moscow: ROSSPEN, 2005.
Tsuchihashi, Takeyasu. *Gunpuku seikatsu shijūnen no omoide.* Tokyo, Keisō shuppan, 1985.
Tzouliadis, Tim. *The Forsaken: An American Tragedy in Stalin's Russia.* New York: Penguin, 2008.
Uralov, Aleksandr. (Avtorkhanov, A.), *Narodoubiistvo v SSSR. Ubiistvo chechenskogo naroda.* Munich: Svobodnyi Kavkaz, 1952.
Uratadze, G.I. *Obrazovanie i konsolidatsiia Gruzinskoi Demokraticheskoi Respubliki.* Munich: Institut zur Erforschung der UdSSR e. V., 1956.
Usmanova, Larisa. *The Türk-Tatar Diaspora in Northeast Asia. Transformation of Consciousness: A Historical and Sociological Account between 1898 and the 1950s.* Tokyo: Rakudasha, 2007.
V.I. Lenin: neizvestnye dokumenty, 1891–1922. Moscow: ROSSPEN, 2000.
Velikanov, Nikolai. *Bliukher.* Moscow: Molodaia gvardiia, 2010.
Villari, Luigi. *Fire and Sword in the Caucasus.* London: T. Fisher Unwin, 1906.
Vita-Finzi, Paolo. *Journal caucasien (1928–1931) suivi de Carnet moscovite (1953)*, tr. Jean-Marc Mandosio. Paris: Inventaire, 2000.

Voennyi sovet pri narodnom komissare oborony SSSR: Dokumenty i materialy. 1938, 1940 gg. Moscow: ROSSPEN, 2006.

Votinov, A. *Iaponskii shpionazh v russko-iaponskuiu voinu 1904–1905 gg.* Moscow: Voenizdat, 1939.

Wheeler-Bennett, John. *The Forgotten Peace, Brest-Litovsk, March 1918.* New York: W. Morrow, 1939.

Wolff, David, David Schimmelpenninck van der Oye, Bruce W. Menning, John W. Steinberg, Shinji Yokote, eds., *The Russo-Japanese War in Global Perspective: World War Zero*, 2 vols. Leiden-Boston: Brill, 2005-2007.

Worringer, Renée, ed., *The Islamic Middle East and Japan: Perceptions, Aspirations, and the Birth of Intra-Asian Modernity.* Princeton, NJ: Markus Wiener, 2007.

Wortman, Richard S., *The Development ofA Russian Legal Consciousness.* Chicago: University of Chicago Press, 1976.

Yakovlev, A.N. *Stalinskie deportatsii 1928–1953.* Moscow: Materik, 2005.

Yamada, Kuniki, and Toshio Sakamoto. *Meiji no kaidanji toruko e tobu: Yamada Torajirō den.* Tokyo: Gendai shokan, 2009.

Yoshimura, Michio. *Zōho: Nihon to Rosia.* Tokyo: Nihon keizai hyōronsha, 1991.

Yume harukanaru: kindai nihon no kyojin Kuhara Fusanosuke. Tokyo: PHP Kenkyūjo, 2009.

Zetterberg, S. *Die Liga der Fremdvölker Russlands 1916-1918. Ein Beitrag zu Deutschlands antirussischem Propagandakrieg unter der Fremdvölkern Russlands im Ersten Weltkriegs.* Helsinki: Finnische Historische Gesellschaft, 1978.

Zhonghua min guo zhong yao shi liao chu bian—dui Ri kang zhan shi qi. Di 3 bia, Zhan shi wai jiao. Taipei: Jing xiao zhe Zhong yang wen wu gong ying she, 1981.

Zhordaniia, Noe. *chemi ts'arsuli. mogonebani* [My past. Memoirs]. Tbilisi: Sarangi, 1990.

Zolling, Hermann, and Höhne Heinz. *Pullach intern: General Gehlen und die Geschichte des Bundesnachrichtendienstes.* Hamburg: Hoffmann u. Campe, 1971.

Zürrer, Werner. *Kaukasien 1918–1921: Der Kampf der Großmächte um die Landbrücke zwischen Schwarzem und Kaspischem Meer.* Düsseldorf: Droste Verlag, 1978.

Articles

Andrew, Christopher. "Codebreakers and Foreign Offices: The French, British and American Experience," Andrew, Christopher and David Dilks, eds., *The Missing Dimension: Governments and Intelligence Communities in the Twentieth Century.* 33-53. Urbana-Chicago: University of Illinois Press, 1984.

Avalishvili, Levan. "The 'Great Terror' of 1937–1938 in Georgia: Between the Two Reports of Lavrentiy Beria." *Caucasus Analytical Digest* no. 22 (1 December 2010): 2-6.

Bammate, Haidar. "The Caucasus and the Russian Revolution (from a Political Viewpoint)." *Central Asian Survey* 10, no. 4 (1991): 1-29.

Baryshev, Eduard. "The General Hermonius Mission to Japan (August 1914–March 1915) and the Issue of Armaments Supply in Russo-Japanese Relations during the First World War." *Acta Slavica Iaponica* v. 30 (2011): 21-42.

Baumgart, Winfried. "Das 'Kaspi-Unternehmen' – Größenwahn Ludendorffs oder Routineplanung des deutschen Generalstabs?" *Jahrbücher für Geschichte Osteuropas* 18, no. 1 (1970): 47-126.

Beillevaire, Patrick. "Apres *la Bataille*: L'égarement japonophile de Claude Farrere." *Les carnets de l'exotisme* v. 5 (2005): 223-246.

Bennigsen Broxup, Marie. "The Last *Ghazawat*: The 1920–1921 Uprising," Bennigsen Broxup, Marie, ed., *The North Caucasus Barrier: The Russian Advance towards the Muslim World.* 112-145. London: Hurst, 1992.

Berton, Peter. "A New Russo-Japanese Alliance?: Diplomacy in the Far East during World War I." *Acta Slavica Iaponica* no. 11 (1993): 57-78.

Biddiscombe, Perry. "Unternehmen Zeppelin: The Deployment of SS Saboteurs and Spies in the Soviet Union, 1942–1945." *Europe-Asia Studies* 52, no 6 (2000): 1115-1142.

Blauvelt, Timothy K. "Resistance and Accommodation in the Stalinist Periphery: A Peasant Uprising in Abkhazia." *Ab Imperio*, no. 3 (2012): 78–108.

Bunin, Sergei. "Samyi znamenityi russkii v Tokio," http://www.sovsekretno.ru/magazines/article/2989 [accessed on 23 November 2012].

Burds, Jeffrey. "The Soviet War against 'Fifth Columnists': The Case of Chechnya, 1942–4." *Journal of Contemporary History* 42, no 2 (2007): 267-314.

Bylinin, K., A.A. Zdanovich, and V.I. Korotaev. "Organizatsiia 'Prometei' i 'prometeiskoe' dvizhenie v planakh pol'skoi razvedki po razvalu Rossii/SSSR." *Trudy Obshchestva izucheniia istorii otechestvennykh spetssluzhb* v. 3. 318-414. Moscow: Kuchkovo pole, 2007.

Catford, J.C. "Mountain of Tongues: The Languages of the Caucasus." *Annual Review of Anthropology*, 6 (1997): 283-314.

Comrie, Bernard. "Linguistic Diversity in the Caucasus." *Annual Review of Anthropology* 37 (2008): 131-143.

Çelikpala, Mitat. "The North Caucasian Émigrés between the World Wars." *International Journal of Turkish Studies* 9, no. 1–2 (2003): 31-59.

Dallin, David. "Between the World War and the NEP," in Haimson, Leopold, ed., *The Mensheviks.* 191-239.Chicago: University of Chicago Press, 1974.

Davies, R. W. "Soviet Military Expenditure and the Armaments Industry, 1929–33: A Reconsideration." *Europe-Asia Studies* 45, no 4 (1993): 577-608.

Derevianko, I.V. "Russkaia agenturnaia razvedka v 1902–1905 gg." *Voenno-istoricheskii zhurnal*, 1989, no. 5: 76-78.

Dickinson, Frederick R. "Toward a Global Perspective of the Great War: Japan and the Foundations of a Twentieth-Century World." *The American Historical Review*, 119, no 4 (2014): 1154-1183.

[Djordjadzé, A.] "La Géorgie et la Fédération du Caucase." *Géorgie, politique et sociale* (Paris) 1903, no. 4: 1-2.

Dündar, Merthan A, and Nobuo Misawa. "Isutanburu no nakamura shōten o meguru ningen kankei no jirei kenkyū." *Tōyō daigaku shakaigakubu kiyō* 46, no. 2 (2009): 181-220.

Eliseeva, N.E. "Chechnia: vooruzhennaia bor'ba v 20-30-e gody." *Voenno-istoricheskii arkhiv* vyp. 2 (1997): 22-26.

Ellman, Michael. "Soviet Repression Statistics: Some Comments." *Europe–Asia Studies* 54, no 7 (November 2002): 1151-1172.

"En marge du conflit." *Prométhée* no. 108 (November 1935): 1-4.

Esenbel, Selçuk. "Seiki matsu Isutanburu no nihonjin," in Ikei, Masaru, and Tsutomu Sakamoto, eds., *Kindai nihon to toruko sekai.* 71-100. Tokyo: Keisoō shobō, 1999.

Esenbel, Selçuk. "Japan and Islam Policy during the 1930s," in Edström, Bert, ed., *Turning Points in Japanese History.* 180-214.Richmond: Japan Library, 2002.

Esenbel, Selçuk. "Japan's Global Claim to Asia and the World of Islam: Transnational Nationalism and World Power, 1900–1945." *The American Historical Review* 109, no 4 (October 2004): 1140–1170.

Furier, Andrzej. "Relacja Józefa Łaszkiewicza o gruzińskim powstaniu antybolszewickim 1924 r." *Pro Georgia* vol. 7 (1998): 137-149

Futrell, Michael. "Colonel Akashi and Japanese Contacts with Russian Revolutionaries in 1904–5." *St. Antony's Papers 2: Far Eastern Affairs* 4 (1967): 7-22.

Galitskii, V.P. "Velikaia otechestvennaia voina 1941–1945 gg. '. . . dlia aktivnoi podryvnoi diversionnoi deiatel'nosti v tylu u Krasnoi Armii'." *Voenno-istoricheskii zhurnbal* 2001, no. 1: 17-25.

Grant, Bruce. "An Average Azeri Village (1930): Remembering Rebellion in the Caucasus Mountains." *Slavic Review* 63, no 4 (2004): 705-731.

Grzywacz, Andrzej, and Grzegorz Mazur. "Ruch Prometejski w Polsce." *Zeszyty historyczne* v. 110 (1994): 74–85.

Hall, Richard C. "The Next War: The Influence of the Russo-Japanese War on Southeastern Europe and the Balkan Wars of 1912–1913." *Journal of Slavic Military Studies* 17, no. 3 (2004): 563-577.

Hara, Teruyuki. "The Japanese Occupation of Northern Sakhalin (1920s)," in Kotkin, Stephen and David Wolff, eds., *Rediscovering Russia in Asia: Siberia and the Russian Far East.* 55-68. Armonk, NY: M.E. Sharpe, 1995.

Harrison, Mark, and P.B. Davies. "The Soviet Military-Economic Effort during the Second Five-Year Plan." *Europe-Asia Studies* 49, no 3 (1997): 369-406.

Hasegawa, Rei. "Nichiro sensō to senjō no chōhōsen." *Gunji shigaku* 42, no. 2 (2006): 118-141.

Kereselidze, G. "sakartvelos damoukideblobis komiteti (1914-1918)" [Committee for the independence of Georgia]. *kartuli emigracia* [Georgian emigration] vol. I (4) (2013): 141-175.

Kereselidze, Leo. "Curriculum Vitae." *Tanamemamule* (Tbilisi) no. 3(24) (2007): 14-16.

Kirichenko, Arekusei [Aleksei]. "Kominterun to Nihon, sono himitsu chōhōsen o abaku." *Seiron* no 10 (2006): 96-114.

Kosok, Pshemakho. "Revolution and Sovietization in the Northern Caucasus." *Caucasian Review* (Munich) no 3, (1956): 45-53.

Kossenko, I. "L'Ukraine D'Extrême orient." *Prométhée* no. 97 (December 1934): 4–8.

Kreiser, Klaus. "Der Japanische Sieg über Russland (1905) und sein Echo unter den Muslimen." *Die Welt des Islams* 21, nos. 1–4 (1981): 209-239.

Kujala, Antti. "March Separately – Strike Together: The Paris and Geneva Conferences Held by the Russian and Minority Nationalities' Revolutionary and Opposition Parties, 1904–1905," in Akashi, Motojirō. *Rakka ryūsui: Colonel Akashi's Report on His Secret Cooperation with the Russian Revolutionary Parties during the Russo-Japanese War. 85-167.* Helsinki: Societas Historica Finlandiae, 1988.

Kujala, Antti. "The Russian Revolutionary Movement and the Finnish Opposition 1905: The John Grafton Affair and the Plans for an Uprising in St. Petersburg." *Scandinavian Journal of History*, no. 5, (1980): 257-275.

Kuromiya, Hiroaki. "Ataman Semenov's Secret Life." *Przegląd Wschodni* 2014, no. 2: 535-556.

Kuromiya, Hiroaki. "The Battle of Lake Khasan Reconsidered." *The Journal of Slavic Military Studies* 29, no. 1 (2016), 99–109.

Kuromiya, Hiroaki. "The Mystery of Nomonhan, 1939." *The Journal of Slavic Military Studies* 24, no 4 (2011): 659-677.

Kuromiya, Hiroaki. "The Promethean Movement and Japan's Diplomacy," in Kornat, Marek. ed., *Ruch Prometejski i walka o przebudowę Europy Wschodniej (1918–1940)*. 137-147. Warsaw: IH PAN, 2012.

Kuromiya, Hiroaki. "The Soviet Famine of 1932–33 Reconsidered." *Europe-Asia Studies*, 60, no 4 (June 2008): 663-675.

Kuromiya, Hiroaki. "Stalin's Great Terror and the Asian Nexus." *Europe-Asia Studies* 66, no 5 (July 2014): 775-793.

Kuromiya, Hiroaki. "Stalin's Great Terror and International Espionage." *The Journal of Slavic Military Studies*, 24, no 2 (2011): 238-252.

Kuromiya, Hiroaki and Paweł Libera. "Notatka Włodzimierza Bączkowskiego na temat współpracy polsko-japońskiej wobec ruchu prometejskiego (1938)." *Zeszyty historyczne* (Paris) v. 169 (2009): *114-135.*

Kuromiya, Hiroaki, and Georges Mamoulia. "Anti-Russian and Anti-Soviet Subversion: The Caucasian-Japanese Nexus." *Europe-Asia Studies* 61, no 8 (October 2009): 415–1440.

Kuromiya, Hiroaki, and Andrzej Pepłoński. "Between East and West: Gaiaz Iskhaki and Gabdulkhai Kurbangaliev." *Nowy Prometeusz*, 2012, no. 2: 89-108.

Kuromiya, Hiroaki, and Pepłoński Andrzej. "Kōzō Izumi and the Soviet Breach of Imperial Japanese Diplomatic Codes." *Intelligence and National Security* 28, no. 6 (2013): 769-784.

Kuromiya, Hiroaki, and Pepłoński Andrzej. "Stalin, Espionage, and Counter-espionage," in *Stalinism and Europe: Terror, War, Domination, 1937-1947*, ed. by Snyder, Timothy and Ray Brandon. 73-91. Oxford University Press, 2014.

"Iaponskie shpiony sredi musul'manskogo dukhovenstva." *Antireligioznik* 1938, nos. 8–9: 66-67.

Inaba, Chiharu. "Franco-Russian Intelligence Collaboration against Japan during the Russo-Japanese War, 1904–05." *Japanese Slavic and East European Studies* vol. 19 (1998): 1-23.

Inaba, Chiharu. "The Question of the Bosphorous and Dardanelles during the Russo-Japanese War: The Struggle between Japan and Russia over the Passage of the Russian Volunteer Fleet in 1904," in Esenbel, Selçuk and Chiharu Inaba, eds., *The Rising Sun and the Turkish Crescent: New Perspectives on the History of Japanese-Turkish Relations.* 122-144.Istanbul: Boğaziçi University Press, 2003.

"L'indépendance de la Mandchourie." *Prométhée* no. 71 (October 1932): 1–2.

Inozemtseva, Elena. "On the History of Slave-Trade in Dagestan." *Iran and the Caucasus*, 10, no. 2 (2006): 181-189.

Jabagi (Cabagi), Vassan-Giray. "Revolution and Civil War in the North Caucasus–End of the 19th—Beginning of the 20th Century." *Central Asian Survey*, 10, nos. 1-2 (1991): 119-132.

Jones, Stephen. "The Establishment of Soviet Power in Transcaucasia: The Case of Georgia 1921–1928." *Soviet Studies*, 40, no 4 (1988): 616-639.

[Jorjadze A.] "ra gadmogvtsa ts'arsulma tse'lma? [The heritage of the last year]." *sakartvelo, kartvel sotsialist'-pederalist'ta sarevolutsio partiis organo* [Georgia, organ of the revolutionary party of Georgian socialist-federalists] (Paris) no. 1(13), (1904): 1-3.

Maghlakelidze, Shalva. "mogonebebi" [Memoirs], in Rtskhiladze, V. *kartvelebi meore msoplio omshi germanuli droshis kvesh* [Georgians in the Second World War under the German Ban-

ner]. 14-224. Tbilisi: Ganatleba, 1994.
Mamoulia, Georges. "L'histoire du groupe Caucase (1934–1939)." *Cahiers du monde Russe* 48, no. 1 (January-March 2007): 45–85.
Mamoulia, Georges. " 'Prometei' do prometeizma: neizvestnye stranitsy iz istorii natsional'no-osvoboditel'nogo dvizheniia na Kavkaze (1922 g.)." *Nowy Prometeusz*, no. 2 (2012): 259-293.
Mamoulia, Georges. "Osobaia troika NKVD Gruzinskoi SSR (1937–1938). Mestnaia specifika i mekhanizm funktsionirovaniia," available http://www.chechen.org/prometheus13.html (accessed 26 December 2012).
Mamoulia, Georges. "Kavkaz i derzhavy Chetvernogo soiuza v 1918 g." *Nowy Prometeusz* no 5 (2013): 125-160.
Manning, Bruce W. "Miscalculating One's Enemies: Russian Military Intelligence before the Russo-Japanese War." *War in History* 13, no. 2 (2006): 141-170.
Marchenko, G.V. "Antisovetskoe dvizhenie v Chechne v 1920–1930-e gody." *Voprosy istorii*, 2003, no. 1: 131-138.
Martin, Terry. "The Origins of Soviet Ethnic Cleansing." *The Journal of Modern History* 70, no. 4 (1998): 813-861
Marshall, Alex. "Russian Military Intelligence, 1905–1917: The Untold Story behind Tsarist Russia in the First World War." *War in History*, 11, no. 4 (2004): 393-423.
Marshall, Alex. "Imperial Russian War Planning for the Eurasian Space and the Impact of the War," in Rotem Kowner, ed., *Rethinking the Russo-Japanese War, 1904–05: Centennial Perspectives*, v. 1. 291-306. Folkestone: Global Oriental, 2006.
Marshall, Alex. "Russian Intelligence during the Russo-Japanese War, 1904–05." *Intelligence and National Security* 22, no. 5 (October 2007): 682-698.
Materski, Wojciech. "Powstanie narodowowyzvoleńcze 1924 r. w Gruzii." *Studia dziejów Rosji i Europy Śródkowo-Wschodniej*, v. 34 (1999): 57-67.
Melkonian, Eduard. "Repressions in the 1930s Soviet Armenia," *Caucasus Analytical Digest*, no. 22 (1 December 2010): 6-9.
Mühlen, Patrick von zur. "Japan und die Sowjetische Nationalitätenfrage am Vorabend und während des Zweites Weltkrieg." *Vierteiljahrshefte für Zeitgeschichte* 21, no3 (1973): 325-333.
"Nam bylo by ochen' vygodno podrat'sia s Iaponiei i osnovatel'no pobit' ee." *Istoricheskii arkhiv*, 2008, no. 6: 3-18.
Nelson, Keith. "The War and British Strategic Foreign Policy," in Kowner, Rotem, ed., *Rethinking the Russo-Japanese War, 1904-05*, vol. 1. 307-318. Folkestone: Global Oriental, 2007.
Nish, Ian. "Japanese Intelligence and the Approach of the Russo-Japanese War," in Andrew, Christopher, and David Dilks, eds., *The Missing Dimension: Governments and Intelligence Communities in the Twentieth Century*. 17-32. Urbana-Chicago: University of Illinois Press, 1984.
Nozadze, Viktor. "gardasrul zhamta ambavni da sakmeni" [Events and deeds of the past]. *kavkassioni* (Caucasus) (Paris) 1964, no. 9: 110-131.
Petrenko, V.M. "Dal'nevostochnyi front nakanune i v period Velikoi Otechestvennoi voiny 1941–1945 gg." *Voenno-istoricheskii zhurnal* 2010, no. 10: 20-25.
Pykhalov, Igor'. "Severnyi Kavkaz. Prichiny deportatsii 1943–1945 gg." *Molodaia gvardiia* 2002, no. 10: 71-98.
"Pis'ma I.I. Vorontsova-Dashkova Nikolaiu Romanovu (1905–1915 gg.)." *Krasnyi arkhiv* no. 26 (1928): 97-126.
van Ree, Eric. " 'Lenin's Last Struggle' Revisited." *Revolutionary Russia* 14, no 2 (December 2001): 85-122.
Rivoire, Georges. (Bammat, H.). "La position de la Turquie." *Le mois suisse: Littéraire et politique. Revue nationale et Européenne* (Montreux) no. 52 (1943): 3-51.

Sakai, Tetsuya. "Nihon gaikō ni okeru soren kan no hensen (1923–37)." *Kokka Gakkai zassi*, 97, nos. 3–4 (1983): 294-324.
Simonova, Tat'iana. "Ustanovlenie Sovetskoi vlasti na Severnom Kavkaze, 1918–1921 gg." *Dialog* 2001, no. 12: 63-68.
"Tainaia voina protiv Rossii," *Istoricheskii arkhiv*, 1994, no. 3: 13-59.
Targalski, Georges. "Les plans polonais concernant l'éclatement de l'URSS, le mouvement 'Prométhée' et le Caucase." *Bulletin de l'Observatoire de l'Asie centrale et du Caucase* 1997, no. 3: 9-14.
Tovy, Tal, and Sharon Halevi. "America's First Cold War: The Emergence of a New Rivalry," in Kowner, Rotem, ed., *The Impact of the Russo-Japanese War.* 137-152. London-New York: Routledge, 2007.
Ts'ereteli, Mikheil. "giorgi dekanozishvili." *'sakhalkho sakme. sakartvelos sotsialist'-pederalist'uri part'iis daarsebis 50 ts'listavi. sagangebo rveuli.* 10-14. [Buenos Aires]: n.p., 1952.
Tugushi, Markoz. "giorgi dekanozishvili (tskhovreba da mokmedeba). sakartvelos sotsialist'-pederalist'uri sarevolutsio part'ia (1901-1906 ts'.ts'.)" [Giorgi Dekanozishvili. Life and Activity. Georgian Socialist-Federalist Revolutionary Party (1901-1906)]. *kavkassioni* [Caucasus] (Paris) 1964, no. 10: 127-163.
Vatshnadze, David. "samshoblos samsakhurshi" [On the service of Motherland]. *iveria* (Paris), no. 35 (1990): 62–92.
"Vtoroe pokorenie Kavkaza: Bol'sheviki i chechenskie povstantsy." *Rodina*, no. 6 (1995): 43-48.
Wehner, Markus. "Le soulèvement géorgien de 1924 et la réaction des Bolcheviks." *Communisme* nos. 42/43/44 (1995): 155-169.
Wojtkowiak, Jakub. "Kontyngent Armii Czerwonej w Mongolii w latach 1936–1938." *Dzieje najnowsze* 40, no 3 (2008): 3-13.
Wolf, David. "Intelligence Intermediaries: The Competition for Chinese Spies," in Wolff, David, David Schimmelpenninck van der Oye, Bruce W. Menning, John W. Steinberg, Shinji Yokote, eds., *The Russo-Japanese War in Global Perspective: World War Zero.* Vol. 1. 305-330. Leiden-Boston: Brill, 2005.
Yaschke, Gotthard. "Le peuples opprimé de Russie et la Conférence de Lausanne en 1916." *Prométhée*, no. 132 (1937): 12–21.
Yoshimura, Michio. "Dai san kai nichiro kyōyaku seiritsu zengo: romō kyōyaku to no kanren ni oite." *Kokusai seiji* 31 (1966): 67-85.
Yoshimura, Michio. "Nichiro sensō go ni okeru nihonjin gunji tantei kengi mondai." *Kokushigaku* 105 (May 1978): 1-23.
Yoshimura, Michio. "Nichiro sensō ki no Nihon no tai-Mōko seisaku no ichimen: 'Kharachin ōfu kenbunroku' ni tsuite." *Seiji keizai shigaku* 300 (1991): 164-188.
Yoshimura, Michio. "Rotan to nihonjin shakai." *Rekishi dokuhon* 49, no. 4 (2004): 140-143.
Zalevkii, K. "Natsional'nyia partii v Rossii," in *Obshchestvennoe dvizhenie v Rossii v nachale xx-go veka*, v. 3. 227-344. St. Petersburg: Obshchestvennaia pol'za, 1914.
"Zenmō ni haru rokoku supaimō." *Tōkyō nichinichi shinbun* (evening edition), 4 October 1933: 1.
Zürrer, Werner. "Deutschland und die Entwicklung Nordkaukasiens in Jahre 1918." *Jahrbücher für Geschichte Osteuropas* 26, no. 1 (1978): 31-59.

List of Figures

Sources of Illustrations

Fig. 2.1: National Diet Library, Tokyo, Japan.
Fig. 2.2: GARF, f. 102, DP PP 1904-II, op. 316, d. 28, l. 47.
Fig. 2.3: National Diet Library, Tokyo, Japan.
Fig. 2.4: Personal Archive of M. Taktakichvili, Paris, France.
Fig. 2.5: National Parliamentary Library of Georgia, Tbilisi, Georgia.
Fig. 2.6: CHAN, Paris, box 345AP/2.
Fig. 2.7: National Parliamentary Library of Georgia, Tbilisi, Georgia.
Fig. 2.8: CHAN, Paris, box 345AP/2.
Fig. 2.9: *La Géorgie*, 1903, Paris.
Fig. 2.10: *Sakartvelo* (Georgia), 1903, Paris
Fig. 2.11: National Parliamentary Library of Georgia, Tbilisi, Georgia.
Fig. 2.12: CHAN, Paris, box 345AP/2.
Fig. 2.13: CHAN, Paris, box 345AP/2.
Fig. 2.14: N. Badual-Kereselidze Family Archive, Aix-en-Province, France.
Fig. 2.15: CHAN, Paris, box 345AP/2.
Fig. 2.16: CHAN, Paris, box 345AP/2.
Fig. 2.17: CHAN, Paris, box 345AP/2.
Fig. 3.1: GSCHA (Tiflis Gendarme Archive)
Fig. 3.2: GSCHA (Tiflis Gendarme Archive)
Fig. 3.3: N. Badual-Kereselidze Family Archive, Aix-en-Province, France.
Fig. 4.1: N. Badual-Kereselidze Family Archive, Aix-en-Province, France.
Fig. 4.2: National Parliamentary Library of Georgia, Tbilisi, Georgia.
Fig. 4.3: National Parliamentary Library of Georgia, Tbilisi, Georgia.
Fig. 4.4: M. Bammat Family Archive, Paris, France.
Fig. 4.5: National Parliamentary Library of Georgia, Tbilisi, Georgia.
Fig. 4.6: Archives d'Ali Mardan-bey Toptchibachi, Le Centre d'études des mondes russe, caucasien et centre-européen, École des hautes études en sciences sociales, Paris, France.
Fig. 5.1: National Parliamentary Library of Georgia, Tbilisi, Georgia.
Fig. 5.2: G. Mamoulia Personal Archive, Paris, France.
Fig. 6.1: Archives d'Ali Mardan-bey Toptchibachi, Le Centre d'études des mondes russe, caucasien et centre-européen, École des hautes études en sciences sociales, Paris, France.
Fig. 6.2: M. Bammat Family Archive, Paris, France.
Fig. 6.3: M. Bammat Family Archive, Paris, France.
Fig. 6.4: M. Bammat Family Archive, Paris, France.
Fig. 6.5: S. Kozliakowsky Family Archive, Tbilisi, Georgia.
Fig. 6.6: M. Bammat Family Archive, Paris, France.
Fig. 6.7: M. Bammat Family Archive, Paris, France.
Fig. 7.2: National Parliamentary Library of Georgia, Tbilisi, Georgia.
Fig. 7.3: Archiv der Kameradschaft "Bergmann," Kronberg, Germany.
Fig. 7.4: M. Bammat Family Archive, Paris, France.

Index